International Business
in the 21st Century

International Business in the 21st Century

Staying on Top: Crucial Issues for International
Business in the 21st Century
Volume 3

Bruce D. Keillor, General Editor

Timothy J. Wilkinson, Editor

Praeger Perspectives

 PRAEGER

AN IMPRINT OF ABC-CLIO, LLC
Santa Barbara, California • Denver, Colorado • Oxford, England

Library of Congress Cataloging-in-Publication Data

International business in the 21st century / Bruce D. Keillor, general editor.
    p. cm. — (Praeger perspectives)
  Includes bibliographical references and index.
  ISBN 978–0–313–37948–2 (hbk. : alk. paper) — ISBN 978–0–313–37949–9 (ebook)
1. International trade. 2. International business enterprises. 3. International economic relations. I. Keillor, Bruce David.
HF1379.I5674   2011
658′.049—dc22   2010048063

ISBN: 978–0–313–37948–2
EISBN: 978–0–313–37949–9

15 14 13 12 11   1 2 3 4 5

This book is also available on the World Wide Web as an eBook.
Visit www.abc-clio.com for details.

Praeger
An Imprint of ABC-CLIO, LLC

ABC-CLIO, LLC
130 Cremona Drive, P.O. Box 1911
Santa Barbara, California 93116-1911

This book is printed on acid-free paper ∞

Manufactured in the United States of America

Contents

Introduction

Bruce D. Keillor

As General Editor, it is my pleasure to introduce the reader to this three-volume set *International Business in the 21st Century*. The objective of this set is to provide the reader with cutting-edge insights from both professionals as well as the academics related to the dynamic and exciting world of international business. This is not a compilation of previously published material and "old" thinking. Myself, and the volume editors, have gone to great lengths to: create a set which can be applied in a real-world setting by firms exploring the possibility of international operations, suggest areas for improving efficiencies for those already operating outside of their home market, and provide insights into the critical issues related to international business in today's world. Each volume is built around a specific theme and represents the most current perspectives of leading government, business, and academic thinkers.

The first volume, *Are You Ready? Preparing for International Operations*, targets topics related to firm preparedness. Beginning with the vital issues of assessing export readiness, evaluating partnership choices in other markets, various market entry options, and obtaining the necessary financing, the volume then moves to more advanced topical areas that address the actual initiation of international operations. These include assessing and avoiding risk in international markets, selecting the appropriate market, or markets, to enter, gaining a clear understanding of the firm's product offering in the market(s) of choice, and coordinating firm strategy. It concludes with the need to consider lessons which can be gained from other firm's mistakes and the use of public relations in international markets. In sum, the first volume is a comprehensive tool for any firm considering entering the realm of international business.

The second volume, *Going Global: Implementing International Business Operations*, is directed at firms who have already committed to operations outside their home market. It opens by addressing the vital question of how to think global and still act local. From there, both internal and external issues are addressed. All of the key internal challenges associated with international operations are covered: expatriate vs. local staffing, how to motivate employees in different cultures, dealing with cultural difference within an organization, and assessing operational effectiveness across markets. From an external perspective, there is a heavy emphasis placed on the important problems related to understanding and connecting with the non-domestic consumers, product and brand strategies, as well as building an international supply chain, dealing with differences in the legal environment, and managing exchange rates. As is the case with the first, the second volume is designed to be a comprehensive tool but is targeted at those firms already operating outside of their home market.

The third, and final, volume, *Staying on Top: Critical Issues for International Business in the 21st Century*, has been designed to cover the truly critical issues associated with international business in the 21st century. Not specifically targeted at any type of firm, or any specific reader, it covers the areas identified by leading professionals and academics as being particularly important. These range from the changing perspectives of cultural differences, the "landscape" of the future international business environment including the role of emerging markets, the problems related to border security and terrorism, emerging macro and micro trends across the globe, the use of e-commerce and social media to reach customers, ethical issues, and using social responsibility as a strategy. In total, the third volume is presented as a "window to the future" for anyone interested in topics which will dominate international business as this century progresses.

My volume editors and I believe that, taken as a whole, this set represents the most comprehensive and useful collection of materials which deals with everything any business professional or academic would need to know in order to understand international business in the 21st century. With its outstanding variety of world-renowned experts providing their own special insights it is very much a unique collection. I am sure it will serve as both a guide as well as an ongoing resource for the future. We are proud to present *International Business in the 21st Century* to you.

Part I

Emerging Issues in the
International Environment

Chapter 1

Security Countermeasures and the Global Supply Chain: Striking the Balance

Andrew R. Thomas

INTRODUCTION

The fundamental security issue facing stakeholders of the global supply chain is which of the many countermeasures put in place after 9/11 will go and which will remain. Moreover, of the measures they keep, how will they integrate them into a systematic approach rather than a scatter-shot one? The answers to these questions, more than almost any other factor, may very well determine much of the future security of the global supply chain.

Effective supply chain security measures represent a combination of activities and techniques that are aimed at giving the system a strong assurance of deterrence, prevention, and detection.[1] Given that security resources are finite and that security measures must be promoted in the context of other constraints, simply buying security by implementing all available measures is not the answer. Trade-offs must be made, and consequently there needs to be a strategy in place to determine which countermeasures are to be employed and how.

Unfortunately, it appears that many governments around the world have been trying to do just the opposite. It seems that anybody with an idea or special technology to peddle is trying to get on the spending train. Almost daily in the popular press we read that some new technology is the magic bullet that will make us safer against Al-Qaeda or other groups or individuals who want to inflict damage on the supply chain.

Around the world stakeholders and industry planners are being asked to trust that whomever is ultimately in charge knows what they are doing. Promises are made that certain countermeasures will dramatically reduce the risk of future attacks: beefed-up passenger and baggage screening in airport terminals; multimillion-dollar X-ray machines at maritime ports; RDID tags; biometrics; and computer profiling technology. Each of these technologies is proclaimed as the next, best answer to the changing threat environment. But most stakeholders, planners, and researchers have almost no idea how to evaluate whether these security measures are ultimately worth the cost.

The purpose of this chapter is to present a baseline conceptual framework for evaluating security countermeasures which will allow for a rational assessment of whether those countermeasures meld with needs of the global supply chain in the post–9/11 environment.

THE SECURITY ELEMENTS OF THE GLOBAL SUPPLY CHAIN

Within the security context, there are four elements of the global supply chain:

- The assets (human, physical, and virtual) of the global supply chain that have to be protected.
- Dangerous groups and individuals—both internal and external—who seek to inflict damage and violence on the system.
- Inherent vulnerabilities that exist within the system which perpetrators seek to exploit in order to accomplish their ends.
- Security countermeasures that are implemented to protect the system's critical parts through the reduction of risk.

A brief summary of each of the first three elements follows here.

Assets of the Global Supply Chain

The global supply chain is one of the world's most important assets. Its growth over the past decades has made it one of the engines for the expansion of the world economy. It has changed the way of life for

Table 1.1
Key Stakeholders of the Global Supply Chain Security System

Producers	Transport firms	Internal contributors
• Consumer products	• Aviation	• Passengers
• B2B products	• Maritime	• Purchasers
• Consumer services	• Intermodal	• Shippers
• B2B services	• Rail	• Bureaucrats
• Manufacturers of supply chain assets	• Multi-modal	• Sellers
		• Re-sellers
		• Handlers
		• Security personnel
Governments		External beneficiaries
• International orgs.		• Customers
• National	**GLOBAL SUPPLY**	• End-users
• State	**CHAIN SECURITY**	• Distributors
• Local	**SYSTEM**	• Passengers
• Regulatory agencies		
• Customs		
• Traffic control		
Services	Infrastructure	Cargo
• Insurance	• Airports	• Freight forwarding
• Leasing/Financing	• Ocean container facilities	• Warehousing
• Distributors	• Highways/ interstates	• Consolidation
• Telecommunications	• Rail systems	• Mail
• Maintenance	• Training centers	• Transport
• Fuel and oil	• Maintenance facilities	
• Inspections	• Traffic control	
• Training		
• Universities		

most human beings on this planet. From a security perspective, the key stakeholders of the global supply chain reveal the scope and magnitude of the system (Table 1.1).

Dangerous Groups and Individuals

The global supply chain provides a tremendous opportunity to individuals or groups seeking to achieve their ends. First criminals and later terrorists came to realize that the global supply chain gave them access to a wide variety of options in order to get what they wanted. Criminals have traditionally looked upon the global supply chain as an environment ripe with offerings. Billions of tons of cargo, plus an individual's ability to move easily, and, more recently, affordably between long distances has lured criminals to use the supply chain as one of the most viable means to enrich themselves. For terrorists, the supply chain has long served as a target-rich environment—a place on the world stage to trumpet their political, social, or religious beliefs.

Criminals

There is no proven scientific explanation as to why certain people commit certain crimes. Criminology, which includes the study of why people commit crime, tends to focus on two main types of theories that try to answer this question: *Microtheories* primarily look at the individual. They explore why individuals become criminals and what might cause them to commit crimes. *Macrotheories*, on the other hand, focus upon how social structure affects criminal behavior. These theories examine what it is in society that makes people behave criminally, and in general look at criminal behavior as it occurs in groups of people rather than in individuals.[2] Whatever the explanation for what makes criminals do what they do, it is clear that the supply chain has always attracted criminals who want to achieve their ends.

According to the Federal Bureau of Investigation, cargo theft costs the United States $15 billion to $30 billion annually. Worldwide, cargo theft accounts for approximately $50 billion in direct merchandise losses. The problem isn't expected to lessen as more high-value goods move through global supply chains.[3]

Terrorists

Terrorism—a word which comes from the Latin *terrere*, "to cause to tremble"—has become a frightening global reality.[4] Scholars have observed that terrorism is most often an action taken as part of a broad strategy, not a random act of violence by wild-eyed psychotic misfits. Terrorism has also changed and evolved in recent decades—for example, the terrorists' ability to organize and the means and levels of violence used to achieve their objectives have all changed.[5] It is important to examine these changes, and to gain an appreciation for the long history of terrorism[6] when developing an understanding of the threat of contemporary terrorist organizations. According to Brian Jenkins, a senior advisor to the RAND Corporation, terrorists have adopted new models of organization and are less dependent on state sponsors; they are also effectively exploiting new communications technologies and can wage global campaigns.[7]

Generally speaking, terrorism has evolved over the last century from a local threat to a transnational phenomenon, facilitated in part by the supply chain's influence on globalization. Indeed, many years ago a terrorist group would have had far greater difficulties exporting their violence (and their extremist ideologies) from one geographic location to another. Ironically, the global supply chain that has aided the terrorists has also been the victim of many terrorist actions.[8]

For most terrorist groups, the appeal of attacking aviation targets may stem in part from the relatively high level of publicity and media coverage each attack receives. Terrorists see these results and conclude that supply chain targets are an effective and relatively low-cost means for gaining public attention about their grievances. During the 1970s and 1980s (when the most airplane hijackings took place) terrorists "adopted the international air carrier and the global supply chain as a podium for proclaiming their organizations' manifestos."[9]

Today, Al-Qaeda's foremost strategic objective is to "bleed" the United States economically and militarily by forcing the United States to spend exuberant amounts of money on protecting its numerous sectors and facilities.[10] An examination of primary Al-Qaeda operational manuals and open-source published literature reveals their ambitious desire to destroy the economy of the United States and other Western powers by striking economic targets in the West and in the Muslim world. They rationalize that if the American economy is derailed, then the United States will crumble and will not be able to sustain its military hegemony and presence overseas.

Terrorists will undoubtedly continue to target the global supply chain because of the potential damage to a nation's economy, along with the psychological impact achieved from the relatively high level of visibility and media coverage that every supply chain disaster receives. These are not the only rationales for targeting the global supply chain, but they do help illustrate the nature of the threat.[11]

A Subset of Terrorists and Criminals: Corrupt Insiders

Another group that is not specifically included within the scheme of perpetrators of violence against aviation but who play an active role is corrupt insiders. They tend to fall within the criminal category. However, they can also be well-placed terrorists who offer assistance to members outside their organization when the time to strike is at hand. The methods of violence they use are the same as criminals and terrorists. Attacks by insiders are not anything new, especially because they typically know their way around the inner workings of the security system and how to circumvent it better than almost anyone else. Personal revenge, a desire to enrich themselves, or any other number of reasons can be the motives for corrupt insiders.

Inherent Security Vulnerabilities of the Global Supply Chain

The dictionary defines the word *vulnerable* as (1) capable of being physically or emotionally wounded and (2) open to attack or damage.[12] The second definition is the one that applies most appropriately to global supply chain security. In its simplest form, a vulnerability is a flaw in the security of a system that an attacker can exploit to commit damage or injury. As with many technical issues, the dictionary definition can only help so much. The issue is much more complex. Vulnerabilities cannot always be defined in a clear-cut manner. With complex systems, supply chain security is a *very* complex system, and what may be a vulnerability in one situation may not be a vulnerability in another.

To get a better sense of what a vulnerability may be, it might be best to start with the broadest possible definition. That is, any access to the system is a potential vulnerability. This may sound somewhat scary, especially since the function of the supply chain is to serve billions of stakeholders around the world. It is impossible to simply block access. It would leave those in supply chain security with the Herculean task of trying to proactively manage risk in a system that is very accessible. It is only when there is no access that there are no vulnerabilities. But that is impossible.

Thus, the next best thing is attempted. Countermeasures which reduce the risk caused by the accessibility to the system are implemented. Yet, attackers will always find some degree of access to the global supply chain. It is an inherent reality.

Vulnerability can also stem from a situation where security measures may do things they weren't expected to do. Unintended consequences of measures and countermeasures are a potential vulnerability. When planners design a measure, it is intended to function in a certain way. Nonetheless, by implementing and putting a measure into action, it tends to become more complex than when it was merely an idea or a plan on the drawing board. This is exacerbated by the complexity of the global supply chain security system.

To be able to plan for all of the contingencies, glitches, and unanticipated problems that invariably arise in a complex system is almost impossible. These types of challenges are what confront those attempting to deal with supply chain security problems—unforeseen problems that may not be very obvious at the outset. In some cases, a long period of time may pass until anyone discovers the unintended vulnerability that a measure has created.

For example, current policies in place allow air marshals, armed pilots, and law enforcement officers to fly with their sidearm. Although the measure is designed in such a way that weapons stay under the control of a trained professional at all times, the mere presence of a firearm in an aircraft cabin can become a vulnerability if an unforeseen human factor enters into the picture.

As has happened in the past on numerous occasions, a law enforcement officer has used the lavatory and removed his firearm. Upon exiting the lavatory, the officer accidentally leaves the weapon behind. In this scenario, firearms in the air cabin may be regarded as a vulnerability according to the broader usage of the word. However, a narrower view of the term holds that such an unforeseen result may fall short of being a true vulnerability. It may be argued that although there is a possibility that a trained professional will leave a firearm in the lavatory onboard an aircraft, the probability of such occurrence helping a terrorist or criminal carry out their aims is quite low. The chance of a potential perpetrator coming across a misplaced firearm is miniscule. Therefore, in this case, a firearm on the aircraft mistakenly falling into the hands of an attacker might not be considered a high risk to the security system.

On the other hand, what about the scenario that a team of terrorists would intentionally cause a disruption on an aircraft to draw out the two or three air marshals that might be on the flight? Suppose that during a flight two terrorists make a beeline to the front of the plane, try to rush the cockpit door, and attempt to force their way in. Because air marshals are trained to work as a team, suppose that each of the marshals on the plane immediately reacted and drew their weapons on the two cockpit intruders. This would identify the marshals and leave them open to assault from the other three terrorists on the plane who had been lying in wait. Such a situation involving firearms on the aircraft could now make the presence of the weapons a vulnerability that could present a much higher level of risk.[13]

The primary concern of supply chain security managers, planners, and researchers should be *exploitable vulnerabilities*, like the air marshal scenario. If air marshals are properly trained to remain incognito and possess the self-discipline necessary to do so while their team member is trying to thwart the attack of the first two terrorists, then the level of risk for this exploitable vulnerability would be dramatically decreased. However, if their fellow air marshals lack the knowledge and control to stay seated, then the risk is much higher that a firearm can be seized by terrorists during a flight. This allows a vulnerability to be used to gain unauthorized access to the system or permits the vulnerability to be leveraged in order to directly attack the system and inflict violence. Unfortunately, such vulnerabilities have been recognized and were widely acknowledged as possible problems, but nothing was ever done to reduce the risk they posed.

A vulnerability can be termed *non-exploitable* if security functions or measures in place prevent exploitation of the vulnerability. If policies were in place that would prohibit the cockpit door from ever being opened during a flight, the vulnerability of the cockpit would be pretty much non-exploitable. However, as we've seen, failing to secure the door by allowing it to be opened keeps the cockpit an exploitable vulnerability.

The majority of the successful attacks on the supply chain security system have historically come from capitalizing on only a few exploitable vulnerabilities. This can be attributed to the fact that attackers are opportunistic, take the easiest and most convenient route, and exploit the best-known flaws with the most effective and widely available attack tools. They count on supply chain security planners not fixing these problems.

SECURITY COUNTERMEASURES AND RISK REDUCTION

Supply chain security, operating as a dynamic system, evolves over time. Discovered vulnerabilities may change and, as a result, security measures must change in response. Effectively implementing supply chain security measures requires an evolutionary systems approach. Security measures need to be advanced in a methodical, not scattershot, manner to ensure an appropriate level of supply chain security.

A major challenge in protecting the supply chain security system is illustrated by the aphorism: "A chain is only as strong as its weakest link." Consider the following as examples of this:

- Recently, several European maritime ports chose to implement a more stringent security measure using high-tech ID cards and access codes. In several cases, employees were terminated. The Information Technology Department, notified by the employee's manager, delayed removing the employee's access code and ID badge from the system because its policies required notification from Human Resources. Human Resources failed to notify IT, believing the department notification was adequate. In the meantime, the fired and now bitter employees still had access to the secure areas at the ports.

- Many cargo facilities around the world use passwords to limit access to secure areas. But many fail to train employees to stop "piggybacking"—allowing a second person to follow the first person through a secure door. The use of passwords in this instance creates a false sense of security.

- Airport checkpoint screeners are trained to better detect prohibited items. However, they are not taught to be on the lookout for lead-lined film bags, which, being perfectly legal, can be purchased at any retail store for around $15.00, and, if not detected, can transport or obscure any prohibited item through the checkpoint.

These examples demonstrate the need to take a holistic approach to supply chain security systems. The evidence is compelling that neither technologies nor policies alone really offer an effective defense for strong supply chain security. Theft of cargo takes place despite the screening of employees and the restriction of access to secure areas. Prohibited weapons flow through checkpoints despite better-trained, better-paid, and more observant workers. To best manage the risks posed by the threats to the supply chain security system, a comprehensive approach needs to be taken: one that embraces both the human and technical dimensions; and one that is not wholly subservient to the needs and wishes of merely a few stakeholders.

The Purpose of Supply Chain Security Measures

The perpetrators of violence—terrorists and criminals—act against the system in several ways and may pose different levels of danger. The severity of the perpetrators' attack is thus a variable. In short, all attackers and all attacks are not the same. The severity of an attack by a drug courier or an upset employee who didn't get a raise is not nearly as strong as a determined terrorist who is on a mission to sacrifice his life in order to kill many more.

The resources of the perpetrator vary as well and may include skills, tools, motivation, and opportunity. The use of these resources can increase or decrease as a function of time. In response to the resources of potential perpetrators, three kinds of supply chain security countermeasures should be implemented:

- *Security measures that reduce the severity of the threat.* Any action, mechanism, device, program, or policy that reduces the severity of a threat can be classified as a security measure.

- *Security measures that reduce the persistence of the threat.* Another type of security measure is one that increases of the resistance of the system to a perpetrator's particular mode of attack. The classic policy of limiting control to secure areas by using identification passwords and identifications is an example.

- *Security measures that reduce value loss to the system.* The third type of security measure reduces the value loss associated with an adverse event. Security measures that work by detecting threats can be thought of as reducing value loss.

The characteristics of the security measure itself are also important. Any security measure has to be set up properly, be tamper resistant, and work whenever it is required. The degree to which these three characteristics are met contributes to the resistance of the security measure against a potential perpetrator's mode of attack.

Evaluating Supply Chain Security Countermeasures

The widespread perception of supply chain security measures is that costs are significant and measurable, whereas the benefits of enhancing security are general and indeterminate.[14] This lack of clarity may stem from the recognition that the evaluation of countermeasures is most often done after the fact. That is, countermeasures are only assessed after they are developed and put into the supply chain.

This section will provide a conceptual framework for planners, managers, and researchers which will give better insight into reaching the balance between risk reduction to the system and countermeasure implementation, maintenance, and delay.

A formula for conceptualizing this relationship between the Inputs and Output would be:

(Amount of Implementation) + (Amount of Maintenance) + (Amount of Delay) = (Amount of Risk Reduction)

Implementation is the initial deployment. It is not time sensitive. Depending on the complexity and scale of the countermeasure, implementation can be a matter of days, weeks, or even years.

Maintenance is what sustains the countermeasure after the implementation phase. It can take on many roles, including updating of technology, retraining, assessment, repairs, or general upkeep.

The third Input, delay, is an inevitable by-product of the implementation and maintenance of a countermeasure. As the global supply chain is driven by the need for increased speed and efficiency, the addition of even a single security countermeasure will slow it down.

Output is defined as the reduction in the risk to the system that the countermeasure provides.

Five points (A, B, C, D, and E) are randomly placed on the continuum. *A* represents a point where the amount of implementation, maintenance, and delay caused (the total of the Inputs) by the countermeasure is low. Accordingly, the amount of risk reduction (the Output) is also minimal.

C illustrates a countermeasure where the amount of implementation, maintenance, and delay is moderate and the related risk reduction is as well. Point *E* is at the high end of the scale. It represents a countermeasure that involves a high degree of implementation and maintenance, while causing considerable delays to the system, yet substantially reducing security risk.

The purpose of this framework is to provide a semblance of rationality for those stakeholders who participate in the global supply chain security equation, either as designers, planners, or implementers of countermeasures. It is intended to provide a launching point for additional research and exploration—*before* the countermeasure is deployed.

SUMMARY

By taking a holistic, system-based approach, the intricate relationships that develop and evolve within the global supply security system can be understood. Taking the extra step towards a full-fledged assessment is the only way to determine the real value of a counter-measure to the system and its stakeholders.

Instead of trying to avoid every possible attack, limited resources must be directed towards countermeasures which provide the best possible protection without stifling the same system it is supposed to protect. Good security isn't perfect. Nor does it have to be. Like good people, effective security only has to do as well as it can to manage the inherent risks that the global supply chain presents. However, too often in their present form, security measures fail to reach this objective because they are not properly evaluated. And this makes the system far less secure than it ever should be.

NOTES

1. Andrew R. Thomas, *Aviation Insecurity: The New Challenges of Air Travel* (Amherst: Prometheus, 2003), 146.

2. Meryvn Bendle, "The Death of the Sociology of Deviance?," *Journal of Sociology* 35, no. 1 (1999): 46.

3. Jonathan Katz, "The Great Supply Chain Robbery," *Industry Week*, November 1, 2007, http://www.industryweek.com/ReadArticle.aspx?ArticleID=15165.

4. Mark Juergensmeyer, *Terror in the Mind of God: The Global Rise of Religious Terrorism* (Berkeley, CA: University of California Press, 2000), 145.

5. John Forest, "Modern Terrorist Threats to Aviation Security," in *Aviation Security Management: A 3-Volume Set*, ed. Andrew R. Thomas (Westport, CT: Praeger, 2008), 167.

6. David C. Rapoport, "The Four Waves of Rebel Terror and September 11," *Anthropoetics* 8, no. 1 (Spring/Summer 2002): 23.

7. Brian Jenkins, "The New Age of Terrorism," in *The McGraw-Hill Home-land Security Handbook*, ed. David G. Kamien (New York: McGraw Hill, 2006), 345.

8. John Forest, "Modern Terrorist Threats to Aviation Security," in *Aviation Security Management: A 3-Volume Set*, ed. Andrew R. Thomas (Westport, CT: Praeger, 2008), 169.

9. Richard M. Wrona, Jr., "Beginning of a War: The United States and the Hijacking of TWA Flight 847," in *Countering Terrorism and Insurgency in the 21st Century: International Perspectives*, vol. 3, ed. James J. F. Forest (Westport, CT: Praeger, 2007), 38.

10. Sammy Salama, "Unraveling Al-Qaida's Target Selection Calculus," in *Terrorism and Political Islam: A Textbook for the FBI New Agent Training Program*, ed. James J. F. Forest (Quantico, VA: FBI, 2007), 47.

11. John Forest, "Modern Terrorist Threats to Aviation Security," in *Aviation Security Management: A 3-Volume Set*, ed. Andrew R. Thomas (Westport, CT: Praeger, 2008), 168.

12. *Webster's Third New International Dictionary*, Unabridged, Third Edition.

13. Andrew R. Thomas, *Aviation Insecurity: The New Challenges of Air Travel* (Amherst: Prometheus, 2003), 188.

14. Barry Prentice, "Tangible and Intangible Benefits of Transportation Security," *Journal of Transportation Security* 1, no. 1 (2008): 13.

Chapter 2

The Sustainability Imperative

Mary McNally and Timothy J. Wilkinson

It is impossible to peruse the management and business literature now without encountering the ubiquitous term *sustainability*. It is everywhere, and used in such a dizzying variety of contexts that it is in danger of becoming misunderstood, even trivialized. In spite of overuse, the underlying fundamentals of the concept of sustainability are having a significant impact on current business practices, and will likely reconfigure international business strategies in the future. Many argue that sustainability will revolutionize and transform capitalism as we know it.[1] This chapter will track the rapidly evolving sustainability revolution and discuss potential implications of what may well become the sustainability imperative.

THE EMERGENCE OF SUSTAINABILITY IN BUSINESS

The most cited early definition of sustainability is from the 1987 Brundtland Commission Report, "Our Common Future."[2] The report defined sustainable development as development that meets the needs of the present without compromising the ability of future generations to meet their own needs. It is significant that the report goes on to specifically discuss both environmental and social/equity implications of sustainable development. In particular, the report notes:

- The concept of sustainable development does imply limits—not absolute limits but limitations imposed by the present state of technology and social organization on environmental resources and by the ability of the biosphere to absorb the effects of human activities. But technology and social organization can be both managed and improved to make way for a new era of economic growth.
- Meeting essential needs requires not only a new era of economic growth for nations in which the majority are poor, but an assurance that those poor get their fair share of the resources required to sustain that growth.[3]

Thus, at its modern inception, the concept of sustainability explicitly recognized the interdependence of economic and environmental well-being, and the importance of social equity.

Around the same time that the Brundtland Commission was convened, a number of related trends were occurring in business practices and literature. One was the increasing prominence of corporate social responsibility (CSR). As with sustainability, definitions of CSR abound, but the concept embodies a commitment to ethical practices and engagement with a range of stakeholders. A core construct of CSR is that, as socially sanctioned organizations, corporations in return need to contribute back to society.[4] And, although there has been debate over the extent of a corporation's social obligation, the CSR movement broadened the scope of that obligation beyond legally making a profit. Over time the effectiveness of CSR has come under scrutiny. The belief that a company could simply "do well by doing good" has been called into question and, as one author recently has noted, two decades after its conception there is a sense of fatigue about the limits of CSR.[5] But the debate over the obligation of business to society that the movement helped to crystallize has only grown.

Along with the emergence of CSR, there was a growing "green" movement, as companies recognized that reducing waste, even preventing pollution, was a more effective approach to environmental concerns than traditional "end of the pipe" mandated solutions. In some ways the improved environmental efficiencies were a result of total quality management practices, which encouraged redesign, process review, and continuous improvement. By the late 1980s a number of companies had implemented environmental practices to help manage risk, improve competitive advantage, and reduce costs.[6] Many of these early initiatives were successful and profitable.

With CSR and the green movement taking hold in industry, the Brundtland Commission Report had a receptive audience. Shortly thereafter there were several notable publications that helped define sustainability and put it front and center in the business literature. One of these was Paul Hawken's 1994 book *The Ecology of Commerce*. Through the title alone, Hawken was trying to connect two seemingly disparate worlds, the natural and the commercial. He drew a stark contrast between the industrial model of commerce, with all its ecological destructive forces, and a new, restorative model.

> To create an enduring society, we will need a system of commerce and production where each and every act is inherently sustainable and restorative. Business will need to integrate economic, biologic, and human systems to create a sustainable method of commerce. . . . Just as every act in an industrial society leads to environmental degradation, regardless of intention, we must design a system where the opposite is true . . . where the natural, everyday acts of work and life accumulate into a better world as a mater or course, not as a matter of conscious altruism.[7]

The key to creating a restorative economy was design—that is, designing commercial practices to align with natural principles. The three fundamental principles Hawken outlined were: waste equals food; reliance on renewable solar power; and thriving through diversity. Thus, for example, the waste that we currently generate, as producers and consumers, would be redesigned to become "food" for subsequent use, through reuse, recycling, or reclamation. Hawken argued that, although business as usual had helped get us to our present state, business is the only institution powerful enough to bring about the necessary changes to create a sustainable, even restorative, future.

Ecology of Commerce had a strong focus on the environmental implications of modern capitalism.[8] There was also growing recognition of the social and equity concerns. The publication, in 1998, of *Cannibals with Forks: The Triple Bottom Line of 21st Century Business*, by John Elkington, integrated the economic with social and environmental.[9] The book's title comes from the Polish poet Stanislaw Lec, who asked "Is it progress if a cannibal uses a fork?" In the foreword to his book, Elkington argues that the emergence of sustainable capitalism, or cannibals with forks, represents a significant improvement over the current system of corporate cannibalism. Elkington, generally credited with articulating what has come to be known as the triple bottom line, argued that business had to focus on economic prosperity, environmental quality, and equity/social justice, and that addressing all three was essential to shaping sustainable capitalism. He echoed Hawken's conviction that business, more than any other entity, was in the "driver's seat" and had the technology, finance, and management skills needed to achieve the sustainability transition. The book also made clear that moving toward sustainability required significant change, including a shift from an exclusive focus on "hard" values (commercial, profitability) to include soft ethical values, such as equity and alleviation of poverty.

The concept of the triple bottom line helped define the broad concept of sustainability. However it is expressed—the three Es representing economy, environment, and equity is common—it is now a widely recognized framework. Until recently, however, the emphasis has been more on the economy and environmental links, and less on the social equity aspects. Arguably, this is due in part to the prominence of environmental issues since the 1970s. But it is also due to the fact that there is no shared understanding about what social equity means, how it should "look," or what role (if any) commerce has in promoting equity.

That began to change with the work of C. K. Prahalad and Stuart Hart, and their focus on the Bottom of the Pyramid (BOP).[10] They defined BOP as the billions of people worldwide who live on less than $2/day, and argued that these people were, in fact, potential consumers and entrepreneurs. Hart in particular went beyond the BOP as potential consumers and urged corporations to move toward developing local producers and community capacity. According to Hart, the objective is indigenous enterprise, co-creating technologies, products, and services to meet local needs and building local businesses from the bottom up.[11] The focus on building local capacity and helping people grow their way out of poverty was not new. In fact, institutions like Grameen Bank had been providing credit and micro-loans to the rural poor since the 1970s. But what had changed was the broader recognition that acute poverty and inequality were issues that business could—and should—address.

In the 30-plus years since the Brundtland Commission put forth its definition, sustainability has assumed a prominent place in the popular lexicon. Although some definitional permutations may remain, there is general agreement about the common elements of sustainability objectives. These include:

- concern for environment, economy, and social equity;
- understanding our dependence on the health of natural systems for our survival and well-being;
- knowledge of the limits of the earth's ecosystems and detrimental impact of unchecked human activities;
- and a long-term, intergenerational perspective.[12]

The work of Hawken, Elkington, Prahalad, Hart, and many others helped bring environmental and social issues to the forefront, and sought to make them integral to business strategy. Although there is now a common framework for thinking about sustainability, there is much less agreement about how to really attain it.

SUSTAINABILITY IN A GLOBALIZED WORLD

The prominence of sustainability—in theory and a range of applications—owes much to the successes and failures of globalization. As the global economy has become more interdependent and interconnected, the impacts of globalization have also become more evident. Even as millions of people rise out of poverty, the gap between the haves and have not's is increasingly visible. The environmental costs of industrial and economic growth, whether calculated in terms of resource depletion, water and air quality, or potential climate change, are also evident. The social and environmental benefits—and costs—of globalization are not uniformly distributed and are not limited by national boundaries. As one author put it:

> The idea of ... "sustainable development" arose in part when people became aware that we could no long maintain our global drive toward continuing economic growth without exhausting our finite resources. ... And no rational person ... would claim that projected global population levels could be sustained at anywhere near the affluence levels found in the United States or other highly developed countries.[13]

Given exponential population growth, the need for improved economic opportunity and quality of life for vast portions of the world, and finite resources, the need for a sustainable approach to global development is inescapable.

But what does that really mean? Essentially a continuum exists of sustainability initiatives, ranging from minimal adjustments to fundamental strategic realignments, even radical systematic change. Does implementing recycling, reducing waste, and/or paying a "living wage" mean a company is operating in a sustainable way? Even if a firm adheres to the comprehensive principles and practices of the Natural Step or similar frameworks, or qualifies for the Dow Jones Sustainability Index (DJSI)—is that sufficient? Or will it require a total transformation of capitalism and the current model of globalization to really achieve a sustainable future? Numerous arguments exist supporting, and opposing, all of these scenarios and this is part of the contemporary confusion about what, in fact, sustainability means.

In some cases ongoing efforts to find new efficiencies or employ new approaches can enhance shareholder value and advance sustainability objectives. Essentially some of these initiatives are an extension of earlier "greening" efforts, but they often continue to be quite successful. A number of companies, MNEs in particular, have taken significant steps to "green" their operations and grow their profits. When a company the size of Wal-Mart embraces a new environmental awareness (and puts some earlier human resources practices aside) it has a significant impact throughout the supply chain, with competition and with customers. Unilever's initiatives in the areas of fisheries, sustainable agriculture, and water quality have kept it at the top of its industry and on the DJSI. These major companies, and many others, continue to find ways to "do well by doing good."[14]

The real challenge comes when sustainability objectives cannot clearly, or profitably, be aligned with business imperatives. A number of individuals, organizations, and businesses have been wrestling with this for some time. For example, the World Business Council for Sustainable Development (WBCSD) is a CEO-led global organization of some 200 companies engaged with business and sustainability. Their mission is to provide business leadership as a catalyst for change toward sustainable development, and to support the business license to operate, innovate, and grow in a world shaped increasingly by sustainable development issues.[15] WBCSD recognizes many of the challenges that exist to moving business forward in sustainable ways. One such impediment, long recognized in environmental and economics literature, is that markets prices do not accurately incorporate environmental values and costs, and that the latter are externalized and outside of traditional business decision-making metrics.[16] WBCSD alludes to this in their report "Sustainability through the Market: Seven Keys to Success." The report supports improving market framework conditions and establishing the worth of the Earth as two of their seven keys, but neglects to advocate how this should be accomplished.[17]

Stakeholder partnerships, innovation, even eco-efficiency may be important steps toward sustainability, but do not adequately address many of the underlying challenges. Eco-efficiency is an instructive example. Eco-efficiency essentially means doing more with less—for example producing the same output while reducing pollution emissions. This is essentially what Wal-Mart and others are doing, with excellent results. Although reducing "the bad" is clearly worthwhile, some argue that it is insufficient because it only works to make the old system a bit less destructive. In effect, being less bad is not good enough.[18]

So what is "good enough"? Some argue that nothing short of a reworking of the basic institutions and rules of global capitalism will take us in a direction of sustainability.[19] For example, in his book *The Bridge at the Edge of the World: Capitalism, the Environment, and Crossing from Crisis to Sustainability,* James Speth, dean of the School of Forestry and Environmental Studies at Yale University, offers a compelling analysis of the increasingly dire state of the environment, and states:

> In short, my conclusion, after much searching and considerable reluctance, is that most environmental deterioration is a result of systematic failures of the capitalism we have today and that long-term solutions must seek transformative change in the key features of this contemporary capitalism.[20]

These long-term changes include transforming markets so they work for the environment; creating a post-growth society, involving alternative measures of social and economic well-being; encouraging green consumption, and less consumption overall; and changing the nature and governance of corporations.

Others believe the transformation must focus on the local level; that is, local communities, economies, and ecosystems. David Korten, for example, argues that a sustainable future rests on networks of local living economies, a concept that is the foundation for the Business Alliance for Local Living Economies (BALLE). A Local Living Economy "ensures that economic power resides locally to the greatest extent possible, sustaining vibrant, livable communities and healthy ecosystems in the process."[21] Korten's most recent book, *Agenda for a New Economy: From Phantom Wealth to Real Wealth* is even more explicit about dismantling traditional capitalist institutions, including Wall Street, decentralizing power, and focusing on invigorating Main Street economies and communities.[22]

One of the most interesting and important ideas to emerge from the cacophony of voices in the exploding sustainability debate is the significance of design. Several different strands exist to this topic, including natural capitalism, biomimicry, and cradle to cradle. Basic principles of natural capitalism were well publicized in a 1999 *Harvard Business Review* article authored by Paul Hawken, Amory Lovins, and L. Hunter Lovins.[23] Essentially, natural capitalism was concerned with advocating new ways of thinking about business and the environment. The three core principles included increasing dramatically the productivity of natural resources (eco-efficiency), shifting to biologically inspired production models (biomimicry), and moving toward a solutions-based business model. In addition to embracing eco-efficiency, natural capitalism advocated redesigning production according to a closed loop model whereby outputs could be recycled into natural or technical nutrients, thus completing the waste equals food biological cycle. The solutions-based business model focused on delivering services as opposed to products—providing illumination, for example, instead of supplying light bulbs. Clearly some of these principles had already been embraced by business, as eco-efficiency had become a driver for many companies. But the natural capitalism model, with its focus on whole system design, was a more comprehensive approach to melding business and sustainability objectives.

Perhaps one of the best-known companies to embrace natural capitalism is Interface carpet. Interface founder and Chairman Ray Anderson, who describes having an epiphany in 1994 as a result of reading *Ecology of Commerce*, became committed to sustainability.[24] The company's journey toward sustainability is extensively documented on Interface's website and in a book written by Anderson himself.[25] Interface has developed its own model, which rests on Seven Fronts, or steps, the company is taking to achieve sustainability. These include eliminating waste; benign emissions; renewable energy; closing the loop; resource efficient transportation; sensitizing stakeholders; and redesigning commerce. Progress and results are verified by third-party standards and organizations, including ISO standards, CRI green label, Leed, and others. Finally, the company has made a commitment to Mission Zero—a promise to eliminate any negative impact Interface has on the environment by 2020.

The principles of biomimicry that natural capitalism embraced were first articulated by Janine Benyus in her 1997 book *Biomimicry: Innovation Inspired by Nature.*[26] According to Benyus, *biomimicry* (a term she created) is a new science that takes inspiration from nature's designs and processes and uses them to solve human problems. Nature is used as a model, measure, and mentor, and the focus is on what can be learned from nature, as opposed to what can be extracted and used from it.

> The classic example of biomimicry innovation is Velcro, whose inventor, George de Mestral, observed that the hooked tips of thistle seeds caused them to stick to the fur of his dog. Today we look ever more systematically to nature for sustainable solutions to a host of practical problems—for which existing solutions are often environmentally unfriendly or energy inefficient. We believe that now is an opportune time for global businesses to develop profitably around some of the ideas nature offers.[27]

Benyus's ideas are having a significant impact on business thinking and innovation. For example, Interface uses biomimicry principles to design eco-friendly and profitable products. The BioHavens developed by an entrepreneur in Montana were designed to mimic the properties of floating islands found in nature.[28] The Biomimicry Institute website offers a number of case studies and links to a database of over 2000 innovations "inspired by nature."[29]

One of the most comprehensive statements about the profound significance of design was captured in the book *Cradle to Cradle.* Written by William McDonough, an architect, and Michael Braungart, a chemist, *Cradle to Cradle* (C2C) is about creating a new industrial re-evolution through ecologically intelligent design. The authors argue that our current system of production is a relic of the Industrial Revolution, wedded to a linear, one way cradle-to-grave model. As the limits of this approach become more acute, many solutions have focused on reducing the impacts—for example, becoming more eco-efficient. McDonough and Braungart offer a very different solution.

> We see a world of abundance, not limits. In the midst of a great deal of talk about reducing the human ecological footprint, we

offer a different vision. What if humans designed products and systems that celebrate an abundance of human creativity, culture, and productivity? That are so intelligent and safe, our species leaves an ecological footprint to delight in, not lament?[30]

Instead of eco-efficiency, C2C argues for eco-effectiveness, creating the right things (products, goods, services) instead of making the wrong things less bad. Two broad principles underlie eco-effectiveness. The first is that waste equals food, meaning that it becomes nourishment for something new. For this to be true, products must be designed so that, at the end of their useful life, they become either biological nutrients (essentially compost) or technical nutrients (upcycled back into use). Products that are technical nutrients (electronics, for example) should be designed to be used by consumers and eventually returned to the manufacturer to be broken down and re-circulated in closed-loop industrial cycles. Thus, instead of constantly buying new cell phones (and trying to dispose of the old ones), consumers would buy the services provided by a cell phone. The second principle is to respect diversity and promote design thinking that reflects the diversity found in nature, cultures, and local places. This includes the diversity found in natural, renewable energy flows and the abundance provided by the sun. The *Cradle to Cradle* book itself is an example of their design principles in action. The book is made from plastic resins and inorganic filler and is waterproof, durable, and recyclable and is a prototype for books as technical nutrients.[31]

The emphasis on waste as a nutrient and nature's need for diversity are evident in other models, and the "product as service" concept is much like the solutions-based approach discussed in natural capital. But the C2C model makes larger claims and envisions a more expansive future than many others. For example, business is not only recognized as a key institution in promotion sustainability; it is viewed as the primary agent of change in terms of realizing eco-effectiveness. In one interview Michael Braungart characterized cradle to cradle as a business model, a strategy to come up with product and process innovation.[32] The website for McDonough Braungart Design Chemistry (MBDC), the consulting business based on C2C, reinforces this through its Transforming Industry message.

More fundamentally, eco-effectiveness seems to reject the idea of limits, and instead celebrates abundance, human creativity, even growth, as long as it is the right kind of growth. The key is to design human industries and systems to get "bigger and better in a way that replenishes, restores, and nourishes the rest of the world."[33] This may be an appealing premise, but it is at odds with many traditional approaches to sustainability, which have focused on efficiency, and reducing environmental impacts. The authors address this head on and in an interesting way by asking how exciting is it to strive to be (only) sustainable? "Natural systems take from their environment but they also give something back. . . . We can follow their cue to create a more inspiring engagement—a partnership—with nature."[34] Their vision is having buildings that are net energy producers, factories whose effluents are drinking water, and business contributing to a world of abundance.

The conscious, ecologically intelligent design concepts embodied in C2C, biomimicry, and natural capitalism are liberating, expansive, and invigorating. They help frame a different way of thinking about almost everything, and put social/human values and environmental principles front and center. The realities, and especially the failures, of globalization have helped drive the sustainability debate, but these emerging models are based on possibility, not fear. In this sense sustainability is about a positive way forward. Instead of focusing on survival, and what we cannot do, it is becoming about how we need to think, and design, and do things differently in order to prosper.

THE WAY FORWARD

It is notable that, even as new thinking is emerging in terms of sustainable practices related to environmental and social realms, there is increasing concern about the fundamentals of existing economic and financial structures. Although critics of globalization, writ large and small, have long offered critiques, recent catastrophic failures of global financial markets and the resulting global recession have renewed broader discussions about where the global system is heading. Now more than ever there is recognition that business as usual, at least as we have practiced it of late, is not working. And, although there may not be consensus about the correct or best way forward, there is recognition that we need to, and must, make changes.

Some of these changes may be relatively straightforward—for example, developing new accounting and financial standards that better account for, and value, environmental services and social investments. Some of this is already under way. Similarly, there has long been recognition that, in order to evaluate and improve initiatives toward sustainability, it is necessary to have metrics to establish benchmarks and track improvements. The earliest and perhaps most recognized example of this is the ISO 14000, a series of international standards for environmental management systems, including lifecycle analysis.[35] Quite a bit of work has been done, especially on the level of individual firms, and although there is still no general agreement on appropriate metrics, considerable progress has been made.[36] In addition, efforts to develop such metrics for larger entities, industries, even communities are also ongoing.

Some other changes, although generally recognized as essential, are less easily implemented. For example, virtually all sustainability models embrace market-based solutions, but there is widespread acknowledgement that, at a minimum, markets need to more accurately reflect real prices and costs. This may be as "simple" as implementing Pigouian taxes or Coasean principles for incorporating real environmental costs into market pricing, or it may entail something more complex to better value nature's ecological services. Continuing to exclude these costs from basic decision frameworks is not acceptable, but implementing such changes is far from simple. The ongoing efforts to include the real cost of carbon emissions into the broader economic, social, and environmental calculus is a current case in point.

Clearly, successfully navigating toward more sustainable business models, even capitalist systems, will involve a variety of changes. One important example of how change may be taking hold is in business education itself. Organizations like the Aspen Institute, through the Center for Business Education, are chronicling the changes in curriculum, programs, even values, in business schools. For example, Beyond Grey Pinstripes, the Aspen Institute's biennial global survey of innovative full-time MBA programs that are integrating issues of social and environmental stewardship into curricula and research, highlights the top 100 such programs. The emphasis on social stewardship is blurring traditional boundaries between for-profit and not-for profit entities, even between business and public policy, as social enterprise and social entrepreneurship programs take shape. Environmental metrics and considerations are increasingly being incorporated in core business disciplines including finance, accounting, production, marketing, and strategy. Although it remains true that many of these changes are occurring in traditional academic "silos" (as exemplified by the proliferation of sustainability/green affiliation groups in professional associations like the American Management Association) there are many interdisciplinary programs emerging as well. The fact that AACSB held its first ever sustainability conference in 2009 is further evidence that this is no longer a "fringe" concept.

The sustainability imperative has been fueled, in part, by fears about irreversible environmental degradation; concern with growing poverty and economic disparity; facing the limitations, even failures of globalization; and uncertainty about our economic future. But emerging thinking about sustainability offers a positive way forward. It presents a different vision—a conscious choice about what the future of capitalism needs to look like. Sustainability recognizes the interconnectedness of systems (natural, economic, social) and the interdependence of all of humanity. It is market driven, but driven by markets that reflect true (environmental and social) costs. Sustainability offers ways of thinking that do not focus on limits as much as innovative, restorative models that can help us re-think the interdependent systems we are all part of, and design organizations, products, and services that help move us toward a different future.

NOTES

1.   See, for example, James Speth, *The Bridge at the Edge of the World: Capitalism, the Environment, and Crossing from Crisis to Sustainability* (New Haven, CT: Yale University Press, 2008); Stuart Hart, *Capitalism at the Crossroads: Aligning Business, Earth, and Humanity* (Upper Saddle River, NJ: Wharton School Publishing, 2007).

2.   The Brundtland Commission, named after its chair, was earlier known as the World Commission on Environment and Development and was convened in 1983 by the United Nations to address concerns about environmental degradation and economic development. Available at: www.un-documents.net/wced-ocf.htm.

3.   Brundtland Report, "Our Common Future: From One Earth to One World," UN Documents, www.un-documents.net/ocf-ov.htm#I.3 (accessed January 29, 2010).

4.   Timothy Devinney, "Is the Socially Responsible Corporation a Myth? The Good, the Bad, and the Ugly of Corporate Social Responsibility," *Academy of Management* (May 2009): 44.

5.   Marjorie Kelly and Allen White, "Turning Point: From Corporate Responsibility to Corporate Design," *Journal of Corporate Citizenship* 33 (Spring 2009): 23.

6.   See, for example, Forest Reinhardt, "Bringing the Environment Down to Earth," *Harvard Business Review* (July–August 1999); Michael Porter and Claas Van Der Linde, "Green and Competitive: Ending the Stalemate," *Harvard Business Review* (September–October 1995).

7. Paul Hawken, *The Ecology of Commerce: A Declaration of Sustainability* (New York: HarperCollins, 1993), Preface xiv.

8. Ibid.

9. John Elkington, *Cannibals with Forks: The Triple Bottom Line of 21st Century Business* (Gabriola Island, BC: New Society Publishers, 1998).

10. Stuart Hart and C. K. Prahalad, "The Fortune at the Bottom of the Pyramid," *Strategy and Business* 26 (2002): 54–67. Both authors subsequently published their own books: C. K. Prahalad, *The Fortune at the Bottom of the Pyramid* (Upper Saddle River, NJ: Wharton School Publishing, 2004); Stuart L. Hart, *Capitalism at the Crossroads: The Unlimited Business Opportunities in Solving the World's Most Difficult Problems* (Upper Saddle River, NJ: Wharton School Publishing, 2005).

11. Hart, *Capitalism at the Crossroads*, 195.

12. Andres Edwards, *The Sustainability Revolution: Portrait of a Paradigm Shift* (Gabriola Island, BC: New Society Publishers, 2005), 7.

13. John Ehrenfled, "The Roots of Sustainability," *MIT Sloan Management Review* 46, no. 2 (Winter 2005), 23.

14. Wal-Mart and several companies are highlighted in Chris Laszlo's, *Sustainable Value: How the World's Leading Companies are Doing Well by Doing Good* (Stanford, CT: Stanford University Press, 2008).

15. World Business Council for Sustainable Development, available at: www.wbcsd.org/ (accessed March 2010).

16. One recent comment gets to the heart of this issue by offering a purely economic definition of sustainability—that is, an activity is sustainable when all costs are internalized. Christopher Meyer, comment on "Leading Green," Harvard Business Review Blog, comment posted June 26, 2008, http://blogs.harvardbusiness.org/leadinggreen/2008/06/we-need-a-definition-of-sustai.html (accessed June 22, 2009).

17. Chad Holliday and John Pepper, "Sustainability through the Market: Seven Keys to Success," *WBCSD*, April 1, 2001, www.wbcsd.org/DocRoot/xs6OhpvANJioGJPFEkBH/stm.pdf.

18. William McDonough and Michael Braungart, *Cradle to Cradle: Remaking the Way We Make Things* (New York: North Point Press, 2002), 62.

19. See particularly John Cavanagh, Jerry Mander, Sarah Anderson, Andrew Kimbrell, Debi Barker, David Korten et al., *Alternatives to Economic Globalization: A Better World Is Possible* (San Francisco, CA: Berrett-Koehler, 2002).

20. Speth, *Bridge at the End of the World*, 9.

21. Business Alliance for Local Living Economies, "Mission, Vision, and Principles," www.livingeconomies.org/aboutus/mission-and-principles.

22. David C. Korten, *Agenda for a New Economy: From Phantom Wealth to Real Wealth* (San Francisco, CA: Berrett-Koehler, 2009).

23. Paul Hawken, Amory Lovins, and L. Hunter Lovins, "A Road Map for Natural Capitalism," *Harvard Business Review* (May–June 1999).

24. Interface Global, www.interfaceglobal.com/Sustainability/Our-Journey .aspx (accessed March 2010).

25. Ray Anderson, *Mid Course Correction* (Atlanta, GA: Peregrinzella Press, 1999).

26. Janine Benyus, *Biomimicry: Innovation Inspired by Nature* (New York: William Morrow, 1997).

27. Janine Benyus and J. M. Pauli, "The Business of Biomimicry," *Harvard Business Review List 2009*, hbr.org/web/2009/hbr-list/business-of-biomimicry (accessed March 2010).

28. Mary McNally and Tim Wilkinson, "Floating Island International," forthcoming.

29. Biomimicry Institute, www.biomimicryinstitute.org/case_studies.php.

30. McDonough and Braungart, *Cradle to Cradle*, 15–16.

31. Ibid., 5.

32. Diana den Held, " 'Criticism on Cradle to Cradle?' Right on Schedule, Says Michael Braungart," interview of Michael Braungart for Duurzaam gebouwd, www.duurzaamgebouwd.nl/index.php?pageID=3946&message ID=1936 (accessed March 2010).

33. McDonough and Braungart, *Cradle to Cradle*, 78.

34. Ibid., 155–56.

35. For a general overview, see the International Organization for Standardization, "ISO 14000 Essentials," www.iso.org/iso/iso_14000_essentials (accessed March 2010).

36. See, for example, the Network for Business Sustainability, "Systematic Review: Valuing Business Sustainability," www.nbs.net/Docs/RNBS_Valuation _2008.pdf (accessed March 2010).

Chapter 3

Emerging Markets, Transitional Economies, and Emerging Market Multinationals

Lance Eliot Brouthers and Ted Barber Randall

INTRODUCTION

In a global economy many companies look to expand internationally to reduce production costs, obtain new resources, and/or to take advantage of new and growing markets. Although developed countries offer relatively safe investment markets, having rule of law established and stable democratically elected governments, relatively open transparent market economies and sound currencies, the cost of entry can be relatively high due to existing competition, start-up costs, or other barriers to entry. For countries willing to take on increased risks, an alternative is to consider investing in emerging markets where risks are higher but potential economic rewards may be significantly greater.

In this chapter, we examine emerging markets. We explain what emerging markets are, examine the big emerging markets (BEMs), describe what transitional economies are and how they may be viewed as emerging markets, and give examples of multinational enterprises (MNEs) that have their roots in emerging markets.

EMERGING MARKETS

In his book *Emerging Economies and the Transformation of International Business*, Jain[1] identifies 28 countries that he considers emerging markets and defines an emerging market as one in the process of moving from a lower state of economic development where the vast majority of the population has little disposable income toward a higher state of economic development where a large proportion of the population has a more significant disposable income. Thus, an emerging market typically has a low-to-middle per capita income.[2]

An emerging market has a semblance of a free-market economy, one where some form of free-market trade and opportunity exists. Some emerging markets are transitioning from command economies to free-market economies. These emerging markets are termed *transitional economies* and include nations such as Russia and other Central and Eastern European Countries (CEEs), and China. In India, like China, trade opportunities are increasing as the existing government assimilates elements of free-market economies into their existing structure. An emerging market exhibits potential opportunities for economic growth for foreign companies.

Various methods exist that look at economies and determine where on the continuum of development a specific economy is currently at, and which direction they are progressing. These measures include, among others, Gross Domestic Product (GDP), Merger and Acquisitions (M&A), Foreign Direct Investment, and the Standard of Living.

Many different lists exist that identify which countries are emerging markets and their status in becoming a developed economy. These lists are generated primarily to aid in investment strategies. They also provide insight to the development of various countries. One of the first lists generated is Standard & Poor's Emerging Market Database. This database was developed in 1973 and is considered one of the premier sources for information and statistics on the stocks in 53 emerging markets.[3] The FTSE Group (FTSE) provides data on 45 emerging markets, classifying the top 22 into two segments, advanced emerging and secondary emerging markets, and the other 23 as frontier markets. FTSE classifies these countries using economic size, wealth, quality of market, and depth and breadth of market.[4] Table 3.1 is a list of the FTSE Global Equity Index Series which has the 45 emerging markets as well as the developed markets that FTSE provides data about.

Another major list is the Morgan Stanley Capital International (MSCI) index. Similar to the FTSE list, MSCI uses their own set of

Table 3.1
FTSE Global Equity Index Series

Developed	Advanced emerging	Secondary emerging	Frontier
Australia	Brazil	Argentina	Bahrain
Austria	Hungary	Chile	Bangladesh
Belgium/Luxembourg	Mexico	China	Botswana
Canada	Poland	Colombia	Bulgaria
Denmark	South Africa	Czech Republic	Côte d'Ivoire
Finland	Taiwan	Egypt	Croatia
France		India	Cyprus
Germany		Indonesia	Estonia
Greece		Malaysia	Jordan
Hong Kong		Morocco	Kenya
Ireland		Pakistan	Lithuania
Israel		Peru	Macedonia
Italy		Philippines	Mauritius
Japan		Russia	Nigeria
Netherlands		Thailand	Oman
New Zealand		Turkey	Qatar
Norway			Romania
Portugal			Serbia
Singapore			Slovakia
South Korea			Slovenia
(September 2009)			Sri Lanka
Spain			Tunisia
Sweden			Vietnam
Switzerland			
UK			
USA			

Source: FTSE, 2008.

indices to identify a list of emerging markets for their financial clients. MSCI uses indices that consist of several index families, spanning 74 markets, designed to address the indexing and benchmarking needs of institutional investors across a range of investment styles.[5] MSCI identifies markets as developed, emerging, and frontier. Table 3.2 contains a list of MSCI market classifications.

Various lists are available from other financial companies such the International Monetary Fund Global Financial Stability Report, HSBC,

Table 3.2
MSCI International Equity Indices—Country and Market Coverage

Developed markets			Emerging markets			Frontier markets				
Americas	Europe	Pacific	Americas	Europe, Middle East & Africa	Asia	Americas	Central & Eastern Europe & CIS	Africa	Middle East	Asia
Canada	Austria	Australia	Brazil	Czech Republic	China	Argentina	Bulgaria	Botswana[a]	Bahrain	Pakistan
United Sates	Belgium	Hong Kong	Chile	Egypt	India	Jamaica[a]	Croatia	Ghana[b]	Jordan	Sri Lanka
	Denmark	Japan	Colombia	Hungary	Indonesia	Trinidad & Tobago	Estonia	Kenya	Kuwait	Vietnam
	Finland	New Zealand	Mexico	Israel	Korea		Lithuania	Mauritius	Lebanon	
	France	Singapore	Peru	Morocco	Malaysia		Kazakhstan	Nigeria	Oman	
	Germany			Poland	Philippines		Romania	Tunisia	Qatar	
	Greece			Russia	Taiwan		Serbia		Saudi Arabia[b]	
	Ireland			South Africa	Thailand		Slovenia		United Arab Emirates	
	Italy			Turkey			Ukraine			
	Netherlands									
	Norway									
	Portugal									
	Spain									
	Sweden									
	Switzerland									
	United Kingdom									

[a]The MSCI Botswana Index, the MSCI Ghana Index, and the MSCI Jamaica Index are currently stand-alone country indices and are not included in the MSCI Frontier Markets Index. The addition of these country indices to the MSCI Frontier Markets Index is under consideration.
[b]The MSCI Saudi Arabia Index is currently not included in the MSCI Frontier Markets Index but is part of the MSCI Gulf Cooperation Council (GCC) Countries Index.
Source: MSCIBarra, 2009.

and others. Although the companies generating these lists may use various indices, and may classify the countries in different ways, they do agree that emerging markets are areas that need to be watched and assessed as potential opportunities of growth.

BIG EMERGING MARKETS

In an attempt to increase exports and thereby increase jobs, the U.S. Commerce Department crafted the United State's National Export Plan in 1993. With growth in developed countries slowing, and the projection that the majority of global growth would come from emerging countries, the Commerce Department identified 10 emerging markets they felt represented the best opportunities for U.S. export growth.[6] Identified as the Big Emerging Markets (BEMs) these 10 countries— Argentina, Brazil, China, India, Indonesia, South Korea, Mexico, Poland, South Africa, and Turkey—represented the best export opportunities in emerging markets.[7]

Chief among the 10 BEMs were Brazil, India, and China. Russia did not make the list, possibly due to the economic and political struggles that country was experiencing during the early 1990s. However, by 2000 Russia was also considered a significant emerging market. Then in 2003 economists from Goldman Sachs published a report entitled "Dreaming With BRICs: The Path to 2050," which focused on long-term projections of GDP growth and size of Brazil, Russia, India, and China, and made popular the acronym BRIC, standing for these four countries.[8] This report estimated that by 2050 the BRIC countries will have eclipsed the original G6—France, Germany, Italy, Japan, United Kingdom, and the United States—in GDP.[9] Assuming that the BRIC countries continue to maintain policies and develop institutions that promote growth, these countries will become a major factor in the global economy.[10]

According to CIA World Factbook, in 2008 the four BRIC countries ranked among the top 10 economies in the world as measured by GDP, and together exceeded the GDP of the European Union (EU). What makes these four countries even more significant is their potential as markets. The population of the BRIC is four times greater than the G6, and almost six times greater than the European Union.[11] As these four countries' economies continue to move toward developed status they have the potential of having significant economic and political clout in the global arena.[12] For this reason, they merit a more in-depth review.

Brazil

Considered the smallest of the BRIC countries, Brazil is still a world power in regards to GDP and size. In 2008, Brazil ranked fifth in population and land area, and ninth in GDP (ppp).[13]

Since the 1930s Brazil's government has vacillated between periods of growth and prosperity that were followed by stagnation and hyperinflation. After years of failing economic and social reform, with the government switching from dictatorship to democracy and back again, the military took over the government in 1964.[14] The years immediately following this military coup saw good economic growth stemming from reforms put in place by the militaristic government. However, as time went on, these reforms began to fail and by the early 1980s the national debt was soaring and the economy was experiencing hyperinflation.[15]

In 1985 the government began a transition from a military dictatorship to a democracy, and in 1989 a newly elected president came to power. With this transition new economic policies involving free trade and privatization of government owned companies were implemented.[16] Companies in the mining, steel, telecommunications, and aerospace industries were privatized. Two such companies, Embraer and Companhia Vale do Rio Doce (branded as Vale), have grown into well-respected multinational enterprises in their industries, with Vale becoming the second-largest mining company in the world (2007).

However, Brazil continues to struggle with sociopolitical problems. Political corruption continues to be a problem. Additionally Brazil is surrounded by what seem to be the strongest socialistic governments in the world with neighbors such as Venezuela and Bolivia.[17] Brazil continues to rank among the top countries in the world with respect to income inequality and has a GDP per capita of just over US $10,000, placing it in the 103rd position in the world.[18]

In spite of the Brazil's problems, its potential remains tremendous. One forecast puts the GDP growth rate of Brazil at more than triple of that of the G6 through 2020 and the GDP is expected to overtake Italy, France, the United States, and Germany by 2036. If Brazil can avoid or significantly reduce, political, financial, and social upheaval, it will emerge as one of the primary markets in the world.[19]

Russia

With a GDP of over US$2.2 trillion, Russia ranks as the seventh-largest economy in the world, and the second largest of the big emerging markets.[20] It has just been in the last few years that Russia has been able to reach this level.

Soon after the collapse of the former Soviet Union in the late 1980s, Russia found itself struggling with its economy, trying to understand what it meant to be a free-market society. The GDP dropped 50 percent, and under Boris Yeltsin's control the doors to the resources of Russia were thrown open and people with experience in a free-market-type society stepped in to take advantage. Many of those with experience were the same people that ran the black markets under communist rule. These black marketers became the new "oligarchs" of Russia and rapidly obtained wealth by snatching up over a trillion dollars worth of factories, mines, metals, transport, oil, gas, iron, coal, and other formerly state-owned resources.[21] By 2004 it was estimated that just 10 groups of oligarchs controlled 35 percent of manufacturing sales.

During the years from 1991 to 1998 many believed that the Russian economy was sound in spite of indicators such as the GDP. Many held to the idea that the hyper-depression which caused the GDP to be cut in half was a statistical illusion due to the improperly inflated values of the former Soviet industry, and companies continued to invest in Russia. The financial crash in August 1998 exposed the reality of the situation to the tune of several billions of dollars in losses.[22] Since the August 1998 financial crash Russia has regrouped and is making significant strides. Russian had an average GDP growth rate of 7 percent from 1998 to 2007 and is emerging as a major market.

As the economy recovered, many of the privatized companies began to look outward and Russian MNEs began to emerge. In the 1990s there was an estimated US$1.9 billion in outward FDI, and by 2007 outward FDI had reached US$45.6 billion and was continuing to grow.[23] Companies like Gazprom, Severstal, and others are major MNEs. Gazprom is the world's largest gas and oil company. Severstal, the largest steel mining company in Russia, has assets in Ukraine, Kazakhstan, United Kingdom, France, Italy, and the United States. One of the major factors in the growth rate is the oil and gas industry. Oil and gas production has played a significant role, contributing to over a quarter of the total GDP and over 50 percent of exports from 2001 to 2004.[24] As a result, Russia's continued growth will be significantly affected by the prices of these products. Because of this, some experts have doubts about the quality and sustainability of Russia's economic growth, claiming that Russia's growth is due exclusively to high oil prices.[25]

The market potential for companies interested in investing in Russia is, like the other BRIC countries, very large. One of the main attractions for Russia, like Brazil, is the natural resources. Russia is the world's largest country by land area. In 2008, Russia's estimated population exceeded 140 million with a GDP US$2.2 trillion, making it the ninth-largest country with the seventh-largest economy in the world.[26] With its high GDP growth and vast natural resources, Russia is a developing opportunity. In 2008 mergers and acquisitions topped US$173 billion, up 71 percent on the year, exceeding those in China by US$29 billion.

In spite of its rocky start Russia is well on the road to once again becoming an economic power. Due to the size of the country and the growth of the GDP many corporations are positioning themselves to take advantage of the opportunity. However, there are risks to entering this market. One must understand the nature of the oligarchic culture and, as in all markets, be well aware of the evolving political situation.

India

With the second-largest population in the world,[27] India has long been on multinational enterprises' lists of potential markets. Unlike the other BRIC countries, India has been a democracy since 1947 when independence was gained from British rule. The new government adopted policies that were primarily socialistic. From 1952 to 1978 India followed the policies of Prime Minister Jawaharlal Nehru, focusing on public investment in heavy industry and tight controls on the private sector.[28] High import tariffs and duties were imposed and India became economically isolated. The policies implemented resulted in a sluggish economy stifled by red tape, excessive bureaucracy and regulation, and corruption was pervasive. Many of the state-governed monopolies were run by people with political connections rather than business experience. During this time the GDP grew 1.7 percent, which was better than during British Rule, but still well below India's potential.[29]

During the period from 1981 to 1991 India saw the beginning of economic reform with the loosening of some bureaucratic tape. Then in 1991 an economic crisis pushed the Indian government near bankruptcy. The International Monetary Fund (IMF) provided a bailout package with gold as collateral and the Rupee devalued significantly. This was the catalyst that brought badly needed reforms. Import tariffs were gradually reduced, private enterprise was encouraged, and globalization was slowly embraced.[30]

In spite of movement toward globalization India still faces major issues. Chief among these is poverty. An estimated 25 percent of the population, or almost 300 million people, lived below the poverty line in 2008,[31] which is estimated at US$1.25 per day in 2005 dollars. The Human Development Index (HDI), which evaluates a country's socio-economic status, ranked India a dismal 132nd in 2006. Comparatively China ranked 94th, Russia 73rd, and Brazil 70th.[32] India also has the world's greatest income inequality with the wealth of 35 families exceeding 800 million poor people.[33]

India, in spite of being a strong democracy for the last 60 years, has had internal conflicts that are based on caste, religion, ethnicity, and language. Its troubled relationship with its nuclear neighbor Pakistan and the militancy in Kashmir continue to demand attention from the government and its resources in that country.[34]

Still the potential in India is tremendous. In 2003, Wilson and Puru-shothaman (2003) estimated that by the year 2035 India's GDP will have exceed all G6 countries except for the United States. That report has since been updated and the forecast now shows India's GDP surpassing all countries, except China, before 2050.[35] If India can stay the course, decrease its poverty numbers, and manage its political unrest then it stands a good chance to become one of the most prosperous nations in the world.

China

No emerging market is bigger than China. China has the world's largest population, is the third largest in land area and already has the second-largest GDP-PPP in the world. Wilson and Purushothaman (2003) estimated that China's GDP-PPP would surpass the United States by 2040. A few years later Poddar and Yi updated that estimate to 2035.[36] With this kind of potential most large MNEs see the importance of entering China, and are adapting their business models to do so.[37]

Like other BRIC countries, following World War II China adopted a policy of isolationism and in 1949 Mao Tse-tung led the country into a Communist style of government. During the first decade the country prospered, but in 1958 Mao implemented a new policy called the Great Leap Forward, which forced collectivization of all property and forced peasants to become urban workers. This policy quickly caused widespread famine and an estimated 20 million people died as a result.[38] Reformists pushed for new policies to reverse the collectivism; in response Mao implemented the Cultural Revolution. This new policy was disastrous and economic output, which was already low, fell 30 percent in 3 years and created a generation of uneducated people.[39]

In 1978, Deng Xiaoping came to power and began implementing new policies, breaking up communes and giving land back to the people. Unlike Russia, China remains a Communist country. The years following Deng's rise to power resulted in staggering economic growth. He implemented many "western-like" economic and business reforms while maintaining tight political control. For instance, Deng established economic zones within the country that allowed foreign corporations to invest and take advantage of low cost labor. This policy and others resulted in a FDI growth rate of greater than 9 percent over the 8-year period leading up to 2007 and a GDP growth rate greater than 9 percent.[40] What was a very impoverished and isolated country has become a world power in the economic arena.[41]

Although this growth has brought a level of prosperity to the country as a whole, like India, China struggles with a significant poverty problem. In essence, two Chinas are emerging, the more affluent industrialized areas and the poorer rural areas.[42] The percentage of the population below the poverty line is only 15 percent, compared to India with 25 percent, with the largest population in the world that still leaves a more than 100 million people living on less that US$1.25 per day.[43]

If China can continue with current foreign policies and come to a resolution of the income disparity problem it is positioning itself to become the leading economic country in the world in the next few decades.

TRANSITIONAL ECONOMIES

In addition to the BRIC countries there is another group of emerging markets called *transitional economies*. Transitional economies get their name from the former second-world countries that are making the "transition" from command economies that are regulated by the government through controlled supply and pricing to free-market economies where resources are allocated and priced through market supply and demand. Generally speaking, transition involves, in approximate sequence, policies to implement market mechanisms, structural changes across and within sectors and firms (in other words, reallocation of resources), improvements in efficiency and new investments; and finally, recovery of output and sustained growth.[44]

Transition implies five broad categories:

- liberalizing economic activity, prices, and market operations, along with reallocating resources to their most efficient use;
- developing indirect, market-oriented instruments for macroeconomic stabilization;
- achieving effective enterprise management and economic efficiency, usually through privatization;
- imposing hard budget constraints, which provides incentives to improve efficiency; and
- establishing an institutional and legal framework to secure property rights, the rule of law, and transparent market-entry regulations.[45]

In 1991 many of the Central and Eastern European Countries (CEEs) went through a transformation depression precipitated by the collapse of the Soviet bloc.[46] Many of the CEEs, such as Hungary, The Czech Republic, Poland, as well as former U.S.S.R. states such as Belarus, Georgia, and Kazakhstan are in the process of becoming free market economies. These transitional economies are at various stages of transition and success. It is a process which involves successes and failures and which varies greatly among CEE countries.[47]

SHOCK THERAPY

With the collapse of the former Soviet Union many of the CEEs were faced with reforming their economies as they transitioned from a command economy to a free-market economy. At the time optimism was high among certain economists and many governments followed the recommendations to implement an economic policy of "shock therapy."[48] Shock therapy is based upon the premise that spontaneous generation of markets and market institutions will occur (and will do so rapidly), given the absence of state interference.[49] Shock therapy has three primary components: price liberalization, rapid privatization, and macroeconomic stabilization through elimination of fiscal deficits.[50]

Although a market economy is widely accepted as the best and oft times only choice with transitioning away from a command economy there is research that proposes there are alternatives. In addition to a market economy a command economy could also transition into either a production economy or an industrial democracy economy.[51]

Whereas a market economy has an environment that produces a short-term profit orientation on the part of business and a focus on increasing labor productivity (i.e., United States), a production economy has levels of regulation that allows companies to focus on long term growth (i.e., Japan). An industrial democracy economy typically has free capital markets with government-regulated labor markets. This type of economy normally has high taxes, extensive regulations, and other policies that encourage full employment (i.e., Germany). Brouthers and Lamb (1995) proposed that CEE nations choose the economy type that most closely emulates historical and cultural commonalities.

Unfortunately Jeffrey Sachs and the World Bank pressured the CEE nations to adopt a uniform emulation of the USA free-market economies through a policy known as "shock therapy," which was touted as the answer to launch the former communist countries into the free-market world. Instead, hyperinflation occurred; the standard of living dropped; and crime, corruption, and income inequality dramatically increased.[52] This occurred, in part, because no attention was paid to institutions and governance: institutions were not considered important for development; public institutions were neither replaced nor created; international constraints were just accepted and implemented; culture, social capital, domestic norms, and values were simply ignored; and path dependency theory was not considered relevant.[53] Transitional economy countries are moving towards free markets at varying rates in large measure due to the problems created by shock therapy.

Three of the most advanced CEE nations experienced major economic/political crises regarding economic reform long before the collapse of the Soviet Union, the 1956 Hungarian Revolution, the Prague Spring in 1968, and the rise of Poland's Solidarity movement in 1980–81.[54] Although each attempt was crushed by the Soviets, each of the three countries (Hungary, the Czech Republic, and Poland) can trace their origins towards free markets to what precipitated each of the three crises. With the collapse of the former Soviet Union, these three countries were the first to make the transition to free markets. By 2004 five more former command economies, Estonia, Latvia, Lithuania, Slovakia, and Slovenia, joined Hungary, the Czech Republic, and Poland as they were validated as free-market economies when they became members of the European Union.

Hungary

One country'that had particular success in the transition to free markets is Hungary. At first glance Hungary started its transition at the collapse of the U.S.S.R. However, a closer look at the history of Hungary reveals a much earlier beginning.

The summer of 1956 found Hungary on the threshold of a revolution. In the years leading up to 1956 the surrounding countries of Poland and Yugoslavia gained small concessions that allowed for slightly more freedom. Encouraged by these concessions Hungary's liberal Communist leaders started distancing themselves from Stalinism. Prime Minister Imre Nagy began implementing changes that tolerated resistance to further agricultural collectivization, released some political prisoners and abolished labor camps. Frightened by such rapid changes, Communist hardliners arrested Nagy in 1955 and expelled him from the Party. As part of this change intellectuals and students formed groups that held open discussions about the political situation.[55]

Then on October 23, 1956, a peaceful student demonstration sparked events that resulted in a complete revolution with a new government, an attempt to withdraw from the Warsaw Pact and the beginning of a new free-market economy. A few days later, on November 4th Hungary felt the might of the Soviet military and by the end of the year the rebellion was over at a cost of over 20,000 lives. The Hungarian people were once again subject to the Communist rule directed from the Kremlin. But the rebellion was not a total loss. More personal freedoms were granted, more contact with the West was allowed, more production of consumer goods was permitted, and the economic exchanges with the U.S.S.R. were made less inequitable.[56]

Of particular significance was the desire to throw off the shackles of Communism which occurred when the Soviet Union collapsed in 1989. Between 1956 and 1989 Hungary's future entrepreneurs acquired a wide spectrum of managerial, organizational, social, and cultural skills that established a basis for success within a short period of time after communism collapsed.[57]

Initially Hungary's GDP growth rate fell drastically, and by 1991 was a negative 11.7 percent. It was not until 1994 that the economy started to turn around and the growth rate became positive. Since 1994 the grow rate has been healthy, exceeding the GDP growth rate of the United States and many Western European countries every year from 1997 through 2007.[58] This growth rate, as well as other factors helped Hungary to become a member of the European Union in 2004.

Czech Republic

Similar to Hungary's 1956 rebellion, in 1968 Czechoslovakia tried to extricate itself from governance by the U.S.S.R. Known as the Prague Spring, elected reformers of the Czechoslovak Communist Party instituted democratic reforms that allowed for greater freedom in Czechoslovakia. Fearing a counter revolution that would destabilize the Communist-controlled region, on August 20, 1968, Brezhnev ordered the Soviet Army to put contingency plans for an invasion of Czechoslovakia into action, and Soviet tanks rolled into Prague. With approximately 100 lives lost, the human cost was nowhere near that of Hungary's rebellion.[59]

The ideal of freedom continued to incubate under Communist rule with other minor non-violent protests occurring. These protests came to the forefront in 1989 with what became known as the Velvet Revolution which occurred in November, during the days following the fall of the Berlin Wall, and ended with the Communist government being replaced before the end of the year. Some Czechs describe the velvet revolution as a simple completion that started during the Prague Spring in 1968, and once the revolution was complete, the mission was accomplished.[60]

Like many of the CEECs, the Czech Republic went through a sharp deflationary period in the early 1990s, followed by good growth until 1997, when weak export competitiveness, a currency crisis, and a decline in international confidence brought a depression which lasted through 1998. In 1999 the Czech Republic rebounded, with accelerating growth and a trade surplus, and in 2004, along with Hungary, Poland, and other CEECs, was allowed into the European Union.[61]

Poland

Like other Eastern Bloc countries, at the close of World War II Poland became a Communist state. From 1950 to 1980 socialism prevailed except for two occasions. In 1956, and then again in the early 1970s, more liberal policies were introduced and briefly existed until the might of Soviet Communism reasserted itself. Then in 1980, with labor in a turmoil, the trade union Solidarity was formed.[62]

Solidarity was the first non-Communist union allowed. This trade union grew to over 9 million members, and in 1981 the Communist leaders began to feel control slipping away. In response to losing control the Polish government, with the support of the Soviet Union, declared martial law, and arrested Solidarity's leaders, driving the union underground. In spite of persecution and the implementation of martial law Solidarity persisted, transforming into a political force that was elected into power in 1989. This event is considered to be one of the major catalysts in the fall of Communism in Eastern Europe.[63]

With the collapse of Communism, Poland adopted "shock therapy" to revitalize its economy. Similar to other CEE countries adopting "shock therapy" Poland's economy took a drastic turn for the worse. National income fell by 13 percent, investment growth dropped by 10 percent, industrial production declined by 22 percent from 1989 levels, inflation reached an annual rate of 585 percent, and unemployment rose to more than 6 percent.[64]

In 1994, following some policy reforms, the economy started to turn around. Unlike the other transitional economies, Poland was able to achieve 1989 GDP levels by 1995, whereas the Czech Republic and Hungary did not achieve 1989 GDP levels until 2001.[65] Brouthers and Lamb (1995) suggest this is because, unlike Hungary and the Czech Republic, the Polish culture more closely resembles the American culture, particularly with respect to entrepreneurial vales and the role of religion.

Since 1995 the economy has gone through periods of exceptional growth and cooling, at times achieving annual growth in excess of 6 percent and at other times leveling off to little or no growth, but overall maintaining an average annual GDP growth rate greater than the European Union. In 2004, Poland joined the seven other CEECs being accepted into the European Union.

HOME-GROWN MNES

When looking at emerging markets MNEs often focus on the potential to compete in those countries. In addition to the potential of new markets, emerging markets also have successful MNEs called *emerging market multinationals* (EMMs) that compete in the global marketplace. The rise of EMMs to global positions has been surprising both in number and rate. In just two years, from 2006 to 2008, the number of companies from the BRIC countries on the FT Global 500 list more than quadrupled, from 15 to 62, and many other companies in emerging markets have set their sights on global markets.[66] Lenovo, Embraer, and Infosys are three such companies, each from emerging markets, perceived leaders in their respective markets, and considered part of the top 100 EMMs by The Boston Consulting Group.[67]

Lenovo

Lenovo is a successful home-grown firm from the emerging Chinese market. Departing from the traditional R&D-based firm that expands into manufacturing and sales, Lenovo started with sales and marketing then expanded upstream into manufacturing, engineering, and finally research.[68] This strategy allowed Lenovo to develop business based on identifying customer needs, recognizing gaps, and then filling those gaps. This approach resulted in Lenovo becoming the leading PC manufacturer and supplier in China.[69] Using this same approach for global expansion, Lenovo identified the lack of brand awareness as their major obstacle to advance in the global marketplace. In response Lenovo acquired IBM's PC business in late 2004 including the prestigious brand name "ThinkPad" and began selling their products with the IBM ThinkPad co-brand. This strategy allowed them to improve their position in China as well as successfully enter Western markets, becoming the world's third-largest PC provider.[70]

Embraer

Embraer was created in 1969 as a mixed private–public enterprise, with the government holding a 51 percent stake and leading the push for manufacturing of its planes.[71] By the 1980s the Brazil was the fifth-largest exporter of military goods with sales to over 40 countries.[72] During this time Embraer exported over 90 percent of their goods to countries in Latin America, Africa, and the Middle East.[73] Embraer's first growth phase was characterized by the Brazilian government's strong market protection, outflows of R&D from military defense institutes to the private sector, and generous subsidies.[74]

In the 1990s the business model dramatically changed, brought by the end of the Cold War and the collapse of the military based government in Brazil.[75] In 1994, Embraer privatized and switched its focus from military to public aircraft. After a couple of failed attempts with other aircraft Embraer launched the ERJ-145, a regional jet that competes directly with the CRJ-200, sold by Bombardier of Canada. The ERJ-145 proved successful due to its lighter and roomier design and lower price of US$18.5 million vs. the US$21 million for the CRJ-200.[76] The Brazilian government provided export financing which was "decisive" in gaining these contracts over Bombardier.[77]

One of Embraer's sustainable competitive advantages is their integration of global supply chains. Embraer set the mark in the aerospace industry, which even Boeing has now followed. Embraer continues to grow and has graduated from regional to long-distance jet competition, taking on Boeing and Airbus in the 100-seat range with the 170 and 190 models.[78]

Infosys

Based in Bangalore, India, Infosys employs over 100,000 people worldwide, sustains 16 India and 9 global development centers, and operates 41 marketing offices across the globe.[79]

In the 1980s the Indian government decided to target IT as a growth sector. The government eliminated significant "red tape" associated with new business formation, offered free or low-cost access to infrastructure, and granted frequent "tax holidays."[80] It was in this environment that Infosys had its beginnings.

Unlike other Indian companies, Infosys focused on business opportunities overseas right from inception.[81] From the 1980s to the present, Infosys' business model evolved through four stages, first offering low-cost labor for offshore outsourcing, then evolving to maintenance contracts for legacy systems. In the late 1990s Infosys moved to marketing of end-to-end solutions and in recent years the model has tightened to focus on specific industries.[82] One of the leading IT companies in the world, Infosys was recognized as one of the Globally Most Admired Knowledge Enterprises by the American Product and Quality Center (APQC), placing them in the company of organizations like Accenture, Amazon.com, BP, General Electric, Toyota, and The World Bank.[83]

SUMMARY

As more companies seek new international markets many are shifting their focus from developed countries where competition is high and growth of GDP is low to emerging markets where for a little more risk there is relatively low competition and high potential of growth. Emerging markets are classified many different ways from GDP and mergers and acquisitions to foreign direct investment and the standard of living. Regardless of the measure, emerging markets are those economies that are in the process of becoming a developed economy, and in many cases are on the brink of doing so. Of particular interest to investors and MNEs alike are those emerging markets that have significant potential for opportunities.

In an effort to promote national exports in 1993 the U.S. government identified 10 emerging markets, called the Big Emerging Markets (BEMs) that it felt had the best potential. These countries are Argentina, Brazil, China, India, Indonesia, South Korea, Mexico, Poland, South Africa, and Turkey. As the 1990s progress and Eastern Europe worked its way through transition from a command economy to a free-market economy, Russia became a stronger presence in the category of emerging markets. Then in 2003 a report from Goldman Sachs identified what they felt were the best four opportunities—Brazil, Russia, India, and China—and coined the term *BRICs*.

The BRICs have higher-than-average GDP growth rates, large populations, and vast natural resources, and in turn attract large amounts of foreign direct investment. Over the next several decades the BRIC nations may emerge as the major markets of the world, potentially eclipsing France, Germany, and even the United States. Gaining a clear understanding of these markets is important for companies choosing to expand globally.

In addition to the BRIC countries, many of the transitional economies of the former second world are emerging as viable and significant participants in globalization. Like Russia, many of the Central and Eastern European countries struggled through the poor economic policy of shock therapy. However, a few countries, the Czech Republic, Hungary, and Poland seemed to move through this transition period easier than other CEEs. This could be due in part to their history of trying to throw off the shackles of Soviet control as early as the 1950s. In 2004 these three countries, and five others—Estonia, Latvia, Lithuania, Slovakia, and Slovenia—were allowed into the European Union.

Along with being important opportunities for MNEs to expand globally, emerging markets are beginning to produce their own set of MNEs. Called Emerging Market Multinationals (EMMs), these enterprises often evolved from and in some cases are still closely linked to state-owned enterprises. They are asserting themselves as significant players in the global market and are taking an increasingly important role in international business.

Emerging markets will continue to play a bigger in globalization; both in opportunities for investment and growth and in roles that EMMs will play. As companies look to the future, if they do not keep an eye on emerging markets they will be left behind on the way to globalization.

NOTES

1. S. C. Jain, *Emerging Economies and the Transformation of International Business* (London: Edward Elgar Publishing, 2006).

2. A. Banerjee, "Private Equity in Developing Nations," *Journal of Asset Management* 9 (2008): 158–70.

3. Standard & Poor's, Emgerging Market Database (2003).

4. FTSE, FTSE Global Equity Index Series Country Classification (2008).

5. MSCIBarra, MSCI International Equity Indices—Country & Market Coverage (2009).

6. N. Slough, P. Miesing, and R. Brain, "The Ten Big Emerging Market Initiative a Decade Later: Measurements and Commentary," in *Proceedings of the Academy of International Business Southeast* (2004).

7. J. E. Garten, "The Big Emerging Markets," *Columbia Journal of World Business* 31 (1996): 6–31.

8. P. N. Bharadwaj, "BRIC Countries—a Competitive Analysis, *Journal of Global Competitiveness* (2006): 52–54.

9. D. Wilson and R. Purushothaman, "Dreaming with BRICs: Path to 2050," *Goldman Sachs Global Paper No. 99* (2003).

10. Ibid.

11. CIA, "References: Guide to Country Comparisons," *CIA World Factbook* (2009).

12. Bharadwaj, "BRIC Countries—a Competitive Analysis."

13. CIA, "References: Guide to Country Comparisons."

14. T. E. Skidmore, "Brazil's Persistent Income Inequality: Lessons from History," *Latin American Politics & Society* 46 (2004): 135–50.

15. E. Amann, "Brazil's Economy Under Lula," *World Economics* 6, no. 4 (2005): 149–69.

16. Ibid.

17. Bharadwaj, "BRIC Countries—a Competitive Analysis."

18. CIA, "References: Guide to Country Comparisons."

19. Wilson and Purushothaman, "Dreaming with BRICs: Path to 2050."

20. CIA, "References: Guide to Country Comparisons."

21. J. Petras, "Global Ruling Class: Billionaires and How They 'Make It,'" *Journal of Contemporary Asia* 38, no. 2 (2008): 319–29.

22. S. Hedlund, "Such a Beautiful Dream: How Russia Did Not Become a Market Economy," *Russian Review* 67, no. 2 (2008): 187–208.

23. S. Filippov, "Russia's Emerging Multinationals: Trends and Issues," *UNU-MERIT Working Papers* (2008).

24. R. Ahrend, "Russia's Post-Crisis Growth: Its Sources and Prospects for Continuation," *Europe-Asia Studies* 58 (2006): 1–24.

25. A. Breach, "Russia's Path to Prosperity in the Postindustrial World," *Problems of Economic Transition* 46, no. 10 (2004): 47–79.

26. CIA, "References: Guide to Country Comparisons."

27. Ibid.

28. A. Maddison, "Shares of the Rich and the Rest in the World Economy: Income Divergence between Nations, 1820–2030," *Asian Economic Policy Review* 3, no. 1 (2008): 67–82.

29. Ibid.

30. OECD, "Economic Survey of India, 2007," *Policy Brief*, Organization of Economic Co-operation and Development (2007).

31. Bharadwaj, "BRIC Countries—a Competitive Analysis."

32. UNDP, "Human Development Report," *United Nations Development Program* (2008).

33. Petras, "Global Ruling Class: Billionaires and How They 'Make It.' "

34. S. Faris, "The Last Straw," *Foreign Policy* 173 (2009): 92.

35. T. Poddar and E. Yi, "India's Rising Global Potential," *Goldman Sachs Global Paper No. 152* (2007).

36. Ibid.

37. N. Pacek and D. Thorniley, *China, Emerging Markets*, 2nd ed. (EIU: Economist Intelligence Unit, 2007), chap. 18, 216–23.

38. D. Yang, "China's Agricultural Crisis and Famine of 1959–1961: A Survey and Comparison to Soviet Famines," 50 (2008): 1.

39. X. Meng and R. G. Gregory, "The Impact of Interrupted Education on Subsequent Educational Attainment: A Cost of the Chinese Cultural Revolution," *Economic Development and Cultural Change* 50, no. 4 (2002): 935–59.

40. H. Hessel, "Recent and Expected FDI Trends in Emerging Market Economies," *Standard & Poor's Ratings Direct* (2007); CIA, "References: Guide to Country Comparisons."

41. D. W. Bromley and Y. Yang, "Understanding China's Economic Transformation," *World Economics* 7 (2006): 73–95.

42. L. Ding, "China's Regional Income Disparity: An Alternative Way to Think of the Sources and Causes," *Economics of Transition* 16 (2008): 31–58.

43. CIA, "References: Guide to Country Comparisons."

44. O. Havrylyshyn and T. Wolf, "Determinants of Growth in Transition Countries," *Finance & Development* 36, no. 2 (1999): 12.

45. Ibid.

46. M. Myant, "Economic Transformation in the Czech Republic—a Qualified Success," *Europe-Asia Studies* 59 (2007): 431–50.

47. P. Tridico, "Institutions, Human Development and Economic Growth in Transition Economies," *European Journal of Development Research* 19 (2007): 569–93.

48. J. Y. Lin, "Viability, Economic Transition and Reflection on Neoclassical Economics," *Kyklos* 58 (2005): 239–64.

49. T. W. Hall and J. E. Elliott, "Poland and Russia One Decade after Shock Therapy," *Journal of Economic Issues* 33, no. 2 (1999): 305–14.

50. Lin, "Viability, Economic Transition and Reflection on Neoclassical Economics."

51. L. E. Brouthers and C. Lamb, "National Ideology, Public Policy, and the Business Environment: A Contingency Approach to Economic Reform in Hungary, Poland, and Eastern Europe," *International Business Review* 1, no. 3 (1995): 355–72.

52. W. Tompson, "Was Gaidar Really Necessary? Russian 'Shock Therapy' Reconsidered," *Problems of Post-Communism* 49, no. 4 (2002): 12.

53. Tridico, "Institutions, Human Development and Economic Growth in Transition Economies."

54. J. Rupnik, "The Postcommunist Divide," *Journal of Democracy* 10, no. 1 (1999): 57.

55. M. Schaff, "The Hungarian Uprising of 1956," *Hungarian Uprising of 1956* (2009a): 1–2.

56. C. A. Macartney, *Hungary—a Short History* (Edinburgh, Scotland: Edinburgh University Press, 1962)

57. M. I. Laki and J. Szalai, "The Puzzle of Success: Hungarian Entrepreneurs at the Turn of the Millennium," *Europe-Asia Studies* 58 (2006): 317–45.

58. CIA, "References: Guide to Country Comparisons."

59. M. Schaff, "Prague Spring," *Prague Spring*: Chapters 1–2 (Great Neck Publishing, 2009b), chap. 1–2.

60. G. E. Castellano and D. Jůn, D., "The Awkward Revolution," *New Presence: The Prague Journal of Central European Affairs* 11, no. 1 (2007), 16–19.

61. Myant, "Economic Transformation in the Czech Republic—a Qualified Success."

62. M. Vojtech, "The Soviet Non-invasion of Poland in 1980–1981 and the End of the Cold War," *Europe-Asia Studies* 51, no. 2 (1999): 189.

63. Ibid.

64. D. A. Rondinelli and J. Yurkiewicz, "Privatization and Economic Restructuring in Poland: An Assessment of Transition Policies," *American Journal of Economics & Sociology* 55, no. 2 (1996): 145–60.

65. GGDC, "Total Economy Database," in ted09I.xls Ed. www.ggdc.net/databases/ted.htm (retrieved 2009).

66. M. Aguiar et al., *The 2009 BCG 100 New Global Challengers Vol. 2009* (The Boston Consulting Group, 2009).

67. Ibid.

68. G. J. Millman, "From East to West," *Financial Executive* 24, no. 10 (2008): 31–33.

69. L. Chuan Zhi, "Lenovo: An Example of Globalization of Chinese Enterprises," *Journal of International Business Studies* 38, no. 4 (2007): 573.

70. Ibid.

71. A. Hira and L. G. De Oliveira, "Take off and Crash: Lessons from the Diverging Fates of the Brazilian and Argentine Aircraft Industries," *Competition & Change* 11, no. 4 (2007): 329–47.

72. R. Gouvea and S. Kassicieh, "From Defence Conversion to Globalisation Strategies," *Journal for International Business and Entrepreneurship Development* 1, no. 2 (2003): 10–17.

73. J. Maldifassi and P. Abetti, *Defense Industries in Latin American Countries: Argentina, Brazil, and Chile* (Westport, CT: Praeger Publishers, 1994).

74. Gouvea and Kassicieh, "From Defence Conversion to Globalisation Strategies."

75. J. Espana, "Explaining Embraer's Hi-Tech Success: Porter's Diamond, New Trade Theory, or the Market at Work?," *Journal of American Academy of Business, Cambridge* 4, no. 1/2 (2004): 489.

76. Hira and De Oliveira, "Take off and Crash: Lessons from the Diverging Fates of the Brazilian and Argentine Aircraft Industries."

77. J. Cassiolato, R. Bernardes, and H. Lastres, "Transfer of Technology for Successful Integration into the Global Economy: A Case Study of Embraer in Brazil" (New York: United Nations, 2007).

78. Hira and De Oliveira, "Take off and Crash: Lessons from the Diverging Fates of the Brazilian and Argentine Aircraft Industries."

79. Infosys, "Fact Sheet—Consolidated Financial Data, First Quarter, 2009–10" (Bangalore: Infosys, 2009).

80. J. A. Narus and D. V. R. Seshadri, "Infosys Technologies Ltd.: Growing Share of a Customer's Business," *Vikalpa: The Journal for Decision Makers* 32, no. 4 (2007): 127–45.

81. R. A. Thillai, "Comparison of Software Service Providers: An Exploratory Study," *IIMB Management Review* 20, no. 4 (2008): 392–404.

82. Narus and Seshadri, "Infosys Technologies Ltd.: Growing Share of a Customer's Business."

83. N. Mehta, S. Oswald, and A. Mehta, "Infosys Technologies: Improving Organizational Knowledge Flows," *Journal of Information Technology* 22, no. 4 (2007): 456.

Chapter 4

An International Marketing Manifesto

Michael R. Czinkota and Ilkka A. Ronkainen

Today might be called the triumph of international marketing. There seems finally to be proof that planned economies are less efficient than market economies. Governments all over the world are encouraging market-based activities. The abolishment of state monopolies, the privatization of state owned companies, the opening of national economies to ward the world market, and the ongoing introduction and enforcement of rules and laws to ensure competitive market conditions are being witnessed. As a change agent, international marketing has brought important benefits to nation-states, firms and their employees, and customers. During the past 30 years, the value of global trade has risen from $200 billion to more than $7.6 trillion.[1] The growth rate of marketing between countries has consistently exceeded average domestic growth rates.[2] The fastest globalizing nations have enjoyed rates of economic growth up to 50% higher than those that have integrated the world economy more slowly.[3] Linked to this growth, these same countries have also achieved relatively greater gains of political freedom, greater increases in life expectancy, higher literacy rates, and better overall standards of living.

Firms have benefited substantially from global marketing expansion. With wider market reach and many more customers, firms in the international market produce more and do so more efficiently than their domestic-only counterparts. As a result, international firms simultaneously achieve lower costs and higher profits both at home and abroad. Market diversification and the stability arising from firms' lack of dependence on any particular market are other positive effects. Firms also learn from their competitors, which often makes their managers more sensitive and responsive to differing environments, thus preparing them for change. In addition, their recruiting can expressly seek out and develop the best talent from all nationalities.[4] The cumulative effect of these dimensions is major. Research has shown that firms of all sizes and in all industries that engage in international marketing outperform their strictly domestic counterparts. They grow more than twice as fast in sales and earn significantly higher returns on equity and assets.[5]

Workers also benefit from international marketing activities. International firms of all sizes pay significantly higher wages than domestic-only firms.[6] Because of their greater profitability and longevity, workplace security is also substantially greater for employees who work in plants of international marketers than for those who work in local firms.[7] Compelled by global media scrutiny, international firms have become greater practitioners of social responsibility—much to the benefit of their employees around the world. Never before have workers benefited to such a degree from benevolent rules implemented by corporations headquartered far away from their locale. For example, the global working conditions set by Nike, for its subcontractors, or by Kmart, for its suppliers, are unique in the annals in global commerce.

Consumers are the greatest beneficiaries of all. They are offered an unprecedented degree of product availability and choice. Furthermore, as a result of international competition, the prices of these products are usually low and offer a better quality and quantity of life to a broad spectrum of individuals. Rising incomes have ensured leaps in purchasing power. For the first time in history, international goods and service availability has gone beyond the luxury of the elite and has become, especially in emerging markets, the reasonable expectation of the masses.

Advocates and activists have had their causes benefit substantially from the spread of international marketing. In 1999, business, labor, and government representatives from 173 countries affirmed core labor standards as fundamental human rights, including freedom of association and the right to organize and bargain collectively. Included was also a call to eliminate child labor, forced labor, and employment-related discrimination.[8] International marketing linkages have also resulted in the emergence of pressure points for activists, which has led to the introduction and implementation of new concepts. The acceptance of "fair trade" and "living wage" requirements has achieved substantial increases in the incomes of the poorer participants in international trade flows.[9]

In spite of these achievements, the academic field of international marketing bears up unsteadily under the weight of these laurels. Some researchers doubt whether the insights they gain from studying and working with other marketing systems broaden their own horizons and increase their abilities to explain marketing phenomena. Many practitioners ignore the academic pronouncement of globalization and still refuse to participate in the global market—judging either the market to be too dangerous or themselves too unprepared. This even applies to the most technologically advanced firms. For example, in the United States, most e-tailers do not accept orders from outside their home market, and more than 55% of U.S. web-merchants do not even ship to Canada.[10] International marketing academics are not deluged by great attention from policymakers. Few marketers are offered chairs at the table in international negotiations, and the writings of international marketers are not often sufficiently part of any great readings package for policymakers.[11]

Most visible is the discontent of consumers. The "Battle of Seattle" and the subsequent confrontations in Washington, D.C.; Davos and Geneva, Switzerland; Quebec, Canada; and Genoa, Italy have alerted the world to the displeasure vocalized by a variety of groups.[12] Simplistic populist messages have turned globalization into a derogatory term and are swaying the sentiments of the general public. For example, after the Seattle summit, a survey found that 52% of the respondents were sympathetic toward the protestors even though they may have been hard-pressed to explain the goals of the protest.[13] Within the United States, many people have come to believe that international marketing undermines U.S. labor and living standards. Outside of the United States, international marketing and its agents, the marketers, are derided as exploiters, destroyers, and Americanizers.[14] Papers by experts are derided as planning for economic rape and pillage; their speeches and meetings are disrupted. International meetings are being shortened and held at inaccessible locations, giving the public impression of a gathering of fiends in the dark. Proponents of international marketing talk about retreat and introspection even though opponents do not offer any coherent alternative economic or social approaches.

Is this an example of the classic Sun Tzu strategy in which the victorious general only attacks already defeated armies? Has international marketing already begun its demise? We think not. We believe that the best is yet to come for international marketing. However, it will take new thinking and new actions by researchers to propel the field forward again. International marketing academics need to be the guardians who separate fact from fiction in policy, practitioner, and consumer discussions. Qualified not by weight of office but by expertise, thoughtfulness, and knowledge (rather than emotions), international marketing researchers must be the guarantors and guides toward free and open markets.

Antiglobalization activists deride international marketing but seem to have difficulties articulating what they are really for. At the same time, government and business arguments in favor of globalization are often vague and based on an abstract long-term vision. No wonder ordinary citizens are left confused, skeptical, and ill-informed, which may lead them to make poor decisions. Given that the public in general does not have a great deal of interest toward international and trade matters, the need is great for outspoken comment on the transformational and uplifting capabilities of market forces. This is a task for marketing scholars. Two examples can highlight this imperative. Antiglobalizers have argued (1) that globalization equals Americanization and (2) that globalization leads to global brands' hegemony and, therefore, global uniformity. In practice, it is evident that cultural imperialism does not sell. In nearly every television market of the world, local production has grown at the expense of imports.[15] More significantly, with the increased facilitation of global production companies, local producers and products have penetrated markets beyond their domestic ones. Although global brands may have gained worldwide prominence in terms of headlines, they constitute only a small percentage of a global marketer's sales in any given market.

The ongoing growth and success of international marketing cannot be taken for granted. As the events of September 11, 2001, show, the international landscape can change with the impact of tectonic-plate adjustment. Even the very essence of international exchange may be called into question. History demonstrates that international marketing has not always persisted in spite of its proven benefits. For example, in 1896, the Empress Dowager Tz'u-hsi, to finance the renovation of her summer palace, impounded government funds that had been designated for China's shipping and its Navy. As a result, China's participation in world trade came almost to a halt. In the subsequent decades, deprived of its means to market internationally, China operated in virtual isolation, without transfer of knowledge from the outside, without major inflows of goods, and without the innovation and productivity increases that result from exposure to international trade.

During the 1930s, the turning away from international marketing came through the Smoot-Hawley Act, which raised U.S. duties to reduce the volume of imports into the United States in the hopes that this would restore domestic employment. However, the result was an increase of duties and other barriers to imports by most other trading nations as well. These measures were key contributing factors in the subsequent worldwide depression and the collapse of the world financial system, which in turn set the scene for World War II.[16]

As global marketing advances to emerging markets, new challenges emerge and old ones may be magnified. For example, international expansion typically results in a more widespread use of intellectual property.[17] More customers should then lead to an increase in the value of such property. However, resource constraints combined with popular demands and political power have delivered different scenarios. Entry into some markets may actually lead to value destruction. The government-induced price revisions of AIDS drugs in Latin America and South Africa and of Cipro, the anthrax antidote, have revealed new problems, which may yet fan local flames into global conflagrations.

The present-day worst-case scenario is frightening. Some people view globalization as a force of oppression, exploitation, and injustice. Might not then extreme actions, such as anarchism and terrorism, be justifiable to correct for its impacts? Successful international marketing scholarship can perhaps become a bulwark against terrorism. Such work does not need to be perceived as apologetic for business interests in promoting international trade. International marketing may well become a key remedy for the world's poor, because scholars should help devise creative strategies for the poor to access the world marketplace.

Given the precarious experiences by the international marketing field in spite of the substantial global improvements due to international marketing activities, steps undertaken by international marketers in academia must be considered to ensure the further progress of an ongoing contribution by the field. Such progress is not viewed narrowly to benefit the academic high priests of international marketing and their acolytes, but rather it is considered imperative in order to have input and guidance for further improvements in the global economy and in the lives of people. Here, we present propositions for the strengthening of the future role of international marketing. We hope that they will lead to introspection as well as to an open and frank exchange of ideas with a subsequent renaissance of international marketing.

REMEMBER THE ROOTS AND PURPOSE OF THE FIELD
INTERNATIONAL MARKETING IS A PRACTICAL FIELD

It is based on the premise that international marketing transactions can be carried out more effectively, that there are many needs that have been left unsatisfied worldwide, and that the field of international marketing can improve the quality of life of individuals. The field requires that its proponents visit with people, institutions, and companies to observe, talk, and understand their activities. The central role of people in international marketing subjects the field to all the vagaries inherent in social sciences. Research gains are not only what researchers can learn about other systems but also what they are forced to learn about their own system in order to understand what happens elsewhere.[18] With this approach, junior researchers do not need to compromise the requirements placed on them for detailed research at the expense of seeing the bigger picture.

Rediscovery of this truth may force some international marketing researchers to shed their "lab coat" syndrome. For some, complexity has become fashionable and esoteric, and analytical tools have become the drivers of research content. On occasion, researchers talk more about models than about people, substitute tools for insight, and examine printouts instead of market participants. Although some international marketers may have chosen the academic profession in a repressed desire to become hard scientists such as physicists or chemists, it is unlikely that a squirt of one compound, a dash of another liquid, or an increase in pressure will precisely manifest itself in international marketing outcomes.

It is critical to develop ways for international marketing to become more accepted by the academic community for its past efforts and the contributions it can make in the future. The field of finance achieved such acceptance through its association with economics; international marketing may want to expand its roots by extending its association with international trade. Perhaps, in the future, international marketing work may then make a scholar eligible for the Nobel Prize. At the same time, senior scholars have the responsibility not only to develop knowledge but also to help grow journals in terms of acceptance and respect. By placing their best work in the internationally oriented outlets, scholars can perform an important service to the profession.

RESIST THE TEMPTATIONS OF OVERSPECIALIZATION

In an academic era of publish or perish, publishing in North America mainly refers to academic journals of the highest order. To avoid becoming academic equivalents of day laborers, international marketing researchers often feel the need to rapidly produce as many top-tier "hits" in as short a time as possible. Top-tier journals, however, together with their editors and reviewers, often tend to adhere to traditional research orthodoxies. Such orthodoxies may involve specific research methodologies, the citation of domestic (e.g., United States) literature, and the analysis of problems, which are considered locally important. We do not believe that such local content requirements[19] are perversely or conspiratorially designed by the gatekeepers to publications, but we recognize how easy it is to fall into that trap.

The problem of publishing is made even more acute by the challenges of conducting research in an international setting, due to data compatibility, definitional equivalence, timing, or funding difficulties. International research typically introduces more noise into data sets. Editors and reviewers need to appreciate and accept a responsible adaptation of evaluative criteria if there is to be more knowledge development and dissemination in the international marketing field.

The expectations set by journals and their evaluators have forced many international marketing academics to become highly specialized special specialists. They often investigate narrower and narrower aspects of problems with tools that are ever increasing in their quantitative sophistication, but in which many unrealistic conditions must be met for the model to work. Many times the results are uninspiring for practitioners or policymakers. The end results are in sights that are decreasingly useful for the discipline or for its social structure. Work in the field must again become more broad-based and linked to the practice of international marketing.

It is important that a discipline have a communication venue in which new approaches, concepts, frameworks, and ideas can be published without the constraints imposed by rigid establishment journals. Thinkers must be allowed to speculate, tease, bully, or just simply visualize and then be able to disseminate their thoughts.

A NEW PARADIGM AND NEW METHODS

There is the emergence of a new approach to furthering the advance of international marketing. Historically, the "case" period can be called an early important approach to international marketing research. Researchers analyzed the activities of one particular firm in great detail and then attempted to generalize the findings to other firms, the industry, or the discipline. This case era was supplemented, and some would even say replaced, by the "numeric" era. Now the goal became the accumulation of quantitative data, which were subjected to rigorous analysis. The goal was to use statistical significances to build stepping-stones for the advancement of knowledge. Taken in conjunction with other tools of analysis and insight, the goal was quite praiseworthy. However, for some, the actual insights obtained were of little concern. Rather, the use and application of new tools became the only issue that mattered—with the motto, Have tool, will apply! Although useful in bringing a scientific perspective to international marketing research, in today's complex times, the singular focus on such an approach has become too limiting.

In our view, today's new paradigm is "boundary-spanning eclecticism." Interdependence requires the recognition of linkages. Progress in international marketing makes it increasingly important to bring together various perspectives from a variety of disciplines to truly understand interactions and consequences. Such an eclectic approach in the international marketing field needs to cover different areas such as jurisprudence and cultural anthropology. In addition, the new eclecticism needs to cover a wide variety of fields and include, for example, history, anthropology, or political science that reflects both qualitative and quantitative insights. Given the newness of some of these linkages and the need to understand and interpret them, this boundary-spanning eclecticism may be today's version of what Bartels labeled the "period of discovery" by early marketing scholars in 1900–10 during the formative years of marketing.[20] Perhaps the celebration of a centennial reflection of marketing will lead to old paths not lately traveled.

The new eclecticism needs to use and define time lines and differentiate between the short-term and long-term outcomes. It also must simultaneously address the issues from the perspective of the key constituencies—business, consumers, and governments—and do so over a growing variety of countries. In addition, the different subcomponents of the business discipline itself need to become reappreciated in their interrelationships so that, for example, the analyst fully understands the repercussion that changing exchange or interest rates have on the international marketing domain. The proof in the pudding? International marketing academics should (again) become comfortable in teaching a broadly focused "Introduction to Global Business" course.

International marketing scholars should join forces periodically with colleagues in other disciplines beyond the conventional ones. Areas such as genetics, health care, history, and linguistics should be considered. By definition, this would also mean becoming familiar with the literature and attending appropriate annual meetings in these disciplines. True cross-fertilization may then result in the application of medical theories of pandemics and resistance to the development of theory for the global diffusion of goods or the application of sociolinguistics to international negotiations. Becoming more interdisciplinary will also be the raison-d'être for outlets such as the *Journal of International Business Studies*.

LOOK TO THE WORLD

In the international marketing field, the world is our oyster. Editors, recruiting committees, and grant-giving organizations should look at the world rather than their comfortable confines as their suppliers of talent and knowledge. Journals need to look for content not just among their traditional constituents but also among the great minds abroad. It must be understood that English, albeit the language of many international marketing transactions, is not the only storehouse of knowledge. It pays to heed the historic lesson that power waxes and wanes depending on the support, input, and actions of allies. When walking the dusty roads of Baghdad, the congested streets of Rome, or the grassy plains of Carthage, one remembers that these locations were once the economic and political leaders of the world.

Although the cradle of marketing may indeed be in the United States, significant contributions to the practice and theory of international marketing have been made throughout the world as the discipline has matured. An examination of the origins of today's academic contributors to the international marketing discipline shows that many of them hail from the Nordic Countries, Central Europe, Turkey, China, India, and Japan. For example, many of the innovations and new thinking in retailing have European roots. The emergent U.S. empire should joyfully acknowledge its magnetism for contributions from around the globe. It should also proudly highlight its emphasis on the protection of all players and its reliance on market forces rather than on the rapaciousness typical of earlier superpowers. Today, if there is demand by the superpower, there is true exchange rather than simple taking. If the practices of centuries past are considered, one current example of comparative advantage would be the burial of U.S. nuclear waste in Africa rather than the western United States.

Academics in the United States in particular should build and maintain contacts with colleagues in other countries, learn other languages, and scrutinize nondomestic literature. After all, it was not long ago when every chemist was expected to know German and every painter had to have been to Italy. Academics dealing with international marketing should also be encouraged to be truly international in their outlook. Listening to the world will make the field better, and doing so in their own tongues will make the sounds so much more understandable. In this context, it should be remembered that the search engines, which have become so instrumental to academic research, tend to pick up only a small portion of actual work carried out and are still heavily biased toward English language publications.

Just as multinational corporations should have substantial international board membership, academic journals should include more members from abroad on their review boards.

Such membership tends to have an effect on the scope of activities. For example, the *European Journal of Marketing*, which carries articles from the broadest national array of authors, boasts 57% of its review board members from outside of the United Kingdom. The non-U.S. share for the *Journal of Marketing* is a mere 4%.[21] International marketing would also benefit from a regularly published volume (or a special issue) of articles not originally published in English from language areas such as Germany, Northern Europe, and Japan.

MAINTAIN THE DIALOGUE

International marketing is principally a dialogue between marketers and their international constituents. Key constituents are consumers, the business community, and policymakers. The international marketing researcher must reach out to them not only to describe phenomena but also to prescribe meaningful action.

All three of these constituencies are unlikely to actively search for pearls of academic wisdom, the existence of which is not necessarily plain to them. Therefore, academics should not shy away from making available an explanation, condensation, and simplification of their research findings. For example, it may be useful to consider distributing summaries of research implications through editorials or electronic means. It also must be clearly indicated what portions of findings are relevant to which community. Subtle hints or slight intonations will not bring out the hidden gem and will only deprive international marketing researchers of the opportunity to contribute through their work to a more prosperous, safe, and responsive international marketplace. Businesses, consumers, and policymakers all need research insights, just as international marketers need them. However, they may be willing to access such insights only through media particular to them. We know that knowledge not communicated rapidly loses its value. Either it finds no application or it may be lost all together. Let us disseminate knowledge!

On the policy side, the importance of communications with constituents and of framing the terminology can be highlighted by the fate of the "fast-track" trade authority sought by President Clinton. Presidents of the United States for decades have had such trade negotiation authority that permits the negotiation of international trade agreements, which Congress could then approve or reject but not change. Lately, however, public misperceptions stirred on by trade foes interpreted the term to mean a railroading of consumers and workers rather than the key to long-term economic benefits. As a result, the request for such authority was denied three times by the U.S. Congress. The Bush administration was forced to change the term to "trade promotion" authority for Congress to even consider and approve it.

It is also imperative to communicate much more with the field's critics (Williams 1984). These opponents are a constituency that must be brought into the tent. Not only are they a source of ideas for research, but they are also a key target group to work with in explaining the benefits of market forces. It is hard to improve the world by pulling on both ends of the rope. Either the rope breaks, or one side (temporarily) eats dirt. Pulling together is far more efficient than a tug-of-war. Thoughtful critics have already acknowledged the worth of trade versus aid and are shying away from the McDonald's-trashing approach.[22]

WORK ALSO WITH THOSE WHO PLACE OR SHOW

There is an innate human tendency to focus on and celebrate winners. Nonetheless, not everyone touched by international marketing will come out a winner. International marketing relies heavily on market forces, which in turn implies a competitive race for limited resources. In any competition, some will arrive first, while others will only place or show.

Working with the ones that benefit from increased resources is usually more fun than standing at the side of the ones who, once again, have missed out. However, to maintain its acceptance by the world community at large, the international marketing field must increase its focus on those who are less likely to emerge victorious from the battle of competition. These firms can eventually become global contenders or out-localize their big-name competitors.[23] These consumers and workers can become major targets of opportunity be it only because of their sheer numbers. There is a future in working with the unserved majority.[24]

Such a focus needs to help, learn, guide, and suggest and is perhaps best accompanied by a good dosage of "tough love." Those who clamor that the rising tide is expected to lift all boats must understand that they are, at least in part, responsible for their own boats. Have they checked their vessel for leakage, for crew training, and for a working sail? Help should also include the identification of trade-offs between current needs and new sources of comparative advantage. For example, developing nations may not, for reasons of pandemic infection and lack of resources, be able to honor and pay for intellectual property rights inherent in pharmaceuticals. There may be reasons and special conditions for using an escape clause, but if countries expect to receive ongoing intellectual property improvements, they need to consider nontraditional forms of compensation rather than simplistic expropriations. This way, perhaps AIDS drugs will someday be paid for with the protection of the rainforest.

Positive solutions must also be found to directly assist the battle-weakened participants in global competition. It should be part and parcel of an international marketer's academic work to consider linkages between policy actions and their effect on disenfranchised communities. For example, should the dumping penalties paid be absorbed by the black hole of a general treasury, or should these funds be used to assist those dislocated by dumped merchandise? Should fees paid for preferred treatment in the work visa granting process be used to strengthen the budget of an agency, or should these moneys help create more domestic workers in that desirable employment category? Should AIDS prevention and treatment campaigns not highlight that AIDS is bad for business and thus encourage businesses to extend health care to their workers?[25] If more such linkages can be built, the benefits of international marketing not only will be better under stood but also will become more acceptable to those who have been exposed to the two-faced, Janus-like effects of the field.

Despite inherently more challenging circumstances, international marketing scholars should be the ones to initiate projects dealing with emerging and developing markets and try to work with colleagues in these countries. This way, they can offer an inside perspective rather than an outside view on the issues. Ultimately, the goal for international marketers is not only to apply existing frameworks to new situations but also to develop new frameworks from the insight that they garner from working in different and diverse environments. These frameworks can then be used to develop new general theories of business.

PROFESS EXPERTISE

Professors are the ones who have chosen to profess, which means to make an open or public declaration of their views, to make protestations, or to affirm and avow their perspectives.[26] All too often, there is an unwillingness of today's academics to publicly step up and separate right from wrong in their field. It often appears as if international marketing academics assume that everyone is keenly aware of the benefits of free trade and exchange. However, not all people are concerned or have had thorough academic training in international marketing. Ignorance and apathy remain key enemies of the truth.

Arguments from university settings may often be dismissed as coming from individuals who are not relevant in the practical sense and who bear no responsibility for their statements. Real-life marketing managers are held accountable by their constituents, a standard that does not always hold for international marketing professors. Such accountability can only increase if professors seek out positions of responsibility, be it as board members in associations, as advisors to local or even national governments, or as consultants to business.

To get to the critical hub linking academia, practice, and public policy, international marketing scholars must do their share. Memberships on boards can be earned through speeches, articles in newsletters, and other constructive contributions. It is necessary to provide cogent, concise, and easily understood information on key issues. For example, there needs to be a widespread understanding of why a reduction of barriers to international marketing is important and what the benefits are. The many misconceptions that abound in the international marketing field must also be addressed and removed. For example, many believe that the World Trade Organization has the power to override domestic laws. This is not the case. Nonetheless, many people believe that this is so—akin to the existence of black helicopters by the United Nations. Similarly, survey research has indicated that in 1981, 12% of U.S. workers were fearful of losing their jobs. In 2000, that fear of job loss had more than tripled, even though unemployment had declined from well over 7% in 1981 to just 4% in 2000.[27] Globalization is blamed for increases in poverty, and yet the number of people in extreme poverty has declined from 20% 25 years ago to less than 5% today.[28]

International marketing academics should be proud of their field and should be cognizant that they may well be the only thin three-striped black line able to keep apart fact, fiction, and emotion. Although it is unlikely that researchers can ever dictate decisions, they should be the ones providing the factual input, so that decisions, however they may come out, have at least a chance of being grounded in reality. For example, in times of global activism, international marketing scholars have a role in assessing both the responsibilities of the companies and the impact that codes of conduct and certifications have on markets and consumers.[29] Just imagine, in days of future International Monetary Fund demonstrations, academics could become the original cast members of an international marketing reality show on television.

IN CONCLUSION

Many academics are disappointed in the lack of appreciation of international marketing by the world. However, worldly reaction clearly indicates that international marketing academics have also fallen short of what the world expects of them. Though perhaps disturbing to some, for marketers who thrive on change, this is a key opportunity. There are new mountains to climb and new frontiers to cross. International marketing researchers have the opportunity to shape activities so that they can continue to be at the center of social change and become the architects of improvements in the quality of life. If international marketing researchers manage to do so, they can be assured that for their discipline, the best is yet to come.

ACKNOWLEDGMENTS

The authors extend their appreciation to Juan Luis Colaiácovo, Masaaki Kotabe, John Ryans, and three anonymous JIM reviewers for their valuable comments.

NOTES

This chapter originally appeared in the *Journal of International Marketing*, Vol. 11, No. 1 (2003), pp. 13–27. © American Marketing Association. All rights Reserved. Reprinted with permission.

1. World Trade Organization, "International Trade Statistics," 2002, http://www.wto.org (accessed February 13, 2002).
2. International Monetary Fund, *International Financial Statistics* (Washington, DC: International Monetary Fund, 2000).
3. Global Business Policy Council , *Globalization Ledger* (Washington, DC: A. T. Kearney, 2000).
4. Ingo Theuerkauf, David Ernst, and Amir Mahini, "Think Local, Organize . . .? ," *International Marketing Review* 13, no. 3 (1996): 7–12.
5. Charles Taylor and Witold Henisz, *U.S. Manufacturers in the Global Marketplace, Report 1058* (New York: The Conference Board, 1994).
6. Business America, "Letter from Secretary Michael Kantor," 117, no. 9 (1996): 9.
7. J. David Richardson and Karin Rindal, *Why Exports Matter: More!* (Washington, DC: The Institute for International Economics and the Manufacturing Institute, 1996).
8. Jay Mazur, "Labor's New Internationalism," *Foreign Affairs* 79 (January–February 2000): 79–93.
9. The Economist , "Globalisation and Its Critics, a Survey of Globalization" (September 29, 2000): 3–30.
10. Jan Putzger, "On-line and International," *Journal of Commerce Weekly* (November 13–19, 2000): 27–28.
11. Michael R. Czinkota, "The Policy Gap in International Marketing," *Journal of International Marketing* 8 (March 2000a): 99–111.
12. Stephen J. Kobrin, "Our Resistance Is as Global as Your Oppression" (paper presented at the 2001 meeting of the International Studies Association, Chicago, February 2001).

13. "Global Growing Pains," *BusinessWeek Online,* December 22, 2001 (accessed April 21, 2001).

14. Richard J. Barnet and John Cavanagh, *Global Dreams: Imperial Corporations and the New World Order* (New York: Simon & Schuster, 1994); Naomi Klein, *No Logo: Taking Aim at the Bullies* (New York: Picador USA, 2000).

15. "Think Local," *The Economist,* April 13, 2002, 12–14.

16. Michael R. Czinkota and Ilkka A. Ronkainen, *International Marketing,* 6th ed. (Fort Worth, TX: Harcourt Inc., 2002), 32; Susan P. Douglas, "Exploring New Worlds: The Challenge of Global Marketing," *Journal of Marketing* 64 (January 2001): 103–7.

17. Michael R. Czinkota and Ilkka A. Ronkainen, "International Business and Trade in the Next Decade: Report from a Delphi Study," *Journal of International Business Studies* 28, no. 4 (1997): 827–44.

18. Reavis Cox, "The Search for Universals in Comparative Studies of Domestic Marketing Systems," *Marketing and Economic Development,* ed. Peter D. Bennett (Chicago: American Marketing Association, 1965), 143–62.

19. Magoroh Mamyama, "Disciplinary Contents Requirement: Academic Non-tariff Barrier in Interdisciplinary Communication," *Human Systems Management* 10, no. 2 (1991): 155.

20. Robert Bartels, *The History of Marketing Thought* (Columbus, OH: Publishing Horizons Inc., 1988).

21. Michael R. Czinkota, "International Information Cross-Fertilization in Marketing: An Empirical Assessment," *European Journal of Marketing* 34, no. 12 (2000b): 1305–14.

22. "New Faith in Free Trade," *The Washington Post,* April 11, 2002, E1, E14; Oliver Williams, "Who Cast the First Stone?," *Harvard Business Review* 62 (September–October 1984), 151–60.

23. Güliz Ger, "Localizing in the Global Village: Local Firms Competing in Global Markets," *California Management Review* 41, no. 4 (1999): 45–63.

24. C. K. Prahalad and Stuart L. Hart, "The Fortune at the Bottom of the Pyramid," *Strategy and Business* 7 (First Quarter 2002): 38–48.

25. Louise Frechette, "Development Cannot Be Imposed from Outside" (speech given at Yale University, New Haven, April 3, 2002).

26. *Webster's New Twentieth Century Dictionary,* 2nd ed. (New York: Simon and Schuster, 1972).

27. Carla Hills, "Getting over the Fear of Free Trade," *The Globalist,* http:// www.theglob alist.com (accessed April 3, 2002).

28. Xavier Sala-i-Martin, "The Disturbing 'Rise' of Global Income Inequality" (discussion paper no. 0102-44, Department of Economics, Columbia University, 2002).

29. Gary Gereffi, Ronie Garcia-Johnson, and Erika Sasser, "The NGO-Industrial Complex," *Foreign Policy* 31 (July/August 2001): 56–65.

Chapter 5

Reaching the International Consumer: An Assessment of the International Direct Marketing Environment

Timothy J. Wilkinson, Anna McAlister, and Scott Widmier

Direct marketing is defined as the use of consumer-direct (CD) channels to reach and deliver goods and services to customers without using marketing middlemen.[1] It allows marketers a more direct response from consumers (generally an order), allows marketers to better target niche markets, and allows marketers to sell product without the expensive and lengthy process of getting it into traditional channels. Direct marketing also presents many benefits to consumers, including avoiding the hassles of traffic congestion, parking headaches, lack of time, shortage of retail help, and lines at checkout counters.

Consumers can browse through a larger selection of products than retail outlets generally carry and price shop by browsing through mail catalogs and online shopping while in the comfort of their home or office. These advantages, for both consumers and marketers, alike have lead to the growth of direct marketing in the USA into a multibillion dollar industry, with $2.3 trillion in U.S. sales in 2004, including 5.2 billion in web-driven sales and $143.3 billion in catalog sales.[2]

Direct marketing is not just an American phenomenon, but a world-wide industry with sales in excess of $101 billion dollars. In 1983, Theodore Levitt argued that globalization was creating an environment in which one should "sell the same thing, the same way, everywhere."[3] While the veracity of these words has been tempered with time, the general thrust of a geocentric approach to business is certainly applicable in the area of direct marketing.

The level of direct marketing activities varies fairly significantly from country to country with the USA still dominating the industry in terms of dollar amount and number of people involved. These variances might be explained by differences in the political, economic, social, and political technological (PEST) environment. These differences create a divergence in the methods and techniques used by direct marketers on a country by country basis and are important to understand because, as this industry internationalizes, variations in the PEST environment will present challenges to firms operating in multiple country markets.

This paper uses PEST analysis to investigate the business environment of international direct marketing and understand its effect on the international direct marketer. This organizing framework—PEST—is the most commonly used tool for environmental analysis.[4] Political factors consist of the laws, regulations, and governmental policies that facilitate or hinder direct marketing. The economic environment includes macro level economic indicators, such as GDP, purchasing power parity (PPP), and wealth distribution that can be used in market selection and macro-segmentation. The social environment includes variables related to consumer behavior and cross-cultural communications. Technology involves both the level of technological and infrastructure development and the breadth of consumer use of technology. Both can have great impact on the method direct marketers used to reach the consumers.

In this paper, the consequences of each element of the PEST environment are described. After examining the PEST environment in general, several issues specific to direct marketing are explored. The implications of the PEST environment for direct marketing firms are also discussed.

POLITICAL ENVIRONMENT

National government regulations and laws are a product of the political systems in which they originate, the socio-cultural backdrop which precedes those systems, and the historical circumstances that give rise to political organization. Not only must businesses be able to negotiate their way through a wide variety of regulations and laws, but they must also understand how those regulations and laws are administered (or not, as the case may be) in country specific situations.

Direct marketing is heavily tied to a free market system and entrepreneurship—the ability of individuals to start and maintain money-making enterprises. Direct marketing offers individuals a means to achieve financial independence and career self-determination with a fairly minimum investment and a great deal of personal effort. In a world where most natural resources are already spoken for, direct marketing gives people the equivalent of the Oklahoma land rush in the modern age, offering money-producing opportunities for those willing to stake their claim with direct marketing. In many countries, this is a capitalistic opportunity unparalleled in history.

The growth of direct marketing salespeople in many countries has its parallels to the growth of the middle class in Victorian England or in the USA with its accompanying changes in political focus and power. Just as the growth of the middle class was resisted by the power establishment, the growth of direct marketing may be resisted by governments because of the political changes it might bring about. One would anticipate this resistance to most often occur in countries run by authoritarian regimes, where individual freedom may threaten the power of the regime.

The complex political economy of China is a case in point. Communism, with central planning at its core, and totalitarianism as its means, is naturally at odds with the capitalistic opportunity presented by direct marketing. Yet, the Chinese government has embraced free markets as a means of achieving economic growth and political stability. This is why many Westerners were taken off guard when the Chinese government banned direct selling in 1998. Companies such as Avon and Amway, that had spent the previous decade entering the Chinese market, suddenly found that their key sales and distribution strategy was undermined by the communist government's control orientation and paranoia concerning perceived threats to its power. The government claimed that meetings of direct marketers created "weird cults, triads, superstitious groups, and hooliganism."[5]

The current regime had reason to feel threatened by the growth of this tool for economic freedom. At the time of the ban an estimated 30 million people participated in direct selling in China.[6] In response, 200,000 people took to the streets—many of them Avon ladies—and engaged in anti-government rioting. In 2005, China lifted the ban on direct sales in China, thereby re-creating an environment which could hold much promise for firms engaged in direct market. Nu Skin Enterprises, for example, has set up 150 stand-alone stores across China. In 2004 the firm had sales of $106 million in China. Sales of $150 million were expected for 2006 as a result of the policy shift.[7] The paradox of Chinese governance necessarily leads to fits and starts in terms of economic and political development.

In contrast to totalitarian regimes, we could anticipate that governments that support capitalism would embrace the opportunities that direct marketing presents to its economic growth and prosperity of its citizens. However, even in these countries direct marketing may run into political difficulties. One problem is brought on by the rapid growth of direct marketing in a capitalistic environment. Politicians in the USA, urged on by a public overwhelmed by telemarketing calls, passed legislation creating the DNC in March of 2003, thereby limiting direct marketers.

Individual laws may also have an impact on direct marketers as they move from country to country. Laws effecting information availability and access to consumers are of concern.

Information Availability

One needed element for direct marketing is information on consumers within the market. At the simplest level this can be names, phone numbers, or addresses. However, additional information such as demographics, lifestyle, shopping habits, and financial data can help the direct marketer further refine the list of targeted consumers, thereby increasing the closing rate of the direct marketing efforts (and thus reducing costs). Privacy laws, rules, and conventions can affect the ability of the direct marketer to asses this vital information.

Different views on the issue of privacy, as exemplified by the USA and the Europe, have led to widely divergent policy approaches to establishing and enforcing privacy rights. The U.S. approach to privacy is largely one of self regulation, with sectoral legislation and limited privacy rights granted to the consumer. Because of historical circumstance, U.S. privacy laws are based on efforts to prevent harm from taking place. The Fair Credit Reporting Act (FCRA) of 1992 was an effort to prevent inaccurate information from being used to evaluate individuals who were applying for credit. This was followed by many other privacy laws, culminating in the Gramm-Leach Bliley Act in 1999, which provides limited protection against the sale of private financial information.

In contrast, the European approach begins with the assumption that individuals should control the information that is associated with their identities. Different laws were put in place, first by the Council of Europe Convention for the Protection of Individuals with regard to Automatic Processing of Personal Data in 1981, followed by the Data Protection directive ratified by the EU in 1995. This perceptive has led to a "consumer focused, top-down regulatory model."[8] For example, personal data is to be collected for purposes which are explicit, specified, and legitimate and may not be further processed in a way that is incompatible with the purposes for which it was originally gathered. Moreover, personal data can be processed only if unambiguous consent is given, must be accurate and up to date, and can be kept "no longer than is necessary for the purposes for which the data were collected."[9]

The European Union has enacted the Data Protection initiative designed to protect the privacy of its citizens by limiting the transmission of information outside of the European Union solely to those countries that meet very specific data protection requirements. The EU Data Protection Directive has had an impact on the privacy laws of numerous countries around the world. It has contributed to a global regulatory environment because EU members are permitted to transfer data to other countries only if those countries have adequate levels of protection for personal data. By limiting the transaction of data to countries which meet their requirements, the EU is extending its regulatory mandates to the home countries of its trading partners. For example, responding to the EU directive, Canada passed national privacy legislation in 2001.[10]

A number of Asian countries have also followed the European approach, including India, Thailand, and Philippines and Japan.[11] The Japanese Diet ratified legislation in 2003, which required direct marketers who wished to trade or rent data to provide consumers with an easy way to opt-out of such data sharing arrangements. The DMA considers this to be an improvement over the previous situation in Japan because in that country "something that is not validated by law is generally considered suspect at best, if not flat out illegal."[12]

Access to Consumers

Laws can limit the access of telemarketers to all or parts of the market within a country. One controversial example of this is the U.S. "Do-Not-Call-List" (DNC) established by the Federal Trade Commission (FTC) in

March of 2003. According to this law, consumers can register their names on a national DNC and telemarketers are not permitted to call anyone on this list. While this afforded many Americans a dinnertime free of telemarketing calls, it had some profound positive and negative effects on the direct marketing industry making the DNC rather controversial. On the positive, the DNC rule did force many unethical firms to close their doors while more legitimate firms had to find new methods of contacting consumers.

On the negative, many firms moved their operations overseas or to Puerto Rico where the DNC did not apply causing a loss of thousands of jobs in the USA. This negative impact was magnified by the fact that most telemarketing firms in the USA are located in small towns providing, in many cases, the only decent employment. For firms overseas, the DNC list provides a goldmine of verified consumer phone numbers to use in telemarketing efforts. The negative impact of the DNC rule highlights the problems created by not recognizing direct marketing as a worldwide industry. European direct marketers have viewed the American DNC rule mostly in negative terms. Responding to the U.S. DNC registry, the Federation of European Direct Marketing (FEDMA) took action to prevent similar regulations from being adopted in Europe.[13]

Despite this move, Telephone Preference Service laws still exist in Europe that are similar to the U.S. DNC rule. Luxemburg, where direct selling is viewed as an intrusion, has taken privacy regulations to such extremes that several direct marketers choose not to do business there. In the UK, there is legislation against door-to-door selling and cold calling. Most field sales representatives there must rely upon referrals and personal relationships in order to gain access to consumers.[14]

Many countries have also enacted laws that allow a "cooling off period" where a consumer is given several days, seven for most of Europe, in which to withdraw their purchases with no monetary penalties. In Japan, the Door-to-Door Sales Law allows for an eight-day "cooling off" period for products valued at more than 3,000 yen (about $25 U.S.) during which a sales contract may be cancelled without penalty. Exemptions include consumable goods if the product has been used, as well as automobiles.[15]

Ability to Recruit and Expand

Much of the rapid expansion of direct marketing is fueled by the ability to recruit part-time salespeople who are seeking to add to their income. One method of quickly expanding a network is multilevel marketing. This technique is used by companies such as Avon, Amway, Tupperware, and Nu Skin. Salespeople in these companies can make money either through commissions from selling product or from selling distributorships to other individuals. Each person in the chain receives a cut of the commissions obtained from their recruits, on down the line.

Many countries have enacted laws either directly aimed at discouraging this form of direct marketing or have employment laws making multi-level marketing problematic. Italy, China, France, and Spain laws exist which define what is a full and/or part time employee along with rules and regulations applying to each.[16] France and Spain requires part time direct marketers to pay social security on their earnings. Even more problematic for some direct marketers are regulations in countries which are aimed directly at limiting multilevel marketing. In China, legislation against "upline and downline relations" was put in place in December of 2005 and is being fought by direct marketers.[17] Germany has had strong regulations in place to avoid "snowball" distribution.

The implications of differences in the regulation of privacy and other issues related to direct marketing suggest that despite the "flattening" of the world, political and legal challenges will continue to impede direct marketing efforts into the foreseeable future. The challenge for international direct marketing is to appropriately select countries for entry where impediments are comparatively low *vis-á-vis* potential market outcomes, and to learn how to work within the constraints of different regulatory regimes. Ironically, not all laws and regulations are bad for the direct marketing industry. In India the growth of direct marketing has been stunted by early scam companies. In response, the India Direct Selling Association has petitioned the Indian government to increase regulation of the direct selling industry.[18]

ECONOMIC ENVIRONMENT

The global economy has been portrayed as both "flat"[19] and "spiky." The former characterization, made in Tom Friedman's bestselling book, *The World Is Flat*, suggests that "ten flatteners" have leveled the playing field in global commerce so that, for example, software engineers in Bangalore can write code as well as Americans in Silicon Valley. These "flatteners" include large historical changes, such as the end of communism and the creation of the Internet, as well as developments of lesser importance, like "open source" software and supply-chain management. In contrast, using some striking visual imagery in the October 2005 issue of *The Atlantic Monthly*, Richard Florida asserts that geography still makes a difference in economic development and innovation. He points out, using quantifiable indicators such as number of patents, light emissions, and scientific citations, that substantial economic activity is concentrated in a comparatively small number of locations around the globe.

It may be that both authors are largely correct, but are simply handling different parts of the elephant. In our opinion globalization should be understood as economic integration. Direct market plays a role as both a facilitator of integration and as a beneficiary of a more interdependent global economy. The reason for this is straightforward. Traditional channels, particularly retail channels, attribute success to three factors; location, location, and location. The best location is close and convenient to consumers with the financial ability and desire to purchase the products carried by the channel. In contrast, direct marketing has no physical location since, by definition, it is a consumer direct channel. Its location is wherever a consumer looks at a catalog or the internet, talks with a field sales representative, or listens to a telemarketing call. As a result, direct marketing is able to go into areas where traditional channels cannot reach. What follows is a discussion of the impact the economic environment may have on direct marketing in developed and developing economies.

Developed Economies

Developed economies have the highest per-capita expenditures in the world making them very attractive to vendors. As a result, developed countries also have the largest numbers of marketers offering a dizzying array of products. This can make it very hard for a marketer to be seen or selected by consumers, thereby requiring fairly significant expenditures of advertising dollars and a sophisticated approach to the consumer. In addition, developed economies are well serviced by a rather high density of retail establishments offering consumers the ability to see, feel, touch, and take home the product all in one trip. This is instant gratification that direct marketing just cannot match.

Despite these challenges, direct marketing has a strong presence in developed economies. Though direct marketing may not have a great share of consumers' expenditures, the level of disposable income available in developed countries makes this small share respectable in dollar amounts. In addition, higher disposable incomes allow consumers to pursue hobbies creating niche markets that direct marketing is uniquely positioned to take advantage of.

The top two direct marketing countries in total sales are developed economies, with the USA at $29.6 billion and Japan at $27 billion. Other developed countries in the top ten of direct marketing sales include the UK ($3 billion), Italy ($3 billion), Germany ($2.9 billion), and France ($1.7 billion). Developed and the prosperous parts of developing nations account for less than 15 percent of the world's population.[20]

Developing Economies

People in developing economies represent over 85 percent of the world's population. However, they have much less individual wealth to spend on products making them less attractive to marketers on a per-person basis. However, as stated previously, direct marketing by nature isn't limited to a location so can make a large population of a country like China or India profitable through large quantities of small transactions. In addition, the lower per capita GDP makes developing countries less attractive to traditional marketers reducing the level of competition in these countries.

The growth of direct marketing in developing countries is aided by high levels of unemployment as people seek ways to earn additional money or gain added income security. In Russia, despite the many challenges including a still-developing banking industry, over 2 million people have become direct sellers and run their own distributorships.[21] When Argentina's monetary crash hit in 1999 and unemployment climbed into double digits in 2001 and 2002, direct selling grew as people sought other ways to make a living.[22]

Developing economies lack the retail infrastructure present in developed economies. As a result, direct marketing has great opportunities to distribute a much wider array of products. "Latin America doesn't have a strong retail infrastructure," said Jane Garrard, Vice President of Investor and Media Relations for Tupperware. "Tupperware functions as a channel there, selling many products through the same channel. On the other hand in the US, Tupperware is a brand market and sells primarily only housewares."[23] Many items that traditionally are sold only through retail channels in developed countries can successfully be distributed through direct marketing in developing economies.

Developing economies that are experiencing rapid growth are known as "emerging markets." The most important recent economic development in emerging markets is the transition of China from a stultified, Marxist regime relying on central planning, to a free market authoritarian regime, testing the limits of capitalism under political repression. China has pursued a gradualist approach to its development. Beginning in the 1970s it liberalized prices, developed a stock market, ended collectivized agriculture and opened up to foreign direct investment. The driving force behind China's embrace of capitalism is the need to sustain employment growth for millions of workers that have previously been employed by state owned enterprises. Today, China is the second largest economy in the world as measured on the basis of PPP. Despite this, great disparities exist between regions, with 150 million Chinese living in poverty.[24]

Targeting Economies

For direct marketing firms that wish to expand into international markets, basic demographic data a key to properly selecting country markets and accurately segmenting consumers. Fundamental to market selection and segmentation is the identification of groups of consumers that possess disposable income. Macroeconomic indicators are a starting place in the effort to identify these consumers. Gross Domestic Income is an aggregate measure of products and services produced by a nation over a period of time. Even though it is a blunt measure of wealth it is available for almost all countries in the world and can be used for simple comparative purposes. PPP is used to take into account difference is prices by measuring a "bundle" of goods and services as denominated in local currencies. With a GDP of $2,228,862, China is a less attractive market than either Japan or Germany. However, on a PPP basis, China moves to second place. Using PPP per capita a different picture emerges. The countries where consumers have the greatest purchasing power on a per capita basis include in order, Luxembourg, Bermuda, USA, Norway and Liechtenstein.

Deregulation, economic liberalization, and global interdependence bode well for the future international direct marketing. For direct marketers, the challenge is to identify high-growth economies that are politically stable and are not overrun with competitors. Emerging markets may provide the greatest opportunities for international direct marketing. According to an A. T. Kearney Inc. report, "If things go right, in less than 40 years the BRIC economies together could be larger than the G6 [Britain, France, Germany, Italy, Japan, and the United States] in US dollar terms." The report states that consumer spending hits a "sweet spot" when per capita income exceeds $3,000 per year. Russia is already there and China and Brazil, followed by India, may reach this level in little over a decade.[25]

In addition to the emergence of attractive consumers in emerging markets, developing countries remain attractive as resource seeking foreign direct investment locations. Wage inflation and the entry of newer, low cost countries into the inventory of possible outsourcing locations, is increasing the flexibility of direct marketers that may wish to move contact centers, back-office processing or other operations, overseas. The combination of low wages and high skill levels make India, by far, the leading services location. Even so, the persistence of burdensome regulation and poor infrastructure are holding the nation back. Nonetheless, good language and IT skills make India the most attractive location for outsourcing direct marketing activities.[26] As a result, direct selling in India has experienced a 15–20 percent annual growth for the past five years.[27]

SOCIAL ENVIRONMENT

The importance of social considerations is tremendous for marketers intending to use direct marketing in an international context. Iyer and Hill argue that factors such as efficient overnight international delivery and improved electronic payment systems have created a marketplace environment that facilitates international trade, by extension, international direct marketing.[28] Evidently, international direct marketing is crossing social boundaries. Here, we examine an aspect of society, namely culture, and how cross-cultural considerations must be accounted for in international direct marketing. Cultural concerns in the delivery of direct marketing messages may include the appropriateness of language used, greetings and salutations, appearance and presentation of marketing materials, and the appropriateness of various different forms of direct marketing.

Whether it is presented in printed form or verbally, language is arguably a primary concern for all direct marketers. When attempting cross-cultural marketing, the use of local language may assist marketers in gaining credibility and building rapport in a foreign environment. However, this is a complicated task and miscommunication often has devastating consequences. It is dangerous to assume that, following a simple direct translation, a message generated for one audience will be appropriate for use in a country whose primary language differs. Two common errors occur here. First, the direct translation may not make sense. Second, despite an accurate translation the message may be culturally insensitive or inappropriate for the cross-cultural audience; it may need additional "tweaking."

Many classic examples of poorly translated marketing messages exist. For example, one Romanian firm produced a beautiful, four color, 12 page pamphlet for use at trade shows. The first sentence reads, "ELSID S.A. was set up in 1984 through brings into operation the production capacity of calcinated petroleum coke and beginning on 1985 the production capacity of graphite electrodes, which [sic] is using in arc furnaces from metallurgy." You can imagine that this brochure did not improve sales!

Sometimes issues with language are not due to translation problems, but may simply be attributed to the fact that a perfectly acceptable company name or slogan in one country reads differently in another. For example, the Italian maker of battery chargers, Powergen, developed a website to facilitate international marketing of its products. Italians may be used to a company name followed by "Italia" to indicate the company's Italian origin. However, the company's website URL, www.powergenitalia.com, caused English-speaking users to be concerned that the website may in fact have been an adults-only site. Powergen has since changed its URL.

There are, however, positive examples where international direct marketing has successfully crossed a cultural divide. In Australia, in 2006, U.S. owned Domino's hit the spot with a successful marketing campaign for their new roast beef and bacon flavored pizza. Flyers in letterboxes around the country read, "Unleash the bloke within . . . Domino's Roast Beef Special." This slogan successfully conveyed the message that the new pizza flavor is manly, since it contains a larger serve of meat than other pizza flavors. The term "bloke" is a uniquely Australian way of referring to a man. It is used with affection down under, but would be relatively meaningless throughout the rest of the world. Here we see that an international corporation, with outlets in more than 50 countries worldwide, has very successfully reached the hearts of its Australian segment via the use of culturally suitable language.

Appropriate greetings and salutations have also been identified as language issues to be considered when engaging in international direct marketing. Despite two different countries having the same primary language, and perhaps even being geographically close, cultural differences such as socio-economic class structure and method of governance may result in a tendency for the audience of potential consumers to prefer to be addressed in a particular manner. Graves illustrates this point via an analysis comparing American and Canadian direct marketing letters.[29] Graves states that culturally sensitive marketing can be complex and requires more than, for example, "replacing the White Sox with the Blue Jays in references." He argues that cultural considerations such as the relatively small power distance between social classes in the United States manifest in direct marketing being worded in such a way as to reduce the power distance between the consumer and the company. As such, direct marketing letters (e.g., invitations to join a credit card company) in the USA typically begin with "Dear Friend" and are worded to assert that "the receiver is virtuous, similar to the sender, or deserving of some reward."[30] In contrast, direct marketing letters targeting a Canadian audience are more likely to acknowledge the power distance that exists in Canada: "The tone is less informal and less likely to attempt to establish a relationship between sender and receiver based on anything other than the business being transacted."[31]

Graves' comparison of American and Canadian direct marketing letters also revealed interesting differences in the presentation of marketing materials—differences that were tied to cultural differences between the countries.[32] Political letters directed to Americans were presented on what appeared to be personal writing paper and were typewritten using a less formal font. Canadians, however, received political letters printed on letterhead with features suggestive of bureaucracy and formality. Graves argues that these differences were underpinned by the relatively strong segregation of marketer from consumer in Canada compared to the U.S. Anecdotal evidence suggests that Australian direct marketing letters tend to align with the U.S. manner of address and presentation, however, research evidence is not currently available to support this contention.

Differences in presentation of marketing materials across different cultural contexts may also have to do with the actual method of direct marketing used. For example, U.S. direct marketers are more likely to reach their audience via the Internet, compared to European direct marketers. In 1996, use of the Internet in Europe was three to four times smaller than in the United States, however, that gap is rapidly closing.[33] Despite the fact that direct marketing has been used in Western Europe longer than in the United States,[34] the United States also uses more frequent database marketing than Europe.[35] According to Eder, international direct marketing within the European Union is complicated by different countries having various local rules, languages, and laws.[36] Sweden, France, and Germany are most restrictive with respect to data protection laws. However, these three countries, along with the United Kingdom, Austria, and Switzerland, are considered to robustly employ direct marketing methods. Eder argues that the highly developed mail delivery service in these countries facilitates direct marketing for mail order businesses.

Contextual differences between various countries in Europe also play a role in determining the European countries to which U.S. international direct marketing is targeted. For example, before the introduction of the Euro U.S. direct marketers tended to be concerned about the ease of converting European currencies into U.S. dollar amounts. As a result, U.S. companies were more likely to target direct marketing to those European countries where credit cards were more frequently used.[37] Prevalence of credit card use appears to have, in the past, been a determinant of direct marketing within the domestic U.S. market also. Researchers have suggested that U.S. direct marketing traditionally paid little attention to the Hispanic population which was previously perceived as "lacking in credit instruments."[38]

The meaning of friendship in different cultures also plays a pivotal role in determining the cultural appropriateness of various methods of direct marketing across different countries. What is considered acceptable in one country may be offensive and brash in another. U.S. based cosmetics company, Avon, has ventured beyond the domestic market and found success in certain foreign countries. In Australia and Mexico, Avon's success may be attributed to the fact that locals welcome the home calls of sales representatives as an opportunity to socialize. In Japan, a cosmetics sales representative can be very successful selling directly to friends, relatives, and neighbors.[39] In contrast, the pyramid selling schemes and home visits are considered intrusive and insincere in Europe, where selling to friends for the purpose of generating profit is offensive. Moreover, as previously described, China in the late 1990s banned Avon, Amway, and Mary Kay from direct selling because "the Chinese public was insufficiently mature to detect fake products or scams."[40]

Although selection of appropriate media is one of the most important decisions to be made when planning international direct marketing, significant differences are rarely seen in terms of the popularity

of various print media.[41] For example, catalogues, magazines, and bro-
chures are the top three printed forms of direct marketing in both the
United States and Europe, while flyers and newspapers have lesser
popularity in both regions.[42] Direct mail-outs are also gaining popularity in China, where production costs such as labor and materials are
relatively low, compared to traditional forms of advertising which are
expensive in Asia. The popularity of direct mail advertisements in
China may also be attributed to the country's cheap and efficient
postal system.

Similarities and Differences

Perhaps an obvious question is whether to assimilate or diversify
when planning a direct marketing campaign that will cross cultural
boundaries. Some researchers argue that the very nature of international direct marketing promotes standardization in order to benefit
from the similarities across consumers from different nations,[43] while
others literally say "No way!"[44] Possibly the key to resolving this
debate is to acknowledge that the direct marketing of certain product
categories is differentially affected by culture. For example, it seems that
Coca-Cola is accepted worldwide. The Coca-Cola Company exemplifies
the geocentric, or standardized, approach to marketing because it makes
only minor adjustments to its marketing mix to suit local regions. In
contrast, when the Mattel Company markets their famous Barbie doll
worldwide, they are forced to adapt to local markets. Now selling in at
least 140 countries worldwide, the Barbie product as well and its
associated marketing have been altered to represent "more than thirty
nationalities with at least forty different career personas."[45] In Japan,
Barbie has brown eyes, darker hair, and a less sexual body than the
original Barbie designed for the American market. In India, the original
Barbie is marketed, but the Ken doll does not sell because open court-
ship is frowned upon in Indian culture.

The marketing of soft drinks and fast food by Coca-Cola and
McDonald's, respectively, may be successfully standardized because
these product categories are more or less universally accepted; drinks
and food satisfy basic human needs and are relatively unobjectionable.[46]
Barbie dolls, on the other hand, carry various cultural meanings.
For example, they are often considered to represent the most coveted
body shape and features in a particular culture. Barbie and Ken dolls
may also provide children with symbols of the accepted conception of
a romantic relationship within a culture.[47] Compared to soft drinks

and fast food, Barbie and Ken dolls may, therefore be considered as objects that are "loaded" with cultural connotations. The key to successful cross-cultural marketing is to standardize the design of international direct marketing only when the product category is relatively universal in its meaning. Standardization of international marketing in that context may be beneficial in terms of reducing production time and associated costs. However, the success of international direct marketing of "culturally loaded" products may rely on carefully tailoring the marketing message to suit individual local markets thereby avoiding offence to consumers.

TECHNOLOGICAL ENVIRONMENT

Technological

Direct marketing is defined as the use of consumer-direct (CD) channels to reach and deliver goods and services to customers without using marketing middlemen.[48] The variety of channels used for direct marketing in the USA continues to grow in response to competitive, customer, and regulatory pressures encompassing technologically dependent channels such as interactive TV, the [I]nternet, and mobile devices. Overseas, however, available technology can impact direct marketing in two ways: 1) availability of channel and 2) consumer expectations.

Availability of Channels

The level of technology of a country or region can have a great impact on what direct marketing channels are available for use. The least technologically dependant method of direct marketing is the field sales call. Avon, a leader in the field of door-to-door sales, has had a great success in moving into international markets moving into many technologically undeveloped portions of the globe with its sales force in 26 developing countries.[49]

Amway corporation, operating in 42 countries, has also experienced great success with the door-to-door method of direct marketing[50] profitably expanding into Latin America and Asia.[51] In Eastern Europe, where many people are looking for ways to become entrepreneurial, Amway's door-to-door sales methods have proven to be very successful. In the Czech Republic Amway Corporation signed up 25,000 Czechs as distributors and sold 40,000 starter kits at $83 each in its first two weeks of business.[52]

Utilizing direct mail and catalogs for direct marketing requires an efficient postal system and effective system for shipping products. For full efficiency, access to a mailing address list and an inbound telemarketing operation is needed. Some catalog companies have found unique solutions to distributing catalogs. For example, Shop America who teamed up with Seven-Eleven Japan to distribute catalogs in its 4,000 stores.[53] In short, direct mail is a viable medium in an increasing number of countries.

Telemarketing requires a reliable telephone infrastructure, large numbers of subscribers, and easily obtained directories. Until the advent of the DNC in the USA in 2004, telemarketing was a good method for direct marketing with 672 out of 1000 people having telephone lines giving coverage of 67%. Other countries pose challenges due to a relatively poor landline infrastructure. India has only 45 lines per 1000 people, Indonesia has 57 lines per 1000, and South Africa has 99 lines per 1000. This means that direct marketers can contact only 4.5% of the population in India, 5.7% in Indonesia, and 9.9% in South Africa.

Many developing countries are leapfrogging telephone technology and going directly into cell-phone technology. In 1999, Hong Kong and Korea were the first to have more wireless subscribers than landlines. Malaysia, New Zealand, Singapore, and Taiwan achieved that in 2000. In the Asian region, the wireless market surpassed the landline market in 2002 and widened the gap in 2003–2004. The number of wireless subscribers increased 21.5 percent to 632.6 million in 2004, while the landline market increased 11.8 percent to 515.1 million.[54]

The primary reason that wireless outnumbering landlines are that wireless requires a less expensive and easier to build infrastructure of towers as opposed to the expense and effort that goes into traditional land-lines. This leapfrog process presents problems for direct marketers wanting to use outbound telemarketing since wireless phone providers may charge customers both for outgoing and incoming calls. The direct marketer risks alienating customers by costing them money for the telemarketing calls.[55]

Wireless, specifically cell-phone technology, also presents wonderful opportunities for direct marketing. Cell-phones not only handle voice calls but they also have the ability to receive text messages all the way up to full multimedia presentations. In Poland, for instance, messages from local retailers scan across cell-phone screens enticing them into the stores.[56] This ability makes cell-phones an ideal and rich one-to-one marketing tool. However, lawmakers are exploring laws to protect consumers from a deluge of marketing on intended for cell-phones.[57]

Direct marketing by television includes advertisements run during regular programming that provide an inbound telemarketing number for the benefit of interested viewers. It also includes dedicated shopping channels such as the Home Shopping Network (HSN) which operates in the USA. These channels provide an unending series of products for sale displayed by a star or salesperson. A sense of urgency is created by the limited quantity available as shown by a countdown timer. In addition, viewers who call to purchase an item may be interviewed live on television. These channels require widespread ownership of televisions along some sort of broadcast infrastructure, as well as access to telephones for in-bound telemarketing.

In countries where penetration of television is not extensive or a direct marketer wants to reach an alternative market, radio may offer a non-visual alternative. In some countries, the USA, South Africa,[58] and Ireland,[59] the percentage of radio listeners is relatively high but experiencing maturity if not some signs of decline. New technology such as [i]Pods, podcasts, and other MP3 technology is cutting into radio's share of the at home and commuter listeners. However, in Asia radio is quickly coming out of the shadow of television and other media. The rise of automobile ownership and the increase of mobile phones that can receive radio have lead to this increase in listeners.[60]

Usage of the World Wide Web for direct marketing has blossomed in the USA due to its richness and speed as well as the number of people who use the [I]nternet. The web is on and able to take orders 24 hours 7 days a week from any location worldwide, making it a relatively inexpensive alternative for direct marketers wanting to go abroad. Web pages can be set up to customize themselves based upon the shopper's input, while at the same time providing the direct marketer a wealth of data. The reach of the [I]nternet is very good in a number of countries including the USA, Australia, Canada, Czech Republic, Finland, Korea, Singapore, Sweden, and the United Kingdom. In New Zealand, 830 out of 1000 people use the [I]nternet (83% of the population)! Reach is rather poor in several developing countries such as Ecuador, Guatemala, Indonesia, Panama, and South Africa. In India only 47 out of 1000 people (4.7%) of the population are [I]nternet users making the [I]nternet less attractive to direct marketers.

Consumer Expectations

The level of technology within a country can influence the expectations customers have of direct marketing, which in turn can directly affect media chosen, products sold, and message used. There are two categories of customer expectations; interactivity and immediacy.

The first category is the level of interactivity of the direct marketing channel, which includes the ability to experience or sample the product and the customizability of the shopping experience. Field sales calls have the highest level of interactivity of any of the direct marketing channels. Avon salespeople customize the makeup products offered to direct observation of the prospect's skin type and complexion. The customer can sample the product and see how the product satisfies his or her needs before purchasing. This interactivity continues to be a driver for the success of field sales companies such as Avon and Amway.[61]

The [I]nternet also interacts with customers. Direct marketers can customize the content seen by prospects through the use of profiles, clicking behavior, and other similar data. Customers can interact with the computer to see products in three dimensions, change color choice on the product, and watch film clips of the product all depending on their needs and choice. As use of the [I]nternet goes up, the use and preference for non-interactive forms of direct marketing, such as catalogs, may decline.

The second category is the immediacy of the direct marketing experience, including the speed by which the purchase is made and the product received. In some countries, such as the USA, if people want products today they can simply climb into their car and drive to a variety of retail establishments and have the product the same day. Cars are used by 479 out of 1000 people and over 50% of the roads are paved in the USA. Thus, direct marketers must offer easy shopping with fast delivery in order to compete with retail establishments. In other countries, such as India where nine out of 1000 people (less than 1%) use a car, direct marketing is a speedier method to purchase products. Consumers in these markets may find their range of retail options is limited by where public transportation or their feet can take them.

Conclusion

In this paper, we used the PEST framework to analyze the international direct marketing environment. We described some of the major legal and regulatory issues facing direct marketers, as wells as matters related to cross-cultural communication and technology. Firms that engage in international direct marketing should make use of the PEST framework for the purpose of market selection as well as for strategic decision making while operating in overseas markets. The PEST environment is not static, and it has both a direct and an indirect impact on firm opportunities and firm performance.

James Barnett, the former Vice President of the Goodyear Tire and Rubber Company, has stated that that when you think of the global economy you should think of the word "complexity". Firms, whether large are small, must make their way through a thicket of complicated issues if they wish to succeed in doing business overseas. Yet the challenge is often worth the trouble because opportunities in international markets are enormous; this is especially the case for firms that bypass traditional distribution channels and market their products directly to their customers.

Emerging markets should be particularly attractive to direct marketers. The GlobalEDGE resource web site and Michigan State University produces an index of market potential indicators which shows which countries are the most attractive for market entry. The twenty-four countries listed in the index include emerging markets in Asia (i.e. China, South Korea, and India), Eastern Europe (Czech Republic, Poland), and South America (Mexico, Brazil, Argentina). These countries have high rates of growth and therefore have a high level of market potential. However, many emerging economies also court a great deal of risk for international firms. For example, Venezuela, Columbia, and Indonesia are included in the 24 country index even though each presents unique and difficult challenges in terms of political, financial and economic risk. The applicability of such risk to particular international firms can be readily assessed using the PEST framework. We recommend that direct marketers actively pursue opportunities in foreign markets, but only after thoroughly assessing the potential benefits and possible costs that those opportunities present.

Globalization, technological innovation, and the spread of free market governance has created new and interesting opportunities for managers who decide to use direct marketing to sell their products overseas. For managers considering international direct marketing, a careful assessment of market prospects and a thoughtful evaluation of the PEST environment should maximize potential opportunities while minimizing the risks associated with foreign markets.

NOTES

This chapter originally appeared in *Direct Marketing: An International Journal*, Vol. 1, No. 1, 2007, pp. 17–37. © Emerald Group Publishing Limited.

1. P. Kotler and K. Kevin, *Marketing Management*, 12th ed. (Upper Saddle River, NJ: Pearson/Prentice Hall, 2006).

2. Direct Marketing Association, "DMA's List Rental Data Card," http://www.the-dma.org/ratecards/listrental.shtml.

3. T. Levitt, "Globalization of Markets," *Harvard Business Review* 61 (1983): 91–102.

4. P. W. Beamish, "European Foreign Investment: Why Go to Canada," *European Management Journal* 14, no. 1 (1996): 76–80.

5. P. R. Cateora and L. B. J. Graham, *International Marketing*, 13th ed. (Chicago: McGraw-Hill, 2007), 508.

6. C. C. L. Wang, "The Rise and Fall of Direct Selling in China: Lessons for International Marketers," *Journal of International Marketing & Marketing Research* 26, no. 3 (2001): 139–50.

7. Betsy Lowther, "Nu Skin Sees Benefit from China Policy Shift," *Women's Wear Daily* 190, no. 83 (2005): 23.

8. http://www.netcaucus.org/books/privacy2000/Part5.pdf.

9. http://www.cdt.org/privacy/eudirective/EU_Directive_.html.

10. Rita Marie Cain, "Global Privacy Concerns and Regulations—Is the United States a World Apart?," *International Review of Law, Computers & Technology* 16, no. 1 (2002): 23–24.

11. Amy E. Worlton, *Asia Opts for EU-Style Privacy* (Washington, DC: WRF Privacy in Focus, 2003), www.wrf.com.

12. Andy Meyers, *How Japan's New Privacy Bill Will Change Direct Marketing in Japan.* (London: Direct Marketing Association, 2003), www.the-dma.org/.

13. C. Arnold, "Law Gives Industry a Buzz," *Marketing News* 38, no. 2 (2004): 11–12.

14. Katherine Ponder, "Selling to 'Neighbours'—Tres European," *Direct Selling News* 1, no. 10 (2005a).

15. Katherine Ponder, "Building Acierto (success) in Latin America," *Direct Selling News* 1, no. 1 (2005b).

16. Ponder, "Selling to 'Neighbours'—Tres European"; Katherine Ponder, "The Billion Dollar Club: How the Top Countries Compare," *Direct Selling News* 2, no. 1 (2006a).

17. Ponder, "Selling to 'Neighbours'—Tres European."

18. Katherine Ponder, "India on the Rise," *Direct Selling News* 2, no. 2 (2006c).

19. T. L. Friedman, *The World Is Flat* (New York: Farrar, Straus and Giroux, 2005).

20. http://www.wfdsa.org/.

21. Ponder, "The Billion Dollar Club: How the Top Countries Compare."

22. Ponder, "Selling to 'Neighbours'—Tres European."

23. Ibid., 70.

24. CIA, *CIA World Factbook* (Washington, DC: CIA, 2005), www.cia.gov/cia/publications/factbook/index.html.

25. A. T. Kearney Inc., *Foreign Policy Globalization Index* (Chicago: A. T. Kearney Inc., 2006a), www.atkearney.com/main.taf?p=5,4,1,127.

26. A. T. Kearney Inc., *Emerging Market Priorities for Global Retailers* (Chicago: A. T. Kearney Inc., 2006b), www.atkearney.com/main.taf?p=5,3,1,141,1.

27. Ponder, "India on the Rise."

28. R. T. Iyer and J. S. Hill, "International Direct Marketing Strategies: A US-European Comparison," *European Journal of Marketing* 30, no. 3 (1996): 65–83.

29. R. Graves, " 'Dear Friend'(?): Culture and Genre in American and Canadian Direct Marketing Letters," *Journal of Business Communication* 34, no. 3 (1997): 235–52.

30. Ibid., 243.

31. Ibid., 244.

32. Ibid., 235–52.

33. P. Eder, "Direct Marketing in Europe: Understanding Differences in Languages, Cultures, and Regulations," *Direct Marketing* 58, no. 11 (2006): 48–50.

34. Iyer and Hill, "International Direct Marketing Strategies: A US-European Comparison."

35. Eder, "Direct Marketing in Europe: Understanding Differences in Languages, Cultures, and Regulations."

36. Ibid.

37. Iyer and Hill, "International Direct Marketing Strategies: A US-European Comparison."

38. P. K. Korgaonkar, E. J. Karson, and D. Lund, "Hispanics and Direct Marketing Advertising," *Journal of Consumer Marketing* 17, no. 2 (2000): 137–57.

39. N. Laidler, *Mary Kay Cosmetics: Asian Market Entry* (Harvard Business School Case No. 9-594-023, rev. July 26, 1996, Boston: Harvard Business School Publishing, 1996).

40. "Living with Your Landlord," *China Economic Review*, 1998.

41. J. Dillon, *Handbook of International Direct Marketing* (Maidenhead: McGraw-Hill, 1996); Iyer and Hill, "International Direct Marketing Strategies: A US-European Comparison."

42. Iyer and Hill, "International Direct Marketing Strategies: A US-European Comparison."

43. Levitt, "Globalization of Markets"; K. Ohmae, *Triad Power* (New York: Free Press, 1985).

44. Eder, "Direct Marketing in Europe: Understanding Differences in Languages, Cultures, and Regulations," 48.

45. J. P. MacDougall, "Transnational Commodities as Local Cultural Icons: Barbie Dolls in Mexico," *The Journal of Popular Culture* 37, no. 2 (2003): 257.

46. A. H. Maslow, *Motivation and Personality,* 2nd ed. (New York: Harper & Row, 1970).

47. MacDougall, "Transnational Commodities as Local Cultural Icons: Barbie Dolls in Mexico."

48. Kotler, Philip, and Keller, *Marketing Management.*

49. "Avon Products Inc.: Earnings Forecast Is Raised on International Performance," *Wall Street Journal*, March 31, 2008, B4.

50. T. A. Foster, "Amway's Dutch Gateway to European Success," *Logistics Management* 42, no. 5 (2003): E65-7.

51. L. Chang, "Amway in China, Once Barred, Now Booming," *Wall Street Journal*, March 12, 2003, B1.

52. Foster, "Amway's Dutch Gateway to European Success."

53. Cateora and Graham, *International Marketing.*

54. B. Wallace, "Assessing Asian Opportunities," *Telecommunications International* 39, no. 6 (2005): S3–S6.

55. P. Kirby, "FCC Aims to Protect Consumers from a Deluge of Wireless 'Spam,'" *Telecommunications Reports* 70, no. 7 (2004): 30–31.

56. D. Wood, "Five Ways to Avoid Cell Regulation," *Brandweek* 46, no. 2 (2005): 20.

57. Kirby, "FCC Aims to Protect Consumers from a Deluge of Wireless 'Spam.'"

58. *Africa News*, "Out of Tune with Listeners," *Sunday Times*, October 2006.

59. E. Oliver, "Podcast Figures Pt to the Test," *The Irish Times*, June 2006, 19.

60. J. Bowman, "Getting Radio Back on Air," *Media, Hong Kong*, May 7, 2004, 22–24.

61. Foster, "Amway's Dutch Gateway to European Success."

Chapter 6

Intellectual Property Protection around the Globe

Masaaki Kotabe

At no other time in economic history have countries been more economically interdependent than they are today. Despite the current global recession, most countries in the 21st century have not shunned globalization and are likely to continue their globalization trend. It has been protected by the belief of firms in the efficiency of global supply chains. Even a firm that is operating in only one domestic market is not immune to the influence of economic activities external to that market. The net result of these factors has been the increased interdependence of countries and economies, increased competitiveness, and the concomitant need for firms to keep a constant watch on the international competitive and technological environment.

As the nature of value-adding activities in the world shifts more and more to information creation, manipulation, and analysis, both developed and emerging nations have started taking an increased interest in international intellectual property protection measures. This shift is comparable to the industrial evolution from agriculture to manufacturing we had experienced in the 12th century. Although the importance of farm products to humankind did not change over the years, the portion of the economy allocated to agriculture has consistently declined, and so have the margins for the agricultural sector. Therefore, farmers moved into manufacturing, or at least into food processing, to maintain margins.

An analogous situation faces a content maker for information-related products such as software, music, movies, newspapers, magazines, and education in the late-20th century headed into the 21st century. In an early civilization, people just knew how to do things, and learning and transferring knowledge to other people was costly and not easy at all. Then people later learned to document their knowledge in written media such as books and drawings. Copying and passing on intellectual property became easier and less costly. In recent years, we use tapes, discs, and other electronic media.

Now with the emergence of the Internet, electronically represented intellectual property can be freely copied anywhere in the world, and knowledge transfer has become virtually instantaneous. Because more and more of value creation in the developed nations is coming from the development and sale of such information-based intellectual property, it is no surprise that developed nations are highly interested in putting strong international intellectual property laws in place. For instance, a recent survey of more than 200 of the largest firms in the United Kingdom disclosed that 83 percent of those firms had experienced different types of cyber crime in 2003. Further, according to an international specialist in computer forensics, roughly 70 percent of UK business professionals have stolen corporate intellectual property through personal e-mails when leaving the employer. Obviously, it is costly for corporations to protect their intellectual property, and to adjust for losses in productivity and perceived damage to corporate brand and share price.[1] The U.S. insistence on the inclusion of provisions relating to intellectual property in the World Trade Organization's (WTO's) Trade Related Aspects of Intellectual Property Rights (TRIPS) agreement is a direct consequence, and is understandable as cyber crime affects all parties with intellectual property. Technology-based protection of electronic information through hardware, software, or a combination thereof in the form of encryption and digital signatures has been suggested as the means of circumventing the problem of unauthorized copying.[2]

Other hurdles exist for content creators with the emergence of electronic commerce (e-commerce). In the past, comparing and contrasting the price and quality of products and services was a time-consuming endeavor. Now, e-commerce operators make it easy for prospective customers to make such a comparison. These vendors even offer customer ratings. E-commerce represents a truly efficient market for information. Information has become transparent. As a result, content creators can no longer maintain a monopolistic advantage for long. This transformation in the form of value creation and ease of dissemination implies a jump in economic integration as nations become part of an international electronic commerce network. Not only money but also products and services will flow faster.

The other consequence of fungible content, information products, and electronic networks is an additional assault on the power of national governments to regulate international commerce. Ford uses a product design process whereby designers in Dearborn, Michigan, pass on their day's work in an electronic form to an office in Japan, which then passes the baton along to designers in Britain, who pass it back to Dearborn the next day. When the information represented in the design crosses borders, how do the governments of the United States, Japan, and Britain treat this information? How will such exchanges be regulated? Less open societies like China and Malaysia, recognizing the power of electronic networks, are already attempting to regulate the infrastructure of and access to the electronic network.

In this chapter, we examine how intellectual property is protected internationally and how this mechanism has been evolving in recent years. Such knowledge is important in an era of globalization as an increasing number of firms, both domestic and international, have begun to realize that intellectual resources that are valuable, rare, and difficult-to-imitate are major sources of their competitive advantage.

INTELLECTUAL PROPERTY PROTECTION

Intellectual property refers to "a broad collection of innovations relating to things such as works of authorship, inventions, trademarks, designs and trade secrets."[3] Intellectual property rights broadly include patents, trademarks, trade secrets, and copyrights. These ideas typically involve large investments in creative and investigative work to create the product, but fairly low costs of manufacturing. As such they are amenable to being duplicated readily by imitators. Imitation reduces the potential returns that would have accrued to the innovator, thereby limiting its ability to appropriate the large investments made. With increasing movements of goods and services across borders, the potential loss of revenues to innovator firms, most of which reside in industrialized countries, is significant.

Few topics in international business have attracted as much attention and discussion in recent years as intellectual property rights.[4] In 2007, the Organization for Economic Cooperation and Development (OECD) released a report estimating the annual value of the international, physical trade of counterfeited consumer products at approximately $200 billion. This equals around 2 percent of the entire world trade and exceeds the GDP of 150 countries.[5] Apart from hurting legitimate businesses and trade, intellectual property infringement leads to the loss of government tax revenue.

Piracy is most rampant in software industry. For example, according to the Business Software Alliance, a global anti-piracy watchdog group, 35 percent of the software installed in 2006 on personal computers (PCs) worldwide was obtained illegally, amounting to nearly $40 billion in global losses due to software piracy. In percentage terms, Central/Eastern Europe topped the piracy rate at 68 percent of all software used, followed by Latin America at 66 percent, Middle East/Africa at 60 percent, Asia Pacific at 50 percent, the European Union at 36 percent, and North America at 22 percent.[6] More concerning is the counterfeiting of medicines, which threatens public safety and poses a growing threat around the world. Between 2000 and 2006, the Food and Drug Administration saw an eightfold increase in the number of new counterfeit drugs cases. In developing countries with weak regulatory systems, approximately 10 to 30 percent of all medicines could be counterfeit. Worldwide sales of counterfeit drugs are forecast to reach $75 billion by 2010.[7]

Various anti-counterfeiting tools and technologies are developed by firms to aid others' anti-counterfeiting efforts, or to enhance their own. Hewlett-Packard's Specialty Printing Systems, for instance, has expanded its offerings to the pharmaceutical industry with the introduction of a new ink cartridge that allows individual capsules or tablets to be marked. Eastman Kodak Co. developed a Traceless System for anti-counterfeiting on its branded rechargeable lithium ion digital camera batteries supplied by Sanyo Electric. With "forensically undetectable" markers put on printed materials, product packaging or product components, the system can help fighting against counterfeiting as only handheld Kodak readers can detect the markers. Also among the firms deploying this anti-counterfeiting technology are DonRuss Playoff and Liz Claiborne. However, in spite of anti-counterfeiting tools and technologies, litigation, as well as legislation that we will discuss later in this section, piracy is still rampant around the world.[8]

Now with the convenient online access, it is even more difficult to ensure that copyright rules are not violated in the cyberspace. Recently, "Google's books online" has been under criticism from American publishing Organization which accuse it of breaching copyright laws. Google aims to put 15 million volumes online from four top U.S. libraries—the libraries of Stanford, Michigan, and Harvard universities, and of the New York Public Library by 2015. The critics worry that if the people can read a book online for free they would not bother purchasing it. As easy as a click to download music online to listen to offline, a recent court ruling clearly states that even though the copyright of music has lapsed, reproducing and distributing the music is a breach to the copyright law. According to the New York's highest court, Naxos was found illegal to release classical recordings by Yehudi Menuhim and others because such recordings were still covered by the common law.[9]

Counterfeiting is not restricted to poor countries, either. Milan, Italy, for example, is a leading producer of counterfeit luxury products; Florida is an international haven for fake aircraft parts; and Switzerland is a big player in pharmaceutical counterfeits production with almost 40 percent of fake medicines seized by the EU. According to the analyst, there is a globalized trend of counterfeiting, like manufacturing. Increasingly, all member countries of the WTO are required to implement Trade Related Aspects of Intellectual Property Rights (TRIPS) to execute intellectual property protection and companies are joining together to fight against the violations.[10]

Patent

A patent, if granted, offers a patent holder a legal monopoly status on the patented technology and/or process for a certain extended period (usually 15 to 21 years depending on a country). Patent laws in the United States and Japan provide an example of the differences in laws across countries and their implications for corporations.[11] The most significant difference between the two countries is on the "first-to-file" and "first-to-invent" principles. Although most countries follow the "first-to-file" principle, only the United States (along with the Philippines) follows the "first-to-invent" principle. In the majority of countries, the patent is granted to the first person filing an application for the patent. In the United States, however, the patent is granted to the person who first invented the product or technology. Any patents granted prior to the filing of the patent application by the "real" inventor would be reversed in order to protect rights of the inventor. The difference between the two principles is no small matter. See Perspective 6.1 for far-reaching implications.[12]

Perspective 6.1: Two Worlds Apart—the "First-to-Invent" Principle vs. the "First-to-File" Principle

First to File vs. First to Invent.

A diplomatic conference to discuss the initial draft of patent harmonization treaty was convened by the World Intellectual Property Organization (WIPO) in May 2002. Most neutral observers would suggest that U.S. domestic politics is one principal impediment to the conference's success. The United States still clings to the old common-law philosophy of "prior use" that should determine the rightful owner of intellectual property. Simply stated, whoever invented it first (i.e., established prior use) is a rightful owner. In the United States, the *first* to *invent* wins the patent, whereas in the rest of the world a patent is awarded to the *first* to *file* an application. The conference examined the virtue of the U.S. "first-to-invent" principle vis-à-vis the "first-to-file" principle espoused in the rest of the world. The conference's recommendation involved changing the law to award patents to the "first to file" instead of to the "first to invent," which has guided the awarding of U.S. patents since Thomas Jefferson looked at the first ones filed in 1790.

Under current U.S. law, an individual applicant for a patent must prove that he or she had the idea first, not simply that he or she won the race to the courthouse. He or she can assert his or her priority to the invention at any time; he or she is entitled to a patent if thereafter he or she has not "suppressed, abandoned, or concealed" the invention. The U.S. system was established to protect the inventor who lacks the resources to keep up a stream of patent applications merely to invoke their priority. Not surprisingly, the system is championed today by resource-poor universities and independent inventors.

Supporters of the "first-to-file" system, largely lawyers and corporations, argue that it would better serve the public because it is simpler and conforms to the systems in the rest of the world. Moreover, it would spur inventors to file for patents earlier and to disclose their inventions sooner, thus speeding the progression from idea to finished product. Many supporters also note that most U.S. companies are equipped to act on a first-to-file basis, because they typically apply for patents as soon as inventions are produced. With the adoption of the first-to-file system, this date would also affect patent rights abroad, and thus provide greater reliability for U.S. patents worldwide.

Many are apprehensive about such a change. The principal objection to the first-to-file system is that it fosters premature, sketchy disclosure in hastily filed applications, letting the courts work things out later. Although unlikely, it leaves open the possibility of someone stealing the profits of an invention from the true inventor by beating him or her to the courthouse steps. In the end, the Patent Office could be deluged with applications filed for defensive purposes, as is the case in Japan where this phenomenon is called "patent flooding."

Sensitive to these criticisms, the commission recommended several other reforms to ensure fairness in implementing the "first-to-file" proposal. These reforms include issuing a provisional patent application at reduced cost while the patent itself is undergoing examination, and establishing a grace period for public disclosure without affecting patentability. Most importantly, the commission suggested adopting the rule of "prior-use right," allowing users of inventions to continue their use under certain conditions, even after a patent on the invention is obtained by another party.

The effect of "first to file" vs. "first to invent" may be best illustrated by the case of the laser, a discovery generally credited to physicist Charles Townes, who won a Nobel Prize for elucidating the principle of the maser, the theoretical father of the laser. Townes owned the patent on the device. Years later, Gordon Gould, a former graduate student at Columbia University, where Townes taught physics, proved by contemporary notebooks and other means that he had developed the idea long before Townes patented it in 1958.

Gould could not have brought his case to the courts in foreign countries that give priority to the first to file. In the United States, however, the court accepted Gould's evidence of priority and awarded him the basic patents to the laser in 1977 and 1979, ruling that Townes and his employer, at the time AT&T Co., had infringed on Gould's idea. Patlex Corp., of which Gould is a director, now collects fees from laser users throughout the world.

Source: Lee Edson, "Patent Wars," *Across the Board* 30 (April 1993)" 24–29; Q. Todd Dickinson, "Harmony and Controversy," *IP Worldwide,* September 2002, 22–24.

The business implications of this difference for U.S. companies as well as foreign companies are significant. To protect any new proprietary technologies, U.S. companies must ensure that their inventions are protected abroad through formal patent applications being filed in various countries, especially the major foreign markets and the markets of competitors and potential competitors. For foreign companies operating in the United States, the implications are that they must be extremely careful in introducing any technologies that have been invented in the United States. A "first-to-file" mentality could result in hasty patent applications and significant financial burden in the form of lawsuits that could be filed by competitors that claim to have invented the technology earlier.

In some extreme situation, governments have broken patent law for public health reasons. For example, Brazil's government, after signing intellectual property protection agreement, announced in August 2001 its plans to break a patent for a drug used to treat AIDS despite the international patent held by Roche, the drug's Swiss-based pharmaceutical company. Federal officials said they were unsuccessful in talks with Roche to lower the prices the country paid for nelfinavir, a drug blocking the HIV virus from replicating itself and infecting new cells.[13] The Brazilian government is not the only one to grab a company's patent rights in the interest of public health. Scared by the anthrax outbreaks in the United States, Canada's health ministry decided that public health came first. It commissioned a generic drug company to make a million doses of ciprofloxacin, a drug used to treat one of the nastier forms of the disease whose patent belongs to German drug giant Bayer.[14]

Copyright

Copyrights protect original literary, dramatic, musical, artistic, and certain other intellectual works. Copyright protection lasts 50 years in the European Union countries and Japan, compared with 95 years in the United States.[15] The difference in the lengths of period of copyright protection could cause tremendous price differences between countries for those products whose copyrights expired in the EU or Japan but are still effective in the United States. Different prices across different markets due to different legal systems motivate gray marketing activities.[16]

For example, copyright protection lasts only 50 years in the European Union and Japan compared with 95 years in the United States. In other words, even if the music recordings were originally made and released in the United States, the recordings made in the early- to mid-1950s by such figures as Elvis Presley and Ella Fitzgerald are entering the public domain in Europe, opening the way for any European recording company to release albums that had been owned exclusively by particular labels. Although the distribution of such albums would be usually limited to Europe, CD-store chains and specialty outlets in the United States routinely stock cheaper foreign imports via gray markets.[17]

A computer program is also considered a literary work and is protected by copyright. A copyright provides its owner the exclusive right to reproduce and distribute the material or perform or display it publicly, although limited reproduction of copyrighted works by others may be permitted for fair-use purposes. In the United States, the use of the copyright notice does not require advance permission, or registration with, the Copyright Office. In fact, many countries offer copyright protection without registration, whereas others offer little or no protection for the works of foreign nationals.[18]

In the United States, the Digital Millennium Copyright Act (DMCA) was passed in 1998 to address a growing struggle in the cyberspace between industries supplying digital content and those arguing against strict enforcement of copyright on the Internet. The DMCA bans any efforts to bypass software that protects copyrighted digital files. Similar laws have been passed in other countries as well. For example, selling "mod" (modification) chips, a device used to play copied games, tinkering with a game console to play legally and illegally copied software, is a practice that has turned into a legal landmine for the video game sector. In 2004, Sony filed a lawsuit against

David Ball, a British national, in Britain's High Court for selling thousands of mod chips called "Messiah 2" for Sony's PlayStation 2 games consoles. He also published information explaining how to install the chips in PlayStation 2 consoles. He was found guilty of violating all counts of UK copyright law.[19]

Trademark

A *trademark* is a word, symbol, or device that identifies the source of goods and may serve as an index of quality. It is used primarily to differentiate or distinguish a product or service from another. Trademark laws are used to prevent others from offering a product or service with a confusingly similar mark. In the United States, registration is not mandatory, because "prior use" technically determines the rightful owner of a trademark. However, because determining who used the trademark prior to anyone else is difficult and subject to lawsuits, trademark registration is highly recommended. In most foreign countries, registration is mandatory for a trademark to be protected. In this sense, the legal principle that applies to trademarks is similar to the one that applies to patents: the "first-to-use" principle in the United States and the "first-to-file" principle in most other countries. Therefore, if companies are expected to do business overseas, their trademarks should be registered in every country in which protection is desired (see Perspective 6.2 for the extent to which U.S. firms could legally protect their own copyright and trademark used by other firms abroad).

Perspective 6.2: Could U.S. Firms Always Protect Their Own Copyright and Trademark Used by Other Firms Abroad? The Answer Is Clearly NO!

Infringement of intellectual property rights is not confined to the United States. Inadequate protection of intellectual property rights in foreign countries could also result in copyrights and trademarks illegally used abroad making their way back to the United States. In many industrialized countries, it is possible to stem illegally used copyrights and trademarks from entering the home country. For example, in the United States, the U.S. Customs Service provides protection to copyrights and trademarks.

Prior to receiving U.S. Customs protection, copyrights and trademarks have to be registered first with the U.S. Copyright Office and the U.S. Patent and Trademark Office, respectively. Then for U.S. Customs protection, each copyright and trademark must be recorded at the U.S. Customs Service Office. The fee is $190. Although there are no standard application forms, the application requirements for recording a copyright and a trademark are listed in Section 133.1–133.7 of the U.S. Customs regulations. An application should include the following information: (1) a certified status copy and five photocopies of the copyright or trademark registration, (2) the name of its legal owner, (3) the business address of the legal owner, (4) the states or countries in which the business of the legal owner is incorporated or otherwise conducted, (5) a list of the names and addresses of all foreign persons or companies authorized or licensed to use the copyright or trademark to be protected, (6) a list of the names and addresses of authorized manufacturers of goods, and (7) a list of all places in which goods using the copyright or bearing the trademark are legally manufactured. Although it is not necessary to submit a separate application for protection of each copyright or trademark, the filing fee of $190 still applies to each and every copyright or trademark being recorded with the Customs Service. Additional information can be obtained by contacting the U.S. Customs Service at the Intellectual Property Rights Branch, Franklin Court, 1301 Constitution Avenue, N.W., Washington, D.C. (Ph. 202-482-6960).

Unfortunately, the U.S. Patent and Trademark Office has little or no legal recourse when it comes to U.S. copyrights or trademarks used by foreign companies outside the United States. For example, in Brazil, America Online's famous "aol.com" domain is legally owned by StarMedia Network, a small Internet services Brazilian company in the fast-growing Latin American market. America Online (AOL) had sued StarMedia Network alleging trademark infringement and contested the Brazilian provider's use of the domain name "aol.com.br." However, the Brazilian court ruled in May 1999 that because Brazil's America Online registered the name first, it would not have to surrender the domain name to its U.S. rival. As a result of the Brazilian court's ruling in favor of StarMedia Network, its shares rose 74 percent in its first day of trading. AOL was then forced to market its Brazilian services under "br.aol.com."

Although no other news leaked on a possible out-of-court settlement on StarMedia's "aol.com.br" vs. AOL's "br.aol.com" recent news articles suggest that AOL may have eventually purchased the right to use "aol.com.br" for an undisclosed sum of money (which would not come cheap).

The decision may touch off concerns about international cybersquatting as many Internet dotcom companies begin to launch overseas operations, only to find that country-level version of the domain name is already registered. For example, the AOL domain had been registered in about 60 countries in addition to Brazil, and not all of these registrations were made by the American company.

Sources: Maxine Lans Retsky, "Curbing Foreign Infringement," *Marketing News,* March 31, 1997, 10; "Brazilian ISP Prevails in AOL Lawsuit" (a news report provided by LatPro.com ejs@LatPro.com), May 31, 1999; "No Free Ride," *Latin Trade,* May 2001, 54; "AOL Latin America Launches Upgraded Wireless E-Mail in Brazil, Mexico and Argentina," *World IT Report,* February 17, 2002, p. N.

Trade Secret

A *trade secret* is another means of protecting intellectual property and fundamentally differs from patents, copyrights, and trademarks in that protection is sought without registration. Trade secrets can be protected in the courts if the company can prove that it took all precautions to protect the idea from its competitors and that infringement occurred illegally by way of espionage or hiring employees with crucial working knowledge. In the United States, the Economic Espionage Act of 1996 makes the theft of trade secrets a U.S. federal criminal offense and lengthens prison sentences and raises fines if done for the benefit of foreign governments.

INTERNATIONAL TREATIES FOR INTELLECTUAL PROPERTY PROTECTION

Although patent and copyright laws have been in place in many countries for well over a hundred years, laws on trademarks and trade secrets are of relatively recent vintage, having been instituted in the late 19th century and beginning of the 20th century.[20] These laws are essentially national laws, and as such, do not automatically protect intellectual property across national boundaries. This is why there are many international treaties to help provide intellectual property protection across national boundaries. Some of the most important treaties are Paris Convention, Patent Cooperation Treaty, Patent Law Treaty, European Patent Convention, and Berne Convention, among others.

Paris Convention

The Paris Convention for the Protection of Industrial Property was established in 1883, and the number of signatory countries currently stands at 140. It is designed to provide "domestic" treatment to protect patent and trademark applications filed in other countries. Operationally, the convention establishes rights of priority that stipulate that once an application for protection is filed in one member country, the applicant has 12 months to file in any other signatory countries, which should consider such an application as if it were filed on the same date as the original application.[21] It also means that if an applicant does not file for protection in other signatory countries within a grace period of 12 months of original filing in one country, legal protection could not be provided. In most countries, other than the United States, the "first-to-file" principle is used for intellectual property protection. Lack of filing within a grace period in all other countries in which protection is desired could mean a loss of market opportunities to a competitor who filed for protection of either an identical or a similar type of intellectual property. The two new treaties, explained below, are further attempts to make international patent application as easy as a domestic patent application.

Patent Cooperation Treaty

The Patent Cooperation Treaty (PCT) was established in 1970, amended in 1979 and modified in 1984. It is open to any signatory member country to the Paris Convention. The PCT makes it possible to seek patent protection for an invention simultaneously in each of a large number of countries by filing an "international" patent application. The patent applicant can file his or her international patent application with his or her national Patent Office, which will act as a PCT "Receiving" Office or with the International Bureau of World Intellectual Property Organization (WIPO) in Geneva. If the applicant is a national or resident of a contracting State which is party to the

European Patent Convention, the Harare Protocol on Patents and Industrial Designs (Harare Protocol) or the Eurasian Patent Convention, the international application may also be filed with the European Patent Office (EPO), the African Regional Industrial Property Organization (ARIPO) or the Eurasian Patent Office (EAPO), respectively.[22]

Patent Law Treaty

The Patent Law Treaty (PLT), adopted in Geneva in June 2000, comes as the result of a World Intellectual Property Organization (WIPO) initiative. Its aim is to harmonize the formal requirements set by patent offices for granting patents, and to streamline the procedures for obtaining and maintaining a patent. Initially, PLT will apply to all European Union countries, the United States, Japan, Canada, and Australia. Eventually it will include virtually all countries in the world. Although the PLT is only concerned with patent formalities, many of the provisions will prove extremely useful when the PLT comes into force for a large number of states, providing speedier and less costly procedures for years to come.[23]

European Patent Convention

The European Patent Convention is a treaty among 25 European countries (as of January 1, 2003) setting up a common patent office, the European Patent Office, headquartered in Munich, Germany, which examines patent applications designated for any of those countries under a common patent procedure and issues a European patent valid in all of the countries designated. The European Patent Office represents the most efficient way of obtaining protection in these countries if a patent applicant desires protection in two or more of the countries. The European Patent Convention is a party to the Paris Convention, and thus recognizes the filing date of an application by anyone in any signatory country as its own priority date if an application is filed within one year of the original filing date. The European Patent Office receives the application in English. The application will be published 18 months after the filing, consistent with the "first-to-file" principle. Once a patent is approved, registrations in, and translations into the language of, each designated country will be required. The European Patent Convention does not supersede any signatories' pre-existing national patent system. Patent applicants still should file and obtain separate national patents, if they would prefer national treatment (favored over pan-European treatment by individual national courts).[24]

Berne Convention

The Berne Convention for the Protection of Literary and Artistic Works is the oldest and most comprehensive international copyright treaty. This treaty provides reciprocal copyright protection in each of the 15 signatory countries. Similar to the Paris Convention, it establishes the principle of national treatment and provides protection without formal registration. The United States did not join the Berne Convention until 1989.[25]

Although there are separate laws to protect the various kinds of intellectual property, there appears to be a strong correlation between the levels of intellectual property in various countries. Although a new study is not available, the 1996 study provides some of the results of a 1996 academic study based on survey questionnaires administered to experts/practitioners in the various countries (see Table 6.1).

A feature that corporations as well as individual managers have to deal with is the growing importance of intellectual property as a

Table 6.1
Ratings for the Level of Intellectual Property Protection in Various Countries (Minimum = 0 … 10 = Maximum)

Country	Patents	Copyrights	Trademarks	Trade Secrets
Argentina	3.8	5.7	7.1	4.4
Brazil	3.3	5.2	3.3	3.3
Canada	8.1	7.7	9.0	7.8
Chile	5.7	5.7	7.6	7.8
China	2.4	2.9	6.2	3.3
Germany	8.6	8.6	9.0	10.0
India	3.3	5.7	3.8	3.3
Israel	7.1	7.1	8.6	8.9
Mexico	3.3	7.6	3.8	3.3
New Zealand	7.1	8.1	9.5	7.8
Philippines	7.1	6.2	7.6	7.8
Singapore	7.1	6.7	8.6	5.6
South Korea	3.3	4.8	3.8	3.3
Thailand	2.4	4.8	6.7	5.6
United States	9.0	8.1	9.0	7.8

Source: Adapted from Belay Seyoum, "The Impact of Intellectual Property Rights on Foreign Direct Investment," *Columbia Journal of World Business* 31 (Spring 1996): 56.

significant form of competitive advantage. The laws to deal with this issue are neither uniform across countries, nor extended across national boundaries (outside of the government pressure). Even if they are similar, the implementation levels vary significantly. Essentially, protection of intellectual property requires registration in all the countries in which a firm plans to do business. Managers need to be cognizant of this and take proactive measures to counteract any infringements.

The most recent development in international copyright protection is the WIPO Copyright Treaty, which entered into force in March 2002, addressing the copyright protection in the Internet era. This treaty updates and supplements the Berne Convention by protecting the rights of authors of literary and artistic works distributed within the digital environment. The treaty clarifies that the traditional right of reproduction continues to apply in the digital environment and confers a rightholder's right to control on-demand delivery of works to individuals.[26]

Further Developments

In 2007 a select handful of the wealthiest countries began a treaty-making process to create a new global standard for intellectual property rights enforcement, the Anti-Counterfeiting Trade Agreement (ACTA). ACTA is spearheaded by the United States, the European Commission, Japan, and Switzerland—those countries with the largest intellectual property industries. Other countries invited to participate in ACTA's negotiation process are Canada, Australia, Korea, Mexico, and New Zealand. Noticeably absent from ACTA's negotiations are leaders from developing countries who hold national policy priorities that differ from the international intellectual property industry.[27]

At the 34th G8 summit held by Japan in July 2008, the eight leaders in their document on the "World Economy" called for finalizing negotiations of the much-debated ACTA by the end of the year. The summit also declared patent harmonization a topic of high importance, asking for accelerated discussions of the Substantive Patent Law Treaty (SPLT), a proposed international patent law treaty aimed at harmonizing substantive points of patent law. In contrast with the Patent Law Treaty which only relates to formalities, the SPLT aims at going far beyond formalities to harmonize substantive requirements such as novelty, inventive step and non-obviousness, industrial applicability and utility, as well as sufficient disclosure, unity of invention, or claim drafting and interpretation.[28]

SUMMARY

When doing business across national boundaries, international business managers almost always face what is perceived to be political and legal barriers. It is because that government policies and laws can be very different from country to country. In most cases, a foreign company has to accept a host country's government policies and laws, as they are usually outside its control. Some large multinational firms, if backed by their home country government, may sometimes influence the host country's policies and laws. However, such an extraterritorial interference may have negative consequences in the long run for a short-term gain.

Despite various international agreements brought about by such international organizations as WTO, G8, and WIPO, which collectively strive toward freer and more equitable world trade, every nation is sovereign and maintains its special interests, which may occasionally clash with those of the international agreements. Although the world has been moving toward a freer trade and investment environment, the road has not necessarily been smooth. When considering entry or market expansion in foreign countries, their country risks need to be assessed. Multinational firms need to be aware of political risks arising from unstable political parties and government programs as well as intellectual property protection in a host country. Political risks are further compounded by economic and financial risks. When disputes arise across national boundaries, they will most likely have to be settled in one country. Therefore, careful planning for establishing the jurisdictional clause in the contract is needed before the contract is entered into.

Various international treaties have been established to protect intellectual property transferred and used by firms across national boundaries. Although these treaties offer some promises of protection and/or expedite the process of application for intellectual property in various countries, they are far from being a panacea in guaranteeing global and uniform protection of intellectual property. The fact still remains that despite the importance of intellectual property protection in international business, it is granted essentially by registration in each country. The United States is pretty much the only exception to this rule in the world. In the United States, "prior use" could determine a rightful owner of intellectual property although registration is recommended, if not mandatory. International business managers, particularly those from U.S. firms, should be aware that domestic protection usually cannot be automatically extended beyond their national boundary.

NOTES

1. DeeDee Doke, "Sniffing Out the Evidence," *Personnel Today*, May 11, 2004, 20–22.

2. Ravi Kalaktota and Andrew B. Whinston, *Frontiers of Electronic Commerce* (Reading, MA: Addison Wesley, 1996). See Chapter 15.

3. Subhash C. Jain, "Intellectual Property Rights and International Business," in *Emerging Issues in International Business Research*, ed. Masaaki Kotabe and Preet S. Aukakh (Northampton, MA: Edward Elgar Publishing, 2002), 37–64.

4. Clifford J. Shultz III and Bill Saporito, "Protecting Intellectual Property: Strategies and Recommendations to Deter Counterfeiting and Brand Piracy in Global Markets," *Columbia Journal of World Business* 31 (Spring 1996): 19–27.

5. Andreas Geiger, "A View from Europe: The High Price of Counterfeiting, and Getting Real about Enforcement," *theHill.com*, April 30, 2008.

6. *2007 Global Piracy Study*, Business Software Alliance, http://www.bsa.org/ (accessed September 20, 2008).

7. Drew Buono, "Counterfeit Drugs a Growing Worldwide Danger," *Drug Store News*, June 23, 2008, 60–62.

8. Jill Jusko, "Counterfeiters Be Gone," *Industry Week*, July 2008, 67–68.

9. "Court Secures Classical Copyright," *BBC News*, http://news.bbc.co.uk/2/hi/entertainment/4415829.stm, April 6, 2005.

10. "Imitating Property Is Theft," May 15, 2003, p. 52; Quality Brands Protection Committee, Chinese Association of Enterprise with Foreign Investment, http://www.qbpc.org.cn/en/about/about/factsheet (accessed February 10, 2006). http://news.bbc.co.uk/2/hi/business/4123319.stm; Drew Buono, "Counterfeit Drugs a Growing Worldwide Danger," *Drug Store News*, June 23, 2008, 60–62.

11. Masaaki Kotabe, "A Comparative Study of U.S. and Japanese Patent Systems," *Journal of International Business Studies* 23 (First Quarter 1992): 147–68.

12. Forty-one nations, including the United States, the European Union, and Japan, reached a basic agreement to draft a treaty for standardizing the patent approval process based on the first-to-file principle in September 2006. If it goes smoothly, the treaty could be adopted as early as 2007. See "Japan, U.S., Others Agree to Craft 1st-to-File Patent Pact," NikkeiNet Interactive, http://www.nni.nikkei.co.jp, September 26, 2006.

13. "Brazil to Break Patent, Make AIDS Drug," *CNN.com*, http://www.cnn.com/2001/WORLD/americas/08/23/aids.drug0730/index.html, August 23, 2001.

14. "Patent Problems Pending," *Economist*, October 27, 2001, 14.

15. "Copyright Revisions Have Japan's Majors Jumping into the Vaults," *Billboard*, April 18, 1998, 52; "Companies in U.S. Sing Blues as Europe Reprises 50's Hits," *New York Times*, January 3, 2003, Late Edition, A1.

16. Gray market channels refer to the legal export/import transaction involving genuine products into a country by intermediaries other than the authorized distributors. From the importer's side, it is also known as a *parallel*

import. Distributors, wholesalers, and retailers in a foreign market obtain the exporter's product from some other business entity. Thus, the exporter's legitimate distributor(s) and dealers face competition from others who sell the exporter's products at reduced prices in that foreign market.

17. "Companies in U.S. Sing Blues as Europe Reprises 50's Hits," *New York Times*, January 3, 2003, Late Edition, p. A1.

18. Subhash C. Jain, "Intellectual Property Rights and International Business," 37–64.

19. "Game over for Mod Chip Dealer," *Managing Intellectual Property*, September 2004, 113–14.

20. Bruce A. Lehman, "Intellectual Property: America's Competitive Advantage in the 21st Century," *Columbia Journal of World Business* 31 (Spring 1996): 8–9.

21. World Intellectual Property Organization, *Paris Convention for the Protection of Industrial Property*, http://www.wipo.int/treaties/en/ip/paris/ (accessed February 20, 2006).

22. World Intellectual Property Organization, *International Protection of Industrial Property—Patent Cooperation Treaty*, http://www.wipo.int/pct/en/treaty/about.htm (accessed February 20, 2006).

23. Q. Todd Dickinson, "Harmony and Controversy," *IP Worldwide*, September 2002, 22–24.

24. Martin Grund and Stacy J. Farmer, "The ABCs of the EPC 2000," *Managing Intellectual Property*, April 2008, 85–88.

25. Nancy R. Wesberg, "Canadian Signal Piracy Revisited in Light of United States Ratification of the Free Trade Agreement and the Berne Convention: Is This a Blueprint for Global Intellectual Property Protection?," *Syracuse Journal of International Law & Commerce* 16 (Fall 1989): 169–205.

26. Amanda R. Evansburg, Mark J. Fiore, Brooke Welch, Lusan Chua, and Phyllis Eremitaggio, "Recent Accessions to WIPO Treaties," *Intellectual Property & Technology Law Journal* 16 (August 2004): 23.

27. "The Anti-Counterfeiting Trade Agreement (ACTA)," *IP Justice*, http://ipjustice.org/ (accessed September 10, 2008).

28. William New, "G8 Governments Want ACTA Finalized This Year, SPLT Talks Accelerated," Intellectual Property Watch, http://www.ip-watch.org/, July 9, 2008; "Substantive Patent Law Harmonization," World Intellectual Property Organization, http://www.wipo.int/patent-law/en/harmonization.htm (accessed February 28, 2009).

Part 2

Social Responsibility, International Ethics, and Threats

Chapter 7

Social Responsibility as Strategy

Tracy L. Gonzalez-Padron

Social responsibility has emerged as a strategic priority for managers as they struggle to address social, environmental, and ethical consequences of their activities. The role of business in society goes far beyond simply meeting obligations to shareholders, with greater societal expectations worldwide now and in the coming years exacerbated by the financial crisis and global economic recession of 2008 to 2009. According to the 2009 Edelman Trust Survey, people trust companies less than a year ago and only 30 to 40 percent of the respondents in the United States and Europe trust business to do "what is right." Globally, more than 94 percent of the public feels that businesses have a role in solving global issues.[1] Although corporate leaders are talking about social responsibility, far fewer are incorporating corporate social responsibility in the ongoing actions and decisions of the firm. According to the *2009 State of Corporate Citizenship in the U.S.*, whereas 69 percent of the 756 executives surveyed believe that corporate citizenship needs to be a priority, only 43 percent report it as an integral part of their business planning process.[2] For international companies operating in multiple countries, local interpretations of environmental, social, and ethical norms challenge global social responsibility strategies.

Porter and Kramer classify social responsibility approaches as responsive or strategic.[3] Responsive strategies include two areas: (1) philanthropy in generic social issues not related to company activities and (2) actions to mitigate harm from value chain activities such as procurement, manufacturing, and distribution. A strategic approach views social responsibility as a means to create value for customers and superior returns for the firm by transforming value-chain activities to benefit society or invest in social issues that strengthen company competitiveness.

Why view social responsibility strategically? Companies adopting a strategic approach to social responsibility can achieve a competitive advantage through lower labor costs, less community opposition, reduced legal costs, stronger leadership, and creation of new marketing opportunities. Corporate social responsibility influences corporate reputation, customer satisfaction, and innovation. Patrick Cescau, Group Chief Executive of Unilever, describes the rationale for a strategic social responsibility approach in a speech titled "Beyond corporate responsibility: Social innovation and sustainable development as drivers of business growth" in 2007:

> Perhaps the biggest catalyst for change has been the increasing awareness within business itself that many of the big social and environmental challenges of our age, once seen as obstacles to progress, have become opportunities for innovation and business development.
>
> I believe that we have come to a point now where this agenda of sustainability and corporate responsibility is not only central to business strategy but will increasingly become a critical driver of business growth. I would go further: I believe that how well and how quickly businesses respond to this agenda will determine which companies succeed and which will fail in the next few decades.[4]

The competitive advantages of strategic social responsibility are particularly evident during economic downturns when firms experience pressures of lower revenues. Although corporate giving and philanthropy decreases, large companies continued to emphasize strategic social initiatives. In 2008, Jeffrey Immelt, the chair and chief executive of General Electric (GE), stresses that social responsibility "must be cost-effective and aligned with the needs of businesses."[5]

The purpose of this chapter is to examine the benefits and challenges in strategic social responsibility in an international business. First, a discussion of the global views of social responsibility highlights similarities and differences. Then, strategic approaches available to companies are defined and compared. Next, industry examples help explain the value of strategic corporate social responsibility by outlining five outcomes that increase competitiveness and foster growth. The chapter concludes with recommendations for management implementing global corporate social responsibility programs.

GLOBAL PERSPECTIVES OF SOCIAL RESPONSIBILITY

An *Economist* article titled "Going Global" has a sub-heading, "CSR is spreading around the world, but in different guises."[6] The warning is clear—international firms should not to expect comparable mind-sets on social responsibility. Management perspectives vary from the narrow view of "the business of business is business" to the broader view of moral responsibilities to contribute to society. Although European, Australian, and U.S. firms recognize corporate social responsibility as a distinct concept, Japanese managers have a strong sense of the "spirit" of social responsibility as a way of doing business (*shobaido*).[7] Before pursuing social responsibility as strategy, it is important to understand the foundations of corporate social responsibility and the basis for disparate views of the role of business in society around the world.

Foundations of Corporate Social Responsibility

Early social responsibility writings in the United States and Europe focused on the ethical duty of business executives to accept responsibility for the consequences of their actions beyond financial performance. Concern for social responsibility developed from Bowen's 1953 book *Social Responsibilities of the Businessman*, where social responsibility is described as "the obligation of businessmen to pursue those policies, to make those decisions, or to follow those lines of action which are desirable in terms of the objectives and values of our society."[8] The notion of business responsibility was further strengthened by calls for business managers to oversee "the operation of an economic system that fulfills the expectations of the public in ensuring that economic and human resources are used for meeting broad social goals."[9] A focus on the thinking of the time was that businesses might lose prized autonomy and economic freedom if not responding to social pressure—termed "negative duty." Managers referred to the "Iron Law of Responsibility" that if the business abuses its power, society might revoke it by increasing regulation. Therefore, social responsibility was primarily a risk management strategy.[10]

Subsequent views of social responsibility in the 1960 focused on "positive duty," representing manager responsibilities to society beyond economic, technical, or legal obligations. Examples of positive duty include providing satisfying and meaningful work careers, ensuring product value and safety, and protecting the ecological system.[11] This idea persists more than 40 years later. For example, McWilliams and Siegel define *corporate social responsibility* as "actions that appear to further some social good, beyond the interests of the firm and that which is required by law."[12] These views of social responsibility distinguish between legal obligations and social obligations based on motivation, voluntarism, or sacrifice. A major contention is whether a corporation achieving economic gain for socially responsible actions is truly embracing the concept of corporate social responsibility. Even executives struggle with differentiating between good management practices and CSR—with over 20 percent indicating that corporate responsibility "is meaningless if it includes things that companies would do anyway."[13]

Corporations require legitimacy to maintain functional, long-term relationships with the various communities on which they depend. Legitimacy is a measure of the attitude of society toward a corporation and its activities, based on cultural norms for corporate behavior. The term *legitimacy* most commonly refers to the right to exist and perform an activity in a certain way, referred to in practice as the "license to operate." Legitimacy views rely upon the notion of a social contract and on the maintained assumption that managers will adopt strategies that show society that the organization is attempting to comply with society's expectations. For example, Portuguese banks seeking to improve their corporate image publish social responsibility disclosures in annual reports and media releases.[14] Managers of multinational corporations in China view social responsibility programs as a way to develop harmonious relationships with the Chinese government and legitimacy to operate in China.[15] In South Africa, export-oriented chemical multinationals adopted a program titled "Responsible Care" to meet the expectations of trade associations and peer networks to improve the industry's image. As one environmental manager commented: "Responsible Care is basically an industry requirement, it's our license to operate."[16]

A relatively recent perspective of corporate social responsibility is sustainability. Sustainability acknowledges the finite limits of nature, and recognizes the need to optimize the economic, environmental, and social elements while minimizing waste. In the 1980s and 1990s, environmental issues came to the forefront of social responsibility conversations. The 1984 Bhopal chemical release and Exxon Valdez oil spill in 1989 raised expectations for companies to protect and conserve natural resources. Around the same time, global attention focused on the deepening poverty brought on by African droughts and childhood deaths from unsafe drinking water. In 1987, the United Nations' Brundtland Commission highlighted that "economic and ecology can interact destructively" and called for sustainable development, or "meeting the needs of the present generation without compromising the ability of future generations to meet their own needs."[17] Companies embracing sustainable business practices look beyond financial profit and look at its impact on social, economic, and ecological resources of the community. Sustainability has become an attractive method for business to view their social responsibilities due to adoption of the term *Triple Bottom Line* (TBL). John Elkington, the author who coined the term in 1994, promoted corporations to focus "not just on the economic value that they add, but also on the environmental and social value that they add—or destroy."[18]

Social Responsibility Mind-Sets

A useful lens for evaluating social responsibility mind-sets is to think of CSR as the firm's obligation to meet economic, legal, ethical, and discretionary expectations that society has of an organization.[19] The economic and legal components refer to the societal expectation that a business produces goods and services at a profit while obeying laws. The ethical component refers to the behaviors and norms that a society expects; and the discretionary component encompasses voluntary and philanthropic activities of contributions of money, time, and talent. Consensus is lacking on the degree of responsibility business have for each of the components and often varies worldwide due to political, cultural, and economical influences.

Economic Social Responsibility

Economic and legal obligations are an inherent part of corporate responsibility, as businesses contribute to social welfare in the form of jobs, products, and innovation. A narrow "classical" paradigm of social responsibility considers that corporate philanthropy is giving away someone else's money and destroys shareholder value, often citing Milton Friedman's argument that the primary social responsibility of business is to make a profit and that the duty of an executive is therefore to create wealth for the company's investors.[20] Economists rely on the agency theory to explain corporate social responsibility, often focusing on the actions of corporate management and effect on shareholder value. An agency theory perspective can imply that corporate social activities signal an agency problem in the firm whereby managers advance their careers or other personal agendas.[21] Corporate governance mechanisms such as forming a charitable foundation and limiting top executive management direct involvement may mitigate certain agency conflicts in the discretionary area of corporate giving or reduce public perceptions of this conflict.

In some regions managers adhere to a classical CSR paradigm more than other countries. A focus on shareholder return is one explanation that charitable donations for disaster relief of Asian firms are significantly lower than European or U.S. firms.[22] Cultural dimensions such as race/ethnicity and religion influence the attention on economic and social responsibilities. Managers from Singapore and Malaysia, particularly the Malay Muslims, are more oriented toward profit than other business priorities such as employee and environmental welfare.[23] Chinese managers of subsidiaries of multinational corporations perceived that "the responsibility of enterprises was to pay taxes, follow laws, provide employment, and develop capital for future growth."[24]

Philanthropy as Social Responsibility

The traditional view of social responsibility as activities beyond economic, technical, or legal obligations stresses philanthropy and charity. The focus is on activities unrelated to the core business, such as donations or encouraging employee engagement in voluntary work. The motivation derives from expected benefits from increased reputation and goodwill. In the United States, approximately 68 percent of businesses provide support cash, in-kind donations, or employee volunteering to support the community in areas of education, health and fitness, and environmental issues.[25] U.S. companies contribute higher values of donations than those of European or Asian counterparts, often attributed to higher GDP and fiscal incentives for philanthropy. However, philanthropy relating to community involvement receives greater attention in developing countries than initiatives relating to business activities. Local companies in Nigeria promote culture and arts to "look good" to their customers.[26] India, with a lower GNP per capita of other Asian countries, has one of the highest levels of philanthropy. This is partly explained by cultural religious philanthropic conditions and partly explained by level of internationalization of business.[27] In countries with a strong social welfare system, charity and philanthropy do not play much of a role in the approach to corporate responsibility. In Finland, for example, company activities to improve living conditions in the 19th century became the responsibility of the state and municipalities. Therefore, Finnish executives in one survey responded "charitable work is neither necessary nor even appropriate for companies paying taxes and fulfilling their obligations to society."[28] Chinese companies expect the government to address social and environmental issues, a sentiment reinforced by the Chinese government's "unwillingness to provide tax incentives for companies' charitable actions."[29]

Stakeholder Perspective

A stakeholder perspective provides another lens for evaluating social responsibilities of a firm. The stakeholder view argues that managers must satisfy various constituents (e.g., customers, employees, suppliers, local community organizations) that would withdraw support for the firm if important social responsibilities were unmet. A widely accepted and popular definition is Freeman's view of a stakeholder as "any group or individual who can affect or is affected by the achievement of the organization's objectives."[30] Firms generally identify two classifications of a company's stakeholders in developing a stakeholder management strategy. Primary stakeholders are those groups whose continued association are necessary for a firm's survival and often include customers, employees, suppliers, investors, and shareholders. Secondary stakeholders can influence the firm or be influenced by the firm, but are not directly necessary for the firm's survival, and typically include consumer advocate groups, media, unions, political groups, scientific community and trade associations. Governments and local communities, whose laws influence company operations and tax obligations while providing infrastructure and markets to the company, can be primary or secondary stakeholders. Some organizations classify the natural environment as a stakeholder, for example, McDonald's has reevaluated packaging continually since

the 1970s to minimize the impact on the environment.[31] Even the judicial system in the United States recognizes the stakeholder concept. At
least 28 states have passed "other constituency" statutes permitting
senior managers and corporate directors, while acting in the best
interests of the corporation, to consider the interests of other stakeholders groups besides stockholders, especially employees and local
communities.[32]

Understanding and addressing stakeholder demands is a complex
undertaking. The importance of a stakeholder varies over a firm's life
cycle and shapes the firm's responsiveness to the stakeholder group.
Powerful stakeholders have various influence strategies to obtain
desired actions from a firm, including consumer boycotts such as that
against StarKist to change tuna fishing practices.[33] Managers should
consider that stakeholders not only interact with the firm, but also
interact with other stakeholders, thus increasing the stakeholder
power to exert pressure. An example is Monsanto's abandoned
attempt to commercialize seed sterilization technology because of
protests initiated by Indian farmers that spread worldwide.[34]

Customers

Customers are key stakeholders that help establish the firm's reputation and identification. The relationship between a customer and a
firm exists because of mutual expectations built on trust, good faith,
and fair dealing in their interaction. In fact, an implied covenant of
good faith and fair dealing exists, and performance cannot simply be
a matter of the firm's own discretion. Customer responses to corporate
social responsibility range from unresponsive to highly responsive to
corporate social responsibility. For example, the 2009 Cone Consumer
Environmental Survey finds that although 70 percent of Americans
indicate that they are paying attention to environmental records of
companies, only 34 percent of American consumers more likely to buy
environmentally responsible products. Furthermore, the findings of
the 2009 Cone Consumer New Media Study are even more telling:
"30 percent have made a purchase based on POSITIVE information
learned about a product, company, or brand; and, 23 percent have
switched brands or boycotted a company based on NEGATIVE information learned about a product, company or brand."[35]

Consumers in different cultures assess the ethics of a situation based
on factors such as religion, cultural values, nationality, and both
gender and age.[36] Distinct ethical consumer behaviors exist in each

European country (Germany, Denmark, Scotland, The Netherlands, Portugal, Spain, Italy, Greece), questioning the ability of organizations to consider even the European Union as one homogeneous market.[37] French and German consumers appear more willing to support responsible businesses than their U.S. counterparts do. Whereas U.S. consumers value highly corporate economic responsibilities, French and German consumers are most concerned about businesses conforming to legal and ethical standards.[38] The majority of Chinese customers do not consider environmental and safety issues in their buying decision; however, consumer awareness of issues like the environment and working conditions is increasing in China and Hong Kong.[39]

Shareholders

In addition to focusing on profits, shareholders influence how a firm responds to multiple stakeholders. Shareholders financially benefit when management meets the demands of multiple stakeholders. Studies of financial performance of *Fortune* 500 firms find that corporate social responsibility is positively correlated to growth in sales.[40] Likewise, firms experience positive stock price reactions from institutional investors upon announcements of corporate governance improvements.[41] J. J. Irani, director of Tata Sons, highlights shareholder focus in India at a conference on corporate and public governance: "There is a drive towards triple bottom-line—financial, environmental, and social. One of the most compelling factors which will drive business towards good ethical practices is the demand from the shareholders, who, in the ultimate analysis, are the owners of the corporation."[42] In response, the Tata Group of India demonstrates a commitment to shareowner and stakeholder values through the Tata Code of Conduct, Tata Business Excellence Model, and the Global Reporting Initiative.

Attention and responsiveness to shareholders have two implications for companies with global operations. First, shareholders can influence multinational corporation decisions to downsize and to relocate overseas.[43] Investors are looking with increasing favor on shareholder proposals, asking companies to disclose and monitor their political contributions, to report on their fair employment policies, and to issue broad-based reports on sustainability.[44] Shareholder resolutions have become increasingly successful at promoting corporate change in global social responsiveness. In 2006, Wal-Mart responded to shareholder resolutions about employee diversity by agreeing to post detailed diversity reports online. The growth of social and ethical investment criteria among shareholders, mutual funds, and pension asset managers demonstrate increased demands for good global citizenship. In Europe, a tradition of greater concern with a broader stakeholder perspective has changed the capital structure, with value-based management common in the United Kingdom, Germany, Switzerland, and Austria.[45]

Employees

Multinational companies with global production or sales facilities have to address employee stakeholder concerns both in their home market and in international markets that may have different social expectations. One example is downsizing due to location of production of goods or services in other countries that can reduce employee loyalty and morale in the home country. Diversity may be difficult to achieve in many markets. For example, in Japan the gap between gender in terms of benefits, salaries, and status is large in comparison to other countries.[46] Production operations overseas often have to address employment issues where legal requirements are less stringent, particularly regarding child labor and low wages. The experience of two companies, Chiquita Brands International, Inc., and Levi Strauss & Company, both with operations in Latin America, underscore the presence of common challenges that accompany the employment of international labor. Although the U.S.-based companies had strong ethical guidelines about labor conditions, local operations in Central America had to address societal expectations requiring employee housing and childcare that were difficult to monitor.[47]

Multinational corporations are the frequent target of activists and NGOs in their human rights advocacy efforts, possibly skewing corporate social responsibility practices by the multinational corporation. For example, initial responses to campaigns on child labor in the sports-goods industry in Pakistan led to many children losing their jobs and working in more hazardous or abusive industries.[48] Japanese managers often struggle in developing countries with human rights issues related to race, class, and faith. One reason is that the homogeneity of the Japanese population causes less experience in these issues.[49]

Suppliers

A socially responsible firm tends to the needs of the supply chain and to socially responsible purchasing practices relating to diversity, environmental, and labor issues. Suppliers expect fair treatment by customers. The network of relationships inherent in the supply chain has resulted in a greater likelihood that organizations shoulder more responsibility for actions of their suppliers. As companies recognize social issues that are related to their supply chain, some include paying more for vendors with good social policies, helping competent vendors become socially responsive, and helping socially responsive vendors to become competent.[50]

Organizations that depend on global suppliers for goods and services have to consider how actions are perceived to avoid supply-chain problems like Nike experienced when exposed for "slave-labor conditions" in Asian countries.[51] One example includes Starbucks, which claims to pay premium prices for coffees, invest in social development projects, and provide access to affordable loans in coffee-growing regions and is considered the most admired corporation in *Fortune*'s survey.[52] Oxfam, a non-profit organization that works to end global poverty, argued that Starbucks is depriving farmers in Ethiopia of $90 million a year by rejecting the Ethiopian government's efforts to trademark three types of local coffee beans. Their campaign generated more than 89,000 faxes from 70 countries asking Starbucks CEO Jim Donald to support Ethiopia's ownership of its coffee names.[53]

Government

Companies operating in multiple countries experience institutional differences in expectation and returns, influencing the relationships with regulatory agencies, governments, and communities, especially in developing countries. Multinational chemical companies recognize a shift of societal expectations increased economic and legal responsibilities in most countries, while the degree of ethical responsibilities and philanthropic responsibilities varied over time and country.[54] Different economic, political, and sociocultural circumstances under which corporations have to operate in developing countries increase the responsibilities of corporations to a full range of stakeholder groups. A study of chemical companies in Mexico and South Africa identified several challenges for the chemical industry in moving forward on CSR: credibility, stakeholder engagement, value-chain accountability, disclosure, and transparency.[55] In addition, the growing regulatory concerns over the environmental impact of corporate practices have begun to influence marketing strategies.

Community

A socially responsible firm focuses on social duties relating to the common good of the host community. Community stakeholders include many nongovernmental organizations and other potential activist groups that have an interest in social issues and have the ability to mobilize public opinion.[56] Community advocacy groups can influence corporate strategy. For example, a chemical company's plans to locate in an economically deprived Louisiana community changed in response to community opinion.[57]

Multinational corporations address a wide range of social issues such as privacy, obesity, offshoring, and pharmaceutical product safety; these issues challenge organizations to adapt to changing ground rules that can impact financial and reputation performance.[58] However, not all social problems escalate to an issue requiring managerial attention. Social issues obtain meaning through the interpretation of the public and other interested parties such as individuals, organizations, associations, governments, and governmental agencies. Popular business press highlights the power of activist groups in escalating a social issue for corporate and regulatory attention. The AFL-CIO and a nonprofit umbrella group, the Center for Community & Corporate Ethics, hopes to get Wal-Mart to alter its employment policies by driving away some business.[59] Student activist demonstrations against Coca-Cola's worker conditions in Colombia cost the beverage company millions of dollars in college contracts.[60] Health and wellness trends and concerns of obesity pressured snack and fast-food companies such as Pepsi, McDonald's, and KFC to change their product offering and marketing strategies.[61]

SOCIAL RESPONSIBILITY STRATEGIES

Peter Drucker argues that a firm ought to convert its social responsibilities into business opportunities. He presents corporate social responsibility as turning "a social problem into economic opportunity and economic benefit, into productive capacity, into human competence, into well-paid jobs and into wealth."[62] However, in practice, companies view aspects of social responsibility in more than one way. One approach is from a compliance view that focuses only on meeting the letter of the law. Another approach is from an efficiency view that looks to gain economic benefits from responsible business practices. A growth approach views social responsibility as a means to create value for customers and superior returns for the firm. Firms adopting innovation perspectives of social responsibility seek pioneering solutions for improving processes and products, thereby gaining a competitive advantage. Viewing social responsibility as strategy creates opportunities for innovation through activities in all three approaches.

Compliance

A compliance approach to social responsibility is a minimalist response in which the focus is on meeting regulatory standards. Regulations seek to create a fair competitive environment for businesses, safeguard natural resources, protect consumers, and ensure safe workplaces. In addressing environmental regulations, one manager expresses a compliance approach by stating, "I think as long as we're compliant and we're not going to get fined we're happy to leave it like that for the time being."[63] A compliance approach considers social responsibility as a "cost of doing business" focusing on adherence to laws relating to business activities in the countries of production, operation and distribution. They feel that such costs reduce resources available for new product development or capital investments. Many firms believe that the costs of regulation outweigh its benefits, thereby support self-regulation, or actively lobby governments for deregulation. In support of this argument, a study of telecommunication firms during a period of lower regulation (1992–1995) showed increases in innovation, which if continued could have resulted in 62 percent more new services to consumers.[64]

However, compliance need not be limiting. Viewing compliance as an opportunity provides first-mover advantages in terms of fostering innovation. For example, U.S. automotive firms reacting to laws requiring reduced pollution and emissions developed defensive product features instead of building more efficient and nonpolluting cars. During the period from 1968 to 1974, the American car manufacturers met emissions regulation by controlling engine spark timing, air-fuel ratio, and using exhaust gas recirculation (EGR) which incurred a significant fuel economy penalty. The reactive focus on compliance especially hurt Chrysler, who was unprepared for the escalating gasoline prices in the 1970s. American consumers turned instead to smaller and fuel efficient Japanese and European cars.[65]

In addition to innovative solutions to regulations, international companies have greater opportunity to view compliance as an opportunity. By complying with the most stringent regulations of all markets, companies benefit from economies of scale through consistent supply-chain operations. Not having to monitor component sourcing and production to multiple standards provides for cost savings. Having a reputation as a global leader in compliance also helps establish an amenable relationship with regulators that bring an opportunity to shape future adoption of legislation. Through diligent attention to current and future regulations, companies may recognize business opportunities first, such as recycling programs to meet imminent legislation in Europe for electronic products disposal.[66]

Efficiency

The business case of cost savings and risk reduction drives many social responsible initiatives relating to core business operations. Companies are finding that many CSR activities, including those that reduce energy consumption or improve employee satisfaction, help reduce overall cost structures, increase productivity, and "mitigate harm from value chain activities."[67] Typically, a stakeholder approach identifies aspects of the business operations on which to focus CSR activities. Managers consider responsibilities in the value chain that they control such as research and development, procurement, production, marketing, and delivery. Focus is on what Porter & Kramer term "Value Chain Impacts," defined as "social issues that are significantly affected by a company's activities in the ordinary course of business."[68] For example, manufacturing controls to ensure product quality and safety demonstrate responsibility towards customers; and intensifies customer loyalty. Fair wages, safe working conditions, and competitive health benefits advance the community's quality of life and increase employee satisfaction and productivity in the entire supply chain.[69] Environmental programs to reduce water use and waste emission ensure a community's potable water supply, while protecting a valuable material for many manufacturers.

Expanding the value chain beyond operations within control of the business offers not only added cost savings and risk reduction, but also opportunities for innovation. Porter and Kramer suggest that social responsibility beyond a reactive response to value-chain issues requires focusing on transforming value-chain activities to benefit society. This is particularly evident when assessing the environmental inputs and outputs of the entire value chain, as vendors can represent 80 percent of the energy, water, and other resources used by a supply chainand they must be a priority in the drive to create sustainable operations. Opportunities for multinational companies include securing reliable and sustainable raw material and components while making positive social changes in the industry. Many examples exist of multinational businesses spreading ethical and responsible behavior among nations. One example is the pulp and paper industry in India, which was identified as one of the most polluting industries in the country, indicating foreign business had a positive influence on environment-friendly behavior.[70]

Growth

A strategic social responsibility approach looks beyond current business operations to emphasize new products and business models for solving social and environmental problems creates new revenue for companies. For this reason, companies are increasingly adopting sustainable innovation even during economic downturns. According to the BSR/GlobeScan State of Sustainable Business Poll 2009, managers focused on two important actions companies should take to improve public trust in business: (1) Create innovative products and business models designed for sustainability and (2) Measure and demonstrate positive social and environmental impacts.[71] Creating sustainable products and business models requires a new mind-set, thinking beyond traditional product features and rethinking ways of meeting customer needs. In the *Harvard Business Review* article, "Why Sustainability is Now the Key Driver of Innovation," the authors provide suggestions for developing sustainable products and business models.

- The capacity to understand what consumers want and to figure out different ways to meet those demands.
- The skills to know which products or services are most unfriendly to the environment.
- The ability to generate real public support for sustainable offerings.
- The management know-how to scale both supplies of green materials and the manufacture of products.
- The ability to understand how partners can enhance the value of offerings.[72]

Businesses seek social responsible initiatives that can create new revenues through social partnerships with NGOs or governments. Social partnerships primarily address social issues (e.g., education, health, and environment) by combining organizational resources to offer solutions that benefit both partners, as well as society. Porter and Kramer argue that a symbiotic relationship develops when collaborative social projects relate to a firm's core competencies, creating stronger businesses and stronger communities. Businesses have enormous resources at their disposal and can provide managerial efficiency, technical expertise, creativity, and access to finance. A social partnership requires a commitment of time and resources by the company. NGOs have expertise and knowledge of the social issue, are mission driven, and better able to reach the market. Therefore, through successful collaboration, these two actors can complement each other and better allocate resources for the common good.[73] A major driver for social partnerships is the United Nations (UN) Global Compact. This voluntary association of businesses encourages companies to seek partnerships in support of broader UN Millennium Development Goals. Partnerships between business, civil society, and government focus on the many areas where private actors and public institutions can engage in win-win relationships, such as poverty reduction, health, education, and community development.[74] A survey of 445 firms by the UN Global Compact and Dalberg Global Development Advisors finds that two-thirds of respondents engaged in partnerships with governments and NGO's to address humanitarian and development challenges, and the majority cited a desire to engage in relevant CSR programs as their primary reason.[75] They classify partnerships into three categories:

Philanthropy and Social Investment—Donating time (volunteers), money, products, and the use of premises

Advocacy and Awareness—Awareness-raising campaigns, projects that influence decision makers, and collective actions that set rules, norms, and standards

Core Business—Creating employment; fostering entrepreneurship; implementing social, environmental, or ethical standards; and/or providing affordable goods and services (projects should be linked to the sourcing, manufacturing, development, distribution, pricing, and end-use of a company's products and services)

BENEFITS OF STRATEGIC CORPORATE SOCIAL RESPONSIBILITY

Corporate social responsibility is found to influence corporate reputation, customer satisfaction, brand equity, and innovation. Strategic CSR strengthens company competitiveness through

(1) developing a talented workforce, (2) achieving a reliable supply of high-quality materials for production, (3) facilitating rules and incentives that govern competition, (4) increasing innovation through new products and services, and (5) providing access to new market segments increase demand for a firm's product and services.[76] The themes relate to the recommendation of Porter and Kramer to invest in social initiatives that foster growth and strengthen company competitiveness. These can include the quantity and quality of available personnel, the rules and incentives that govern competition, the size and sophistication of demand, and the availability of suppliers (Table 7.1).

Table 7.1
Outcomes of Strategic CSR

	Outcomes	Examples
Competitive environment		
Talented workforce	Develop skilled labor pool	Honeywell partners with the National Aeronautics and Space Administration (NASA) in a middle school science education program to promote future supply of scientists, engineers, and technologists
	Reduce costs generated by employee attraction and turnover	Apache Footwear reduced labor turnover by building one-story, red-brick buildings for staff, organizing Saturday night movies and dances, and hiring its employees' relatives
Reliable supply chain	Secure consistent, long-term, and sustainable access to safe, high- quality raw materials and products	Pepsi shares its expertise about potato farming under desert conditions with the Chinese Ministry of Agriculture to ensure materials for snack foods marketed in China

(continued)

Table 7.1 (Continued)

	Outcomes	Examples
Favorable rules and incentives	Reduce costs and regulations within the industry	General Electric, Cinergy, and Bechtel developed solutions to reduce coal emissions in energy plants, meeting environmental regulations and at a lower cost than traditional practices
	Reduce local resistance to entry in new markets	Altria Group works with governments to secure fair excise tax structures in many of its key markets

Growth

	Outcomes	Examples
New product and services innovation	Create products to meet unmet social needs and increase differentiation	Heinz partners advisory groups from around the world to guide development of healthier foods meeting diverse dietary needs
	Develop cutting edge technology for unmet social or environmental needs	Ecolab developed a new washing process for hotel and healthcare laundries using an innovative process to conserve energy and water
New markets and customers	Gain access to new markets	Hindustan Lever is improving health conditions in rural India through its education programs on hygiene while creating demand for soap products
	Increase demand through education and infrastructure development	Cisco Systems, Hewlett Packard, and Nokia are partner organizations in the United Nations Information and Community Technology task force to encourage universal access to information technology
	Foster brand loyalty and goodwill	

Talented Workforce

Companies with an integrated social responsibility program are more likely to attract, develop, and inspire employees. International Business Machines Corporation (IBM) offers a Global Citizen Portfolio program for employee training and development opportunities including 600 employee assignments to engage in solving social problems in emerging and developing markets. IBM feels that the program will "sustain the company's commitment to its employees and the communities in which they live and work, reinforce a culture of trust and responsibility, and ultimately contribute to business success."[77] Hewlett Packard supports technology centers at 12 Russian universities to focus on building practical IT -related business skills, with top performers hired as interns at HP labs.

Collaborative initiatives between businesses and government in education benefit society while providing a personnel pool for industry. For example, Honeywell partners with the National Aeronautics and Space Administration (NASA) in a middle school science education program in anticipation of a "talented workforce of scientists, engineers and technologists."[78] In China, once-abundant factory laborers are more selective of employers due to information-sharing through the Internet and competition for workers. Therefore, multinationals have gone beyond complying with labor laws to provide an environment attractive to migrant factory laborers. A supplier for Adidas, Apache Footwear, reduced turnover of factory workers in the city of Qingyun by providing private living quarters, organizing Saturday night movies and dances, and giving job preference to its employees' relatives.[79]

Reliable Supply Chain

Strategic social responsibility focusing on the supply chain can provide for a reliable supply of products and raw materials for production. Starbucks is known for its work with organizations to help coffee farmers to improve their quality of life, including collaborating with farmers to implement new and sustainable farming techniques. Pepsi shares its expertise about potato farming with the Chinese Ministry of Agriculture to ensure materials for snack foods marketed in China. Similarly, Water is a key ingredient in beverages, resulting in strategic social responsibility projects by Pepsi and Coca-Cola to preserve and conserve water. For example, Coca-Cola invested in over

200 community water projects in 60 countries during 2005 to 2009.[80] Hershey works with the World Cocoa Foundation to ensure that cocoa is grown responsibly and to support income improvement for cocoa-growing families. Even companies that are not marketing internationally have social responsibilities relating to supply from international markets. For example, although Target does not have stores outside the United States, they source products from global markets like India and Central America. Their 2009 Corporate Social Responsibility Report outlines their social initiatives relating to their supply base for their North American department stores:

> With team members and vendors located worldwide, we are committed to helping communities abroad as well. Since 2003, the Target International Giving Program has helped children, families, and communities in need in countries including China, India, and Guatemala. In 2008, the program awarded more than 75 grants to Non-Governmental Organizations (NGOs) in 18 countries where our team members and vendors live and work.[81]

Favorable Rules and Incentives

Social responsibility projects may alter the competitive environment of the firm through facilitating changes to rules and regulations within the industry. General Electric, Cinergy, and Bechtel developed solutions to reduce coal emissions in energy plants, meeting environmental regulations and at a lower cost than traditional practices. Altria Group discusses their "success working with governments to secure fair excise tax structures in many of its key markets, with numerous countries adopting minimum excise taxes and several considering the adoption of minimum reference prices."[82] These projects can result in growth through access to new market segments. FedEx Express attributes its competitive advantage in the Chinese market to "a very good relationship with the Chinese government . . . to ensure we are continuously balancing market demands with government regulations."[83]

New Product and Services Innovation

Companies adopting strategic approaches to social responsibility may experience improvements in products or services through innovation. Heinz sponsors studies and symposiums with leading nutritionists, dieticians, and physicians from around the world for bolstering nutrient content and reducing sodium and fats in ketchup, soups, sauces, and frozen foods. IBM engages with governments, universities, and NGOs to develop innovative capabilities, products, and services in response to emerging trends in technology, society, and culture. Ecolab, Inc., has become a global industry leader by developing cleaning, sanitizing and food safety products that consider the total impact on the environment, from the formulation, production, packaging, and customer usage. An innovative hotel and healthcare laundry system recycles energy and water, earning Ecolab an environmental award in Germany.[84] Strategic approaches also result in innovative new service offerings. For example, Allstate mentions that by working closely with state officials, they are able to provide better insurance protection against hurricanes.

New Markets and Customers

Increasing demand for a firm's product and services is another outcome of strategic social responsibility within the computer industry. Two general approaches to develop future demand include promoting product usage and enabling capacity. Some projects focus on educating consumers on the use of products and services offered by the company. Hewlett Packard states that their "engagements in underserved communities are strategic to our business as much as they are philanthropic. By introducing digital solutions in emerging economies, we learn how our portfolio might be leveraged in ways we never imagined."[85] The computer firm has a number of collaborative projects in Africa, including one with the South African government to train residents of a local community in PC literacy. Intel also has a number of programs to help enable a worldwide computing ecosystem. They state in their 2004 Annual Report, "We are working with governments in several countries on programs aimed at increasing PC and Internet literacy, and making computing more accessible to larger segments of the population."[86] Colgate-Palmolive works with the Royal Society for the Prevention of Cruelty to Animals in Australia to counsel pet adopters on the importance of nutrition and the benefits of Science Diet pet food. Aetna sponsors a public education campaign with the Financial Planning Association to help women understand how to choose and use their health benefits better.

Unilever has a comprehensive strategic program to tap a new market of consumers through education on health, nutrition, and hygiene.

One joint project with UNICEF provided Ghanaians' access to affordable iodized salt to overcome an iodine deficiency linked to impaired brain development. Unilever also collaborates with the World Dental Federation to fund oral health projects in 38 countries, including mobile dental vans in Nigeria. In rural India, Hindustan Lever is improving health conditions through its education programs on hygiene, including waving an ultraviolet-light wand over the hands of pilgrims seeking to bathe at in India's sacred rivers to show where germs and dirt resided.

> "It's not enough for the company to look at market-share increase," says Anand Kripalu, 42, the company's head of detergents and a creative thinker behind many of the company's rural-outreach strategies. "We want to spread the message of hygiene and really use the Lifebuoy brand to deliver that benefit to consumers. This isn't just good for us as a brand; it's good for the country."[87]

Some companies collaborate with government and other industry partners to develop an infrastructure that supports future demand for products and services. One example is a Jordanian government initiative to develop a knowledge economy by partnering with HP, Microsoft Corporation, and Cisco Systems to develop curricula, provide technology support and equipment, and work with local companies to enhance the country's information technology industry. Cisco Systems, Hewlett Packard, and Nokia are partner organizations in the United Nations Information and Community Technology (UNICT) task force. UNICT includes actors from all societal sectors—industry, government, and non-governmental organizations—that work to bridge the digital divide and provide universal access to information technology. Nokia recognizes the new growth markets from improvements in the world's communication infrastructure on their corporate website, stating:

> The number of new mobile phone users in high-growth markets is growing dramatically and we aim to play a leading role in boosting this growth. As a market leader, we estimate that there will be available and affordable mobile communications for half the world's population by 2015.[88]

MANAGERIAL IMPLICATIONS

A global view of corporate responsibility is imperative as companies engage in the expanding marketplace. For the optimal return on CSR investments, managers must develop capabilities to deal with cultural and institutional differences in the expectation and benefits of social responsiveness. Integration of ethical and responsible management principles throughout the value chain establishes a foundation for strategic social responsibility. Adaption of a stakeholder orientation that includes the global and local stakeholders allows companies to respond rapidly to changing market conditions, enabling the organization to sustain a position of competitive advantage.

Ethical Leadership Throughout Value Chain

A strong ethical program transcending organizational boundaries to include subsidiaries and global suppliers is a condition for realizing benefits of a strategic corporate social responsibility. Ethical leaders at the executive and management level are the champions for responsible management, and "embody the purpose, vision, and values of the organization and of the constituents, within an understanding of ethical ideals."[89] A strong ethics program communicates and monitors to employees and suppliers the ethical values and legal requirements, thereby reducing the risk of ethical misconduct and legal sanctions that can damage a firm's reputation.

Ethical misconduct or illegal activities in the global supply chain can include human rights violations, tainted products, and environmental disasters. The network of relationships inherent in the supply chain has resulted in a greater likelihood that organizations shoulder more responsibility for actions of their suppliers. Corporate social activities can help protect a positive reputation, but may not be able to repair a negative reputation. Research shows that positive social responsiveness increases firm performance through enhanced reputation, but harmful activities without positive actions reduce both reputation and financial performance. Therefore, a strong ethical and compliance program permeating throughout the global supply chain is the best method of protecting reputation.

Stakeholder Orientation

Growth strategies in social responsibility require a capability to understand what consumers want and to figure out different ways to meet those demands. A stakeholder orientation refers to the extent to which a firm understands and addresses stakeholder demands in daily operations and strategic planning. Adoption of a stakeholder orientation provides firms an opportunity to understand its impact on stakeholders, anticipate changing societal expectations, and use its capacity for innovation to create additional business value from superior social and environmental performance. A stakeholder orientation requires a balanced evaluation of stakeholders and their competing demands, recognizing that complex marketing strategies may alienate a particular group. Multinational corporations need to consider both global and local stakeholder groups in developing a strategic CSR approach.

A stakeholder orientation includes three activities: (1) the organization-wide generation of intelligence pertaining to the nature of stakeholder issues, (2) the dissemination of this intelligence throughout the organization, and (3) the organization-wide responsiveness to this intelligence.[90] The generation of stakeholder intelligence essentially consists of identifying relevant stakeholders, clarifying stakeholder issues, and evaluating the organization's impact on these issues. Various actors generate stakeholder intelligence at different organizational levels and locations. Subsequently, organizational members require the dissemination of stakeholder intelligence about the issues driving stakeholders' needs and the organization's involvement with these issues. The organization-wide responsiveness to stakeholder intelligence designates initiatives taken by the organization at two levels—globally and locally. One approach is for a centralized CSR strategy defined in general terms (i.e., water conservation, workforce development, infrastructure generation) to be used as a framework for local implementation of social and environmental programs. Partnerships with governments and NGO's can provide valuable expertise for social responsible initiatives that meet each locale's specific needs.

CONCLUSION

Considering social responsibility as strategic provides an advantage for global companies through both a favorable competitive environment and innovative growth. However, managers should understand the disparate views of the role of business in society among cultures, including the similarities and differences of perspectives regarding corporate social responsibility. As illustrated, the degree that business is expected to address economic, legal, ethical, and philanthropic responsibilities often varies due to political, cultural, and economical influences. Through integrative ethical leadership and effective stakeholder engagement, companies can achieve a competitive advantage in the global marketplace.

NOTES

1.   Edelman, "Edelman Trust Barometer," 2009, http://www.edelman.com/trust/2009/docs/Trust_Book_Final_2.pdf.

2.   Bradley Googins et al., "State of Corporate Citizenship 2009: Weathering the Storm," Boston College Center for Corporate Citizenship, Chestnut Hill, MA, 46, www.BCCorporateCitizenship.org.

3.   Michael E. Porter and Mark R. Kramer, "Strategy & Society: The Link between Competitive Advantage and Corporate Social Responsibility," *Harvard Business Review* 84, no. 12 (2006): 78–92.

4.   Patrick Cescau, "Beyond Corporate Responsibility: Social Innovation and Sustainable Development as Drivers of Business Growth" (speech at INSEAD's INDEVOR Alumni Forum on Integrating CSR into Business Strategy, Fontainebleau, May 25, 2007), www.unilever.com.

5.   Alyson Warhurst, "The Future of Corporate Philanthropy; in the Downturn, Corporate Chiefs Like GE's Immelt Say Social Responsibility Will Remain Vital, but It Must Be Cost-Effective and Fit Corporate Needs. (Viewpoint)," *Business Week Online*, 2008.

6.   "Going Global," *Economist: A Special Report on Corporate Social Responsibility,* January 19, 2008.

7.   K. Fukukawa and Y. Teramoto, "Understanding Japanese CSR: The Reflections of Managers in the Field of Global Operations," *Journal of Business Ethics* 85 (2009): 133–46.

8.   Howard R. Bowen, *Social Responsibilities of the Businessman* (New York: Harper & Row, 1953).

9.   William C. Frederick, "The Growing Concern over Business Responsibility," *California Management Review* 2 (1960): 54–61.

10. Keith Davis, "Can Business Afford to Ignore Social Responsibilities?," *California Management Review* 2 (Spring 1960): 70–76.

11. William E. Halal, "A Return-on-Resources Model of Corporate Performance," *California Management Review* 19, no. 4 (1977): 23–34.

12. Abagail McWilliams and Donald S. Siegel, "Corporate Social Responsibility: A Theory of the Firm Perspective," *Academy of Management Review* 26, no. 1 (2001): 117.

13. "The Next Question," January 19, 2008, *Economist: A Special Report on Corporate Social Responsibility.*

14. Manuel Castelo Branco and Lúcia Lima Rodrigues, "Communication of Corporate Social Responsibility by Portuguese Banks," *Corporate Communications* 11, no. 3 (2006): 232.

15. M. L. L. Lam, "Beyond Credibility of Doing Business in China: Strategies for Improving Corporate Citizenship of Foreign Multinational Enterprises in China," *Journal of Business Ethics* 87 (2009): 137–46.

16. Nicola J. Acutt, Veronica Medina-Ross, and Tim O'Riordan, "Perspectives on Corporate Social Responsibility in the Chemical Sector: A Comparative Analysis of the Mexican and South African Cases," *Natural Resources Forum* 28, no. 4 (2004): 302–16.

17. World Commission on Environment and Development, *Our Common Future* (Oxford; New York: Oxford University Press, 1987).

18. Adrian Henriques and Julie Richardson, *The Triple Bottom Line, Does It All Add Up?: Assessing the Sustainability of Business and CSR* (London; Sterling, VA: Earthscan, 2004).

19. Archie B. Carroll, "A Three-Dimensional Conceptual Model of Corporate Performance," *Academy of Management Review* 4, no. 4 (1979): 497–505.

20. "The Social Responsibility of Business Is to Increase Its Profits," *New York Times Magazine*, September, 2009.

21. Abagail McWilliams, Donald S. Siegel, and Patrick M. Wright, "Corporate Social Responsibility: Strategic Implications," *Journal of Management Studies* 43, no. 1 (2006): 1–18.

22. A. Muller and G. Whiteman, "Exploring the Geography of Corporate Philanthropic Disaster Response: A Study of Fortune Global 500 Firms," *Journal of Business Ethics* 84, no. 4 (2009): 589–603.

23. A. Yong, "Cross-Cultural Comparisons of Managerial Perceptions on Profit," *Journal of Business Ethics* 82, no. 4 (2008): 775–91.

24. Lam, "Beyond Credibility of Doing Business in China: Strategies for Improving Corporate Citizenship of Foreign Multinational Enterprises in China," 137–46.

25. Googins et al., "State of Corporate Citizenship 2009: Weathering the Storm," 46.

26. Foluso Philips, "Corporate Social Responsibility in an African Context," *Journal of Corporate Citizenship*, no. 24 (2006): 23–27.

27. Wendy Chapple and Jeremy Moon, "Corporate Social Responsibility (CSR) in Asia: A Seven-Country Study of CSR Web Site Reporting," *Business & Society* 44, no. 4 (2005): 415–41.

28. Juholin Elisa, "For Business or the Good of All? A Finnish Approach to Corporate Social Responsibility," *Corporate Governance* 4, no. 3 (2004): 20.

29. Lam, "Beyond Credibility of Doing Business in China: Strategies for Improving Corporate Citizenship of Foreign Multinational Enterprises in China," 137–46.

30. R. Edward Freeman, *Strategic Management: A Stakeholder Approach* (Englewood Cliffs, NJ: Prentice-Hall, 1984).

31. Michael Jay Polonsky, "A Stakeholder Theory Approach to Designing Environmental Marketing Strategy," *Journal of Business & Industrial Marketing* 10, no. 3 (1995): 29.

32. Ronald M. Green, "Shareholders as Stakeholders: Changing Metaphors of Corporate Governance," *Washington and Lee Law Review* 50, no. 4 (1993): 1409.

33. Jeff Frooman, "Stakeholder Influence Strategies," *Academy of Management Review* 24, no. 2 (1999): 191–204.

34. Stuart L. Hart and S. Sharma, "Emerging Fringe Stakeholders for Competitive Imagination," *Academy of Management Executive* 18, no. 1 (2004): 7–18.

35. Cone "2009 Cone Consumer Environmental Survey," http://www.coneinc.com; Cone, "2009 Cone Consumer New Media Study."

36. Bettina Cornwell et al., "A Cross-Cultural Study of the Role of Religion in Consumers' Ethical Positions," *International Marketing Review* 22, no. 5 (2005): 531; Jim Fisher, Gordon Woodbine, and Sam Fullerton, "A Cross-Cultural Assessment of Attitudes Regarding Perceived Breaches of Ethical Conduct by Both Parties in the Business-Consumer Dyad," *Journal of Consumer Behaviour* 2, no. 4 (2003): 333; Andrew Chan, Simon Wong, and Paul Leung, "Ethical Beliefs of Chinese Consumers in Hong Kong," *Journal of Business Ethics* 17, no. 11 (1998): 1163; Robert C. Erffmeyer, Bruce D. Keillor, and Debbie Thorne LeClair, "An Empirical Investigation of Japanese Consumer Ethics," *Journal of Business Ethics* 18, no. 1 (1999): 35.

37. Michael Jay Polonsky et al., "Consumer Ethics in the European Union: A Comparison of Northern and Southern Views," *Journal of Business Ethics* 31, no. 2 (2001): 117.

38. Isabelle Maignan, "Consumers' Perceptions of Corporate Social Responsibilities: A Cross-Cultural Comparison," *Journal of Business Ethics* 30, no. 1 (2001): 57.

39. B. Ramasamy and M. Yeung, "Chinese Consumers' Perception of Corporate Social Responsibility (CSR)," *Journal of Business Ethics* 88 (2009): 119.

40. Bernadette M. Ruf et al., "An Empirical Investigation of the Relationship between Change in Corporate Social Performance and Financial Performance: A Stakeholder Theory Perspective," *Journal of Business Ethics* 32, no. 2 (2001): 143.

41. Armand Picou and Michael J. Rubach, "Does Good Governance Matter to Institutional Investors? Evidence from the Enactment of Corporate Governance Guidelines," *Journal of Business Ethics* 65, no. 1 (2006): 55.

42. J. J. Irani, Subir Raha, and Suresh Prabhu, "Corporate Governance: Three Views," *Vikalpa: The Journal for Decision Makers* 30, no. 4 (2005): 1–10.

43. Nick Collett, "Shareholders and Employees: The Impact of Redundancies on Key Stakeholders," *Business Ethics* 13, no. 2–3 (2004): 117; Julian Birkinshaw et al., "Why Do Some Multinational Corporations Relocate Their Headquarters Overseas?," *Strategic Management Journal* 27, no. 7 (2006): 681.

44. Meg Voorhes, "Support Grows for Social Proposals," 2006, http://blog .riskmetrics.com/gov/2006/09/support-grow-for-social-proposalsubmitted-by-meg-voorhes-social-issues-service-director-and-carly.html.

45. Roger W. Mills and Bill Weinstein, "Beyond Shareholder Value—Reconciling the Shareholder and Stakeholder Perspectives," *Journal of General Management* 25, no. 3 (2000): 79.

46. Fukukawa and Teramoto, "Understanding Japanese CSR: The Reflections of Managers in the Field of Global Operations," 133–46.

47. Tara J. Radin, "The Effectiveness of Global Codes of Conduct: Role Models That Make Sense," *Business and Society Review* 109, no. 4 (2004): 415.

48. Jem Bendell, "In Whose Name? The Accountability of Corporate Social Responsibility," *Development in Practice* 15, no. 3/4 (2005): 362–74.

49. Fukukawa and Teramoto, "Understanding Japanese CSR: The Reflections of Managers in the Field of Global Operations," 133–46.

50. Minete E. Drumwright, "Socially Responsible Organizational Buying: Environmental Concern as a Noneconomic Buying Criterion," *Journal of Marketing* 58, no. 3 (1994): 1.

51. S. L. Bachman, "The Political Economy of Child Labor and Its Impacts on International Business," *Business Economics* 35, no. 3 (2000): 30.

52. Anne Fisher and Telis Demos, "America's Most Admired Companies," *Fortune* 153, no. 4 (2006): 65.

53. "Business: Storm in a Coffee Cup; Starbucks vs. Ethiopia," *The Economist* 381, no. 8506 (2006): 74.

54. Tammie S. Pinkston and Archie B. Carroll, "A Retrospective Examination of CSR Orientations: Have They Changed?," *Journal of Business Ethics* 15, no. 2 (1996): 199.

55. Acutt, Medina-Ross, and O'Riordan, "Perspectives on Corporate Social Responsibility in the Chemical Sector: A Comparative Analysis of the Mexican and South African Cases," 302–16.

56. Subhabrata Bobby Banerjee, Easwar S. Iyer, and Rajiv K. Kashyap, "Corporate Environmentalism: Antecedents and Influence of Industry Type," *Journal of Marketing* 67, no. 2 (2003): 106.

57. Gregory R. Berry, "Organizing against Multinational Corporate Power in Cancer Alley: The Activist Community as Primary Stakeholder," *Organization & Environment* 16, no. 1 (2003): 3.

58. Sheila M. J. Bonini, Lenny T. Mendonca, and Jeremy M. Oppenheim, "When Social Issues Become Strategic," *The McKinsey Quarterly* 2 (2006): 19–31.

59. "Declaring War on Wal-Mart," *Business Week*, February 7, 2005.

60. " 'Killer Coke' or Innocent Abroad?," *Business Week*, January 23, 2006.

61. "Business: The Blog in the Corporate Machine; Corporate Reputations," *The Economist*, February 11, 2006.

62. Peter F. Drucker, "Converting Social Problems into Business Opportunities: The New Meaning of Corporate Social Responsibility," *California Management Review* 26, no. 2 (1984): 53.

63. D. Williamson, G. Lynch-Wood, and J. Ramsay, "Drivers of Environmental Behaviour in Manufacturing SMEs and the Implications for CSR," *Journal of Business Ethics* 67, no. 3 (2006): 317–30.

64. James E. Prieger, "Regulation, Innovation, and the Introduction of New Telecommunications Services," *Review of Economics & Statistics* 84, no. 4 (2002): 704–15.

65. Anil Menon and Ajay Menon, "Enviropreneurial Marketing Strategy: The Emergence of Corporate Environmentalism as Market Strategy," *Journal of Marketing* 61, no. 1 (1997): 51.

66. Ram Nidumolu, C. K. Prahalad, and M. R. Rangaswami, "Why Sustainability Is Now the Key Driver of Innovation" (cover story), *Harvard Business Review* 87, no. 9 (2009): 56–64.

67. Porter and Kramer, "Strategy & Society: The Link between Competitive Advantage and Corporate Social Responsibility," 78–92.

68. Ibid.

69. Arno Kourula and Minna Halme, "Types of Corporate Responsibility and Engagement with NGOs: An Exploration of Business and Societal Outcomes," *Corporate Governance* 8, no. 4 (2008): 557.

70. Gopinath Pradhan and Kaustuva Barik, "Environment-Friendly Behaviour and Competitiveness: A Study of Pulp and Paper Industry in India," *Environmental and Resource Economics* 14, no. 4 (1999): 481.

71. BSR, "BSR/Globescan State of Sustainable Business Poll 2009 Fact Sheet" (survey report, 2009), http://www.bsr.org/research/reports.cfm.

72. Nidumolu, Prahalad, and Rangaswami, "Why Sustainability Is Now the Key Driver of Innovation," 59.

73. Sandra A. Waddock, "Building Successful Social Partnerships," *Sloan Management Review* 29, no. 4 (1988): 17–23.

74. Robert W. Nason, "Structuring the Global Marketplace: The Impact of the United Nations Global Compact," *Journal of Macromarketing* 28, no. 4 (2008): 418–25.

75. UN Global Compact and Dalberg Global Development Advisors, "Business Guide to Partnering with NGOs and the United Nations," Dalberg Global Development Advisors, Denmark.

76. Tracy L. Gonzalez-Padron and Robert W. Nason, "Market Responsiveness to Societal Interests," *Journal of Macromarketing* 29, no. 4 (2009): 392–405.

77. Robin Guamieri and Tina Kao, "Leadership and CSR—a Perfect Match: How Top Companies for Leaders Utilize CSR as a Competitive Advantage," *People & Strategy* 31, no. 3 (2008)" 41.

78. Honeywell International. Annual report (Morristown, NJ: Honeywell International, Inc., 2004), 24.

79. Dexter Roberts, "Waking Up To Their Rights," *Business Week*, August 22, 2005. Iss. 3948, p. 122.

80. Coca-Cola February 2009, "Achieving Water Balance through Community Water Partnership," http://www.thecoca-colacompany.com/citizenship/pdf/cwp_2009.pdf.

81. Target Corporation 2009. "2009 Corporate Responsibility Report," http://sites.target.com/images/corporate/about/responsibility_report/2009/full_report.pdf.

82. Altria Group Inc., Annual report (New York: 2004), 6.

83. FedEx Corporation, Annual report (Memphis, TN: 2004), 26.

84. Ecolab USA, Inc., "Ecolab 2008 Sustainability Report" (St. Paul, MN), 15.

85. Hewlett Packard Company, HP Annual report (Palo Alto, CA: 2004), 17.

86. Intel Corporation, Annual report (Santa Clara, CA: 2004).

87. Rekha Balu, "Hindustan Lever," *Fast Company* no. 47 (2001): 120–36.

88. Nokia, "Business Benefits," 2009, http://www.nokia.com/corporate-responsibility/ethics/business-value.

89. R. Edward Freeman and Lisa Stewart, "Developing Ethical Leadership" (Business Roundtable Institute for Corporate Ethics, 2006), http://www.corporate-ethics.org/pdf/ethical_leadership.pdf, p. 3.

90. AjayK. Kohli and Bernard J. Jaworski, "Market Orientation: The Construct, Research Propositions, and Managerial Implications," *Journal of Marketing* 54 (1990): 1–18; Isabelle Maignan and O. C. Ferrell, "Corporate Social Responsibility and Marketing: An Integrative Framework," *Journal of the Academy of Marketing Science* 32, no. 1 (2004): 3–19.

Chapter 8

Business Ethics across Cultures

Terri L. Rittenburg

Business ethics is a topic that seems to wax and wane; interest in it heightens when consumers and policy makers become concerned about particular issues or events. The recent business corruption scandals have raised the profile of business ethics as a topic of importance to schools and businesses.

What do we mean by business ethics? In simplest terms, we are talking about matters of good and bad, right and wrong in making business decisions. More formally, we think of business ethics as the application of moral philosophy to the realm of business. A related term with which we should be familiar is *corporate social responsibility*. By social responsibility, we mean maximizing positive impacts on society while minimizing negative impacts.

Do all businesses agree on how ethics and social responsibility should be implemented? Or whether they should be implemented? Of course not! Even within one culture, there are varying perceptions and opinions about how ethics should be applied to business. In the international arena, when business crosses cultures, the difficulty is considerably magnified. Why should this be the case? Different cultures have their own values and norms, so the bases for ethical decision making can be quite different. By values we mean the fundamental aspects of culture that drive people to think and feel as they do. Norms are the guidelines for behavior that reflect these values. For example, U.S. culture values individualism, so we see many business decisions made by individual managers, whereas Japanese culture values collectivism, so more decisions are the result of a group orientation.

WALKING A TIGHTROPE

The differences in values and norms across cultures create a balancing act for the international manager, like walking a tightrope between the two cultures. The manager must satisfy the cultural expectations in both the host country's culture, where the business is operating, and the home or parent country's culture, where the company is based. Although it is imperative that one is sensitive to the cultural values of the host country, one's own values don't go out the window. In international business, a manager must be sensitive to other cultures, but make decisions with which he or she can live. This dilemma might be thought of as a conflict in interests, where both interests are salient, and one must satisfy the needs of both.

Multiply this situation times all the countries in which a multinational enterprise operates, and you have quite a balancing act. Even businesspeople who are motivated to act ethically face a conundrum in the international arena. How to act ethically provides a stumbling block within the context of a particular culture. The norms of that society apply. Even with the best of intentions, finding the "right" actions may create complexity.

What sorts of aspects are we talking about? Geert Hofstede's[1] extensive research has identified five dimensions of culture: power distance, uncertainty avoidance, individualism vs. collectivism, masculinity vs. femininity, and long-term vs. short-term orientation. He defines power distance as different solutions to the basic problem of human inequality; uncertainty avoidance related to the level of stress in a society in the face of an unknown future; individualism vs. collectivism related to the integration of individuals into primary groups; masculinity vs. femininity as the division of emotional roles between men and women; and long-term vs. short-term orientation as the choice of focus for people's efforts, the future or the present. These dimensions help us to understand how cultures differ, thus how people's perceptions in different societies will vary.

EXTERNAL INFLUENCES

In addition to the environmental influence of culture and its attendant values and norms, other factors may act as constraints or facilitators in doing business. These additional macroenvironmental factors combine to create the context in which business operates: legal systems; political systems; economic systems; technological systems; the natural environment; and social influences, such as demographic trends, religions, social stratification, and social issues of importance in a society. All of these macroenvironmental areas contribute to relevant differences across societies that may be important in considering ethical questions in business. For example, disparities in economic development may mean consumers in a particular country (or subgroup within a country) do not have access to the highest levels of technology. These disparities will have practical implications for doing business there, but perhaps also ethical implications for what approaches are appropriate. Where literacy rates are low, for example, promotional methods that rely on written words may not only be ineffective but may mislead or leave out some consumers with a need for the product.

INTERNATIONAL BUSINESS ETHICS ISSUES

What are some of the sticky issues related to international business ethics? It is impossible to include here an exhaustive list of all the ethical problems international businesspeople face, but it may be helpful to consider a few of the major issues. These include:

Bribery and Corruption

One of the most researched topics with respect to international business ethics is bribery and corruption. Whether one refers to a million dollars under the table to be assured the awarding of a contract or a small grease payment as facilitation, bribery is problematic because of cultural differences. In some cultures, historical practices have become a way of life. Outsiders who regard such payments as questionable or wrong wrestle with the home country–host country divide. For U.S.-based firms, bribery became a legal issue when the Foreign Corrupt Practices Act was passed in the 1970s. This law was controversial for several reasons, including: (1) it is an extraterritorial law, governing what U.S. firms may do outside U.S. borders, (2) some companies argue that it creates a competitive disadvantage for U.S. firms in the global marketplace, and

(3) it may be seen as ethical imperialism, imposing U.S. values on actions of firms doing business within other countries and cultures. Regardless of legalities, the practice of bribery is fraught with difficulty for many businesspeople around the world. Part of the difficulty stems from differences in values, and part of it resides in the hidden aspects of bribery, in that sometimes payments are couched as gift giving or tipping, so that it is not outwardly obvious to foreigners.

Child Labor

The role of children in households and societies has evolved over the centuries. Historically, in agrarian societies, children were viewed as assets and resources to be employed. In wealthy societies today, children are seen quite differently as resource users rather than suppliers. Children still work on farms and ranches around the world; the major controversy applies in poor countries when children work outside the home in factories, stores or, infinitely worse, in prostitution. Although some observers believe all child labor should be abolished, others believe it will die a natural death as a result of economic development. So the crux of the matter for ethicists is: Do we wait for child labor to go away on its own, or should pressure be applied to end it immediately? Pros and cons exist to its immediate ending, because children losing their jobs may face starvation or go underground into worse occupations. So businesses operating where child labor occurs face a dilemma in terms of the child labor itself, and another dilemma of public opinion and consumer activism in rich countries where knowledgeable consumers boycott goods made with child labor. The issue is not child's play!

Poor or Unsafe Working Conditions

Countries' laws vary widely in protection of workers from unsafe conditions. Companies that outsource manufacturing to countries with lower wage rates also often benefit from fewer rules and restrictions regarding safety standards and working conditions. Even in countries with fairly stringent employment laws, sweat shops exist under the radar. In the United States, for example, illegal immigrants working in the meat-packing industry sometimes work under very poor conditions; because of their immigration status, they are not in a position to complain. Most of us consumers may seldom hear about the poor working conditions unless a catastrophe occurs, such as the Bhopal disaster in India 25 years ago,[2] when deadly gas exploded out of a faulty tank in a pesticide factory and spread into people's homes. About 20,000 people died, and many survivors suffered bodily damage and multiple diseases that still plague them today. For international business ethicists, the question becomes: What are reasonable standards and how should they be enforced?

Discriminatory Practices

Schools and businesses discriminate every day, between those who are smarter, more skilled, or harder working, and those who are not. In modern society, we have come to view the term *discrimination* negatively, although each of us uses discrimination in ways we see in a more positive light: we discriminate among the fruit we select in the grocery store, among the people we date before selecting a spouse, and among the candidates we vote for in elections. It is when discrimination is used to undermine or reject a whole group of people that we object to it. In the business sector, most societies outlaw discrimination in employment and product sales/pricing; thus, a job candidate cannot be rejected simply because of his or her religion, and a consumer cannot be charged more for a product because of the color of his or her skin. In the United States the Equal Employment Opportunity Commission was created to protect employees (and potential employees) from just such discrimination. Do all societies feel the same way about needing this protection and about who should be protected? Clearly not. In Norway, gender equality and egalitarianism are taken very seriously, whereas in Muslim societies such as Saudi Arabia, views regarding women's roles are quite different. Whether the issue is race, religion, gender, sexual orientation, marital status, or age, there are chasms of cultural difference around the world with regard to this issue.

Piracy and Counterfeiting

One needn't travel very much to run across counterfeit or pirated goods. The author has seen pirated compact disks and DVDs on display in China, and once in Tijuana, Mexico, was startled by a sign boldly promoting "Rolex Copy" watches. But even in the United States, knockoff handbags and bootlegged music and software are widely available. From a business perspective, the costs are huge in terms of lost sales, lost tax revenues, and sometimes damage to company reputations because of low-quality products parading as "genuine." One illustration of the backlash against pirated and counterfeit goods can be found in the case of these products targeted toward tourists in Italy. Is there controversy regarding this issue? Yes, in at least two facets: (1) Cultural differences appear in views about intellectual property and its legitimacy. In Asian cultures, historically one would not expect remuneration because others wanted to copy something he had created; rather, one would be honored that others held his work in such esteem. Countries such as China do have laws protecting intellectual property today, largely in order to play in the global economy, not because they are consistent with local culture. (2) Because of the rich-poor divide, the question is raised: Should the poor be denied access to music, software, or other products because the branded versions are so far out of financial reach for them?

Human Trafficking

An issue only recently researched in the business disciplines is that of human trafficking. Today it might be considered the ugly side of free markets. The sale of human beings as servants or sex slaves is certainly not new in the history of the world, but its continued existence is a sad commentary on how far civilizations have advanced (or not advanced).

Product Safety

We as consumers rely on the safety of the products and services we purchase, whether the source of those products is domestic or foreign. In recent years, international scares regarding mad cow disease and bird flu have brought to the fore dangers that can exist in basic products such as food. Clearly there are legal issues related to product safety and political issues regarding trade relationships between countries. What are the ethical issues? They are associated with the responsibility businesses have to ensure consumer safety and to stand by their products.

Materialism and Promotion of Unneeded Products

Consumers have many needs, both physical (or functional) and psychological. A basic tenet of marketing is that marketers do not create needs; marketers create wants in consumers to fulfill their needs in particular ways. That said, the field of marketing is sometimes criticized for promoting materialism and emphasizing the fulfillment of human needs through the acquisition of more things. In a world of finite resources and limited space for disposal of packaging and used goods, there are ethical questions related to promotion of the instant-gratification, throw-away society.

Environmental Degradation

Regardless of one's position regarding climate change, there is no question that the earth's resources are finite. The impacts of increased population and consumer lifestyles on the planet in terms of pollution, use of natural resources, and waste disposal are critical for future generations. Environmental issues are global in nature. Pollution does not respect human political boundaries. Thus, from a business ethics perspective, there is a responsibility not to harm others through our actions.

MICRO APPROACHES

The previous discussion outlined a number of challenges facing international businesspeople today. In facing these challenges, business ethics can be examined from both micro, or individual firm, and macro, or entire business system, levels. We will first consider a micro perspective, focusing on tools that companies can adopt to aid in making ethical decisions. Many approaches for examining business ethics are ethicists. Nonetheless, we can identify some general directions and emphases. As stated earlier, business ethics is the application of moral philosophy to business; some ethicists focus on the major philosophical frameworks.

Moral Philosophy

The frameworks most often applied in business settings are consequentialism, particularly utilitarianism; deontological, or rule-based, frameworks, such as the Golden Rule, Kant's categorical imperative, or Ross's prima facie duties; contract-based theories, such as social contracts theory or Rawls's theory of social justice; and virtue ethics, based on the idea of forming good habits.[3] Table 8.1 presents a summary of these four categories of ethical theories.

As a practical matter, most people are unlikely to adopt just one framework that applies in all situations. When faced with an ethical problem or dilemma, we are more likely to think it through drawing on multiple approaches (i.e., what are the likely consequences of an action? what rules apply? is the action just or fair to all stakeholders? is the action consistent with the habits I have formed to instill a

Table 8.1
Summary of Major Ethical Theories Applied in Business

Category	Description	Examples
Teleological theories (Consequentialism)	Ethicality is judged based on outcomes or consequences of actions.	*Utilitarianism*: Action taken should produce the greatest good for the greatest number of individuals.
Deontological theories	Ethicality is judged based on adherence to a rule or set of rules.	*Golden Rule*: Do unto others as you would have them do unto you. *Kant's Categorical Imperative*: Act only on maxims that you can will to be universal laws of nature.
Contract-based theories	Ethicality is judged based on fidelity to obligations of the social contract.	*Rawls's Theory of Social Justice*: Applies two principles of justice, the liberty principle and the difference principle. The liberty principle ensures each person an equal right to the most extensive liberty compatible with a similar liberty for others. The difference principle states that social and economic inequalities are to be arranged so that they are to the greatest benefit of the most disadvantaged. These principles should be applied under an ideal system of justice whereby, if we did not know what our station in life would be, we would rationally choose to minimize the harm done to those most disadvantaged in society.
Virtue ethics	Ethicality is judged based on the embodiment of specific virtues as part of an individual's character.	*Aristotle's Virtues*: truthfulness, justice, generosity, and self-control.

Source: Compiled from Patrick E. Murphy and Gene R. Laczniak, *Marketing Ethics: Cases and Readings* (Upper Saddle River, NJ: Pearson Education, Inc., 2006), 9–29.

virtuous character?). Hybrid frameworks integrate various approaches to ethical decision making into one model to illustrate how decision makers draw on them in the ethical decision process. A model developed by Hunt and Vitell provides a good example of such integration.[4] This framework provides a descriptive representation of how decision making appears to be accomplished. Major components of the Hunt-Vitell theory consist of influences on the decision maker, such as factors in the cultural, professional, industry, and organizational environments, and personal characteristics of the decision maker; perceptions about the ethical problem, perceived alternatives, deontological norms leading to a deontological evaluation, and perceptions about consequences leading to a teleological evaluation; ethical judgments; intentions; behavior; and consequences of that behavior. This process model illustrates how multiple ethical frameworks may enter into a decision maker's thinking in reasoning through an ethical decision. From an international perspective, the Hunt-Vitell theory of ethics incorporates the influence of culture, specifically incorporating the influences of religion, legal system, and political system on the decision maker's perceptions. Thus, it provides a comprehensive view of the decision process within an organization, illustrating how both teleology and deontology may be incorporated into the process.

A hybrid model developed by Ferrell, Gresham, and Fraedrich[5] incorporated many of the same elements as the Hunt-Vitell model, but framed them along the decision process: awareness—cognitions—moral evaluations—determination—action. This model also recognizes influences such as the social and economic environment and a feedback loop of consequences on these influences. It integrates deontology, teleology, and judgments in the moral evaluation stage. These integrative models may be helpful for decision makers in visualizing the ethical decision process and the various factors that shape it.

Practical Guidelines

A popular approach to business ethics seems to be development of practical behavioral guidelines for companies. Often we can identify the roots of moral philosophy's theories in these guidelines, but such frameworks are not presented as applications of moral philosophy, but rather as realistic rules of thumb useful for business decision makers. As with the previous section on moral theories, it is beyond the scope of this chapter to provide an exhaustive list of these types of guidelines, but we will touch on a few of the major tools that are available for businesses.

Richard DeGeorge compiled a list of five general norms for multinational firms:[6]

- Do no direct international harm.
- Produce more good than harm for the host country.
- Respect the rights of employees and of all others affected by one's actions or policies.
- To the extent consistent with ethical norms, respect the local culture and work with and not against it.
- Multinationals should pay their fair share of taxes and cooperate with the local government in developing equitable laws and other background institutions.

DeGeorge states that the guidelines are suggestive of the content of specific codes and that, in cases of possible conflict in their application, common sense and ethical reasoning should be applied.[7] Guidelines such as these provide a practical tool for companies doing business internationally. As with any ethical framework, they do not purport to give the user an algorithm that automatically creates a perfect solution; rather, they remind us of some basic norms that are fairly widely accepted and urge us to take these into consideration in making business decisions across cultures.

Similarly, Kathleen Getz distilled codes of conduct for multinational companies which were developed by four international organizations into one code of conduct.[8] This compilation included the areas of economic and development policies, laws and regulations, political involvement, technology transfer, environmental protection, consumer protection, employment practices, and human rights, combining overlapping items in codes developed by the International Chamber of Commerce (ICC), Organization for Economic Cooperation and Development (OECD), International Labor Organization (ILO), and the United Nations Center on Transnational Corporations (UNCTC).

Taking this research a step further, Getz analyzed the common elements from these four codes of conduct and identified the underlying values reflected in the items.[9] These values are:

- *National sovereignty:* National governments possess ultimate authority over the activities that take place within their boundaries and should be free from interference from foreign governments.

- *Social equity:* It is good and appropriate for social burdens and benefits to be fairly, though not necessarily equally, distributed among all individuals and groups in society.
- *Basic human rights:* Natural and legal rights, and corresponding duties to honor those rights.
- *Market integrity:* Arises when markets are unimpaired or when market imperfections are corrected. This occurs in a competitive marketplace in which contracts are honored and sellers and buyers have freedom of choice and perfect information.
- *Organizational autonomy:* The legitimate authority of private organizations to direct their own activities, free from governmental interference.

This set of values represents a beginning toward identifying some universal principles for international business.

Thomas Donaldson also has developed a set of guidelines; these focus specifically on international human rights:[10]

- The right to freedom of physical movement.
- The right to ownership of property.
- The right to freedom from torture.
- The right to a fair trial.
- The right to nondiscriminatory treatment.
- The right to physical security.
- The right to freedom of speech and association.
- The right to minimal education.
- The right to political participation.
- The right to subsistence.

A number of these rights are consistent with codes later developed by the United Nations and other organizations. Although clearly not all of these rights are respected in all societies, globalization seems to be putting pressure on governments to accept and uphold human rights such as these.

We see striking similarities to Donaldson's list in the more recently developed United Nations Global Compact,[11] 10 principles in the areas of human rights, labor, the environment, and anti-corruption derived from the Universal Declaration of Human Rights, the International Labor Organization's Declaration on Fundamental Principles and Rights at Work, the Rio Declaration on Environment and Development, and the United Nations Convention Against Corruption. The 10 principles are:

Human Rights

- *Principle 1*: Businesses should support and respect the protection of internationally proclaimed human rights; and
- *Principle 2*: make sure that they are not complicit in human rights abuses.

Labor Standards

- *Principle 3*: Businesses should uphold the freedom of association and the effective recognition of the right to collective bargaining;
- *Principle 4*: the elimination of all forms of forced and compulsory labor;
- *Principle 5*: the effective abolition of child labor; and
- *Principle 6*: the elimination of discrimination in respect of employment and occupation.

Environment

- *Principle 7*: Businesses should support a precautionary approach to environmental challenges;
- *Principle 8*: undertake initiatives to promote greater environmental responsibility; and
- *Principle 9*: encourage the development and diffusion of environmentally friendly technologies.

Anti-Corruption

- *Principle 10*: Businesses should work against corruption in all its forms, including extortion and bribery.

Although the work of DeGeorge, Getz, and Donaldson may not have reached a large number of decision makers in multinational corporations, the United Nations Global Compact should have the broad reach to do so. As with all other guidelines, there is a level of common sense and judgment in applying these principles, but they are a huge step forward in creating universal standards of behavior for business around the world.

A discussion of practical guidelines would not be complete without mentioning the concepts of sustainability and the triple bottom line. The concept of sustainable development was introduced by the Brundtland Commission, formally known as the World Commission on Environment and Development which took the name of its chair, Gro Harlem Brundtland, from Norway. The commission's report, "Our Common Future," defined sustainable development as development that meets the needs of the present without compromising the ability of future generations to meet their own needs.[12] The idea of sustainable business practices has far-reaching implications for businesses, particularly with respect to issues related to social and economic development and environmental protection. The environmental principles of the UN Global Compact clearly mirror these concerns, and the principles of human rights and labor standards may be pertinent too inasmuch as they relate to a society's development. Companies are jumping on the sustainability bandwagon, and are making a point of communicating their sustainability activities to consumers. For example, Coca-Cola's home page touts their sustainability efforts.[13]

The phrase "triple bottom line" was coined in 1994 by John Elkington,[14] to capture the three pillars for measuring organizational (and societal) success: economic, ecological, and social (or people, planet, and profit). These triumvirate measures are advocated in order to achieve sustainability.

Although the concepts of sustainability and the triple bottom line do not provide specific guidelines for behavior, they suggest broadened measures of business performance and success. In most all pursuits in life, people do that for which they are rewarded. These concepts remind us that, if we want businesses to help achieve global sustainability, reward systems are needed that incentivize appropriate behaviors.

Implementation

A key challenge for businesses lies in implementation of ethics as a part of day-to-day operations. It is far easier to create a code of conduct that sits on a shelf or work through a case situation in a training session than it is to incorporate ethics into business activities. Laczniak, Murphy, Bowie, and Klein suggest a number of methods for implementing ethics into a business organization.[15] They categorize these methods into formal corporate policies and informal approaches designed to create a corporate culture conducive to ethical behavior.

Formal policies include corporate ethics statements and training programs. Ethics statements take several forms: a *corporate credo* is a short (one page or less) document that lists corporate beliefs and/or responsibilities to stakeholders; a *corporate code* provides rules for conduct; a *values statement* represents the guiding principles of the firm; an *Internet privacy policy* outlines the company's position on what will be done with information collected from consumers. Ethics training programs may take either a compliance approach, focusing on following rules and codes of conduct, or a values/integrity approach, using the credo or values statement as an aspirational goal.[16] Both approaches may be incorporated into a company's training program. When implemented diligently, these formal approaches can be quite effective in providing clear guidelines for employees. Many multinational firms have explicit credos, codes, and values statements available on their websites, easily accessible to employees and external audiences alike. For example, Johnson & Johnson is well known for their corporate credo,[17] corporate codes of conduct are easily accessible online for Caterpillar[18] and Nokia,[19] Coca-Cola shares their values statement,[20] and Disney explicates their business standards and ethics training on their company's home page.[21]

Corporate culture is a critical factor in reinforcing values and behavioral expectations. It is crucial that ethical values are communicated from top management throughout the organization. A supportive atmosphere where employees feel free to ask questions when facing difficult or ethically ambiguous situations can go a long way in facilitating ethical behavior. Reward and punishment systems must uphold those values; otherwise they are meaningless. Observers note that Enron had a well-developed code of conduct, but their formal document obviously could not compete with the informal culture of the organization. Employees need role models and will take their cues from top management in understanding what is considered appropriate within that company's milieu. J. C. Penney Company's corporate culture is discussed on their website, drawing on the early days of James Cash Penney's Golden Rule store, making clear the moral values espoused by the founder. GE specifically talks about the link between their reward systems and ethical performance.[22]

The best plan in the world has no value unless it is effectively implemented. The same is true of ethics. The best code of conduct can accomplish nothing unless it is vigorously enforced. Global firms face huge challenges in order to develop a global ethical policy and reinforce this through a global corporate culture. The corporate examples to which we have referred in this section are multinational enterprises that, at a minimum, are communicating their intentions to achieve this goal. We as consumers may judge how successful we believe their efforts are.

MACRO PERSPECTIVE

The focus of the previous section was micro in orientation, identifying approaches companies could use as tools in ethical decision making. Assuming companies are motivated to act in an ethical manner, these frameworks and guidelines provide the means for arriving at ethical decisions.

A contrasting view is to consider ethics in international business from a macro perspective, focusing on the system-wide array of stakeholders and institutions that create the context within which businesses operate. At the macro level, ethical practices on the part of businesses bestow benefits on societies and the various stakeholders that are affected by those businesses' actions. If we consider this notion in crudest terms—the sectors of business, government, and consumers—ethicality on the part of businesses creates a better relationship with consumers and fewer problems (i.e., legal, regulatory) for governments. But also from a macro perspective, we must contemplate the macro environment within which businesses operate. Is it an environment that nurtures and encourages ethical action? In other words, does the system reward companies that adhere to the triple bottom line in setting goals and measuring performance? Ferrell and Hartline argue that a climate of ethics within a firm creates trust among a firm's stakeholders.[23] In their estimation, ethical firms perform better because of this trust, which inculcates loyalty among consumers.

On the other hand, the fact that the United Nations, as well as several other organizations, has adopted a convention against corruption implies that the global environment for ethical business needs improvement.[24] At the aggregate level, if the rules of the game were reinforced, or even agreed upon, a discussion of international business ethics would be moot. Clearly this is not the case; we recognize differences in values, laws, norms, and expectations around the world, and businesses still struggle with both doing right and understanding what is right to do.

Global Business Citizenship

Perhaps what is needed is a new paradigm that links micro and macro considerations. A framework which may help us address this concern is the concept of Global Business Citizenship. A *global business citizen* is defined as "a multinational enterprise that responsibly exercises its rights and implements its duties to individuals, stakeholders and societies within and across national and cultural borders."[25] Global business citizenship (GBC) is offered as a path to applying universal ethical principles while simultaneously respecting local cultural variations. It is posited that this approach not only benefits the individual organization, but the global community as well. In fact, the authors advocate GBC as a private pathway to a collective good, in other words, a way of making capitalism sustainable.[26] They argue that, if businesses engage in unethical practices that harm societies, those societies are free to choose other systems for distributing goods and services, to the detriment of capitalism, which has expanded in many of the world's economies since the end of the cold war.

The GBC concept offers a necessary bridge between micro and macro that is lacking in many other approaches to international business ethics. Wood et al. have created a process for balancing the home country values against host country values; they recommend analysis and experimentation to deal with problems of fit, conflicts, and contradictions.[27] Whether this framework represents the panacea for which we search remains to be seen, but it certainly offers promise as a process for businesses, with both micro and macro benefits.

Rich vs. Poor

From a macro perspective, there are clearly "haves" and "have nots" in the world. The most straightforward way of approaching the topic is to look at differences in economic development. C. K. Prahalad likens the gap to a pyramid in which about four billion people, or over half of the world's population, lives on less than US$2 per day.[28] Paul Collier has researched the poorest of the poor, the "bottom billion," in an attempt to understand why poverty prevails in the face of various types of aid.[29] The Millenium Development Goals[30] (MDG) include the eradication of extreme poverty and hunger. Is poverty an ethical issue? Do businesses have a role to play?

On a micro company level, businesses work to achieve their own objectives; they work within the macro environmental context to make a profit and provide benefits for their stakeholders. On a macro level, the business sector's actions in aggregate contribute to the macro environment. If companies bribe corrupt government officials, target only affluent societies with useful products, outsource to poor countries in order to take advantage of lenient environmental laws or low safety standards for workers, or hire child labor, these companies are contributing to the status quo. Businesses are not nongovernmental organizations (NGOs), and their missions are not philanthropic in nature, but that doesn't mean businesses cannot do good while making a profit.

Prahalad argues that companies need to look more closely at the opportunities at the Bottom of the Pyramid where there is great need for reasonably priced goods and services.[31] He has demonstrated through a number of case studies that such ventures can be profitable while improving the lives of the very poor. He suggests innovation as a way of lowering costs, making product offerings feasible. Wood advocates business participation in achieving the Millennium Development Goals,[32] including rethinking technology, design, production process, and content in order to bring costs and prices down. These arguments indicate that businesses can focus on their business and profit without contributing to greater poverty. A social responsibility position would propose businesses bring about greater positive impacts than negative, thereby helping to alleviate poverty. In a recent example, the Norwegian company Voxtra is working to develop a supply chain for low-cost treadle pumps for farmers in the state of Asam in northern India. A small investment in a treadle pump and fertilizer allows a farmer to irrigate and harvest three crops per year instead of one crop. It is estimated that the treadle pump will produce a 300 percent return on investment in the first year. Although Norway is a leading country in foreign aid, the new trend recognizes that entrepreneurship and business are part of the poverty solution.[33]

According to Collier, the poorest countries share several characteristics that appear to be related to their continued poverty. He calls these poverty traps: the conflict trap, the natural resource trap, landlocked with bad neighbors trap, and bad governance in a small country trap.[34] Briefly, the conflict trap refers to the tendency for very poor countries to suffer from civil wars or coups d'état that are costly both financially and socially. The natural resource trap is a problem for countries in various economic strata; for the poorest countries, wealth in natural resources raises prices, political systems fail, wealth does not reach most of the population, and paradoxically a country rich in natural resources continues in poverty. Countries that are landlocked face major constraints to engaging in international trade. If their neighboring countries either are not favorable markets or have major problems, such as internal conflict, themselves, this exacerbates the effects of being landlocked. A country's government determines the shape of its economic policies and legal system. Bad governance can be devastating to an economy. Africa, a region plagued by poverty, has a number of countries that suffer from one or more of these poverty traps. Collier argues that aid alone will not be enough to solve the problems of the bottom billion.[35] Access to export markets and assistance in developing offerings that affluent consumers want to buy is also needed in order to end the cycle of poverty. As Farmer argued over two decades ago,[36] the way for poor countries to get rich is to get involved in the global economy. Closing themselves off from the outside world will only increase their problems. They must be open to importing new technology, materials, and whatever else it takes in order to make world-class products that others in the world want to buy. What does this mean for the business sector? Consider developing countries as both potential markets and locations for foreign direct investment, not simply to exploit human and natural resources, but to benefit both the company and the country. As DeGeorge admonished, produce more good than harm in the host country.[37] Good global business citizens contribute to a better macro environment for all, which increases the probability that countries will continue to support capitalism as an economic system.

REVISITING THE ISSUES

Up to this point, we have been exploring international business ethics largely from the standpoint of generalities and abstractions. Whereas these general approaches to ethics lay the groundwork for decision making, it might be helpful to revisit some of the key ethical issues that are problematic in conducting business in the global economy. Several of these issues are reflected in the Millennium Development Goals,[38] so let us first consider these:

- Eradicate extreme poverty and hunger.
- Achieve universal primary education.
- Promote gender equality and empower women.
- Reduce child mortality.

- Improve maternal health.
- Combat HIV, AIDS, malaria, and other diseases.
- Ensure environmental sustainability.
- Develop a global partnership for development.

These goals represent a tall order for the global community, and one that many are skeptical about reaching by the target deadline of 2015.

Bribery and Corruption

Although cultural differences regarding this issue have not disappeared, a number of developments have occurred in recent years to combat bribery and corruption and level the playing field for firms who do not engage in these types of activities. Several regional and global organizations have adopted conventions against bribery, including the OECD, the OAS, the African Union, and the United Nations. Bribery is still a problematic issue for international businesses, but the emergence of these conventions against bribery suggests some convergence in global opinion. From a macro perspective, bribery is economically inefficient, so markets are allowed to operate more smoothly without it. Also, the recognition of the role corrupt governments play in the maintenance of poverty may have influenced cooperation in the movement to eradicate bribery and corruption. This sticky issue is still far from being solved, but it seems as though there is evidence that more governments are including its solution as part of their agendas.

Child Labor

Though not directly addressed as an item in the Millennium Development Goals, the goal of universal primary education suggests that the world community views children's role as one of becoming educated for future employment rather than as productive members of the workforce. Of course, ending child labor may fly in the face of the first goal, to eradicate poverty and hunger. This issue, too, is far from being solved.

Poor or Unsafe Working Conditions

The frameworks of DeGeorge, Donaldson, and the UN Global Compact reinforce the importance of respecting employees' human rights and providing safe working conditions. In addition, a phenomenon that has gained considerable momentum in recent years is the fair trade movement. Fair trade is a market-based model of international trade that provides minimum prices to farmers and farm workers in developing countries. Its goals include empowering farmers to ensure favorable working conditions and protection of the environment. Through fair trade certification, consumers can be assured they are buying fair trade goods, thereby making a conscious decision to help alleviate poverty. Fair trade principles specifically include: fair prices, fair labor conditions, direct trade, democratic and transparent organizations, community development, and environmental sustainability. As more and more consumers opt for fair trade coffee, tea, handicrafts, and other products, it increases pressure on businesses to give more attention to these principles.

Discriminatory Practices

Principle 6 of the UN Global Compact is the elimination of discrimination in respect of employment and occupation. As discussed earlier, this principle mirrors items included in Donaldson's international human rights and universal values identified by Getz. Only one area of discrimination, gender equality and the empowerment of women, is detailed in the Millennium Development Goals, arguably because of its controversy across cultures or its importance to economic development in poor countries. Whatever the reasons, clearly discriminatory practices are under fire by various international groups.

Piracy and Counterfeiting

Although laws and international conventions are designed to protect companies' intellectual property, their enforcement continues to be problematic. Even in wealthy countries, counterfeiting and piracy are common; for example, it is estimated that 33 percent of Canada's software is pirated.[39] Nonetheless, companies are exploring innovative methods for dealing with this issue. Rather than relying on enforcement of laws, companies such as Microsoft, Philips, and Warner Bros. are using managerial approaches to find a balance between sharing new technology, pricing it at affordable rates, and protection of intellectual property.[40]

Human Trafficking

We would be hard pressed to identify worse human rights abuses than trafficking in human beings. Principle 4 of the UN Global Compact is the elimination of all forms of forced and compulsory labor.

Researchers define human trafficking as the moving of human beings across borders for the purpose of enslaving them; human trafficking may be in the sex trade, forced labor or service, extraction of body parts, or other forms of exploited labor or debt bondage.[41] The authors' findings suggest that the magnitude of human trafficking activity has probably been considerably underestimated to date. From a macro perspective, participation in illicit markets for human beings, drugs, or other illegal activities harm capitalism as a global economic system.

Product Safety

DeGeorge exhorts businesses to do no direct international harm. Products may be inherently dangerous, such as tobacco, or dangerous due to misuse, such as alcohol. Further, products that are contaminated or poorly made may present dangers to consumers. Of course, these concerns are relevant domestically too; internationally, problems may be compounded due to cultural differences and differences in levels of economic development. A classic example was the marketing of infant formula in developing countries in the 1970s; mixing the powdered formula with contaminated water led to infant disease and death. Caution in marketing needs to be balanced, however, with the recognition of markets at the bottom of the pyramid that have needs and wants for new technologies.

Materialism and Promotion of Unneeded Products

This criticism of marketing may underscore cultural differences more than any other. Materialism is often associated with the West, particularly U.S. culture. The issue of promotion, however, gets at the heart of basic rights: What rights do companies have to communicate their wares? What rights do consumers have to be informed and to make personal choices about what they want? Individualistic cultures defend these rights, whereas collectivistic cultures are more concerned about the welfare of the group. From a macro perspective, some people in the world have much more than they need and some have much less than they need. Given reliance on market economies, disproportionate distribution is likely to continue. Solutions at the bottom of the pyramid are complex, relying on philanthropy, aid, entrepreneurship, and economic development to better the situation of the "have nots." Whose job is it to promote simpler lifestyles to the more affluent in the world? Does business have a responsibility to demarket and encourage consumers to consume less? These are difficult questions for cross-cultural ethicists.

Environmental Degradation

As discussed earlier, the world's physical environment is a crucial global problem. The UN Global Compact devotes three principles (7, 8, and 9) to environmental issues. Environmental sustainability is one of the Millennium Development Goals. It has been suggested that a whole new paradigm is needed in order to tackle the challenges of environmental sustainability.[42] Global cooperation is the only way to attain this goal, and systems that reward responsible individual actions are needed in order to provide the incentives for people to change their everyday behaviors. The global environment represents the fundamental notion of a commons, and people will use it as such unless they are restricted from doing so. Questions of energy usage, pollution, and disposal of waste can pit "haves" against "have nots," developed countries against developing countries, individualists against collectivists, and so on.

What solutions might business ethics approaches provide to assist with environmental issues? If clean air and water are considered basic human rights, perhaps as elements of subsistence, then current and future generations have those rights. Utilitarians are concerned with the greatest good for the greatest number, which suggests preserving the environment for all. Deontologists would consider rule-based approaches to caring for air and water and recycling substances. A virtue ethics approach would suggest developing good habits in the environmental realm. The ethical tools can aid in reaching environmental sustainability if the will exists to do so.

LIMITATIONS

The purpose of this essay has been to discuss some basic business ethics approaches, identify some of the ethical issues that arise in the global environment, and demonstrate the complexities of applying business ethics across cultures. Within the confines of one chapter, it is impossible to do justice to all of the ethical frameworks and issues that exist today. Moreover, one of the fundamental challenges of cross-cultural ethics is in the perspective of the observer, forever tied to her own culture. The author faces this same challenge and is the first to admit that a Western bias exists in the views expressed here.

The scenario of the individual decision maker considering ethical ideas and alternatives has cultural content embedded in it. It is inescapable and can be recognized but not totally eliminated.

CONCLUSIONS

Companies face hard decisions every day: How should we do business? Where should we do business? Where do we draw the line on activities we consider unethical? Choices are made and consequences occur. In an ideal situation, a company can act ethically and reap rewards, but there is no guarantee this will always be the case. Nice guys finish first in Hollywood movies, but not always in real life. When cultures clash with the values of the firm and its leaders, companies sometimes choose not to do business rather than compromise their values. These decisions are not easy to make.

Many tools are available to aid business firms in their ethical quests. Whether a firm chooses the route of a values-oriented approach or a compliance-oriented approach, it is clear that leadership at the top is a crucial factor in implementing an ethics program. A comprehensive line of attack that emphasizes open communication about ethical issues and encourages employees to ask questions is vital in effecting ethical behavior. People will do that for which they are rewarded; if ethical actions are rewarded, they will occur. Unless ethics is part of the bedrock of corporate culture, its execution is likely to be problematic.

Global business citizenship is a relatively new approach that may provide a process for companies to navigate the rough seas of cross-cultural ethical decisions. This framework recognizes the balancing act companies face between ethical imperialism and ethical relativism. It seems a fruitful direction to consider. It does, however, rely on identification of a set of universal principles, which presents some difficulty. Nonetheless, from a macro perspective, the future of capitalism may depend upon global business citizenship or something like it.

Finally, companies doing business internationally are bound to run into ethical questions. Such is the nature of the world. It is not the problems we face, but our handling of them, that reveals the nature of our character. A motivational video from 1972 was entitled, "You pack your own 'chute." [43] The main character faced her fear of skydiving with the lesson that, when you pack your own parachute, you know it is reliable. Each of us packs our own 'chute, psychologically speaking, every day. Companies pack their own 'chutes too. Through managerial processes of selection, hiring, training, and motivation, companies pack their 'chutes for success. The same applies to ethics. Companies pack their 'chutes with leaders who provide role models, corporate credos, codes of conduct, values statements, development of corporate cultures, reward and punishment systems. Companies instill values and virtues among employees. When the time arrives to make the big jump from the metaphoric plane, or indeed, navigate the tightrope of the international manager, those who have packed their 'chutes are ready to face whatever ethical challenges lie ahead of them.

NOTES

1. Geert Hofstede, *Culture's Consequences* (Thousand Oaks, CA: Sage Publications, 2001), 29.

2. Subodh Varma, "Bhopal Gas Tragedy: Endless Nightmare," *The Times of India*, December 3, 2009.

3. Patrick E. Murphy and Gene R. Laczniak, *Marketing Ethics: Cases and Readings* (Upper Saddle River, NJ: Pearson Education, Inc., 2006), 18–29.

4. Shelby D. Hunt and Scott Vitell, "The General Theory of Marketing Ethics: A Retrospective and Revision," in *Ethics in Marketing*, ed. N. C. Smith and J. A. Quelch (Homewood, IL: Richard D. Irwin, 1991), 775–84.

5. O. C. Ferrell, L. G. Gresham, and J. Fraedrich, "A Synthesis of Ethical Decision Making Models for Marketing," *Journal of Macromarketing* 11 (1989): 55–64.

6. Richard T. DeGeorge, "Ethics in International Business—a Contradiction in Terms?," *Business Credit* (September 2000): 50–52.

7. DeGeorge, "Ethics in International Business—a Contradiction in Terms?," 51.

8. Kathleen Getz, "International Codes of Conduct: An Analysis of Ethical Reasoning," *Journal of Business Ethics* 9 (1990): 567–77.

9. Kathleen Getz, "Trans-ideological Business Values in International Codes of Conduct," *International Journal of Value-Based Management* 8 (1995): 117–34.

10. Thomas Donaldson, *The Ethics of International Business* (New York: Oxford University Press, 1989).

11. United Nations, *United Nations Global Compact*, 2007, http://www.unglobal compact.org/AboutTheGC/index.html.

12. World Commission on Environment and Development, *Our Common Future, Report of the World Commission on Environment and Development*, General Assembly Resolution 42/187 (United Nations, December 11, 1987).

13. The Coca-Cola Company, home page (2009), http://www.thecoca -colacompany.com.

14. John Elkington, "Towards the Sustainable Corporation: Win-win-win Business Strategies for Sustainable Development," *California Management Review* 36 (1994): 90–100.

15. Patrick E. Murphy, Gene R. Laczniak, Norman E. Bowie, and Thomas A. Klein, *Ethical Marketing* (Upper Saddle River, NJ: Pearson Education, Inc., 2005), 214–24.

16. Murphy et al., *Ethical Marketing*, 214–22.

17. Johnson & Johnson, *Corporate Credo* (2009), http://www.jnj.com/connect/about-jnj/jnj-credo/.

18. Caterpillar, *Code of Conduct* (2009), http://www.cat.com/code-of -conduct.

19. Nokia, *Code of Conduct* (2009), http://www.nokia.com/corporate -responsibility/ethics/tools/code-of-conduct.

20. The Coca-Cola Company, *Mission, Vision, and Values* (2009), http://www.thecoca-colacompany.com/ourcompany/mission_vision_values.html.

21. The Walt Disney Company and Affiliated Companies, *Business Standards and Ethics Training* (2009), http://corporate.disney.go.com/corporate/cr_business _standards.html.

22. GE, *GE Citizenship* (2009), http://www.ge.com/citizenship/priorities _engagement/operational_excellent_co.jsp.

23. O. C. Ferrell and Michael D. Hartline, *Marketing Strategy*, 4th ed. (Mason, OH: Thomson Higher Education, 2008), 78–79.

24. United Nations, *United Nations Global Compact*.

25. Donna J. Wood, Jeanne M. Logsdon, Patsy G. Lewellyn, and Kim Davenport, *Global Business Citizenship: A Transformative Framework for Ethics and Sustainable Capitalism* (Armonk, NY: M. E. Sharpe, Inc., 2006).

26. Wood et al., *Global Business Citizenship*.

27. Donna J. Wood, *Business Ethics: Text and Workbook* (Cedar Falls, IA: Woodhaven Press, LLC, 2007).

28. C. K. Prahalad, *The Fortune at the Bottom of the Pyramid* (Upper Saddle River, NJ: Wharton School Publishing, 2005), 4.

29. Paul Collier, *The Bottom Billion* (Oxford: Oxford University Press, 2007).

30. United Nations, *Millennium Development Goals* (2009), http://www.un.org/millenniumgoals/.

31. Prahalad, *The Fortune at the Bottom of the Pyramid*, 48–62.

32. Wood, *Business Ethics: Text and Workbook*, 334.

33. Rasmus Falck, "A Treadle Pump Makes a Difference," *Norwegian American Weekly* (November 13, 2009): 4.

34. Collier, *The Bottom Billion*, 17–74.

35. Ibid., 191.

36. Richard Farmer, "Would You Want Your Granddaughter to Marry a Taiwanese Marketing Man?," *Journal of Marketing* 51 (1987): 111–16.

37. DeGeorge, "Ethics in International Business—a Contradiction in Terms?," 51.

38. United Nations, *Millennium Development Goals*.

39. NationMaster, *Fifth Annual BSA and IDC Global Software Piracy Study* (2010), http://www.nationmaster.com/red/graph/cri_sof_pir_rat-crime -software-piracy-rate.

40. Philip R. Cateora, Mary C. Gilly, and John L. Graham, *International Marketing*, 14th ed. (NewYork: McGraw-Hill/Irwin, 2009), 200.

41. Julia R. Pennington, A. Dwayne Ball, Ronald D. Hampton, and Julia N. Soulakova, "The Cross-National Market in Human Beings," *Journal of Macromarketing* 29 (2009):119–34.

42. William Kilbourne, Pierre McDonagh, and Andrea Prothero, "Sustainable Consumption and the Quality of Life: A Macromarketing Challenge to the Dominant Social Paradigm," *Journal of Macromarketing* 17 (1997): 4–24.

43. Eden Ryl, *You Pack Your Own 'Chute* (Newport Beach, CA: Ramic Productions, 1972).

Chapter 9

The Risk of Adopting Disruptive Technology to Gain Global Competitive Advantage

Nancy Napier, Gary Garrison, and Michael Harvey

INTRODUCTION

Given today's uncertain environment, some managers in global organizations might prefer to avoid risk altogether. Yet, this may in fact be the best time to recognize that risk is likely to be a normal part of the future. As a result, managers should consider which risk makes best sense to pursue. The past year's disconcerting and often shrill general business and news press would have us believe we will face a "new normal," in which organizational success will be tougher and fewer firms will achieve it. Thus, although risk would seem less attractive, forward thinking managers may in fact see risk as a future strategic choice. In this chapter, we discuss an approach to using risk: the decision to adopt disruptive technology as a way to achieve long-term competitive advantage.

THE RISK OF BEING INNOVATIVE AND TECHNOLOGICAL LEADER

Risk is a rather amorphous topic, with different perspectives from various types of researchers and managers. Decision theory researchers view risk as relating to risk and returns: the possibilities and the distribution of outcomes, the probability of each outcome, and the value of each outcome if it occurs.[1] The decision theory bottom line is the link between what a decision maker expects or predicts and the returns on given alternatives. The decision maker will likely assume the expected value of her decision will be positive. Therefore, when managers make technology decisions, the risk is the cost of making the decision relative to the probability of the decision leading to positive outcomes for the decision maker.

A managerial perspective on risk takes into account the context/environment during decision making. Given this, at least three different risk-taking positions exist for global managers: (1) decision makers are optimistic about positive outcomes and thus see risk as relatively low; (2) decision makers think about risk in terms of the probabilities of bad outcomes (i.e., the total number of potential outcomes relative to the chances for a positive outcome); and (3) decision makers consider risk to have several dimensions and frequently refrain from reducing the concept to a single quantifiable construct (i.e., they move beyond either/or decision making).[2] The notion that global managers can take any of three positions relative to technology decisions is consistent with the idea that intrinsic motivational factors tie risk taking to the personality/experience of the decision maker. This may suggest that risk taking is less related to organizational incentives and more related to personal characteristics, such as the propensity to take risk as a personal prerogative. Managerial propensity to take risk may vary across managers based upon incentives and experience as well as context or environments. This makes it difficult to understand how decision makers analyze risk, especially as we move into looking at decision opportunities relative to taking on a new technology.

To understand the possible impact of risk on decisions related to adopting technology, it is important to examine relevant dimensions of risk. At least six dimensions of risk seem critical: (1) willingness to be exposed—how open are managers to considering adoption of a new technology; (2) ability to control the consequences—can global managers reverse or change decisions, if they wish to; (3) time—to what extent can intended benefits occur more rapidly than anticipated or how can an undesirable outcome be postponed; (4) knowledge of risk situations—will global managers will know more about and focus more on positive outcomes, such as keeping what works rather than focusing on potential risks); (5) magnitude of impact—to what extent are technology decisions viewed as having a high probability of small losses rather than low probability of larger losses; and (6) group/individual factors—what norms at the individual, group, and organizational levels exist for accepting perceived risk.[3] Decision making relative to risk is important when the decision pertains to making technology decisions that can affect the organization for the foreseeable future. Further, the risk of selecting the "wrong" technology may be tied directly to the level of disruptiveness of the technology. We discuss that possibility in the following section.

DEFINING DISRUPTIVE TECHNOLOGIES

Disruptive technologies are radically new scientific discoveries that provide organizations the capability or foundation to alter the business environment by destroying the value of existing technical competencies.[4] History highlights many examples of how disruptive technologies, radically superior to existing technologies, have made obsolete the competitive landscape of selected business industries.[5] Compared to existing technologies, disruptive technologies promote a unique value proposition characterized by different product or service characteristics[6] (see Table 9.1). Additionally, they tend to come from small organizations and result in worse performance of existing technology, at least in the early stages of market introduction.[7] However, disruptive technologies provide novel features that their early adopting customers value. Products based on disruptive technologies tend to be less expensive, less complex, smaller and more convenient to use. As they improve overtime, these technologies grow to capture a major share of the established market and alter the competitive landscape.

Table 9.1
Comparison of Sustaining and Disruptive Technology

Sustaining technology	Disruptive technology
Superior performers	Under performers (near-term)
Incremental improvement	Application uncertain
Established market (near-term)	Emerging market
Greater profit margins	Lower profit margins
Exceeds users' abilities	Smaller/Simpler/Easier to use
Greater development expense	Cheaper development expense
Meets existing needs	Value uncertain

Disruptive and sustaining technologies describe different forms of technological innovations. Disruptive technologies represent fundamental changes in technology that become revolutionary innovations signifying clear departures from existing practice.[8] On the other hand, sustaining technologies are incremental adjustments in current technology. Thus, the major difference between the two is the degree of new knowledge embedded in the technology and the risk of introducing a technology that deviates from the present technological orientation.[9] Further, disruptive technologies have different key success factors than sustaining technologies; therefore, managers may differ in their evaluation and adoption of these technologies based on their level of familiarity and experience.

STRATEGIC RISKS ASSOCIATED WITH BEING AN EARLIER ADOPTER OF DISRUPTIVE TECHNOLOGIES

Disruptive technologies continue to reshape the manner in which organizations operate. Thus, the strategic use of information technology is increasingly critical for organizations. Organizations that have succeeded in the transition toward disruptive innovations have ignored the characteristics and capabilities of existing technology and sought to develop new ways to use disruptive technology.[10] In contrast, organizations that were toppled by disruptive technologies accepted the established technology and avoided searching proactively for new ways to create value with the new technology. Essentially, the non-early adopter organizations inappropriately applied a sustaining technology approach in their analysis of the new disruptive technology.

Interestingly, managers can view the same (disruptive) technology in very different opposite ways. Some managers see a potentially disruptive technology as insignificantly small and cannibalistic to their existing information technology infrastructure.[11] Future-oriented managers, however, view the same technology and recognize opportunity for new growth. The two opposing managerial views stem in part from managers' judgment errors in assuming that investing early and aggressively in disruptive technologies is an irrational financial decision. However, managers who understand the principles of disruptive technologies can be extremely effective at managing the most disruptive of innovations.

Increasingly, emergent advances in technology threaten to disrupt established products and markets. This is creating an atmosphere of turmoil and difficult decision-making for managers in global organizations,[12] in industrial and emerging economies alike. However, these potentially disruptive technologies can ultimately provide organizations with enormous global competitive advantages, if they learn how to recognize and use them. Those organizations most capable of exploiting the advantages of disruptive technologies do so by sensing and responding to information as soon as it changes. They then implement aggressive strategic initiatives, such as investing early in disruptive technologies, which will create opportunities for competitive advantage. Thus, predicting the organizational factors that influence the early adoption of disruptive technologies is necessary for organizations' future viability in the digital economy.

Information technology adoption and diffusion research has long tried to predict the factors that lead to its adoption and use.[13] However, research on organizational propensity to be an early adopter of disruptive technologies is scarce. Understanding the factors that influence an organization's likelihood to be an early adopter of disruptive technologies is thus critical to understanding how to turn the adoption into a competitive advantage. We examine next why some organizations have a higher propensity to be early adopters of disruptive technologies than others. More specifically, what organizational factors significantly influence an organization's tendency to be an early adopter of disruptive technology? Finally, how does the early adoption of disruptive technology impact organizational performance, especially in global settings?

Constructing a model of adopters of disruptive technology can help us understand where organizations fall on the range of adoption. In addition, such a model may help us understand future effectiveness of organizational adoption strategies targeting disruptive technologies. We have sought to build a model that combines existing thinking in research while incorporating practical aspects facing managers.

Much discussion in the academic and general press focuses on how long it takes to build and show a sustained competitive advantage. Some argue for a long "calendar time period."[14] Others claim a competitive advantage is sustained when the advantage remains after all efforts to duplicate it have expired.[15] Finally, in terms of technology, a competitive advantage may exist when an organization receives a return on investment that exceeds the industry norm and continues long enough that it alters the nature of its industry's competition.[16]

Several characteristics are common. First, a resource or capability must be valuable. This means it offers the ability to improve an organization's efficiency and effectiveness. Related to this, it could have the ability to exploit opportunities and combat environmental threats. Second, to consider itself a source of competitive advantage, a resource or capability must be heterogeneously distributed within its industry. In other words, a capability is heterogeneous if it is rare, and not simultaneously possessed by many competing or potentially competing organizations.[17] However, if the resource is valuable, but not rare, then it is considered a value-added resource or capability leading to competitive parity. Thus, when a resource or capability is valuable, rare, and not held by many organizations, it can offer at least a temporary source of competitive advantage.

Third, a resource or capability must be imperfectly mobile. This suggests that those organizations lacking a rare and valuable resource or capability cannot easily obtain it. Four criteria describe this characteristic of being imperfectly mobile. First, its historical conditions (place and time the capability was first acquired) make it difficult to move. Second, the resource or capability is causally ambiguous (poorly understood). Third, the resource or capability is socially complex.[18] Finally, a resource or capability must not have strategically equivalent substitutes (a similar resource or capability) that another firm could use to implement similar strategies.[19] In summary, a resource or capability is considered a source of sustained competitive advantage when it is *valuable, rare,* or *heterogeneously distributed* across organizations and *imperfectly mobile*. This also means that other organizations will face a cost disadvantage in developing, obtaining, and implementing strategically equivalent resources or capabilities and are unable to duplicate their benefits. However, not all organizational resources have the potential of becoming sources of sustained competitive advantage.

RESOURCE-BASED VIEW OF THE FIRM AND ITS LINK TO DISRUPTIVE TECHNOLOGY ADOPTION

About 20 years ago, researchers developed an approach to understanding how information technologies provide organizations with opportunities to create sustained competitive advantages. Called the *resource-based view of the firm*, or *RBV*, the approach rests on assumptions, as we suggest previously, that resources that are valuable, rare, and immobile come from an organization's ability to envision, integrate, and exploit new technologies. In addition, the approach assumes that organizations within an industry can gain competitive advantage by using a value-creating strategy not being used by a current or potential competitor. Finally, the RBV approach assumes that a firm can sustain its competitive advantage so long as a current or potential competitor is unable to duplicate the benefits of that value-creating strategy.

The resource-based view suggests that organizational resources fall into three broad types of capital resources: physical, human, or organizational. Physical capital resources include plant(s) and equipment, location, physical technology, and access to raw materials.[20] Human capital resources comprise managerial insight and tacit knowledge (i.e., not easily put into words), experience, social networks, intelligence, and entrepreneurship. Finally, organizational capital resources involve formal reporting structures, informal and formal planning, controlling and coordinating systems, culture, and within organizational networks.[21]

As managers learn how to discover potentially disruptive technologies, process relevant information, and use knowledge in specific situations, those distinct capabilities will likely lead to sustainable competitive advantage.[22] These activities may occur in many locations as firms become more able to use knowledge globally and as technologies develop in various parts of the world. Global managers may in turn proactively develop strategies to exploit opportunities through early adoption and diffusion of disruptive technologies.

Diffusion of Innovations

Diffusion of innovations, particularly with regard to information technology (IT) adoption, has been of interest to managers and researcher for years. The research has focused on the goals for diffusion and predicting which factors lead to the adoption and use of various technologies.[23] Most adoption of technology innovation occurs over time, not as a compulsive act of acquisition. The process usually involves several individuals, each playing a different role in the adoption-decision process. Finally, the adoption of innovation usually requires some adaptation in both the organization and the technology.

One model of the innovation-decision process consists of five stages of decisions or actions, where each stage leads logically to the following stage. In addition, for organizations to use disruptive technologies to their optimal performance levels, they need to integrate the technology in a proactive process, where the technology "fits" the organization's needs.

Physical Capital Resources

So what factors influence organizational adoption of technology or physical capital innovations? Organizational size and slack resources can affect innovation adoption, although research results vary on how size is measured (e.g., number of employees vs. annual sales) and the stage in the adoption process.[24]

Organizational size may be important early in the adoption of disruptive technology because size provides an organization with more opportunities to discover an innovation. For example, recent studies on commercial banks and insurance[25] found that larger organizations tend to adopt technologies more often. This may happen because larger organizations have more people interacting with the external environment,[26] which offers more ways for new information to enter and diffuse within the firm.

Other studies show that in industrialized countries, larger firms tend to adopt technology sooner than smaller firms. This holds across several industries, including numerically controlled technology, software, and database systems.[27] However, one researcher[28] found that smaller organizations are more efficient than larger ones at adopting technologies. This stems in part because, as organizations grow, they may become more structurally rigid, potentially constraining the ability of managers to innovate.[29] Finally, it appears that a firm's network may allow it to receive and disseminate information and knowledge.[30] A larger firm, therefore, should be better able to acquire new information because of its more extensive network.

An organization's slack resources may be another important factor in its willingness to adopt innovation technology. Slack resources give an organization flexibility in terms of financial and human resources so it may avoid outcomes of poor adoption decisions. Slack resources may help encourage creativity and experimentation[31] and adoption of innovation.[32] Such slack resources could also allow the firm to acquire necessary managerial and technical talent to implement an innovation. Therefore, slack resources should give organizations an opportunity to pursue riskier strategies, because it provides a type of buffer against failures.

Given the lack of research, it is difficult to know the impact of slack resources on innovation adoption in firms based in emerging economies. Some may argue that managers in emerging markets will be less willing to adopt new technology that cannibalizes their existing technology, because any innovation in technology is hard to obtain in emerging markets. As a result, a manager may hold onto older technology as long as it is operational, fearing that once it is gone, the replacement may be less effective. Conversely, however, some managers in emerging markets are accustomed to cannibalizing existing technology. When they lack spare parts, they may have an attitude that any technology is better than none and they will "make it work," regardless of what they have.

Research shows that IT can add value to an organization[33] and improve efficiency when management is actively involved in the adoption, use, and/or replacement of technology.[34] However, creating organizational value by increasing efficiencies and lowering costs does not constitute a source of sustained competitive advantage.

One of the first scholars to use the resource-based view to understand how information technology may be a source-sustained competitive advantage, argued that an organization's hardware and software can be duplicated by competing firms. So, these resources alone cannot be sources of sustained competitive advantage. However, the manner in which organizations use IT may enable IT to become a potential source of sustained competitive advantage.[35]

Human Capital Resources

Managerial IT skills could be a source of sustained competitive advantage for many reasons. First, managerial IT skills take years to develop and require much learning through trial and error.[36] Therefore, over the long run, managerial IT skills could be rare and immobile. Second, the IT expertise created and held by a manager could have strategic value to an organization's operational effectiveness.[37] Such tacit knowledge could emerge from many small decisions over time, making IT knowledge difficult to imitate. Finally, many IT managerial skills develop and accumulate through an IT manager's through long-term relationships, both within and out of the firm, making it also a socially complex process and thus hard to replicate by other firms.[38]

IT management skills vary widely. Some examples that could create sustained advantage include an IT manager's ability to: (1) provide new approaches for analyzing a technological innovation; (2) evaluate immediate and future implications of an innovation in terms of its new value networks; (3) envision future organizational needs and possible ways to address these needs; (4) anticipate other stakeholders' needs and be able to develop IT applications for them; (5) create and promote a culture that encourages the creation and diffusion of new ideas throughout an organization; and (6) willingness to cannibalize existing IT infrastructure.

Top management's advocacy of an innovation is critical for at least three reasons. First, it affects decisions regarding allocation of organizational resources to new product development.[39] In particular, top management's advocacy may encourage lower-tiered managers to allocate the necessary resources for sensing and responding to potentially disruptive technologies. Second, such advocacy helps create an entrepreneurial culture within an organization.[40] Finally, their advocacy helps foster technological opportunism,[41] which is important because disruptive technologies may make existing IT obsolete. Therefore, top managers play an important role in the willingness to cannibalize existing IT infrastructure to support new technology.

Organizational Capital Resources

Organizational culture comprises a complex set of values, beliefs, assumptions, and symbols to shape the way an organization conducts business and interacts with its environment. Similarly, organizational culture can be viewed as a system of shared beliefs and values that mold the organization's structure and its members' actions to produce behavioral norms.[42] For organizational culture to be a source of sustained competitive advantage, it must meet three conditions. First, a culture must create an environment that encourages the conception and dissemination of new ideas throughout the organization. This means the culture does not penalize managers for failing when they try to add value (e.g., financial and image) to the organization. Second, an organization's culture must be heterogeneously distributed across other organizations within its industry. In other words, the culture's attributes and performance enhancing characteristics must be rare. Third, a culture must be imperfectly mobile, in that other organizations cannot duplicate its benefits and/or face a cost disadvantage in developing, obtaining, and implementing a strategically equivalent culture.

Research suggests organizational culture can be a source of sustained competitive advantage, especially if it can exploit value-creating opportunities resulting from uncertainty in its external environment. Ouchi argued that cultures provide organizations the flexibility to perform various value-added functions that would be difficult for competitors without such a culture.[43] However, not all organizational cultures, even when they encourage potentially value-added activities, have positive effects on organizational performance. In fact, some scholars[44] argue that sometimes an organization's culture can reduce a firm's effectiveness.

A culture may, for example, prevent managers from seeing competitive and operational options or even from choosing the best option to meet its operational and competitive needs.

An organization's culture helps to shape how its members interpret problems and view the competitive environment. For instance, an entrepreneurial culture promotes risk taking, tolerates failure, is future-oriented, and encourages continuous change and seeking of opportunities.[45] Others suggest entrepreneurial cultures actively search for information. Therefore, such organizations should be better informed about potentially disruptive technologies than organizations that are more centrally or hierarchically structured.[46] Additionally, an entrepreneurial culture would encourage organizational members to search for opportunities in uncertain business environments and then determine the capabilities needed to successfully exploit them.[47] Such has been the case with organizations that have succeeded in the face of disruptive innovations.

An organization's culture may also influence the firm's willingness to cannibalize its existing technology/IT infrastructure. Cannibalizing decisions are often more difficult because of their complexity and the changes required to fully optimize a disruptive innovation. However, entrepreneurial organizations that proactively monitor their environments should be better able to assess how disruptive technologies may help or hurt them. As a result, they should be more willing to cannibalize. In contrast, more hierarchically/centrally structured cultures may be less willing to cannibalize, because these innovations usually require changes in existing organizational routines, markets, and IT infrastructure. Because such changes require enormous switching costs,[48] employees may resist, making it harder to adopt new innovations.

Technological opportunism gives a firm the capability to sense and respond to new technologies. Those technologies can, in turn, create sources of competitive advantage.[49] So firms that are technologically opportunistic proactively search for innovations by exploring technologies they see as potential opportunities or threats to their competitive posture. Further, managers aware of potentially disruptive technologies would be more apt to press for change within their organization, possibly giving their firm a better chance to respond properly to environmental shifts. Therefore, technologically opportunistic organizations may be more willing to cannibalize existing IT to invest in and adopt sooner disruptive technologies, if they view the innovation as a potential source of competitive advantage.

Willingness to Cannibalize

Willingness to cannibalize is the extent to which an organization is prepared to reduce the actual or potential value of its existing technology in favor of new technology. Disruptive technologies have the potential to destroy core competencies and make obsolete a firm's long-term costly investments. Therefore, in times of disruption, successful organizations tend to be more willing to cannibalize their investments than unsuccessful ones. Willingness to cannibalize permeates top management's attitude and the organization's culture and thus may increase a firm's propensity to be an early adopter of disruptive technology.

Cannibalization is one way organizations can reduce the actual or potential value of their invested resources. Organizational resources can include tangible resources, such as IT hardware and software or intangible resources, such as tacit knowledge, expertise, and standard operating procedures.[50] These routines develop over time as operational efficiency, but may become irrelevant if the firm adopts a disruptive technology. Therefore, future competitive advantage may rest with management's willingness to cannibalize existing resources to adopt a disruptive technology, particularly at an early stage.

For more than a decade, researchers have examined the relationship between information technology and organizational performance. Often, researchers have employed a resource-based view of the firm to broaden our understanding of the impact IT on business value and organizational performance.[51] To date, however, no universal measure or financial metric exists to analyze the impact IT has on organizational performance. In fact, researchers have used numerous approaches to assess organizational performance and various methodologies at multiple levels of analysis.[52] When traditional accounting metrics and measures falter because they are ineffective and unnecessary, researchers have turned to a range of measures associated with operational efficiency. They include, for example, time-to-market and customer satisfaction, cost reduction, revenue enhancement, competitive advantage, return on assets, market share, and sales growth. Others also claim that perceptual measures should be added to financial and usage metrics.[53]

Although IT appears to have a positive impact on organizational performance, it is unlikely that greater IT investment alone will guarantee superior organizational performance.[54] Also, organizational structure and technology need to change during an innovation-decision process.

Previous research has mostly looked at the impact sustaining technologies have on organizational performance, rather than on disruptive technologies. In fact, early adoption of disruptive technologies can result in worse organizational performance, at least in the short term.[55] Still, as these technologies become more main stream, early adopting organizations realize their wealth creating potential and become industry leaders.

DIFFUSION OF INNOVATIONS AND STAGES OF ADOPTING RISKY DISRUPTIVE TECHNOLOGY

Diffusion of innovations has been studied by researchers in many fields, including sociology, marketing and consumer behavior, geography, economics, and management information systems (MIS). Most studies look at the simple adopt/reject dichotomy as the outcome. The principle drivers examined in the past include an innovation's characteristics and the chronology of the innovation process. In sum, the research classifies organizations in terms of when they adopt an innovation and implement it into their daily routines, in other words "are they early or late adopters" and what characteristics might be common across firms by stage of adoption.[56] There are five accepted adopter categories and the approximate percentage of organizations in each category. They include: (1) innovators (2.5%), (2) early adopters (13.5%), (3) early majority (34%), (4) late majority (34%), and (5) Laggards (16%) (Rogers, 1995). This classification system is not exhaustive as non-adopters are excluded from the list of categories; however, the five categories of adoption are mutually exclusive.

Innovators—the first to adopt an innovation—tend to have greater slack resources that allow them to better absorb the possible loss from unprofitable adoption. They are better able to comprehend and apply complex technical knowledge that allows them to cope with an innovation's high degree of uncertainty throughout the adoption process. Further, innovators play a crucial role in the diffusion process because they knowingly or unknowingly diffuse information about the innovation throughout their system. Organizational culture may play a crucial role in terms of an organization adopter category, as innovators tend to proactively seek information about innovations and new ways to implement them.

Early adopters tend to be more embedded within a social system than innovators and are prone to leadership opinions when making an adoption decision. Because most early adopters are highly respected within their social system and are known to make shrewd decisions, they tend to reduce uncertainty for other potential adopters, who watch their moves closely. Thus, early adopters act as change agents for catalyzing the diffusion process; as they provide potential adopters with much needed information about an innovation.

Early-majority adopters make up the largest adopter category with roughly one-third of the adopters belonging to this category. Early-majority adopters tend to adopt an innovation right before the average member of a system, and provide a vital link in the diffusion process. They spend more time in the innovation decision-making process than innovators and early adopters. Early-majority adopters tend to take on a follower's strategy as they are more risk averse than the innovators and early adopters.

Late-majority adopters, also a large category, differ from early-majority adopters in that these organizations adopt innovations just after the average organization within their industry. Adoption is a reactive measure, rather than as a proactive move to maintain viability. Late-majority adopters approach an innovation with great uncertainty; also, their slack resources are scarce compared to those organizations in the preceding categories. Therefore, they adopt after their counterparts more as a means of uncertainty reduction.

Laggards make up the final innovation adoption category. They tend to be isolated from their social system and lack opinion leadership. Laggards rely mostly on their past actions as a means of survival and interact primarily with other organizations with similarly conservative cultures. Laggards' innovation decision process takes longer than any other group: they must be positive that a new innovation will be successful because they do not have the slack resources to combat failure.

Within the field of MIS, information technology adoption and diffusion research has been inspired by the motivation to predict what influences its adoption and use.[57] The impetus of these studies is how IT adoption is influenced by a potential users' perception of the innovation. The objective of diffusion of innovations is to predict patterns of innovation adoption over time based on the innovation attributes that influence its diffusion and the categorization of adopters having dissimilar characteristics.[58] To more clearly understand diffusion of innovations it is important to identify and define the two important terms underlying the theory. First, diffusion is the timely process of communicating an innovation among members of a social network. It is a type of communication. It also involves some uncertainty that implies poor predictability of structure and information. Second, an innovation is a physical object, an idea, or practice that is perceived to be new by an individual or organization. The technological aspect of an information technology innovation usually has two components: (1) Hardware, comprised of the tool that personifies the technology (e.g., processors, hard drive, etc.) and (2) software, comprised of the information base for the tool (e.g., code, programs, operating system that allows individuals to use the tool). The software component is usually less visible than the hardware component. Therefore, a technology comprised of only a software component has a slower rate of diffusion; as the degree of uncertainty reduction is greatly decreased along with the degree of benefit (Rogers, 1995).

SUMMARY/CONCLUSION

Managers in organizations willing to consider and use information technology as a global competitive advantage must be willing to "think differently" than they traditionally have. The main changes include recognition that existing technology and IT can be a competitive advantage, the ability to act entrepreneurially, and the willingness to cannibalize existing technology and infrastructure to develop and maintain that competitive advantage, and finally, the understanding of and decision of when/how to adopt and diffuse technology within the organization.

Taking risks appears to be one of the means to be competitive in the global marketplace. The adoption of disruptive technology by firms attempt to gain a competitive advantage appears to be on the increase, particularly in the IT arena. The problem with this strategy is there will be strategic winners as well as losers. The focus is on how to win rather than what to do with the disruptive technology is just that, disruptive. Can the risk taking have a deleterious impact of the entire company to the point that recovery and/or sustainability is in question. There needs to be additional research on the overall impact on risk taking under the guise of gaining global competitive advantage.

NOTES

1. J. Pratt, "Risk Aversion in the Small and in the Large," *Econometrica* 32 (1964): 122–36; J. March and Z. Shapira, "Managerial Perspectives on Risk and Risk Taking," *Management Science* 33, no. 11 (1987): 1404–18.

2. K. MacCrimmon and D. Wehrung, *Taking Risk: The Management of Uncertainty* (New York: Free Press, 1986).

3. I. Baird and H. Thomas, "Toward a Contingency Model of Strategic Risk Taking," *Academy of Management Review* 10, no. 2 (1985): 230–43; F. Gluck, S. Kaufman, and H. Walleck, "Strategic Management for Competitive Advantage," *Harvard Business Review* 58, no. 4 (1980): 154–61.

4. W. Abernathy and C. Clark, "Innovation: "Mapping the Winds of Creative Destruction," *Research Policy* 14, no. 1 (1985): 3–22; P. Anderson and M. Tushman, "Technological Discontinuities and Dominant Designs: A Cyclical Model of Technological Change," *Administrative Science Quarterly* 35, no. 6 (1990): 604–33; J. Bower and C. Christensen, "Disruptive Technologies: Catching the Wave," *Harvard Business Review* 73, no. 1 (1995): 43–53.

5. C. Christiensen, "Strategy and Innovation: Breakthrough Insight and Ideas for Driving Growth," *A Newsletter from Harvard Business School Publishing and Insight* 1, no. 2 (July–August 2003): 1–4; J. Utterback, *Mastering the Dynamics of Innovation* (Boston: Harvard Business School Press, 1994).

6. C. Charitou and C. Markides, "Responses to Disruptive Strategic Innovation," *MIT Sloan Management Review*, 44, no. 2 (Winter 2003): 55–64.

7. C. Christensen, *The Innovators Dilemma: When New Technologies Cause Great Firms to Fail* (Boston, MA: Harvard Business School Press, 1997).

8. T. Duchesneau, S. Cohn, and J. Dutton, *A Study of Innovation in Manufacturing, Determination Processes and Methodological Issues* (Orono, ME: Social Science Research Institute, University of Maine, 1979), 1.

9. R. D. Dewar and J. E. Dutton, "The Adoption of Radical and Incremental Innovations: An Experimental Analysis," *Management Science* 32 (November 1986): 1422–33.

10. C. Christensen, *The Innovators Dilemma: When New Technologies Cause Great Firms to Fail* (Boston, MA: Harvard Business School Press, 1997).

11. Christiensen, "Strategy and Innovation: Breakthrough Insight and Ideas for Driving Growth," 1–4.

12. J. Borck, "Dawn of Disruption," *InfoWorld*, January 7, 2002, 38.

13. R. Thompson and G. Rose, "Information Technology Adoption and Use," in *Proceedings of the Administrative Sciences Association of Canada (ASAC) Annual Conference* (1994), 16–26.

14. M. Porter, *Competitive Advantage* (New York: Free Press, 1985).

15. J. Barney, "Firm Resources and Sustained Competitive Advantage," *Journal of Management* 17, no. 1 (1991): 99–120; R. Rumelt, "Towards a Strategic Theory of the Firm," in *Competitive Strategic Management*, ed. R. B. Lamb (Englewood Cliffs, NJ: Prentice Hall, 1984), 566–70.

16. W. Kettinger, V. Grover, S. Guha, and A. Segars, "Strategic Information Systems Revisited: A Study in Sustainability and Performance," *MIS Quarterly* 18, no. 1 (March 1994): 31–58.

17. D. Hambrick, "Top Management Teams: Key to Strategic Success," *California Management Review* 30 (1987): 88–108.

18. I. Dierickx and K. Cool, "Asset Stock Accumulation and Sustainable Competitive Advantage," *Management Science* 35, no. 6 (1989): 1504–11.

19. J. Barney, "Firm Resources and Sustained Competitive Advantage," *Journal of Management*, 17, no. 1 (1991): 99–120.

20. O. Williamson, *Markets and Hierarchies, Analysis and Antitrust Implications: A Study in the Economics of Internal Organization* (New York: The Free Press, 1975).

21. G. Becker, *Human Capital* (New York: Columbia, 1964); J. Tomer, *Organizational Capital: The Path to Higher Productivity and Well-Being* (New York: Praeger, 1987).

22. M. Peteraf, "The Cornerstones of Competitive Advantage: A Resource-Based View," *Strategic Management Journal* 14, no. 3 (1993): 179–91.

23. R. Cooper and R. Zmud, "Information Technology Implementation Research: A Technological Diffusion Approach," *Management Science* 36 (1990): 123–39; E. Rogers, *Diffusion of Innovations*, 3rd ed. (New York: The Free Press, 1983); E. Rogers, *Diffusion of Innovations*, 4th ed. (New York: The Free Press, 1995).

24. F. Damanpour, "Organizational Innovation: A Meta-Analysis of Effects of Determinants and Moderators," *Academy of Management Journal* 13 (1991): 555–90; F. Damanpour, "Organizational Size and Innovations," *Innovation Studies* 13 (1992): 375–402; P. Nystrom, K. Ramamurthy, and A. Wilson, "Organizational Context, Climate and Innovativeness: Adoption of Imaging Technology," *Journal of Engineering and Technology Management* 19 (2002): 221–47.

25. S. Gopalakrishan and F. Damanpour, "The Impact of Organizational Context on Innovation Adoption in Commercial Banks," *IEEE Transactions on Engineering Management* 47 (2000): 14–25; M. Liberatore and D. Breem, "Adoption and Implementation of Digital-Imaging Technology in the Banking and Insurance Industries," *IEEE Transactions on Engineering Management* 44 (1997): 367–77.

26. M. Tushman, "Special Boundary Roles in the Innovation Process," *Administrative Science Quarterly* 22 (1977): 587–605.

27. S. Globerman, "Technological Diffusion in the Canadian Tool and Die Industry," *Review of Economics and Statistics* 57 (November 1975): 428–34; A. Romeo, "Inter-Industry and Inter-Firm Differences in the Rate of Diffusion of Technological Innovation," *Review of Economics and Statistics* 5 (1975): 311–19; R. Zmud "Design Alternatives for Organizing Information Systems Activities," *MIS Quarterly* 8 (1984) 79–93; L. Ball, I. Dambolena, and H. Hennessey, "Identifying Early Adopters of Large Software Systems," *Data Base* 19 (1987): 21–27.

28. R. Yeaple, "Why Are Small R&D Organizations More Productive?," *IEEE Transactions on Engineering Management* 39 (1992): 332–46.

29. D. DeTienne and C. Koberg, "The Impact of Environmental and Organizational Factors on Discontinuous Innovation within High-Technology

Industries," *IEEE Transactions on Engineering Management* 49, no. 4 (November 2002): 352–64.

30. H. Ibarra, "Network Centrality, Power and Innovation Involvement: Determinants of Technical and Administrative Roles," *Academy of Management Journal* 36 (1993): 471–501; H. Scarbrough, "Introduction," in *The Management of Expertise*, ed. H. Scarbrough (London: MacMillian, 1996), 1–6; M. Kelley and S. Helper, "Firm Size and Capabilities, Regional Agglomeration, and the Adoption of New Technology," *Economic Innovations and New Technology* 8 (1999): 79–103.

31. A. Meyer, "Adapting to Environmental Jolts," *Administrative Science Quarterly* 27 (1982): 515–37; M. Rosner, "Economic Determinants of Organizational Innovation," *Administrative Science Quarterly* 12 (1968): 614–25.

32. R. Cyert and J. March, *A Behavioral Theory of the Firm* (Englewood Cliffs, NJ: Prentice-Hall, 1963).

33. F. Mata, W. Fuerst, and J. Barney, "Information Technology and Sustained Competitive Advantage: A Resource-Based Analysis," *MIS Quarterly* 19, no. 4 (December 1995): 487–505; R. Santhanam and E. Hartono, "Issues in Linking Information Technology Capability to Firm Performance," *MIS Quarterly* 27, no. 1 (March 2003): 125–53.

34. J. Allen, "The Selective Adoption of Information Systems: Assessing Practicality, Trustworthiness, and Fairness," in *Facilitating Technology Transfer through Partnership*, ed. Tom McMaster, Enid Mumford, E. Burton Swanson, Brian Warboys, and David Wastell (London: Chapman and Hall Publishers, 1997), 145–60; R. Cooper and R. Zmud, "Information Technology Implementation Research: A Technological Diffusion Approach," *Management Science* 36 (1990): 123–39.

35. E. Clemons, "Corporate Strategies for Information Technology: A Resource-Based Approach," *Computer* 24, no. 11 (November 1991): 23–32.

36. R. Katz, "Skills of an Effective Administrator," *Harvard Business Review* 52, no. 5 (September–October 1994): 90–102.

37. R. Grant, "Toward a Knowledge-Based Theory of the Firm," *Strategic Management Journal* 17 (Winter 1996): 109–22.

38. Mata, Fuerst, and Barney, "Information Technology and Sustained Competitive Advantage: A Resource-Based Analysis," 487–505.

39. C. Christensen, *The Innovators Dilemma: When New Technologies Cause Great Firms to Fail*; J. Howell and C. Higgins, "Champions of Technological Innovation," *Administrative Science Quarterly* 35 (June 1990): 317–41.

40. D. Ireland, M. Hitt, and D. Sirmon, "A Model of Strategic Entrepreneurship: The Construct and Its Dimensions," *Journal of Management* 29, no. 6 (2003): 963–89.

41. R. Srinivasan, G. Lilien, and A. Rangaswamy, "Technological Opportunism and Radical Technology Adoption: An Application to E-Business," *Journal of Marketing* 66, no. 3 (July 2002): 47–60.

42. J. Barney, "Organizational Culture: Can It Be a Source of Sustained Competitive Advantage?" *Academy of Management Review* 11, no. 3 (1986): 656–65;

G. Dess and J. Picken, *Beyond Productivity: How Leading Companies Achieve Superior Performance by Leveraging Their Human Capital* (New York: AMACOM, 1999).

43. W. Ouchi, *Theory Z* (Reading, MA: Addison-Wesley, 1981).

44. M. Porter, *Competitive Strategy* (New York: Free Press, 1980); N. Tichy, *Managing Strategic Change: Technical, Political, and Cultural Dynamics* (New York: Wiley, 1983).

45. L. Johnson, "The Organizational Identity Trap," *MIT Sloan Management Review* 43, no. 4 (2002).

46. Srinivasan, Lilien, and Rangaswamy, "Technological Opportunism and Radical Technology Adoption: An Application to E-Business," 47–60.

47. J. Covin and D. Slevin, "The Entrepreneurial Imperatives of Strategic Leadership," in *Strategic Entrepreneurship: Creating a New Mindset*, ed. M. Hitt, R. Ireland, S. Camp, and D. Sexton (Oxford: Blackwell Publishers, 2002), 309–27; R. McGrath and I. MacMillan, *The Entrepreneurial Mindset* (Boston, MA: Harvard Business School Press, 2000).

48. R. Chandy and G. Tellis, "Organizing for Radical Innovation: The Overlooked Role of Willingness to Cannibalize," *Journal of Marketing Research* 35 (November 1998): 474–87.

49. Srinivasan, Lilien, and Rangaswamy, "Technological Opportunism and Radical Technology Adoption: An Application to E-Business," 47–60.

50. R. Grant, "Toward a Knowledge-Based Theory of the Firm," 109–22; R. Henderson and K. Clark, "Architectural Innovation: The Reconfiguration of Existing Product Technologies and the Failure of Established Firms," *Administrative Science Quarterly* 35 (January 1990): 9–30.

51. A. S. Bharadwaj, "A Resource-Based Perspective on Information Technology Capability and Firm Performance: An Empirical Investigation," *MIS Quarterly* 24, no. 1 (2000): 169–96; E. Clemons, "Corporate Strategies for Information Technology: A Resource-Based Approach," *Computer* 24, no. 11 (November 1991): 23–32; R. Santhanam and E. Hartono, "Issues in Linking Information Technology Capability to Firm Performance," *MIS Quarterly* 27, no. 1 (March 2003): 125–53.

52. M. Nigel, K. Kraemer, and V. Gurbaxani, "Review: Information Technology and Organizational Performance: An Integrative Model of IT Business Value," *MIS Quarterly* 28, no. 2 (2004): 283–322.

53. J. E. Maglitta, "Beyond ROI," *Computer World* 31, no. 43 (October 1997): 73–78; S. Devaraj and R. Kohli, "Information Technology Payoff in the Health-Care Industry: A Longitudinal Study," *Journal of Management Information Systems* 16, no. 4 (2000): 41–67; Nigel, Kraemer, and Gurbaxani, "Review: Information Technology and Organizational Performance: An Integrative Model of IT Business Value," 283–322; J. Lee and U. Bose, "Operational Linkage between Diverse Dimensions of Information Technology Investments and Multifaceted Aspects of a Firm's Economic Performance," *Journal of Information Technology* 17 (2002): 119–31; P. P. Tallon, K. L. Kraemer, and V. Gurbaxani, "Executives' Perceptions

of the Business Value of Information Technology: A Process-Oriented Approach," *Journal of Management Information Systems* 16, no. 4 (2000): 145–73.

54. E. Brynjolfsson and L. Hitt, "Paradox Lost? Firm Level Evidence on the Returns to Information Systems Spending," *Management Science* 42, no. 4 (1996): 541–58; R. Kohli and S. Devaraj, "Measuring Information Technology Payoff: A Meta-Analysis of Structural Variables in Firm-Level Empirical Research," *Information Systems Research* 14, no. 2 (2003): 127–45.

55. C. Christensen, *The Innovators Dilemma: When New Technologies Cause Great Firms to Fail.*

56. Rogers, *Diffusion of Innovations*; L. Brown, *Innovation Diffusion: A New Perspective* (London: Methuen, 1981); P. Stoneman, "Technological Diffusion: The Viewpoint of Economic Theory," *Richerche Economiche* 40 (1986): 585–606; R. Wolfe, "Organizational Innovation: Review, Critique and Suggested Research Directions," *Journal of Management* 5, no. 3 (1994): 221–40.

57. R. Cooper and R. Zmud, "Information Technology Implementation Research: A Technological Diffusion Approach," *Management Science* 36 (1990): 123–39; Thompson and Rose, "Information Technology Adoption and Use," 16–26.

58. Rogers, *Diffusion of Innovations*.

Chapter 10

Terrorism: Vulnerability and Risk

Llewellyn D. Howell

TERRORISM: WHERE DID IT COME FROM?

There is no war on terrorism. Let's start there. There is a war with radical Islamists. They use terrorist tactics. Underlying the conflict between a state, the United States, and an organization, Al Qaeda, is a culture war that will not be resolved in a generation or probably more. We—in the United States—are not yet addressing it.

There are two sides in this conflict. From the American side, we are trying to kill individual members of Al Qaeda and their associate organizations. From their side, they are trying to destroy the American system. Al Qaeda's goals are strategic. American goals are tactical. Even though the United States is employing nonconventional tactics in its fight against Al Qaeda in Pakistan, Afghanistan, Somalia, and Yemen, its primary goals are still to kill the enemy. Al Qaeda wants to kill America, its culture, its social fabric, and especially its economic system.

The bombings of the U.S. embassies in Kenya and Tanzania 1988 were not new events for Americans nor were they the most proximate instances of terrorism that the United States has encountered. The surprise for all was the rapid and extra-legal response by Washington. For the first time, the United States had entered into the simmering war against Islamic terrorists with a response in kind.

The missile responses against terrorist-linked facilities in Sudan and Afghanistan were thought of by many as somehow "uncivilized." There was no warning. These military attacks were undertaken without submitting them to the formal American processes of war-making. Sovereign territory was invaded without regard to consideration of the nations involved.

The rules of war have been undergoing a process of degradation since World War II. As war has shifted from being between nations to being conflicts within nations and between ethnic, racial, cultural, and religious groups, the enforcers of the rules of war—national governments and international organizations—have been powerless to intervene. The rules have fallen one by one.

Weapons with field testing (or actual use) include chemical and biological agents. Civilian women are the explicit targets of rape and sexual molestation as has been highlighted by recent events in the Congo, with the clear intent of destruction of cultures and their will to fight on. Captured soldiers and even civilians are subject to mass execution and burial in unmarked graves, lost forever to families and societies.

Terrorism is merely the downward linear extension of such conduct. It is indeed a degradation as relations among human beings deteriorate in an inexorable regression toward the primitive.

Military historians often note the argument of Prussian Gen. Carl von Clausewitz, who, in his three-volume On War (1911), contended that "war is . . . a continuation of policy by other means. It is not merely a political act, but a real political instrument, a continuation of political intercourse, a conduct of political intercourse by other means." I would argue the opposite, as English philosopher Thomas Hobbes did more than four centuries ago, that the primitive and natural state of man is violence. Government and the rule of law is the civilizing veneer, the more "developed" state of man. War is not a "continuation of political intercourse," but, rather, a falling back from political acts to acts of base violence. The use of terrorism is, in this line of thinking, a further falling back to even rawer instincts.

Four factors in the nature of human life seem to offer themselves most prominently to explain the expansion of terrorism: rising population; increasing disparities in wealth and benefits; the expansion of religious extremism; and increased technology and knowledge of it. The first three are related to the perception of threat.

Despite arguments that the Earth can handle even larger populations, this is not apparent to most humans who find their available space diminishing. A simple formula explains the perception: More people, less space per person; more interactions, more opportunities for conflict; more conflict, more preparation for conflict. Poet Robert Frost observed the basic human sentiment, without necessarily agreeing with it, that "good fences make good neighbors." As populations have grown, sufficient numbers of fences have become impossible to build. The intrusion of too many neighbors competing for a limited number of resources has produced anxiety that leads to striking out, sometimes in the form of terrorist activity.

Another important function derived from population growth is a mathematical opportunity outcome. It takes just one person to make and carry a bomb into a crowded terminal. The more people there are, the more likely it is there will be one willing to do it. Still just one. The larger the population, the greater the opportunity to resort to the primal behavior that is terrorism.

Population growth is almost always seen, even in its threat form, as arithmetic. However, in the terms that we need to understand for dealing with terrorism, population growth has to be seen as exponential. Two people compose a dyad with two relationships. Add a third person and there are now six relationships. Add a fourth person and there are now 12 relationships. It is this ever-expanding number of relationships among human beings that is of concern rather than civil population expansion. In a population of four people, one person has the possibility of impacting 12 interactions. Within a population 6 billion, one person has the possibility of impacting trillions (Impact = $n (n-1)$). The point is that with small or large populations it still only takes one to set it afire.

Partly because of increasing populations, but also because of variance in culture and capabilities, there is a widening disparity between the developed and less-developed worlds, and increasing disparities even within societies—like in the United States The rich are getting richer and the poor poorer. This was especially so during the Bush administration and after tax decreases for the wealthiest segment of the American population. While it may be possible to reverse this trend, growing populations and resistance from the "haves" (however it is argued) have exacerbated the problem. With the classical demonstration effect from development economics magnified by access to television, videos, cell phones and iPhones, Blackberries, Facebook, and the Internet, disparities and awareness of them will continue to expand. Whatever the have-nots deserve, some of them are likely to strike out to obtain the gold at the end of the rainbow.

If rapid population growth, especially in the developing world, depletes resources relatively and the economic system is one that has left many impoverished without hope, fundamentalist, extremist, and radical religion offers an opportunity for escape. Fundamentalist religion became a much more common recourse in the late 20th century, and it is the organizing influence behind most terrorism. This includes fundamentalist radicals among Muslims and Christians, Hindus and Jews, Buddhists and animists. As the ranks of radical fundamentalists swell, more potential terrorists will emerge with the belief that their sacrifices will be rewarded in heaven, and the numbers of terrorists will increase.

Thus, there is a rising number of potential terrorist agents, with a growing number of perceived threats, greater unhappiness about the distribution of health and wealth, and further theological justification for acting in a violent manner. Add to this mix greater knowledge of the means of destruction. Technology has added not only the means of learning how to create such weapons, but the means of movement on a global basis such that terrorists can strike anywhere.

How do we protect ourselves against terrorists? It isn't by killing a few of them, although that might be a temporary deterrence for those who remain. It isn't by stooping to the lowest common denominator in tactical violence. Ultimately, it has to be by addressing the sources of terrorism, rather than just the symptoms. The sources lie in the human condition, not in the attributes of the few.

THE 21st CENTURY WAR: TERRORISM

It was a new world with many corners turned at the onset of a new millennium in 2001. Among the most critical of corners was in the conduct of war.

The major changes in the conduct of war haven't been linked with particular counts of years, whether millennia or centuries. Firing from cover was a monumental change in tactic for Western armies that arose in the mid-18th century following encounters with savages in the colonies. American revolutionaries were seen as terrorists. Armored ships and vehicles entered the war picture a century later in the American Civil War. In the mid-20th century, atomic weapons intruded on the primitiveness of human fighting by initiating the use of mass destruction in international conduct.

Now, however, the fast pace of technological change, an increasing level of knowledge in every imaginable party and group, easy access across borders made more porous for the purpose of international trade and investment, and a rapidly increasing global population combine to shift not only the tactics and strategies but also the very nature of war itself. The weapons of choice have now become airliners, backpack bombs (or underwear), computer viruses and cyber theft, biological viruses, and chemicals delivered in the mail. Military units are no longer divisions and battalions but are instead teams of two or ten. Terrorism is another stage of war.

Armies were needed not only to wield the weapons of war but also to occupy the land of the enemy, like the Germans occupied much of Europe for a time or the Japanese occupied China and Korea. Modern war won't involve occupation. Americans will never occupy China or Russia and no one will occupy America. The United States couldn't occupy Vietnam and NATO forces can't really occupy Kosovo or Afghanistan, even with a mostly friendly and appreciative population. An army of occupiers is no longer the name of the game. The game is now the dramatic explosion or chemical attack that generates fear and destroys economic functions. The objective is no longer to kill or capture or bring down the government but instead is to undermine, panic, hinder, or get simple revenge.

The shift to terrorism as the means of conducting war for the 21st century poses a dramatic problem for which we are still unprepared. The key issue is defense. A war by a country's armed forces can be responded to by another country's armed forces. There is a matching of military power measured in men, weapons, and technology. How is an act of terror to be matched? More importantly, how is it to be prevented? The best defense for the moment seems to be the errors and simple clumsiness of the terrorists themselves.

The origins of conventional war were always in governments. In the 21st century, even individuals can wage war but the most frequent use has been by small groups, whose power is multiplied exponentially by the change in the nature of weapons. But their power also lies in the lack of a defense. Armies, no matter how well trained or equipped, can't search every truck, car, and individual crossing the border into the United States let alone cordon off the vast stretches of American border that are open and untended.

Most critical, on the defensive side, is that modern states cannot apply the old aphorism that "the best defense is a good offense." The enemy of the state could be any one of six billion individuals. The nationality, sex, color, or religion of the enemy can never be consistently known, although Muslims, Arabs, the unshaven, and others are profiled. Governments sometimes directly back terrorists but often not, out of concern that the weapons of terrorism could be turned on them.

Given the wide and increasing availability of the weapons of terrorism, the critical variable in defense is determining *intent*. The key ingredients in Timothy McVeigh's bombing of the federal building in Oklahoma were low-tech ammonium nitrate and a rental truck. These are the weapons of modern war. What made them weapons was what was in Timothy McVeigh's mind. The U.S.S. *Cole* was heavily damaged and nearly sunk and 17 Americans were killed by two men in a small boat who seemed friendly until the moment of impact. What were their beliefs that allowed them to sacrifice their lives?

There has been greatly increased attention to defense in the United States against terrorism over the three decades since the American embassy was seized in Tehran. Training in counter-terrorism by government agencies and even businesses has expanded greatly in recent years. Counter-terrorism measures (our defense) include the sensitive acts of infiltration, interception of mail and phone calls, and the sharing of information about the characteristics and behaviors of profiled individuals and groups. Even local police forces in the United States are training and preparing for the worst terrorist catastrophes.

The trends in the impact of terrorism are not heartening. A study in the *Journal of Conflict Resolution* by Walter Enders and Todd Sandler showed convincingly that although the numbers of terrorist incidents have declined (not counting incidents in Iraq and Afghanistan), those that are still occurring are even more deadly. Each incident is now much more likely to result in death or injury than those of the 1980s, more than making up for the decline in occurrences.[1]

They also note that there has been a dramatic shift from politically based acts to religious-based terrorism. The origins of this phenomenon are not in easily identified governments and nation-states but are instead in group ideologies, cult beliefs, and religious dogma. Targets of terrorists, usually shifting away from defended facilities and secure installations, have become office buildings, market places, power plants, and transportation facilities. The objective in this altered form of modern war is not conquest or change of government. It is simple terror aimed at social conflagration, economic destabilization, or simple religious merit on behalf of a cause.

For American political or military leadership, the question of the nature of a defense for a new form of war for a new century is key. Should the focus of a defense strategy and budget be on conventional war-fighting power, anti-ballistic missile capability, electronic warfare in space, or detecting and disrupting intent and capability of groups and individuals who focus on killing of civilians, instilling fear, and creating chaos? The forces of economy and familiarity drive governmental strategies toward technology and raw power, while the real threat and vulnerability lies in the hearts and minds of men.

SAMUEL HUNTINGTON's "CLASH OF CIVILIZATIONS"

The first decade of the 21st century has been filled with fear. Even in that context, we still need to be able to sit back and reason a bit to be able to understand the origins of the terrorist attacks on September 11, to in turn be able to respond to them meaningfully. We need to choose a paradigm to structure causality, to then select a response. As in medicine, the sequence is theory, diagnosis, prescription. The tool has to be the correct one for the task. And an excellent theory with no prescription is worthless.

Broad categories of theories and diagnoses were dispersed in the news and social science analyses in the aftermath of the attacks. They range from the simple to the complex and are often intermingled. One was the sentiment that the attacks were an act of "evil." This thought was persistently employed throughout the Bush administration. By ascribing the deeds to the existence of evil in the world, we also incapacitate ourselves since this explanation requires calling upon a deity or religious resources to expunge the source of the problem. Another is to argue that the terrorists are "nihilists" out to destroy all of humanity. Like anarchists, whose acts are in themselves the objectives, nihilism can be responded to only by eliminating the true believers or by convincing them one by one to replace their belief systems.

Some have argued that the attacks were "criminal." The individuals who carried them out were societal deviants motivated by base instincts, limited intelligence, or an inability to perform even near the mainstream of human society. If the actions are criminal, they are perpetual and can only be policed, not eliminated. There will always be a fringe to society and non-conforming acts will always be represented in the actions of that fringe, requiring perpetual police and a police state.

Many have suggested that these were the actions of primitives, undertaken by the "uncivilized" against the "civilized." The act was so heinous, one DOD official said, that "maybe even some of those in the uncivilized world now realize that they are on the wrong side." The "barbarian" paradigm has the virtue of making the world into a simple "us and them." It provides us with targets and justification for immediate response and serves the purpose of a paradigm. If the problem is that there are people somewhere who are uncivilized, the solution is that we civilize them or, in the short term, that we eliminate them, by capturing, imprisoning, or killing them to remove the threat of future cataclysms.

This explanation, though, removes the rallying motivation of war. War isn't waged against the ignorant or the primitive. It isn't waged against hooligans, even highly successful ones. It is waged against entities. Entities like nation-states or civilizations. The Bush administration declared that terrorists were an entity and, as one, where the enemy. Thus, the "war on terrorism."

So if it's war, where is the paradigmatic explanation that involves an entity? In a 1993 *Foreign Affairs* article titled "The Clash of Civilizations?" and later in his book *The Clash of Civilizations and the Remaking of World Order*, Harvard's Samuel P. Huntington initiated a debate about the best paradigm to replace the Cold War construct that had explained so much in international affairs in the 40 years after the Berlin Wall. He cites Thomas Kuhn's classic text *The Structure of Scientific Revolutions* in arguing that what is the best explanation is the most useful explanation. Huntington's hypothesis is that "the fundamental source of conflict in this new world will not be primarily ideological or primarily economic. The great divisions among humankind and the dominating source of conflict will be cultural. ... The clash of civilizations will dominate global politics ... conflict between civilizations will supplant ideological and other forms of conflict as the dominant global form of conflict."

Huntington's thesis about the nature of human conflict was met with considerable opposition. References to it in the numerous analyses of the sources of the terrorist attacks are mostly in dismissal. The argument, in the minds of some, is a formalizing of racism, a legitimizing of the use of religion and ethnicity in the intentional division of human society. To others it was an overestimation of the power of culture or missed the subtleties of cultural accommodation. For many of us it is simply that this is not the way we want the world to be. But the frequency of reference indicates that the thesis has struck a chord.

Arguments against the clash of civilizations thesis for the most part miss a critical point. It is not whether we are choosing to wage a war on Islam or any civilization but rather, are they waging war on us as a civilization? Engaging Huntington's hypothesis, were the terrorist attacks a clash with the American government, the American military, or American culture? The strikes at Wall Street and the military establishment, it has been argued, were strikes at symbols of American culture, at the financial system that supports it, at the American way of life. The Taliban employed this paradigm themselves in arguing that a responding U.S. attack on Afghanistan would be an attack on all of Islam, a response of one civilization to another.

Some sense of goodness in many of us wants to deny that races and linked cultures are at the origin of this war. "But if not a clash of civilizations, then what?" Huntington countered his critics with this same challenge. If this was evil, how do we respond to evil? If nihilism, what then? How do we deal meaningfully with the uncivilized, the primitive? Can we hate them?

If the problem is that there are gaps between civilizations, we must find ways in which differences can be accommodated or reduced. In rebutting Huntington at the origin of the 1993 debate, Johns Hopkins scholar Fouad Ajami argued that the process of accommodation between civilizations is already under way, fed by the drive for the economic rewards that the West has generated and demonstrated to the rest. "In making itself over the centuries, the West helped make the others as well," he notes.

Ironically, Ajami inadvertently posits that there *has been and is* a clash between civilizations, although a nonviolent one, and that the West was winning. The implication is that the clash of civilizations can be pursued without war and that the best way to reduce the lines of conflict is for the West to absorb immigrants, to educate the world, to feed its poor—just what we have been doing.

Ajami, the lead critic to Huntington's thesis in the 1993 *Foreign Affairs* article, had changed his mind by 2008. Initially, Ajami had wagered against Huntington's view that there "was no 'universal civilization.' " Huntington had argued that there was only a pretense of what he called the " 'Davos culture' [representing the West], consisting of a thin layer of technocrats and academics and businessmen who gather annually at the watering hole of the global elite in Switzerland." By 2008, Ajami's

sense was that "nearly 15 years on, Huntington's thesis about a civiliza-
tional clash seems more compelling to me than a critique I provided at
that time."

These acts of terrorism, by a radical subgroup of Islam, were undertaken by an organization on behalf of a culture, of what they see as a
civilization. Huntington's paradigm may not satisfy the demand for a
perfect explanation but it's better than the others in telling us why this
happened and what to do about it—continue to be a civilization of
enlightenment and reason, not the vindictive angel of war.

IS THERE A "WAR ON TERRORISM"?

President Bush and many Republicans continually referred to everyone not on our side in Iraq as "the terrorists." Unfortunately, this has
been directly appropriated by every government that wants to get in
on "the War on Terrorism" as a way of fighting old tribal enemies, killing off long-standing insurgents, and suppressing minorities. The War
on Terrorism has morphed into the War on Resistance. Now the
United States China, Russia, Thailand, the Philippines, India, Yemen,
and others are all fighting "terrorists." And, today, they are all Muslims.

Even history has been revised to fit the Bush administration's concept of a War on Terrorism. In Randall Law's *Terrorism: A History,*[2] virtually every revolution (including the French but not the American)
can be seen through the terrorist prism. Law argues that "Terrorism
is as old as human civilization. ... The weapons, method, and goals
of terrorists constantly change, but core features have remained since
the earliest times." This argument leads to taking tactical responses to
terrorist actions without examining how to deal with the motivational
aspect behind today's Islamic terrorists. In other words, no long-run
strategy. The Obama administration has carried over the tactical
approach of the Bush administration, unable to overcome the inertia
of war fighting.

There is a long list of errors that we have made in our pursuit of
Islamic and radical terrorists. But key among them is the fact that there
isn't really any war at all on terrorism. You can't have a war against a
concept. It didn't work with the War on Poverty and it will never really
go anywhere with terror either.

The fact that there is no War on Terrorism is reflected in the Bush
administration's conflating of the war in Iraq with the War on Terrorism. In his ongoing effort to achieve simple common denominators,

Bush glossed over the obvious complexity of who is at war in Iraq and, in the meantime, misidentified who our forces should be fighting, helped create the very havoc that fosters terrorism, and missed the opportunity to combat actual terrorists.

We seem to know neither who it is we are fighting nor what it is we should do to fight them. Identifying where it is that we are fighting the War on Terrorism is most of the game. Locating the war should involve locating where it is that terrorists actually are.

They were not in Iraq until the Americans arrived. The fighting there is not the War on Terrorism. A "win" in Iraq by the United States—even once we determine what a win is—will not be a defeat for terrorists (although a loss will help them in their recruitment), and Islamic terrorists will continue attacking the United States and the non-Muslim developed countries and their multinationals whatever the Iraq outcome. And at this point it isn't clear that Iraq can ever be made whole. Divisions between Kurds and Arabs, in particular, making Iraq divided into sub-states for the indefinite future. Add to that the distinctive religion- and culture-based separation between Sunni and Shia and we have a volatile mix that is unlikely to be repaired in our lifetimes.

WHAT IS TERRORISM?

George Bush and Secretary of Defense Donald Rumsfeld should have started with a definition of terrorism instead of using it as a simple pejorative. From September 11 on, Bush intentionally commingled terrorism with revolution, rebellion, criminality, ethnic conflict, anarchy, war, and evil.

Louise Richardson, in her book *What Terrorists Want*,[3] draws from her decades-long study of terrorism to define it with seven components. First, a terrorist is politically [or religiously] inspired. Second, a terrorist act involves violence. Third, the point of a terrorist act is to send a message, that is, induce terror, *not to kill the enemy*. Incidental deaths are likely but terrorists target symbols and systems. Fourth, in doing this, the act and the victim have symbolic significance. The psychological impact has to be greater than the physical act. Fifth, terrorism is an act of individuals or groups, not nation-states. If a nation-state commits a violent act, it is war, not terrorism.

Sixth, in a terrorist act the victim of the violence and the target audience that the terrorist is trying to reach are not the same. Terrorists want to inculcate fear in a much larger population than just the few (even 3,000) that they can kill. Terrorists' objectives are far beyond the reach of weapons and are often multidimensional (political, religious, social, economic, universal, and/or global).

Lastly, there is no soldier class in terrorism. Anyone can carry out a terrorist act and anyone can be a victim. We are far beyond lines of musket-firing professionals in uniform, whether red or camouflage. Civilians are the preferred targets.

The terrorists we are fighting today are radical Muslims. At the fringe there are some attempted exceptions, namely the Philippines' effort to rename the Communist rebellion that has been going on for 50 years as "terrorism." There are Islamic radicals in the southern Philippines, specifically from the Abu Sayyaf and the Jemaah Islamiya groups, that are employing terrorist tactics against the Philippines government and other states in Southeast Asia.[4] But we are not worried about any secular, Buddhist, Hindu, Christian, Jewish, Green, or Communist terrorists (although there are a few of all of these). The sources of the many plots against the West (including Russia) are rooted in the Islamic world.

Fifteen of the 19 highjackers who flew into the World Trade Center were Arabs from Saudi Arabia, as is Osama bin Laden. Few of those we have identified officially as terrorists are from other religions and cultures. Five ethnic Uighurs (Muslims) from China were held at Guantanamo but were released to Muslim Albania. Other Uighurs from Guantanamo has subsequently released to other non-Muslim countries and were not returned to China. Were they terrorists? Or still separatists fighting for independence of the 100 million or so Muslims from Beijing's control?

In attacking Afghanistan in 2001, the United States and its allies went after the support system for a terrorist organization, Al Qaeda, and after one leader, Osama bin Laden. The individual proved illusive and the support system was far more deeply embedded than just the Taliban in the government. After sitting for seven years in the deep shadow of the Iraq invasion, and after a reinvasion with tens of thousands of American and NATO troops, Afghanistan appears to be no more stable nor progressive nor violence free than it was five or ten or twenty years ago.

Bob Woodward noted in his book *State of Denial* that President Bush refused to look (or couldn't look) beyond the simplest of divisions of his own religious belief, that the world was divided into good and evil.[5] The United States and Great Britain invaded Iraq to rid the world of an evil Saddam Hussein without taking the time—or maybe having the ability—to understand the very gray world of political violence. They ended up with an array of physical and psychological conflicts but employing a unidimensional and unadaptive tool—a conventional army looking for the enemy.

But the opposing forces in Iraq are not a single entity. What we face is a complex configuration of sometime allies, often enemies, and occasional opportunistic bystanders. To have any hope of success against terrorists, we have to differentiate among and understand the differences between, the various groups:

Arab Sunnis. A relatively small minority in Iraq who, behind Saddam Hussein (the Baathists), brought unity to Iraq for decades. Not terrorists but willing to shoot Americans who get in the way. *Arab Shia.* A long oppressed minority with a visceral hatred of the Sunnis that is based in a millennium of growing religious conflict with the larger global Sunni sect. Not terrorists, willing to shoot Americans but more interested in killing Sunnis. *Insurgents.* A growing number of Iraqis, mostly Arabs, who see the Americans as an interfering force and foreign dominator. Includes both Sunnis and Shia. *Kurds.* Sunnis but not Arabs, a separate ethnic group that already has some autonomy from the Iraq government.

Militias. Fighters aligned with a particular school of religious thought in Iraq. They are defenders of a particular sectarian faith and are as likely to fight each other as they are national armies or the Americans. *Tribes.* Either Shia or Sunni but with local interests first. *Criminals.* There were criminals, both petty and organizational, in Iraq before the arrival of the Americans in 2003. They can be from any ethnic group. By naming anyone who opposed the U.S.-led invasion as criminals—as President Bush did early on—the distinction was lost regarding motivation in acting against the U.S. forces. But criminals don't commit suicide. *Foreign fighters.* Islamist *Jihad* has become the romantic as well as religious adventure for those without purpose in life. *Jihad* gives direction and maybe salvation. Since the foreign fighters blend into the Al Qaeda–directed efforts, we can cast them as terrorists although their motivation is initially quite different.

Al Qaeda in Iraq. These are some of the terrorists. Their numbers are small but their reach is great because they have direction, religious conviction, political organization, and financing. They know how to play the other actors in Iraq and Afghanistan. But Al Qaeda in Iraq is only a manifestation of a much larger school of thought that has adherents throughout the Islamic world. Al Qaeda and Islamic terrorists generally have sympathizers in Indonesia, Malaysia, Thailand, the Philippines, Pakistan, Nigeria, and other countries outside the Arab world, as well as throughout the Arab Middle East.

Troops fight armies, whether they are bands, clans, tribes, militias, companies, or battalions. They can't fight ideologically based conspiracies. And a conspiracy only takes two. A terrorist conspiracy can take a week to mature or twenty years. There's no hurry. Motivation to commit an act of terrorism that will have the desired impact is the key.

A War on Terrorism has to attack three things. First, it has to try to find conspiracies and conspirators, as in the search for Osama bin Laden and the Al Qaeda leadership. This leadership has, of course, long ago transformed into a greatly dispersed semi-organization with many heads, and Osama may even be dead. This search involves intelligence organizations, not soldiers. An obtrusive search risks alienating the very populations that a War on Terrorism is supposed to protect, witness the issues of tapping phones and the suspension of *Habeus Corpus* in some circumstances in the United States

Second, a War on Terrorism needs to be pursued in the global financial systems through which the many plots are funded. For example, a radiation bomb attack on a major U.S. harbor through use of a container or a small ship involves payments for support of a small crew (maybe 5–7), purchase of a ship and fuel, bribes for port disguises and exits, purchase of a radiation bomb and ancillary materials, and other support systems (phones, communications). The money has to come from somewhere and be processed.

Third, a War on Terrorism has to be pursued against the ideological and religious motivation of terrorists. We can never capture, imprison, or kill them all, especially when they enjoy a global distribution. Somewhere, somehow we have to be able to stop them from being created. There is good evidence that there are more willing terrorists in the Islamic world now than there were before we invaded Iraq.

A War on Terrorism has to be addressing the religious, cultural, educational, and economic circumstances from which terrorists arise. Are we now really pursuing such a war? The evidence seems to indicate that we are still just killing insurgents and not striking at the underpinnings or motivations of today's Islamic terrorists.

"Misunderestimating the War against Terrorism"

George Bush paid the price for never having studied international politics in his Harvard MBA academic career. It's clear from his policy statements and addresses to the nation that he never got a grip on the basic structures that underlay his problems with terrorism, dictators, and Israeli foreign policy. The confusion in the speeches can't be blamed on the speech writers or the president's advisors. If he takes the credit, he gets the blame. Where is it that he, and his policy, went wrong?

Error Number One: The most critical error the administration made is its confusion of Iraq and the events of 9/11. The Bush administration repeated the suppositional relationship between Saddam Hussein and the attacks of 9/11 so often that polls are finding that most Americans believe that there actually *was* a relationship. In every other world but Bush politics, it was always clear that there was none.

Well before Al Qaeda became an influential international actor, it was clear that Saddam's regime had taken a far more secular course than the religious zealots of Al Qaeda would or could accommodate. That secularism was a necessary means of dealing with the tribalism and religious divisions in Iraq. Al Qaeda, in fact, regularly referred to Saddam Hussein's regime as an "infidel" government. Even Pres. Bush's later modification of his claim to argue that Saddam and Al Qaeda were linked but that Saddam had no role in 9/11 belies the cleavage that existed between them. By insisting on a connection—without any evidence—between the two, Pres. Bush appeared to have a basic misunderstanding of what the problem is in the Middle East and, in fact, in the interchange between the West and the Islamic world.

Error Number Two: The Bush administration did not have a working definition of terrorism. The 9/11 attacks were acts of what we commonly known as terrorism. Al Qaeda was behind them with the primary individual actors being Saudis, including Osama Bin Laden. The intent of a terrorist act is to intimidate, to create fear, to undermine the will to fight. The terrorists carried out their acts by committing suicide. Terrorism takes many forms, including acts by the Ku Klux Klan in recent U.S. history.[6] However, most terrorism has not involved suicide. To commit only one act of terror, and to die in doing it, involves very powerful beliefs—beliefs in another life. Religious terrorism, in this sense, is distinct from other forms. These people clearly believed in something more important than their individual lives. This was clearly not the principle of the sybaritic Saddam regime.

Error Number Three: "We are rolling back the terrorist threat to civilization," said Pres. Bush on Sept. 7, 2003. But we weren't. We are not "civilization" and these religious terrorists are not the "uncivilized" attacking us. Reading—and understanding—Huntington, would have been helpful here. It had been 10 years since Huntington provided his seminal theory and discussion of it was widespread. Muslims—even radical Islamic fundamentalists—have their own civilization, culture, and history. By making an assumption that these religious terrorists are barbarians we automatically underestimated them . . . and certainly overestimated our own capabilities and relative attractiveness in the global competition for social and political development.

Error Number Four: There is no such thing as "ideologies of terror." Terrorism is a means to an end, not the objective itself. If we substitute the acts of terrorism for goals, we end up ignoring and not understanding the motivations of these terrorists. By this same measure, the terrorists of Al Qaeda are not "the enemies of freedom," as Bush repeatedly stated. Their objective is to advance the cause of their particular version of Islam, to undermine American strength and global influence so that their own vision of societal order may succeed. And as hard as it might be for us to accept this, America is not synonymous with freedom. The "freedom" to own an AK-47 is hardly coveted on a universal basis.

Error Number Five: The Bush Administration believed that the conflict between Israel and the Palestinians could be resolved without international intervention. Based in deeply set religious beliefs, the objectives of the Israelis and the Palestinians are mutually incompatible. Each side holds as divine absolutes something that the other side is unwilling to sacrifice. Many Palestinians believe that the land of Israel is Palestine (as it once was). Many Israelis believe that some or all of the West Bank is an inherent component of Israel. To bring the Israel-Palestine conflict to a stage of truce, a referee will be absolutely necessary. This means separating the two sides with an international force placed there . . . for the foreseeable future.

Error Number Six: Bush believed that the war on terrorism could be won without first resolving the Israeli-Palestinian conflict. It cannot. Before the invasion of Iraq, Europeans were expressing consternation with the underlying battle plan put forth by the Americans and British. They were putting it this way: "Bush is trying to kill the alligators, one by one; a better long term approach would be to drain the swamp." "Draining the swamp" in this case would be to take away the motivation. In Islamic countries well beyond the Arab domain, the Palestinian cause is the primary one. In Malaysia, for example, far off in Southeast Asia, sociometric surveys from the 1970s to the late 1990s showed that Israel and Israelis were more reviled by Muslim Malays than any other government or nationality and the PLO was resoundingly praised. The

Palestinian cause resonates throughout the Islamic world and provides a commonality that would not exist otherwise. Take it away and the mosaic of Islam, with its great diversity, would shine through. Leave that cause in place and the motivation for this terrorist war will remain a potent one for generations.

The Economics of Terrorism: An Attack on America

Most American businesspeople don't realize that there is insurance for foreign investors against losses generated by political or social causes in developing countries. Especially that there is insurance against war damage or against acts of terrorism. The Overseas Private Investment Corporation (OPIC), a U.S. government-owned insurance and guarantee company, and the Multilateral Investment Guarantee Agency (MIGA), OPIC's counterpart at the World Bank, both provide risk insurance against such possibilities as expropriation and damage to investors from political violence, domestic or international, terrorist or other. Many private insurers such as AIG do likewise.

The management choice of purchasing some form of political risk insurance can be guided by some consultation with companies or specialists who conduct political risk assessments or who monitor political violence. Even among those that do know about political risk assessment and political risk insurance, it is not well known that risk assessments of the United States Japan, and other developed countries have been available for more than 30 years.

Commercial risk assessment companies such as The PRS (Political Risk Services) Group and BERI (Business Environment Risk Intelligence) have routinely provided political risk assessments of the United States and Western countries since the 1970s. VRA, Inc., a Massachusetts-based research company, monitors violence globally, for all countries, with highly developed computer software that can provide real-time intelligence for foreign investors.

We can thus prepare, in some senses, for the expansion of political violence, including terrorist attacks, that has occurred in the 21st Century. We can be on alert. We can buy insurance that will help us recover from losses of facilities, materials, and production. We can be defensive and manage risk and prevent some losses. There has been a quantum change in the meaning of "political risk" with the advent of mass destruction terrorism. All of this had been previously on a micro level.

But the system of political risk assessment and management is set up for businesses operating as individual units. What about system-wide risks? For the state or the country? Terrorism, and our response to it, has much larger consequences for businesses than those that OPIC can help them with. The accumulation of U.S. business—the American economy—has to be defended by the larger entity—the U.S. government.

Where does this economic defense need to occur? Let's look at some critical examples of where we have been hurt economically by after-effects resonating from the terrorist acts of September 11.

Foreign investment in the United States: Just as it is a little known fact that risk assessments are done of the United States and other developed countries, few Americans recognize the importance of foreign invest-ment in the United States Globally, there has been exponential growth in foreign investment since the 1970s. Within that, as American capital has left the United States to take advantage of low wages in the develop-ing world, foreign capital has come to replace it to take advantage of America's high technologies and high labor/productivity ratios.

But those foreign investors are now being deterred by not only the threats from terrorists in the United States but also by the U.S. govern-ment's response to them. Regulations on foreign investment are being tightened by financial regulations and investigations in the search for al-Qaeda money. Anti-foreign sentiment is on the rise generally, making it difficult for foreign investors to be present in the United States Even preliminary efforts to investigate investment opportunities are being made more difficult by newly enacted visa requirements and entry reg-ulations. Given the hundreds of billions of dollars invested in the United States even a small percentage downturn could have a profound impact.

U.S. investment abroad: U.S. investments abroad have now become targets, especially in the Muslim world, which is more than a quarter of all countries. Businesses like McDonald's, American Express, or Chase Manhattan Bank that have U.S. identities have become potential targets, along with the individuals who come and go from them. As U.S. investors become more cautious about going abroad, both the opportunities for income and development prospects for Third World economies and democracies will diminish.

Tourism: Tourism is a major and growing industry globally. International tourists spend about $80 billion per year in the United States according to the Travel Industry Association of America. More is spent by domestic tourists, many of whom ordinarily fly to their des-tinations. Tourism has a very unique quality of businesses in that it has no real limits in terms of expansion possibilities. U.S. tourism destinations like Hawaii are heavily dependent on it and could face financial disaster without it. In addition to the greatly increased entry limitations faced by foreign tourists, the fear of flying and of being near tall buildings further impedes both growth and maintenance of this important source of income for Americans.

Worldwide, revenues from tourism shrank 2.6 percent last year, with the United States being among the hardest hit with a drop of 11.9%. Estimates are higher for some selected locations like Hawaii at about 20%. The losses in foreign tourist revenue will be about $2 billion, according to TIAA. While it can be argued that some of the drop has resulted from economic slowdown unrelated to terrorism, this is a difficult case to make given the broad reshaping of the international economy as globalization proceeds.

International students: Few Americans realize that a major industry in the United States is higher education. Hundreds of thousands of international students make their way to the United States every year to take advantage of our high quality tertiary institutions. They bring with them U.S. dollars that circulate as international currency. Now, visa regulations and cultural suspicion are beginning to hinder entry and discourage applications. The Europeans and others are jumping into this fray to try to draw that business and income away from the United States As they do, the American economy will suffer. Growth in many U.S. universities depends in great part on an international student clientele and institutional investment. We will suffer both financially and intellectually if there is a decline in this industry.

There are more problems stemming from the attack on America. What is important for Americans to understand is that the consequences of political violence in the United States and in the world have become much more about economics than we might have ever expected. If the destruction of the United States was a goal of the terrorists who struck on September 11, the diversion and limitation of the U.S. economy is certainly the way to get there. We can't insure against this risk. The core of the War on Terrorism—if it is have any more than symbolic effect—has to be a defense of the American economy, and killing Al-Qaeda fighters one by one isn't the solution.

STRIKING AT THE HEART OF DEVELOPMENT: A CASE STUDY

The October 2002 attack on tourists in night clubs in Bali turned the world of travel and tourism in Southeast Asia upside down. Bali had always been an island of tourist tranquility in Indonesia. Its history dates to the powerful Madjapahit empire that existed from 1100 to 1500 AD on eastern Java and the adjacent islands. The Madjapahit political dynasty traced its origins to the Indian Hindu polities that led to the development of all Southeast Asian states except Vietnam. Most of Madjapahit was eventually subjugated to the expanding Islamic empires that followed the founding of Malacca in 1400 AD but Bali escaped with its Hindu culture intact.

It is that Hindu culture that has made Bali the most attractive vacation site in the region for the last half century. The more permissive atmosphere of Hinduism allowed sunbathing, partying, and general relaxing by Australians, Europeans, and Americans that didn't fit the local culture in the rest of Islamic Indonesia. The hotels and resorts of Bali have been bringing hundreds of millions of dollars steadily into foreign currency–starved Indonesia for decades.

The bombing in Bali killed more than 190, mostly Australians but other tourists as well, including seven Americans, in a tactical hit for their cause. But it was also a strategic strike at the heart of Indonesia and the region. It reflected a desire on the part of many fundamentalist Muslims to quell the constant intrusion of Western influences into the country and incidentally served to send a message to the Hindu population of the island. Where Bali's domestic population gained from the interaction with the flow of tourism, now there has been a leveling to the least common denominator. Jakarta's Center for Labor and Development estimates that 150,000 tourism-related jobs will be lost on Bali and close to a million for Indonesia as a whole.

The bombing was a powerful message across the region. Those countries with fundamentalist and radical Islamic populations— whether in large numbers or small minorities—are now deemed physically vulnerable to attacks on Westerners. These states include Indonesia, Malaysia, Thailand, Brunei, Singapore, the Philippines, and India. The United States Australia, and Britain issued warnings to their citizens about visiting these countries, and if they do, about avoiding groups and some locations.

There were sufficient departures and trip cancellations that the meeting of the heads of state of the Association of Southeast Asian Nations (ASEAN) in November 2002 began with a focus on the devastating effect the drop in tourism revenue was having. The two-day summit of the ten heads of state resulted in pledges of further cooperation among law-enforcement bodies to protect both visitors and investors and the establishment of an anti-terrorism center to be located in Malaysia.

But these measures are probably too late. The lessons of the Bali explosions for the tourism industry have compounded those already provided by attacks—by Islamic radicals—on tourists and civilian targets at Luxor and other sites in Egypt, in Algeria, in Sabah in Malaysia, and, especially in 2010, in the southern Philippines.

The lessons are, first, that Western tourists are viable targets for terrorists. Second, that the danger is global. No country or location is immune. Third, that Islamic populations are the source of active terrorism. While the war on terrorism may not be a war against Islam, there is a very high correlation between attacks on tourists and instigation by Islamic terrorists, rather than Hindu, Buddhist, or Christian. No amount of political correctness can disguise this evident fact from tourists, tour organizers, and insurance companies.

As a corollary to that, fourth, culturally diverse societies—if one of the subcultures is Muslim—are likely to be hotspots for Western tourists. This is critical to the tourism industry since the culturally diverse destinations have been the most interesting ones.

Fifth, that open societies that allow unrestricted internal travel are more vulnerable to terrorist attacks than others. Hence, the strength of the tourism case for countries like Vietnam that have tight controls over both the practice of religion and travel into and within the country. There is a small Muslim population in Vietnam but all religions in Vietnam function under a restrictive official institution sanctioned by the central government.

As the tourism industry suffers through the reaction to danger and deaths, the fear factor infects other industries as well. Bali garment makers were concerned that buyers would not arrive as scheduled in December 2002 to place orders for 2003. If that industry falls, employment could greatly diminish in an industry that employs an eighth of the island's population, on top of the tourism losses. Nike confirmed plans to shift most of its shoe production lines from Indonesia to Vietnam. Businesses that have no portability, such as Exxon Mobile in northern Sumatra and Freeport McMoran Copper and Gold in West Papua at the other end of Indonesia, have had to step up security, adding considerable cost to their extraction products and, ultimately, reducing income for the countries in which they are operating.

It's the ultimate irony. Those who have argued that the wave of terrorism over the last decade has its roots in poverty and economic disparity now see a far greater negative impact of terrorist actions on those societies than elsewhere. Tourism is Indonesia's third largest industry after oil and textiles. It generated nearly $5.5 billion last year. J. P. Morgan forecasts that up to $3 billion in Indonesia tourism revenues will be lost in the year following the Bali attack and 2003 economic growth will be cut by nearly a percent, a loss that poverty-stricken Indonesia cannot afford. The attacks on tourists have become as much of an attack on the societies that host them as on the Western visitors themselves.

Ironic, too, is the fact that the countries that will benefit from the attacks—both in tourist revenues and in direct investment—are repressive societies like Vietnam that control their religions and their populations. In this very odd twist, what were the risks of the recent past have now become very attractive alternatives in a world filled with danger, but one that is also seeing an exponential growth in both interest and financial capability on the part of would be sightseers and students of the human condition.

A final irony is that the terrorists who planned the bombing in Bali apparently intended to kill Americans, not Australians. Maybe the terrorists were as much in need of cross-cultural training and experience as Americans are. The target remains the same, however. Even nearly a decade later, the target is the West and the tool is terrorism.

ANOTHER ATTACK ON AMERICA?

We have several fundamental questions about terrorism but we in the United States haven't yet addressed in any realistic way. The first is are we really "at war." If we are, we have never really mobilized for it. Second, if we are at war, who is the enemy? Does the enemy include Taliban combatants in Afghanistan, Nigerian discontents, and mentally disturbed American doctors who are Muslims? Third, if we are at war with terrorists, why haven't we labeled the war as such? That is, instead of it being a war on terrorism, why isn't it a war *with* terrorism? They are attacking too and they are fighting back. The fact that we haven't addressed these questions leads us in a state of political and legal confusion in America.

We have never really determined whether a terrorist is a criminal or a soldier, the only two categories we have for bringing those suspected of acts of violence to trial. We also haven't actually decided on what a "war on terrorism" is. Is it like World War II (declared)? The Vietnam

War (undeclared)? Or the War on Poverty or the War on Drugs (a campaign)?

Short of deciding on a legal basis for the paramilitary and police actions against those who are planning terrorist acts as well as committing them, we have to operate with the available tools.

After George Bush's attempt at Military Tribunals at Guantanamo and the Supreme Court's rejection of them in 2006, the controversial but still formally legal Military Commissions Act was promulgated to insert a third way to approach trying terrorism suspects. But the Military Commissions have failed to provide the alternative intended. A good share of the case for a civilian trial for Khalid Sheikh Mohammad is that the Military Commissions have been both thoroughly challenged and unsuccessful. They have resulted in only three convictions thus far.

In addition, there are a number of problems with this option simply on the face of it. First, we can't assume that a Military Commission would be held in Guantanamo. The Obama administration is in the process of closing the prison there and, despite delays on its part, shutting the doors will have to occur before the election cycle of 2010 envelops the legal arguments. If Obama doesn't keep this campaign promise, there will be an uprising on the left instead of the right. Obama already has enough trouble with his party's left.

Second, contrary to claims from Republican critics, a Military Commission trial is no guarantee of a conviction, let alone an assured death penalty. Challenges have arisen within the U.S. military itself regarding what appears to be railroading of detainees toward conviction. The media will never let a secret trial pass without inordinate attention to whatever they can get in the way of dramatic coverage. As of early 2010, only three military commissions at Guantanamo have come to a conclusion.

Third, the eyes of the world will be on any Commission, its processes, and its outcomes. A guilty conviction involving evidence obtained in possibly coerced testimony (read "torture") would produce global outrage and undermine American diplomatic—and perhaps military—efforts everywhere.

Lastly, and most importantly, an execution at Guantanamo would be more likely to produce a negative global reaction affecting America and its citizens than could possibly result from almost any anti-terrorist action we're taking in the field. It would undo some very positive changes Barack Obama has made in America's relations with the world. Can any American imagine the United States executing a prisoner in a secret prison—located on expropriated foreign soil—after a secret trial, after possible use of torture to get information?

It's unlikely that we'll ever be able to execute these men. But if we want to pursue a death sentence, it will have to be on U.S. soil, in U.S. civilian courts. That is, we'll have to declare that the war on terrorism is not really a war.

The Obama administration has little choice in picking between a civilian court and a Military Commission for Khalid Sheikh Mohammed and the other suspected perpetrators of the 9/11 attacks. Venue, police protection, cost for the trial, and political theatrics are all secondary issues. A cornerstone of the American judicial system is the right to transparent demonstration of proof when accused. This applies to criminals and enemies, especially when we can't distinguish between them. And we are America, after all. We should do it right, and we can. There is a moral question here.

However, there's actually a larger problem with a civilian trial in New York City. It's not that security there is not up to the challenge, or that New Yorkers will be particularly burdened or endangered. The problem is that we are again underestimating the Islamic radicals who are behind the terrorist attacks on the United States and the West. These are smart people, as they continue to demonstrate and we continue to forget. They have already mounted a successful attack on New York City and the heart of the American financial system. They mounted an attack not only on people but also on our economy. The Islamic radicals are planning strategically, and we are responding reflexively. This is the way the conservative mind works.

If they have the resources—and the resourcefulness—to attack again, why go back to the same target? Why not Chicago? Or Los Angeles? (Or even Detroit, with an underwear bomb?) Or especially ports like New Orleans or Long Beach, California? Cargo ship containers are notoriously difficult to examine even at the docks, let alone some distance offshore. The Halifax, Nova Scotia, explosion of 1917 especially gives us pause. In that accidental explosion of one ship carrying what was at the time conventional munitions, a fireball of one cubic mile was created. Nineteen hundred people were killed and 9,000 injured. Sixteen hundred buildings were destroyed and 12,000 houses damaged. Six thousand people were made homeless and 25,000 more were left with inadequate housing in the middle of a bitter winter. That was nearly 100 years ago and deep, now, in technological history.

While conventional explosives such as those are the most readily obtained weapon, police forces worldwide are already preparing for biological, chemical, radiological, and nuclear attacks on the United States. So are the Islamic radicals.

So, while American attention is focused on New York City and a handful of radicals already sacrificed (the right hand), why not hit at the economic heart of the western United States (with the left hand)? Radical magic. More than $100 billion in trade moves annually through Long Beach. According to its website, the port "supports more than 30,000 jobs in Long Beach, 316,000 jobs throughout Southern California and 1.4 million jobs throughout the United States. It generates about $16 billion in annual trade-related wages statewide." And more, with ramifications across the country and throughout the American economic system.

The Congressional Research Service reported that Al Qaeda estimated the economic costs of the 9/11 attacks to the U.S. economy at $1 trillion. Maybe that can't quite be matched with attacks on other targets. New York City is a special place. But it is now the most heavily guarded place in the world. Al Qaeda isn't going to rescue KSM, so other targets beckon. Will we be ready?

BIBLIOGRAPHY

Achcar, Gilbert. *The Clash of Barbarians: The Making of the New World Disorder.* Boulder, CO: Paradigm Pubs., 2006

Ajami, Fouad. "The Clash," *The New York Times,* January 6, 2008.

Chandler, Michael, and Rohan Gunaratna. *Countering Terrorism: Can We Meet the Threat of Global Violence.* London: Reaktion Books, 2007.

Clarke, Richard A. *Against All Enemies: Inside America's War on Terror.* New York: Free Press, 2004.

Clarke, Richard A. *Your Government Failed You.* New York: Harper Collins Pubs., 2008.

Dean, John. *Worse Than Watergate: The Secret Presidency of George W. Bush.* New York: Little Brown and Company, 2004.

Draghici, Carmen. "Terror and Beyond: Moral and Normative Dilemmas," *International Studies Review* (review article), 11, no. 4 (December 2009): 755–59.

Duffy, Helen. *The "War on Terror" and the Framework of International Law.* Cambridge, UK: Cambridge University Press, 2005.

Endeers, Walter, and Todd Sandler. *The Political Economy of Terrorism.* Cambridge, UK: Cambridge University Press, 2006.

Ensalco, Mark. *Middle East Terrorism: From Black September to September 11.* Philadelphia, PA: University of Pennsylvania Press, 2008.

Filkins, Dexter. *The Forever War*. New York: Alfred A. Knopf, 2008.

Flynn, Stephen. *The Edge of Disaster: Rebuilding a Resilient Nation*. New York: Random House, 2007.

Forest, James JF, ed. *Teaching Terror: Strategic and Tactical Learning in the Terrorist World*. Lanham, MD: Rowman & Littlefield, Pubs., 2006.

Forst, Brian. *Terrorism, Crime, and Public Policy*. Cambridge, UK: Cambridge University Press, 2009.

Gabriel, Brigitte. *They Must Be Stopped: Why We Must Defeat Radical Islam and How We Can Do It*. New York: St. Martin's Press, 2008.

Halper, Stefan, and Jonathan Clarke. *America Alone: The Neo-Conservatives and the Global Order*. Cambridge, UK: Cambridge University Press, 2004.

Hoge, James F., Jr., and Gideon Rose, eds. *Understanding the War on Terror*. New York: Council on Foreign Relations, 2005.

Howell, Llewellyn D. "Act of War: Terrorism in the Clash of Civilizations." *USA Today Magazine* 131, no. 2686 (July 2002): 19.

Howell, Llewellyn D. "The Economics of Terrorism: An Attack on America." *USA Today Magazine* 131, no. 2688 (September 2002): 23.

Howell, Llewellyn D. "Is the New Global Terrorism a Clash of Civilizations? Evaluating Terrorism's Multiple Sources." In *The New Global Terrorism: Causes, Symptoms, Solutions*, edited by Charles W. Kegley, Jr. Boston, MA: Prentice Hall, 2003, 173–84.

Howell, Llewellyn D. "Managing Political Risk in the Age of Terrorism." In *Global Risk Management: Financial, Operational, and Insurance Strategies*, edited by Jay J. Choi. London: Elsevier Science, 2002, 131–33.

Howell, Llewellyn D. "Terrorism and the Politics of Tourism." *Honolulu Star Bulletin*, November 22, 2002, p. C6.

Howell, Llewellyn D. "Terrorism: The 21st Century War." In *Readings in American Government*, edited by Mack C. Shelley, II, Jamie Swift, and Steffen W. Schmidt. Chicago, IL: Cengage, 2003.

Howell, Llewellyn D. "Terrorism's Violence Warp." *USA Today Magazine* 133, no. 2716 (January 2005): 65–67.

Huntington, Samuel. *The Clash of Civilizations and the Remaking of World Order*. New York: Simon & Schuster, 2006.

Kean, Thomas H., and Lee H. Hamilton. *Without Precedent: The Inside Story of the 9/11 Commission*. New York: Alfred A. Knopf, 2006.

Kegley, Charles W. Jr., ed. *International Terrorism: Characteristics, Causes, Controls*. New Jersey: Prentice Hall, 1990.

Kegley, Charles W. Jr., ed. *The New Global Terrorism: Characteristics, Causes, Controls*. New Jersey: Prentice Hall, 2003.

Law, Randall D. *Terrorism: A History*. Cambridge, UK: Polity Press, 2009.

Mendelsohn, Barak. "Bolstering the State: A Different Perspective on the War on the Jihadi Movement." *International Studies Review* 11, no. 4 (December 2009): 663–86.

Muller, Jerry Z. "Us and Them: The Enduring Power of Ethnic Nationalism." *Foreign Affairs* (March/April 2008): 18–35.

Posner, Richard A. *Countering Terrorism: Blurred Focus, Halting Steps.* Lanham, MD: Rowman & Littlefield Pubs., 2007.

Richardson, Louise. *What Terrorists Want: Understanding the Enemy, Containing the Threat.* New York: Random House, 2006.

Ross, Marc Howard. *Cultural Contestation in Ethnic Conflict.* Cambridge, UK: Cambridge University Press, 2007.

Smith, Paul J. *The Terrorism Ahead: Confronting Transnational Violence in the Twenty-First Century.* Armonk, New York: M. E. Sharp, 2008.

Smith, Paul J., ed. *Terrorism and Violence in Southeast Asia.* Armonk, New York: M. E. Sharp, 2005.

Stern, Jessica. *Terror in the Name of Good: Why Religious Militants Kill.* New York: Harper Collins, 2003.

Von Clausewitz, Carl. *On War.* London: Routledge, 1962.

Woodward, Bob. *State of Denial: Bush at War III.* New York: Simon & Schuster, 2006.

Woodward, Bob. *The War Within: A Secret White House History, 2006–2008.* New York: Simon & Schuster, 2008.

Zakaria, Fareed. "The Jihad against the Jihadis: How Moderate Muslim Leaders Waged War on Extremists—and Won." *Newsweek* (February 22, 2010): 26–32.

NOTES

Portions of this chapter are reprinted with permission from *USA Today Magazine*, January 1999, March 2001, and January 2003. Copyright © 1999, 2001, and 2003 by the Society for the Advancement of Education, Inc. All Rights Reserved.

1. Walter Enders and Todd Sandler. "Is Transnational Terrorism Becoming More Threatening?," *Journal of Conflict Resolution* 44, no. 3 (2000), 307–33.

2. Randall D. Law, *Terrorism: A History* (Cambridge, UK: Polity Press, 2009).

3. Louise Richardson, *What Terrorists Want: Understanding the Enemy, Containing the Threat* (New York: Random House, 2006).

4. Paul J. Smith, ed., *Terrorism and Violence in Southeast Asia* (Armonk, New York: M. E. Sharp, 2005).

5. Bob Woodward, *State of Denial: Bush at War III* (New York: Simon & Schuster, 2006).

6. Law, *Terrorism: A History.*

Chapter 11

Global Web and Culture

Nitish Singh and Hongxin Zhao

The global online population has now reached almost 1.08 billon users and about 70 percent of these users are now non-English speaking (internetworldstats.com). Studies are now showing that this large non-English speaking online segment prefers to shop and browse web sites localized for their countries and in their local languages.[1] According to a recent survey of 2,400 worldwide Internet users, more than half of the sample buys only from web sites that present information in their local language.[2] Businesses expanding their e-business find understanding language and cultural expectations and building online trust as most challenging.[3]

The World Wide Web is evolving to be the new frontier in international business, as it provides unprecedented advantages to companies attempting to tap the global market. In the past, size and the financial strength of a company were critical competitive advantages in reaching global consumers. Today, with the fast worldwide diffusion of the Internet and the rapid internationalization of e-commerce companies, the Web allows companies of all sizes instant global reach and the immediate ability to interact with customers spread all over the world.[4] Web has in fact lowered the barriers of entry for small and large companies around the world. This is creating a more level playing ground for companies to compete on a global basis, regardless of their size. Web has also been instrumental in reducing information asymmetry, enhancing interactivity to enable direct communication with members of the value chain and external customers, and most importantly the Web has led to disintermediation of the global distribution leading to easy access to global markets.

However, the Web also has led to emergence of several challenges such as: lowering of entry barriers means local companies are now exposed to global competition, decreasing information asymmetry also translates into better informed purchase decisions and pressure on prices and margins, and increasing customer choice and ease of switching from one company site to another has created new challenges for global customer acquisition and retention.

Thus, the Web is not only the key to global success but also the highway to global competition. To succeed globally companies have to cater to the needs of their global audiences and implement strategies to attract and retain their global online customers. However, many companies have not yet adapted their e-commerce efforts to meet the needs of a global-online market. Various studies have shown that marketers are not really localizing their international sites to cater to the needs of their global audiences.[5] Although many hurdles exist to this internationalization process, an *InternetWeek* survey found that one of the major obstacles for companies was an understanding of the cultural and language differences between countries.[6] This problem is reflected in the English language dominance of URLs, search engines, and web sites. Recent estimates by Internet World Stats show that only one third of all Internet users are now English speaking.[7] Furthermore, a survey of 2,400 worldwide Internet users found that more than half of the sample buys only from web sites that present information in their local language.[8] Notably, studies on e-commerce have suggested that country specific and culturally sensitive web content enhances usability, reach, and web site interactivity.[9] This web site interactivity then leads to more business related activity on the Web. Therefore, the issue of the cultural adaptability of the Web content is directly linked to business performance and is worthy of study.

Therefore, culturally adapted web sites are now seen as a necessary strategy to effectively tap international online markets.[10] A survey of multinational executives also found that 71 percent of these executives consider localization of web sites as a strategic priority for successful international expansion.[11] This may be because company web sites provide a major opportunity to impart and promote a corporate image and to sell products and services, but the effectiveness of the web site depends on the value of its localized content.[12] An effective web site is the one where the consumers invest a considerable amount of time reviewing the content of interest, requesting more information, and buying the goods or services offered.[13] As such, the quality and value of a web site will be influenced by how the web site mirror's the culture of the nation for which it has been designed.[14] Consequently, the adaptation of Web contents to local cultures becomes increasingly important as global e-commerce provides international marketers an exceptional channel to reach their potential customers worldwide.

CULTURE THE MISSING LINK IN WEB LOCALIZATION

The differences in cultures require international businesses to find ways to make their web sites communicate with different cultures in different parts of the world. As such, the key acronym that has emerged in this new arena of business operation is GILT or globalization, internationalization, localization, and translation.[15] Globalization, Internationalization, Localization, and Translation (GILT) is commonly associated with the process required to create multilingual international web sites.

Globalization (G11n): Globalization addresses all of the enterprise issues associated with making a company truly global. For the globalization of products and services this involves integrating all of the internal and external business functions with marketing, sales, and customer support in the world market.[16] From a more technical view point, web globalization includes two complementary processes: Internationalization and Localization.

Internationalization (I18n): Internationalization is the process of generalizing a product so that it can handle multiple languages and cultural conventions without the need for redesign. In more technical terms, it is the process through which back-end technologies are used to create modular, extendible, and accessible global web site templates that support front-end customization.[17] Internationalization takes place at the level of program design and web document development.

Localization (L10n): Localization involves taking a product and making it linguistically and culturally appropriate to the target locale (country/region and language) where it will be used and sold. Web site localization is specifically the process of the front-end customization, whereby web sites are adapted to meet the needs of a specific international target market.[18]

Thus based on these definitions it is clear that internationalization (i18n) serves as the backbone of the multilingual international web site and provides a modular and supple web design which can be localized to different markets and languages. However what customers see on the website is the direct result of web site localization. Web site localization as defined above constitutes efforts to translate and culturally adapt the web site to specific language, locale or country. For example, localizing web site for French speaking Canada is locale-level localization; localizing web site for Japan is country-level localization; and localizing web site to specific language (Japanese, Chinese, French, etc.) is language-level localization. To help companies effectively localize the web site a whole industry called the localization industry has emerged. The localization industry can trace back its roots to early 1980s when the software industry was emerging as an upcoming sector of the U.S. economy, and felt a need to translate software products in multiple languages.[19] As the application of software grew across a cross-section of industries and with the growth of the Internet, the localization industry also saw sustained growth. Now the localization industry is seeing a growth phase with the need for translation and localization of software, manuals, packaging, and most importantly multilingual web sites. However, most of the localization companies generally serve and compete on providing translation services and do not help much with regard to the cultural customization efforts. This is evident from the past studies by Singh and Boughton, wherein in their sample of several hundred multinational sites they could not identify well culturally adapted sites.[20] Similarly several academic studies have found that multinational sites have still a long way to go in terms of culturally adapting their web sites. Some of the reasons for this lack of cultural customization efforts could be the lack of knowledge, expertise, and resources available to companies to understand several cultures and then adapt their sites accordingly. However, emerging sources of knowledge can help companies culturally customize their sites. For example, Singh and Pereira have provided in their book a step-by-step process to culturally customize web sites to almost any country in the world.[21] More recently in 2009 Saint Louis University business school has started to offer an online executive certificate in web globalization. Thus, the hope is that as such resources emerge and the expertise is readily available companies could effectively localize their sites by not just translating them but also culturally customizing them.

In the remaining section of this chapter we attempt to summarize and present in a managerially relevant format some academic findings that can help companies better understand the importance of cultural customization of web sites. The goal is to show that culture is an important ingredient of any local web site and web sites of different countries depict local cultural values. Second we also highlight what impact does cultural customization of web site has on online consumers.

IMPORTANCE OF CULTURAL CUSTOMIZATION OF WEB SITES

Although culture is often seen secondary to other elements of international marketing strategy because of its soft aspect,[22] it provides acceptable ways of behaving and acting in particular situations and shapes our motivations, lifestyles, and product choices.[23] For this reason, several researchers have emphasized the importance of using country-specific values in international advertising campaigns and communication material.[24]

The Web is not culturally neutral, but it is filled with cultural markers which make web sites unique to the local culture.[25] So, if Web users come across foreign languages, signs, and symbols, or culturally incongruent web content, they feel more cognitive stress, and consequently have less control over the interaction and lose focus.[26] However, when web users are confronted with culturally congruent web sites, they feel less anxiety and find it easier to interact with the web sites.[27] Thus, web users in a specific country prefers web site features customized to their needs in terms of navigation, security, product information, customer service, shopping tools, and other features.[28]

There has been not enough research on the importance of culture in Web communications, but several studies found that international consumers prefer locally adapted Web content.[29] Singh, Zhao, and Hu examined cultural values depicted on the web sites of China, India, Japan, and the United States and found that local web sites of companies from each country represent local cultural values.[30] According to the study by Singh et al, German, Chinese and Indian consumers found web sites of American multinationals which are culturally adapted to their country to be more effective (in terms of presentation, navigation, purchase intention, and attitude toward the site) than web sites that are not.[31]

Culture has been shown to impact how individuals develop trusting relationships and interact with members of society.[32] However, there is a dearth of research investigating how culture impacts online trust creation or how online trust differs cross-culturally. Gefen and Heart strongly urge more research with regards to cross-cultural aspects of trust creation.[33] Few studies have attempted to study online trust in cross-cultural context. Studies by Jarvenpaa et al. and Gefen and Heart have researched how online trust or attributes of online trust differ based on cultural values such as individualism/collectivism, power distance, uncertainty avoidance, and masculinity/femininity.[34] A study by Cyr et al. compared consumer preference for Web design features and consumer trust on local vs. foreign sites with mixed findings.[35] Given these mixed results and limitations, Cyr et al. like Gefen and Heart also urged more in-depth investigation to study impact of culture on online trust.[36]

CULTURAL ADAPTATION

It has been confirmed that web sites are not culturally neutral but they show they demonstrate great differences across cultures. The research of Singh et al. found that local web sites of China, India, Japan, and United States mirror cultural values of each country, showing significant differences on cultural dimensions.[37] For example, the local Chinese web sites are characterized by the repeating images of the family theme, whereas many Japanese web sites include online clubs, family themes, and links to local companies, which reflects the Japanese people's mentality of looking out for others in the group.

To examine cultural adaptation on the Web, Singh et al. compared the U.S.-based international companies' domestic web sites and their Chinese web sites in their research and found that cultural adaptation is practiced by the U.S. firms on their Chinese web sites.[38] The appearance and structure of the Chinese web sites were significantly different from the domestic web sites. For instance, the Chinese web sites were characterized by bold colors and animation which stand for high contextuality and harmony with nature along with traditional theme. In addition, the Chinese web sites frequently included images which symbolize Chinese culture, such as the Great Wall of China, Chinese festivals, and the Chinese flag. In the U.S. domestic web sites, however, realism theme is dominant, information is set forth more directly, and fantasy and imagery are not seen as often. Superlatives and a hard sell approach are other features of the U.S. web sites that strike contrast to the Chinese ones.

IMPACT OF CULTURAL CUSTOMIZATION OF WEB SITE ON ONLINE CONSUMERS

There has been growing recognition of the importance of the cultural impact on global business in the information system literature.[39] Studies have showed that culturally adapted Web content improves usability, accessibility, and web site interactivity.[40] Luna et al. found that culturally congruent Web content is easier to navigate and induce favorable attitude toward the web site by reducing cognitive effort to process information.[41] This can be explained by cultural schemas which are shared by everybody in the group, who knows everyone else know the schemas.[42] The cultural schemas result from adaptation to the environment and the way we have learned to see things in our culture, and they facilitate interpreting culturally congruent communication.

Among many theories explaining cross-cultural differences in shopping behavior, the theory of planned behavior seems to be most convincing because it not only takes into account consumers' motivational influence, but also their perception of behavioral control, which is important on the Internet as Web users cannot touch and feel the products.[43] In this theory, beliefs are conditioned by the directive force of cultural system, early childhood socialization, and the sense of responsibility in societal rules and norms, and they precede attitude, subjective norms, and perceived behavior control.[44]

Attitudes: People's attitudes are greatly affected by the cultural values of a society.[45] Thus, Web users will have more favorable attitude toward web sites that are adapted to their own cultural values. The attitude-behavior link and attitudinal preferences are determined by culture. Aaker and Mahehswaran argue that attitudinal and behavioral differences between members of Western and Eastern cultures are explained by individualism and collectivism respectively.[46] Furrer et al.. and Tsikriktsis also showed that consumers' attitudes toward service encounters are affected by the level of power distance of a society.[47]

Subjective Norm: Subjective norm refers to the shared beliefs and expectations by a society that are observed by its members on their own accord. Thus web sites filled with local values and norms will have more favorable attitude than web sites that are not.

Perceived Behavioral Control: According to Pavlou and Chai,[48] culture influences the degree of perceived behavioral control an individual exhibits. It has been confirmed by many studies that that cultures high on uncertainty avoidance are generally slow in technology (Internet) adoption, because they turn to interpersonal information sources to fee more perceived behavioral control.[49] Luna et al. found that cognitive effort to navigate is lower when Web users are confronted with culturally congruent Web content and this in turn leads to higher perceived control over the navigation experience.[50]

Behavioral Intention: People's behavior patterns depend to a great extent on their cultural value orientation.[51] Thus, culture guides our products choices and purchase decisions in addition to determining our attitudes and structuring our subjective norms. In brief, culturally congruent Web content will induce favorable behavioral intention toward a web site by activating the cultural schemas.

Implications

On the one hand, World Wide Web is a global communication medium where technology makes mass customization possible. On the other hand, a standardized Web marketing is justified with global integration and the emergence of transnational Web style. Considering the complicated context of the Web, the debate on the appropriateness of standardization vs. localization seems to continue. People for standardization argue that contend that convergence of national cultures driven by technology development and its global diffusion will lead to a homogenous global culture. However, some studies challenge this argument by demonstrating that standardization does not really impact financial performance of firms. Thus, considering the diversity of the international marketing environment in terms of cultures, product usage conditions, economic, political and legal environment, firms are recommended to adapt their marketing programs to the conditions in a specific target market.

One of the best examples that employed both internationalization and localization approaches on their web sites is 3M. According to the study by Boudreau and Watson,[52] 3M showed local responsiveness in several ways: (1) the global gateway page guides visitors to find country-specific content; (2) each country-specific web site is in the country's most used language; (3) content is specifically targeted to local customers; (4) geolocation function. Several aspect of global integration on 3M web sites are: (1) a standard global Web template;

(2) most local web sites should be accessed from the main web site; (3) some key functionality is in English in all country-specific web sites.

In conclusion, it is unquestionable that today's business environment is greatly affected by global factors. At the same time, however, most companies are confronted with the challenging demand for local responsiveness to fully leverage global opportunities. However, the extent of cultural adaptation represented on the country-specific Websites is still at an early stage. Because it is obvious that culture is an integral part of Web communication, managers and Web designers of multinational enterprises should carefully study each country's culture when they develop country-specific web sites.

NOTES

1. Marc Ferranti, "From Global to Local," *InfoWorld* 21, no. 41 (1999): 36; Patrick D. Lynch and John C. Beck, "Profiles of Internet Buyers in 20 Countries: Evidence for Region-Specific Strategies," *Journal of International Business Studies* 32, no. 4 (2001): 725; N. Singh and A. Pereira, *The Culturally Customized Web Site: Customizing Web Sites for the Global Marketplace* (Burlington, MA: Elsevier, 2005).

2. Donald A. DePalma, Benjamin B. Sargent, and Renato S. Beninatto, "Can't Read, Won't Buy: Why Language Matters on Global Websites. An International Survey of Global Websites" (Massachusetts: Common Sense Advisory, Inc., 2006).

3. Mary J. Culnan and Pamela K. Armstrong, "Information Privacy Concerns, Procedural Fairness, and Impersonal Trust: An Empirical Investigation," *Organization Science* 10, no. 1 (1999): 104–15; Sirkka L. Jarvenpaa, Joam Tractinsky, and Michael Vitale, "Consumer Trust in an Internet Store," *Information Technology and Management* 1, no. 1–2 (2000): 45–71; Singh and Pereira, *The Culturally Customized Web Site*; Bob Violino, "E-Business Lurches ABROAD," *InternetWeek* 853 (2001): 1.

4. Hongxin Zhao, Seung Kim, Taewon Suh, and Jianjun Di, "Social Institutional Explanations of Global Internet Diffusion: A Cross-Country Analysis," *Journal of Global Information Management* 15, no. 2 (April–June 2007): 28–55; Yadong Luo, Hongxin Zhao, and Jianjun Du, "The Internationalization Speed of E-commerce Companies: An Empirical Analysis," *International Marketing Review* 22, no. 6 (2005): 693–709.

5. Singh and Pereira, *The Culturally Customized Web Site*.

6. Violino, "E-Business Lurches ABROAD."

7. Internet World Stats (2008), http://www.internetworldstats.com.

8. DePalma et al., "Can't Read, Won't Buy."

9. H. Fock, "Cultural Influences on Marketing Communication on the World Wide Web" (paper presented at the Multicultural Marketing Conference in

Hong Kong, September 2000); S. J. Simon, "The Impact of Culture and Gender on Websites: An Empirical Study," *Database for Advances in Information Systems* 32, no. 1 (2001): 18–37.

10. Dianne Cyr and Richard Lew, "Emerging Challenges in the Software Localization Industry," *Thunderbird International Business Review* 45, no. 3 (2003).

11. B. Petro, G. Muddyman, J. Prichard, K. Schweigerdt, and N. Singh, "Strategic Role of Localization in MNE" (paper presented at the meeting of the Applied Business Research Conference, Honolulu, Hawaii, January 2007).

12. R. W. Pollay, "Measuring the Cultural Values Manifest in Advertising," in *Current Issues and Research in Advertising*, ed. J. H. Leigh and C. R. Martin (Ann Arbor: MI: University of Michigan Press, 1983), 72–92.

13. C. Liu, J. Marchewka, and C. Ku, "American and Taiwanese Perceptions Concerning Privacy, Trust, and Behavioral Intentions in Electronic Commerce," *Journal of Global Information Management* 12, no. 1 (2004): 18–40.

14. Singh and Pereira, *The Culturally Customized Web Site*.

15. A. Lommel, *LISA, The Localization Industry Primer*, 2nd ed. (2003), 1–50, www.lisa.org.

16. The Localization Industry Standards Association, "What Is Globalization?," lisa.org/What-Is-Globalization.48.0.html (accessed July 28, 2008).

17. N. Singh and P. Boughton, "Measuring Web Site Globalization: A Cross-Sectional Country and Industry Level Analysis," *Journal of Web Site Promotion* 1, no. 3 (2005): 3–20.

18. Ibid.

19. The Localization Industry Standards Association, *Globalization Industry Primer (LISA)*, (2007), www.lida.org.

20. Singh and Boughton, "Measuring Web Site Globalization."

21. Singh and Pereira, *The Culturally Customized Web Site*.

22. D. M. Mooij, "The Future Is Predictable for International Marketers," *International Marketing Review* 17, no. 2 (2000): 103–13.

23. N. Feather, "Values, Valences, and Choice," *Journal of Personality and Social Psychology* 68 (1995): 1135–51; David K. Tse, Russell W. Belk, and Nan Zhou, "Becoming a Consumer Society: A Longitudinal and Cross-Cultural Content Analysis of Print Ads from Hong Kong, the People's Republic of China, and Taiwan," *Journal of Consumer Research* 15, no. 4 (1989): 457.

24. Nancy D. Albers-Miller and Betsy D. Gelb, "Business Advertising Appeals as Mirror of Cultural Dimensions: A Study of Eleven Countries," *Journal of Advertising* 25 (Winter 1996): 57–70; Sang-Pil Han and S. Shavitt, "Persuasion and Culture: Advertising Appeals in Individualistic and Collectivistic Societies," *Journal of Experimental Social Psychology* 30 (July 1994): 8–18.

25. Barber and Badre, "Culturability."

26. David Luna, Laura A. Peracchio, and María D. De Juan, "Cross-Cultural and Cognitive Aspects of Web Site Navigation," *Journal of the Academy of Marketing Science* 30, no. 4 (2002): 397–410.

27. Barber and Badre, "Culturability."

28. Dieter Fink and Ricky Laupase, "Perceptions of Web Site Design Characteristics: A Malaysian/Australian Comparison," *Internet Research* 10, no. 1 (2000): 44–55; Luna et al., "Cross-Cultural and Cognitive Aspects of Web Site Navigation"; Simon, "The Impact of Culture and Gender on Websites"; and Nikos Tsikriktsis, "Does Culture Influence Web Site Quality Expectations? An Empirical Study," *Journal of Service Research* 5, no. 2 (2002): 101.

29. Ibid.

30. Nitish Singh, John Zhao, and X. Hu, "Analyzing Cultural Information on Web Sites: A Cross-National Study of Web Site from China, India, Japan, and the U.S.," *International Marketing Review* 22, no. 2 (2005).

31. Nitish Singh, Georg Fassott, Mike C. H. Chao, and Jonas A. Hoffmann, "Understanding International Web Site Usage," *International Marketing Review* 23, no. 1 (2006): 83–97.

32. Dianne Cyr, Carole Bonanni, John Bowes, and Joe Ilsever, "Beyond Trust: Web Site Design Preferences across Cultures," *Journal of Global Information Management* 13, no. 4 (2005): 25–54; Patricia M. Doney and Joseph P. Cannon, "An Examination of the Nature of Trust in Buyer-Seller Relationships," *Journal of Marketing* 61, no. 2 (1997): 35; Patricia M. Doney, Joseph P. Cannon, and Michael R. Mullen, "Understanding the Influence of National Culture on the Development of Trust," *Academy of Management Review* 23, no. 3 (1998): 601–20; Jaebeom Suh, Janda Swinder, and Seo Sunhee, "Exploring the Role of Culture in Trust Development with Service Providers," *Journal of Services Marketing* 20, no. 4 (2006): 265–73.

33. David Gefen and Tsipi Heart, "On the Need to Include National Culture as a Central Issue in E-Commerce Trust Beliefs," *Journal of Global Information Management* 14, no. 4 (2006): 1–30.

34. Jarvenpaa et al., "Consumer Trust in an Internet Store"; Ibid.

35. Cyr et al., "Beyond Trust."

36. Ibid.; Gefen and Heart, "On the Need to Include National Culture."

37. Singh, Zhao, and Hu, "Analyzing Cultural Information on Web Sites."

38. Nitish Singh, J. Zhao, and X. Hu, "Cultural Adaptation on the Web: A Study of American Companies' Chinese Web Sites," *Journal of Global Information Management* (JGIM), (2002).

39. M. D. Myers and F. B. Tan, "Beyond Models of National Culture in Information System Research," *Journal of Global Information Management* 10, no. 1 (2002): 24–32.

40. Fock, "Cultural Influences on Marketing Communication"; Simon, "The Impact of Culture and Gender on Websites."

41. Luna, Peracchio, and De Juan, "Cross-Cultural and Cognitive Aspects of Web Site Navigation."

42. Roy G. D'Andrade, ed., *A Folk Model of the Mind* (London: Cambridge University Press, 1987).

43. Icek Ajzen, "From Intentions to Actions: A Theory of Planned Behavior," in *Action-control: From Cognitions to Behavior*, ed. J. Kuhlandand and J. Beckman (Heidelberg: Springer, 1985).

44. Roy G. D'Andrade, *Schemas and Motivation* (Cambridge: Cambridge University Press, 1992).

45. M. D. Mooij, *Global Marketing and Advertising. Understanding Cultural Paradox* (Thousand Oaks, CA: Sage Publications, 1998).

46. L. Jennifer Aaker and Durairaj Mahaeswaran, "The Effect of Cultural Orientation on Persuasion," *Journal of Consumer Research* 24 (December 1997): 315–28.

47. Olivier Furrer, Ben Shaw-Ching Liu, and D. Sudharshan, "The Relationships between Culture and Service Quality Perceptions: Basis for Cross-Cultural Market Segmentation and Resource Allocation," *Journal of Service Research* 2, no. 4 (2000): 355–71; Tsikriktsis, "Does Culture Influence Web Site Quality Expectations?"

48. A. Paul Pavlou and Lin Chai, "What Drives Electronic Commerce across Cultures? A Cross-Cultural Empirical Investigation of the Theory of Planned Behavior," *Journal of Electronic Commerce Research* 3, no. 4 (2002): 240–53.

49. C. L. Ferle, S. M. Edwards, and Y. Mizuno, "Internet Diffusion in Japan: Cultural Considerations," *Journal of Advertising Research* 2, no. 1 (2002): 55–79; and Mooij, "Global Marketing and Advertising."

50. Luna, Peracchio, and De Juan, "Cross-Cultural and Cognitive Aspects of Web Site Navigation."

51. Mooij, "Global Marketing and Advertising."

52. Marie-Claude Boudreau and Richard T. Watson, "Internet Advertising Strategy Alignment," *Internet Research* 16, no. 1 (2006); 23–38.

Part 3

How to Stay Ahead of the Competition

Chapter 12

Demographic Trends: The Changing "Face" of the Global Market

Tracy Scott and Dana-Nicoleta Lascu

Worldwide demographics are changing rapidly, presenting a continuous challenge to marketers' efforts to understand, segment, and successfully target consumers. Firms exploring long-term market opportunities require a clear understanding of consumers, especially of those consumers who will make up the markets of the future. Changing consumer demographics will have an important impact on the level of demand and preferences for products and services in different parts of the world; consequently, understanding demographic trends constitutes a critical step in the process of determining the optimal marketing strategies for reaching tomorrow's consumers.

A more populated planet offers global firms more possibilities than ever; but it also requires firms to rethink their marketing to achieve a better fit with the highly differentiated consumer desires in the older—literally and figuratively—markets of high-income countries, and with the limited pocketbooks in the much younger low- and middle-income countries. For the global population, the most dramatic changes are in size, density, and distribution: the roughly 6.7 billion people living on earth today—more than ever—is expected to grow to 9 billion by 2050.[1] That means that 2 billion consumers, not yet born, will need products and services that address their unique needs and wants. Although this figure demonstrates the enormous scale of predicted growth, examining the specific patterns of expansion is more critical in understanding the vast political, business, and social implications of this new world population.

Changing birth-rate dynamics are hastening a massive population imbalance between regions. More than 85 percent of children born today live in low- and middle-income countries in Asia, Latin America, and Africa. India and China will continue to represent the largest populations in the world, with India expected to outpace China by 2050; and the United States will maintain its distant third ranking.[2] The population of India is almost four times as large as that of the United States.[3] And the gap is widening at an accelerated pace: more than 27 million people are born in India each year, more than three times the population of New York City.[4] Yearly, more than 16 million children are born in China; in comparison just over 4 million are born in the United States.[5] Table 12.1 illustrates the disparate population growth rate in high-income countries such as the United States, Japan, and Germany, compared to those in India and China.

For long-term planning, it is important to note that the population boom of the coming years is not expected to last. According to the U.S. Census Bureau International Database,[6] the years 1985 and 1990 saw the fastest human population growth rate, based on the number of people born, in history. The current growth rates have slowed from a peak of roughly 2 percent per year in the 1960's to just over 1 percent

Table 12.1
Population Growth Rate in China, Germany, India, Japan, and the United States (in thousands)

| Country | Year | | | | |
	1950	2009	2015	2025	2050
China	545	1,346	1,396	1,453	1,417
Germany	68	82	81	79	71
India	372	1,198	1,294	1,431	1,614
Japan	83	127	126	121	102
U.S.A.	158	315	332	359	404

today. And, due to the use of more effective contraceptive methods, government policies regarding family size, and later marriage, population growth rates are expected to continue declining in the coming decades.

Further decline in the population growth rate is also attributed to economic performance: in the long term, the health of the economy has had a strong and direct impact on birth decisions. Specifically, fertility has been shown to be a lagging indicator of economic performance, particularly in Western nations: as overall income rises, more children are born, whereas, during periods of recession, births decline, accordingly.[7]

Yet, even as the population growth rate is gradually decreasing, the population boom of recent years is a force to reckon with for already overburdened governments and national and local infrastructures, and for natural resources. On the other hand, the impact on business will be, for the most part, positive, prompting a number of questions that managers should examine. First and foremost, what consequences will the coming decades of population growth have for businesses? What are the profitable markets of the near future and what opportunities and challenges do they present? What and how will 9 billion consumers buy? How will large population clusters manifest internally and internationally in terms of consumption or production? Individual consumer buying power, lifestyles, and preferences will transform the nature of commerce locally and internationally. Most notably, the transfer of wealth and power from West to East will alter traditional patterns and assumptions; it is likely, for instance, that the next blockbuster global brands, the new Coca-Colas or Starbucks, will come from the East.[8] How will those brands perform in Western nations and what existing brands will they challenge around the world? How will the West maintain its relevance, and, most importantly, its influence?

In addition, more people drawing on the earth's resources is expected by many to lead to scarcities in commodities and natural resources including fresh water, proteins, oil, and food. It is likely that these scarcities will impact not only the relationships between rich and poor nations, but between future generations. Scarcities will lead to lifestyle changes, as consumers move away from products that are more expensive, wasteful, or harmful to the environment. And scarcities will also cause inflation, which will affect demand patterns. There is no doubt that scarcities will lead to both significant threats and opportunities for businesses, from sourcing to public relations.

This chapter examines the demographic trends that will shape the character and composition of global markets, and considers the consequences of those trends on the strategies of multinational firms. These trends include the changing age makeup of high-income and low- and middle-income countries; the changing income distribution worldwide; changes in the population distribution resulting from migration and urbanization; the changing role of women; the changing family structure; and the role of education.

DIVERGENT AGE STRUCTURES: AGING POPULATION IN HIGH- AND MIDDLE-INCOME COUNTRIES, AND THE YOUTH BULGE IN LOW-INCOME COUNTRIES

Although the earth's population size is quickly expanding, regional population growth is disparate. Throughout history, population age structures have been a dynamic consequence of economic, political and social forces, disease, and war in a region. Today, there are two critical opposing trends: low- and middle-income countries are quickly getting younger on average, whereas industrialized, high-income countries are aging. Differing fertility rates between regions explain the differences. Europeans, for example, have one or two children at most, and Asians have between two and three, whereas sub-Saharan African families consist, on average, of more than five children.[9] To provide a comparison, in 2009, France's population grew at a rate of 0.55 percent, whereas Ethiopia's population grew at a rate of 3.21 percent.[10] Most of the population boom will take place in developing countries. Three regions, Asia, Africa, and Latin America, will account for virtually all population growth in the coming 20 years—in fact, all of the top 10 countries with the highest population growth rates are located in the Middle East and Africa; meanwhile, less than 3 percent of growth will take place in Western nations.[11]

This disparity in population growth rates between East and West and low- and middle-income countries at one end and high-income countries at the other, will have noteworthy social, political, and economic consequences. Within nations, changing age structures will affect saving and consumption patterns, social interaction, family and household structures, and demand for products and services. Between nations, it will impact competition for resources, trade relationships, immigration and diplomacy. These trends are explored in more detail later.

The Aging Population in High- and Middle-Income Countries

Around the world, lower fertility coupled with a decreased death rate, means populations are older on average than ever before. This is especially true in Western countries. The age of a nation's population is a critical factor in determining productivity, and thus economic output. As people age, they tend to reduce work or retire from the workforce entirely; consequently, an aging population will eventually result in lower productivity. Currently, 70 percent of the population in developed, high-income countries is of working age, between 15 and 64. By 2025, there will be one senior for every three working-age individuals in high-income countries vs. a one-to-four ratio today.[12] In fact, the median age of the world's population ranges from 23.9 years in 1950 to 38.1 years in 2050. This trend is most dramatic in Western Europe, Japan, and in other developed Asian economies such as those of Hong Kong, Singapore, Korea, and Taiwan, where empty nesters aged 40 to 59 are a fast-growing group, growing at a rate of 30 percent.[13] In another example, the United Kingdom has more people over 60 than under 16 and the gap continues to grow: by 2031, it is projected that 2.9 million people (4 percent) will be aged 85 or more, of whom 59,000 will be aged 100 or more.[14] Likewise, 23 percent of individuals in Japan and 20 percent in Germany are over 65. Low-income countries, on the other hand, provide a stark contrast; only 4 percent of Pakistanis, for example, are over 65.[15]

Multiple factors have contributed to the reduced number of children born to the average woman in middle- and high-income countries. Women's improved standing in society and the advent of birth control have changed behavior related to birth management. Social security and a transition away from agrarian culture in developed nations have reduced the economic incentive to have a large family. At the same time, individuals are living longer than ever thanks to better healthcare and nutrition. The large Baby Boomer generation in the United States, for example, is expected to outlive previous generations. Yet, although Western countries represent many of the extreme examples of maturing populations, much of the global aging trend can be attributed to Asia due to its relatively larger portion of the world's population. By 2035, 60 percent of the world's population over 65 years old will be living in Asia.[16] China is the primary driver in this aging trend due to its sheer population size. Due to a longstanding policy of limited childbirth, or "one child policy," the size of China's working age population will begin to decline around 2015.[17] Japan is aging the fastest of any high-income nation.[18]

The financial and economic impact that the large segments of aging people will have on society is considerable. As this once small group begins to represent a larger proportion of society, the behavioral tendencies of a few will develop into widespread trends with far-reaching effects. One example relates to capital markets and savings vs. investment: because elderly households have been found to draw down assets, rather than increase savings, it is likely that the overall savings rate will be reduced in aging countries.[19] As large groups of investors move to a distribution phase of the investment cycle, it is important to ascertain the impact of this phenomenon have on market-wide sentiments and on investor behavior. Where are the investment reductions most likely to occur and where do the opportunities lie on the spending side? Although nations with more mature populations anticipate having a slower economic growth, they also tend to be more democratic, developed and secure,[20] which, in turn, reduces investment risk and concerns about social unrest. The balance that results will determine the economic future of aging nations.

From a public policy perspective, aging populations will create unprecedented strains on local and national systems of government. Financially, the cost of pensions and healthcare will weigh on the governments and the working individuals who produce the taxes to support them. The Japanese, for example, have proactively developed innovative programs to address the needs of the elderly. Long-term care insurance was instituted in 2000 to help ease the burden of caring for the elderly for family members. And there has been significant new investment in technologies, research and development to improve medicine and healthcare for the elderly, as well as find a way to counteract the economic impact of reduced manpower.[21]

Socially, the impact will be equally high. An aging population also means an increase in one-person households with unique needs and challenges. Due to a longer relative lifespan, the majority of the older population will be female, a particularly vulnerable group who tend to have lower educational attainment, suffer financially, and who tend to live alone.[22]

Although the elderly in developed nations are encouraged to leave the workforce through pensions or forced retirement, those in less developed nations will continue working well into old age. In developed nations, a reintroduction into the workforce or continuing employment on a part-time basis has been addressed at length. Part-time employment may offer several advantages, such as the ability to tap into the experience and wisdom of an older generation as also providing a better quality of life for aging individuals, and the positive mental value of socialization, as well as increased earning power.[23, 24]

The impact of aging populations will vary worldwide, based on changing family structures and cultural norms. In many countries, multi-generational households will increase as older individuals go to live with their children and grandchildren. Transforming cultural and family dynamics, however, mean that both the capacity and willingness of a family to provide care to the elderly are changing. In general, caring for aging parents will create financial and time pressures for children. In situations where children are a proportionally smaller group, and thus there is less potential division of responsibility among the offspring, this stress may be exacerbated. In China, for instance, many only children are poised to inherit the care giving accountability for two aging parents. In Thailand, migration to cities and smaller family sizes has meant that the number of older persons living with their children has dropped from 77 percent in 1986 to only 59 percent in 2007.[25] Throughout Asia, changing earning dynamics and weakening filial attitudes may mean that many parents are less likely to be able to rely on their children.

Some Implications for Marketing

A significant restructuring of industries and services to serve the large aging population in high- and middle-income countries is inevitable. Existing industries providing critical care giving, such as long-term, in-home, and transportation assistance will continue to grow. Similarly, companies will continue to develop medical devices aimed at elderly consumers and other profitable health-related products, such as pharmaceuticals. In one example, Procter & Gamble's $500 million osteoporosis drug, Actonel, has met with great success, and its top markets are, in descending order, Japan, Italy, France, the rest of Western Europe, followed by the United States.[26]

There will also be a greater demand for innovative services and products that provide simple solutions to age-related needs and wants. This will inform changes across the marketing spectrum, from product design to packaging. Examples include products that address the functional impairments of aging. From easy-grip kitchen tools to mobile phones with larger keys, companies that address the physical and lifestyle needs of the elderly will see increased opportunities.

Among examples of successful targeting of the elderly market are the following: Toymaker Takara Co. Ltd. gained a foothold in the respective market with products such as a two-seater mini electric car, home karaoke systems, and robots that open beer cans; Motorola Inc. offers phones with features appealing to aging consumers, such as a zoom function to bump up the font size on the tiny screen and internal speakers that connect with hearing aids; and Yamaha Corp. created an easy-to-play electronic guitar for Baby Boomers who grew up on the Beatles and Japanese folk rock.[27]

Physical limitations that come with age are accompanied by attitudinal and behavioral changes. As individuals age, they also individualize, becoming less a clone of peers. Consequently, although historically there has been a tendency to group the elderly into one group, in the future, it is likely that there will be many more unique segments in the aging market. Understanding the distinctive needs and wants of these disparate segments will be critical in effectively targeting the elderly population. Selling to older consumers means learning more about the cultural and historical influences shaping their values, whereas selling to younger consumers is much easier, as they are more willing to spend and they all "speak MTV."[28]

Because the older market is highly heterogeneous, marketers are advised to abandon the age variable as a segmentation variable in the adult market and, instead, develop segmentation strategies that include cohort, health status, goals, and task and context characteristics,[29] among other variables. A gender focus has been proven to be a winning strategy for companies such as Procter & Gamble, which, among others, successfully launched a toothpaste for aging women, called "Rejuvenating Effects" in the United States and a blockbuster beauty product, its Olay anti-aging cream, which it rolled out first in Western Europe and the United States.[30]

The Youth Bulge in Low- and Middle-Income Countries

Although industrialized nations are concerned with the retirement of a large elderly population, many of the world's poorer nations have experienced a recent baby boom. This "youth bulge" extends from the Andes of South America across to Sub-Saharan Africa, the Middle East and northern parts of South Asia, resulting in large cohorts of children and young adults in these areas.[31] Compared to the rest of the world, these areas exhibit very high fertility rates, where the average woman gives birth to four or more children in her lifetime. Today, roughly 65 percent of people living in North Africa and the Middle East are under 30 years old.[32] And, as the offspring of the current bulge begin having children, this growth will be further compounded in future decades. Thus, countries such as Pakistan, Iraq, Nigeria, Afghanistan, and Sudan will see their populations double in the next 35 years.[33]

This trend has been a focus of international policy concern, especially in situations where unemployment and dissatisfaction have led to social unrest and terrorism. The National Intelligence Council calls this phenomenon a "perfect storm" that drives conflict in areas of failed governments, religious extremism, and poverty.[34] Throughout history, this dynamic has been shown to negatively impact stability and social and economic growth. Eighty percent of the world's civil conflicts have occurred in countries where 60 percent or more of the population was under the age of 30.[35] In North Africa and the Middle East, 60 percent of the 330 million population is under 25 years old, and, as the population grows to 400 million over the next decade, growing shortages in cultivatable land, food, water, and earning opportunities will continue to create hardship and foster discontent—two-fifths of the population in the Arab world lives in poverty today and the trend is worsening.[36] The consequences of these pressures have worldwide significance. The Islamic resurgence in the Arab World, including the September 11 Terrorist Attacks and Al Qaeda, have been linked to youth bulges in areas of slow economic and social progress.[37]

On the upside, however, youth bulges in poorer countries carry great economic potential. A young population translates to an increase in available workers; in areas where these workers are highly educated, this has the potential to provide a competitive advantage. A large working-age population requires jobs to employ those workers. A youthful age structure in Asia, for example, if met with the right policies, is expected to result in economic dividends based on an increased labor supply, higher savings rates, and more investment in human capital, such as education and health care.[38] Thus, public policy, both within regions and by regions affected by the social and economic security of youth bulge nations, will be a major determinant in harnessing the human capital and labor potential these countries hold. Long-term market opportunities will exist in nations where governments and politics are poised to capitalize on these economic opportunities.

Some Implications for Marketing Practice

At the consumer level, much of the growth for international companies has come from developing markets, where young adults do spend more freely than older adults: They are quick to pick up on new technologies, and readily open their wallets.[39] Companies have built low-cost factories in these markets to manufacture their branded products so that local consumers can afford them. For example, Procter & Gamble built a low-cost diaper factory in Vietnam, where it sells diapers for 15 cents each; in fact, all the products that it sells to consumers in low-income countries are half or even less than half the price in developed markets.[40]

For many middle-class consumers in developing countries, the Internet is the consumption, creation, and sharing platform of choice for youth.[41] Brands can thus use this venue to appeal to young consumers. For urban youth, who typically travel by public transportation, eye-level and commute-focused outdoor advertising in captive environments such as buses, trains, and elevators are a good choice for marketers.[42] Even in low-income countries where young consumers do not have access to running water or electricity, it is possible for them to have access to computer terminals at local shops that provide low-cost Internet service.

Income Inequality: Extremes in Wealth Distribution

Income inequality is measured both within and between nations. The distribution of income impacts political, social, and business structures within a country and the resulting relationships among countries and regions. At the extremes are the very wealthy and the very poor. The last 150 years have seen a transition from the most extreme income inequality existing within nations (between individuals or groups of individuals) to the largest income differences prevailing between nations. But that trend may be reversing, as the last 20 years has seen within-nation inequality accelerating. Both measures are required to understand the real worldview of income distribution, from the poorest individuals in low-income countries to the wealthiest individuals in high-income countries.[43] Because income inequality both within and between nations affects economic and social stability, as well as the size and composition of the marketplace, it is a key factor in determining business risks and opportunities in a region. A firm's profits are closely related to the income distribution of its customers because the demand for certain kinds of goods, from food to medicine, and the price individuals are willing to pay for those goods depends on the level of income. It is interesting to note that the breakdown in consumption patterns is often related more to income and relative prices than to regional differences. Thus, consumers in poor countries tend to consume like consumers in other poor countries; and consumers in wealthy countries consume like consumers in other wealthy countries.[44]

Income distribution within nations has become a topic of growing policy interest over the last two decades. Although different societies have diverse attitudes about income inequality, there is much discussion about the negative effect that extreme income distribution can have on growth and development, especially in developing nations. This is because the very poor countries also tend to have the greatest income gaps. The most extreme examples are in Africa (Namibia vs. South Africa) and South America (Paraguay vs. Brazil). In areas where policy and markets allow inequality to translate into increased incentives for individuals and a lure for outside investment capital (due to low wages), disproportionate income levels can drive growth for a country. Examples of this dynamic include Brazil, China, and India. On the other hand, in nations where leadership and imperfect markets prevail, these factors reinforce "destructive inequality" characterized by economic discrimination and privileges for the rich.[45] This is the case with many countries throughout Africa and Latin America. Income inequality also continues to grow in many developed nations, including the United States, Germany, Norway, and Canada. Generally this is due to the rich improving their income at a higher relative rate than middle and low-income individuals. Mexico, Greece, and the United Kingdom, on the other hand, have seen incomes become more equal in recent years. And post-communist countries, as well as countries such as Germany, Austria, and the Scandinavian countries demonstrate the highest income equality.[46, 47]

Some Implications for Marketing Practice

Within countries, the common practice of dividing population groups into "classes"—high, middle, and low—creates a helpful construct that managers can use to understand consumption patterns and relationships. It should be noted, however, that this approach carries limitations when it used to draw comparisons between countries. The lifestyle, net income, and buying power of an individual considered "wealthy" in Sub-Saharan Africa vs. a "wealthy" individual in Western Europe are markedly different. For example, consumers

Table 12.2
A Comparison of 18 of the Wealthiest Countries (by GDP/capita) and 13 of the Poorest Countries

| | Budget shares | |
Commodity	Rich countries	Poor countries
Food	29.59	40.44
Clothing	9.17	9.29
Housing	16.35	11.41
Durables	9.04	8.43
Medicine	5.06	3.77
Transport	12.37	9.72
Recreation	7.49	5.93
Other	19.94	11.02

Source: Kenneth W. Clements and Ye Qiang, "The Economics of Global Consumption Patterns," *Journal of Agricultural and Applied Economics* 35 (2003): 28.

in low-income countries perceive a fast-food restaurant such as McDonald's to be a luxury, special-occasion service offering that they would not afford to indulge in on a frequent basis. This same McDonald's restaurant is seen as a lower-quality restaurant alternative in high-income countries.

In general, very poor consumers tend to live fairly homogenous lives worldwide, with food representing a much higher portion of the budget, from 50 to 70 percent of income for families in developing countries.[48] Table 12.2 compares consumption in 18 of the wealthiest countries in the world with consumption in 13 of the poorest countries in the world based on GDP per capita.

Over the years, however, due to advances in agrarian technology, purchasing power for food has increased, and the average calorie availability in the developing world has increased from about 1,950 to 2,680 Kcals per person per day since the 1960s.[49] Access to better and cheaper food creates a healthier population with earnings left to spend on other products.

For businesses targeting wealthier consumers, however, budget allocation against different kinds of commodities is only part of the story. Within commodity groups, what kinds of consumption patterns will exist? Evidence exists that, in spite of—and potentially because of—the technology and product convergence that is happening worldwide, consumers will begin to resist homogenization, opting for products that align with national values and identity.[50] This is especially true of food products and dress, which are both closely linked to tradition. Thus, understanding local cultures will continue to be critical in understanding purchase behavior and preferences.

The Growing Global Middle Class

One of the most significant population trends of this century will be a growing middle class. Globalism has created unheralded opportunity for many people living in low-income countries. By working to create the goods and services the world marketplace demands, individuals have been able to earn a living that ends generations of subsistence living; this new class of earners is often called the "global middle class" and they represent the fastest-growing segment of the world's population, projected to grow from 440 million in 2005 to 1.2 billion, or 15 percent of the world's population, in 2030.[51] Most of this new wealth is taking place in emerging markets. Whereas 56 percent of the global middle class lives in developing countries today, by 2030 that number is expected to reach 92 percent; at the same time, average per capita income in developing countries will grow from $4,800 in 2007 to $11,000 in 2030.[52] Many of the large countries in Latin America, especially, are experiencing a booming middle class. Exceptions to this trend, such as Venezuela and Bolivia, are usually due to a government policy that sustains economic inequality by limiting opportunity for self-advancement.[53] Yet most of the new wealth creation is taking place in Asia, especially China, where the middle class is growing faster than any other country. China's wealthy class is expected to grow from 1.6 million today to 4.4 million by 2015, which means that over half of the consumers in China who will be wealthy five years from now are not wealthy today.[54] In India, the average household income is expected to triple in the next 20 years; India's middle class is expected to grow to more than 40 percent of the population (vs. 5% today) to become the world's fifth-largest consumer market by 2025.[55]

As mentioned previously, it is important to understand that the common definition of "middle class" is relative: it relates to buying power, not actual dollars. In India, for example, the average "middle-class family" spent roughly $6,600 in 2005.[56] This is vastly less than the typical level of a middle-class family in the United States. Ultimately, relevant products that can be priced with the understanding of the realities of this middle-class budget will succeed. Marketers should pay close attention to the behavior of these new consumers.

It is expected that brands will not be able to overcome poor product quality. Thus, brands that stand for quality (and deliver) will be in good position.

Some Implications for Marketing Practice

What can we expect from these upwardly mobile middle-class consumers? As incomes rise, so does consumption—but what exactly will be consumed? A rising middle class means a growing market of consumers with discretionary income to purchase a larger array of products. It can be expected that demand for services, especially education, health and tourism will increase. Likewise, there will be a growing demand for non-essential products that disposable income affords. These non-essential products create a leisure economy, where categories such as travel and entertainment are likely to thrive. At the same time, the market for modern domestic appliances (air conditioners, dishwashers, and refrigerators) and related goods will grow as many individuals will, for the first time, have the resources to ease household burdens.

As the first family members to part with generations of poverty, the lifestyles of the new middle class will be markedly different than those of their parents and grandparents. Which traditional values and priorities will carry forward as earning power increases? Beyond convenience goods, how will this cultural legacy be translated into consumer preferences and how will new levels of income change the culture itself? Access to goods outside of the traditional markets will expand and test new tastes and preferences. Evidence exists, for instance, that the newly wealthy in the East may begin to prefer a more Western diet.[57]

Around the globe, there will be myriad opportunities to bring global brands of products and services to a market of consumers hungry for goods that support and enhance their new lifestyles. Yet, evidence indicates that the tastes and purchase behavior of the world's middle class will not be uniform. The newly wealthy Chinese cohort, for example, behaves and thinks differently than their counterparts around the world: they tend to be much younger and care, on average, more about the functionality and durability of a product than its luxury brand status.[58] Wealthy Indian consumers, on the other hand, tend to live in cities where they have access to and a taste for the same kinds of goods as their counterparts in developed countries: brand names, high-end electronics, vacations and luxury cars.[59]

Urbanization: Cities Are the Future

In every area of the world, urban centers continue to grow as people leave the country for opportunities in the city. The larger the income difference is between urban and rural areas, the higher the incentive is to migrate. This trend geographically both exposes and accelerates the income gap described earlier: the wealthy live in the cities and the poor live in the country. By 2025, 57 percent of the world's population will live in urban areas, up from 50 percent today.[60] This development is most pronounced in Africa and Asia where the percentage of the population living in rural areas is expected to increase by 14.8 percent and 15.7 percent, respectively, by 2030.[61] By 2025, eight new megacities will be added to the world, all located in Asia and Sub-Saharan Africa.[62]

This massive shift from farming to factory will put intense pressure on growing metropolitan areas. Urbanization helps drive infrastructure and transportation development within and across borders; however, in many cases the speed and size of the migration has overwhelmed the infrastructure, utilities, and law enforcement of cities: The urban population of Burundi, in Sub-Saharan Africa, for example, has been growing 6.8 percent per year since 2005,[63] and the situation is similar in many countries in the surrounding area, such as Rwanda, Burundi, and most parts of the Democratic Republic of Congo. No infrastructure could possibly absorb and accommodate so many people in such a short time span. The resulting oversaturation often means enormous rings of slums begin to grow around the outskirts of urban areas, and, by 2030, it is predicted that 2 billion of the world's population will live in slums.[64] In the most extreme cases, such as Sudan, Ecuador, and Chad, over 90 percent of the urban population live in slums.[65] These areas of high poverty often translate into dangerous areas of high crime and limited social mobility, and they accentuate the social unrest that results from the contrasting extremes of poverty and wealth.

Historically, it has been a rule of thumb that the wealthiest individuals also lived in cities. But, as the middle class expands, second and third-tier cities will house many wealthy consumers. In China, for example, while 50 percent of the wealthy live in the 10 largest cities, 75 percent of the new wealth creation is expected to happen outside of the large metropolitan areas, in smaller towns and cities. It is expected that these newly wealthy individuals, with ties to their home, will stay put, rather than migrate to larger urban areas.[66]

Some Implications for Marketing Practice

Urbanization changes consumer preferences and consumption patterns, as cities offer increased product selection and access, especially
in low- and middle-income countries. Products typically not used in
rural areas, such as household appliances, are increasingly becoming
necessities and/or objects of status consumption. In addition, grain
consumption falls as consumers move to urban areas, whereas meat
and liquor consumption tend to increase as urbanites frequent the
growing restaurant market; in China, the nature of these changes is
also cultural, as the Chinese tradition is to wait until all diners have
finished their liquor before eating grains, such as rice or wheat.[67]
Across the globe, growing consumer demand for new and different
food selections impacts the way food is processed, delivered, and
served.

In urban areas, consumers, proportionately, are more likely to use
service providers for services performed traditionally by the extended
family in rural areas. For example, hair salons, massage parlors, and
mental health professionals have replaced services that were originally
offered by family members. Food service providers have replaced the
traditional family meal—in China, for example, massive urban growth
has corresponded with an increase in "eating out."[68]

Migration and Its Impact on the Ethnic and Religious
Makeup of the Population

Throughout human history, people have traveled great distances for
the opportunity of a better life. Large groups of ethnic minorities have
and continue to move across regions and borders, within country and
between countries, to take advantage of jobs that exist in more developed areas. Today, roughly 3 percent of the world's population, or
200 million people, are immigrants.[69] These immigrants tend to be
younger, and they make the transition in many different ways—some
are permanent while others are temporary, some are legal while many
are undocumented. Their decision to come or stay in new lands may be
forced or voluntary.

In Europe, new migrants number one million per year. Many of
these immigrants come from Muslim countries in North Africa and
Asia. In 2006, for example, almost 10 percent of the population in the
United Kingdom were born overseas.[70] In the coming years, as wages
improve in developing countries, migration will also likely occur in

Table 12.3
Migration Patterns by Income Classification

	High-income OECD	High-income non-OECD	Low income	Middle income	Total
Migrants from (in millions)					
Low-income countries	11.0	6.6	16.2	7.9	41.8
Middle-income countries	49.9	9.6	2.2	30.3	91.9
High-income countries	28.7	1.1	0.3	3.8	34.0
Total	89.6	17.3	18.7	42.0	167.6

Source: Adapted from Dilip Ratha and W. Shaw, "South-South Migration and Remittances," World Bank Working Paper, January 19, 2007, http://siteresources.worldbank.org/INTPROSPECTS/Resources/South-SouthmigrationJan192006.pdf.

new centers of industrialization in China, southern India, and, possibly, Iran and Turkey. The United States has long received labor migration from all parts of the world, especially Mexico. In the future, as Mexico's own industrial economy grows and the population declines, this influx of workers is expected to decline. Workers throughout South America will gravitate toward Brazil and the "southern cone" of South America for work opportunities and Australia will receive immigrants from South East Asia.[71] Table 12.3 offers an illustration of current migration patterns from low-, middle-, and high-income countries.

Migrants tend to be young, they are likely to have children at a younger age, and they tend to have more children than the nationals of the destination country. Over time, the differences in fertility between immigrants who remain in the new country and the native population will change the ethnic and religious composition of these areas. By 2025, minority populations could reach 15 percent or more in most Western European countries.[72] These high levels of fertility will help counteract the aging populations of high-income countries, but it can also cause tensions related to ethnic, religious, and income differences. The pace of ethnic diversification can strengthen intolerance and xenophobic attitudes. A prime example is the growing anxiety related to immigration in Western Europe. A Eurobarometer survey found that 15 percent of European Union members reported being disturbed when they are in the presence of people of another nationality and 14 percent had a problem with being around individuals of another religion.[73] In France, for example, ethnic conflicts have grown between French citizens and the 5 million Muslim immigrants living in France. The riots which erupted in 2005 in poor French suburbs were partially linked to the anger of youth immigrants in regard to perceived racism toward their families.[74]

In addition to economic migration, another cause behind transnational migration is inter-country marriages. Due to disproportionate ratios of men to women, an international marriage migration trend has developed, especially in Asia. Policies limiting childbirth have lead to an imbalance between males and females. In Taiwan, for example, 32.2 percent of marriages are to foreigners and foreign women are responsible for 13.4 percent of babies born. Brides are recruited in Thailand, the Philippines, and Vietnam to marry men in Taiwan. But the trend extends beyond Asia. Of the over 170,000 Filipino women married to foreigners, 30 to 40 percent are married to men residing in the United States or in Japan.[75]

It is also important to consider the areas that are left behind by immigrants, the impacts of the reduction in working population, and, in many cases, the brain-drain, the human capital flight of individuals with technical skills from developing countries to developed countries. In low- and middle-income countries, "ghost villages" often remain in areas where the population has left to pursue earnings available in far off urban centers. But although the villages, cities, and countries which migrants leave behind are affected by the loss of their young citizens, they also benefit from the remittances that these workers send home. For example, due to economic hardship and geographic proximity, Morocco has been a major source of non-skilled workers to Western Europe since the 1970s; rather than returning home as expected, many of these migrants permanently relocated, effectively setting up networks and opportunities for future immigration.[76] In 2004, with a country population of 30 million, almost 3 million individuals of Moroccan descent lived abroad; they represent a valuable resource for a nation which has come to depend on the remittances from workers abroad. In 2003, migrants sent $3.6 billion back to Morocco.[77] This outside capital helps fund markets in home countries. The family separation that results from immigration also drives demand for products and services that provide for the transfer of communication, money, and goods between family members.

Although many migrants establish residence in the places where they find work, migration is not always permanent. Migrants are frequently seasonal and even long-term migrants often maintain strong ties to their home countries and eventually return. This reverse migration is often attributable to increased buying power abroad and family and cultural ties, but in some cases, it is also encouraged by incentives offered by countries of origin. Immigrants take with them the education and earnings from their time abroad. This is especially impactful at higher skill levels. The highly skilled and technical individuals who left for better opportunities abroad eventually increase the competitiveness of their home countries once they return home; examples of this "reverse brain drain" phenomenon exist particularly in China, Brazil, India, and Mexico. This group will likely introduce new tastes, returning with a demand for products and services to which they were exposed during their time abroad.

Some Implications for Marketing Practice

What market opportunities will be created by international migration? Immigrants often desire the goods and services of their home country or culture. Businesses that provide these home-country products and services or address other unique needs of immigrants, such as language-related products (translation services or language education) will find new market prospects. Examples of businesses that serve the needs of immigrants are the sari shops in North Chicago, selling clothing for the Indian and Pakistani community, as well as electronics and appliances for use in the Indian subcontinent; Turkish bakeries selling baklava and local restaurants selling Döner kebab (rotating lamb roast) in Berlin, Germany's Kreuzberg—Little Istanbul—neighborhood; and the many small shops selling Indian food and clothing in the large cities in East Africa.

Entering a new market with products targeting a specific group requires an understanding of the geographical distribution of ethnicities within a region. Looking at broad statistics (such as birth rates), can be misleading, because clustering is likely, especially with first-generation immigrants. Thus, local market–concentrated media and messaging is often a cost-effective method for reaching a specific target, especially in situations where ethnicities tend to group together in neighborhoods or blocks.

Women's Economic Advancement: Tomorrow's Noteworthy Market Opportunity

The female demographic is quickly gaining significant power and influence in markets worldwide. Women's increased autonomy and participation in the global economy, both as producers and consumers, will change all aspects of the marketing continuum, from product development to point-of-sale purchase behavior. In the coming 5 years, women will be responsible for 70 percent of consumer dollars spent worldwide and will create 70 percent of the global growth in household income; and women control $10 trillion of the $15.3 trillion spent in the top 20 consumer markets today—by 2028, women will control 72 percent of global consumer spending.[79] Thus successfully marketing to the female population is critical. Companies that recognize and transform to meet the needs of the female target will see significant competitive advantage; missing the target with the female consumer will be costly.

Women's presence in the workforce has increased across the globe. Between 1998 and 2008, the female adult employment-to-population ratio increased in every region in the world except East Asia and Southeast Asia, where there is already a relatively higher rate of female employment; and, of the 3 billion people employed worldwide in 2008, 1.2 billion (40.4 percent) were women.[80] A number of factors contribute to the trend of more women in the workforce. Improvements in technology have resulted in timesaving household appliances and increases in food availability and preservation. At the same time, there has been a decrease in the average number of children born to each woman, made possible through birth control measures and changing societal norms. These transformations mean that women are less constrained by traditional household roles, resulting in an increased capacity for external activities. In addition, as jobs are created and wages go up, the economic incentive to pursue work outside the household increases. Moreover, women's increased education and earning power is also a mechanism for improving outcomes for other members of the household: an increasing number of women in the workforce reduces poverty levels for children; and women's increased education leads to healthier, more educated children.[81, 82]

Thus, women are major participants in the trends of globalization and urbanization. The global economy has created these earning opportunities in services and industry for women, increasing the number of women migrating from rural areas to take manufacturing jobs in the city. Between 2002 and 2007, women's income (globally) increased from $6.8 trillion to 9.8 trillion. By 2014, it will reach $15.6 trillion.[83]

Exceptions to the trend of increased female employment exist on opposite ends of the income spectrum. In wealthier nations, some women can afford to remain unemployed because of the earning power of their spouse; in the less developed nations, many women remain tied to the household due to cultural obligations.[84] In Japan, for instance, 85 percent of elderly family care-giving is performed by women.[85]

Yet although the economic freedom, influence, and earning power of women continues to grow on average, significant regional differences in female economic participation, especially between high- and low-income countries) and gender disparities with regard to wages, unemployment levels, and education persist. Worldwide, women earn an average of 15 percent less than men for each hour worked, and North Africa and the Middle East show the largest gaps.[86]

Education, the primary factor in women's economic advancement, continues to see a gender imbalance, especially in low-income nations. The Middle East, North Africa, South Asia, and West and Central Africa show the greatest gender parity in primary and secondary education.[87] In Pakistan, for example, only 22 percent of girls complete primary schools vs. 47 percent of boys.[88] In much of the Arab World, women have limited opportunities for advancement: societal norms and official laws discriminate against women both economically and politically.[89] Worldwide, the quality and security of the jobs available to women also varies significantly as does the corresponding economic and social empowerment that comes with working. The type of employment in which women engage is the primary determinant of earnings potential: most female employment (46%) is in the growing services sector, followed by relatively lower-wage-earning agriculture (35.4%).[90]

In less developed regions, agriculture is the primary employment activity for women. Half of the world's food production comes from women working in agriculture: in South Asia and Sub-Saharan Africa; for example, 60 percent of working women are engaged in agriculture.[91] Industry, where the higher wages can be earned, accounts for only 18.3 percent of women's employment compared to 26.6 percent for men.

Although women's empowerment is not growing uniformly worldwide, even small changes in the role and attitudes of women will change market behavior. In some Muslim countries, for example, women are making different choices than their mothers, often related to their increased education and new forms of media. Yet, although they are finding new opportunity and potential, there are also limitations to their freedom. In Yemen, for example, a conservative Muslim country, women are expected to preserve the family's honor through modesty and seclusion from men.[92] Yemen has the highest gender parity (only 41 girls for every 100 boys) in secondary education.[93] Yet, due to a variety of demand factors, the formal employment of women climbed from 5.6 percent in the 1980s to 23.7 percent in 2006. As a result of this increased participation in society, women's lives and tastes have changed. Urban university-educated women often do not have a taste for the same kind of traditional religious gatherings that their mothers do. Modern education, time-constraints and exhaustion with political messaging have created a preference for new forms of religious experience: the entertainment of televangelists, who forego political messages, concentrating more on emotion and piety, and a more modern Muslim woman, are more pertinent.[94]

Some Implications for Marketing Practice

As women contribute more to household income through outside wage earning, their impact on household spending decisions increases as well. The role of the woman increasingly stands as a critical component in understanding buying behavior in relation to specific products and brands. Yet, companies continue to lose significant revenue opportunities with women worldwide. A new BCG global survey of 12,000 women in 22 countries shows that women are "over-worked, over-extended, over-stressed and under-served" by businesses.... They want time leverage, more value and suppliers that specifically understand them."

Demands on women's time were the greatest challenge that the women surveyed mentioned. According to the study, companies are coming up short with women in five ways: "poor product design and customization for women; clumsy sales and marketing; inability to address the need for time-saving solutions: inability to provide a meaningful hook and differentiation; and failure to develop community."[95] This disconnect—the purchasing power of women contrasted with their widespread dissatisfaction—equates to considerable business opportunity. Organizations that proactively change business processes to address the specific needs of women will succeed in this environment.

Household Composition and Consumption

In every region of the world, the family stands as a significant economic building block, and is thus a subject of great social and political concern. For marketers, household composition is a critical factor in understanding and forecasting consumer demands. The family makeup in a single home affects spending decisions as the income divided among the family members informs market consumption. Family formation, marriage timing, and childbearing are all defining characteristics of the family. In recent decades, industrial modernization and urbanization have also modernized the structure and dynamics of the family. The number of people in a household and the roles they perform are changing in many parts of the world. Lower fertility rates in developed nations have led to smaller households, whose members often benefit from increased spending power per individual. On a market level, these smaller households lead to increased disposable income and thus increase spending on non-essential goods and services.

International migration also affects family composition, often diverging both from the country of origin and that of the host country. In the United States, for example, Mexican immigrants tend to live with a family dynamic under one roof that is different than those found in Mexico: the extended family for immigrants often reaches beyond traditional generational depth (grandparents) to a width that includes cousins, uncles, and aunts.[96] The state of families left behind by migrants traveling to larger urban areas or abroad, is also affected: although household earnings can benefit from remittances, relationships and decision making are affected by time spent apart.

Another common factor affecting household composition, and thus buying behavior, is divorce: around the world, divorce has seen a dramatic rise over the last few decades. Even in recent years, the divorce rate continues to climb. In Brazil, for example, the number of divorces per year climbed 33 percent between 2003 and 2007, and China's divorce rate rose 57 percent over that same period.[97] The same countries that have seen a decrease in fertility have also seen an increase in non-traditional forms of living, such as cohabitation and births out of wedlock.[98] These tendencies are highest in Scandinavian countries.

Education and Market Knowledge

Across the world, globalization and urbanization will accelerate the positive relationship between education and opportunity. As urban centers consolidate wealth, people and industries which values increased skills, educational centers and opportunities will emerge.[99] The differences are significant: in developing countries, 30 percent of children living in rural areas are out of school, compared with 18 percent of children in urban areas.[100] In the decades to come, education will stand as a primary determinant in the health and future economic prosperity of individuals, communities and nations. The effects of education are far-reaching: higher quality and availability of education have many positive outcomes from an increase in earnings-potential and productivity to decreases in fertility levels and infant mortality.[101] In Israel, for example, the average hourly pay of someone with a university degree is three times that of an unskilled worker.[102]

In areas with a youth bulge, discussed earlier, where there is a large labor supply, the value and quality of that labor is dependent upon skills and education.[103] Additionally, there is evidence that improved education policies may reduce extremes in income distribution.[104] For marketers, a more educated marketplace likely means a wealthier and more sophisticated buyer. Education levels inform and expand media selection and messaging development. As education levels and the corresponding access to information increase, buyers gain power and increase knowledge about products and product selection. Education is also a critical component in women's advancement in society, as education can increase autonomy and offer increased access to labor markets.

Unfortunately, educational attainment is still low in much of the world. Seventy-five million children worldwide fail to complete primary school each year, either having never attended or only attended for a short time.[105] Worldwide, 776 million adults (two-thirds women) lack basic literacy skills, and rates of illiteracy are highest in sub-Saharan Africa and Southwest Asia.[106] In many parts of the world, the quality of education is dependent on access to both skilled educators and vital technological resources, such as personal computers, educational software tools, and Internet access. Educational institutions are frequently the link to educational information and technology tools that would otherwise be unavailable to many individuals. Between and among regions, inequalities in digital educational tools continue to exist. In Latin America, for example, there are significant disparities: in 2003, for example, 27.7 percent of people in Chile had a personal computer and 13.1 percent had Internet access compared to 4.5 percent and 1 percent, respectively, in Peru.[107]

Because income follows education, marketers will be wise to identify current and future educational levels and outlets in evaluating a given market. More educated consumers will mean more disposable income and expanded demand across product categories. Urban markets will continue to lead the way, especially with luxury and niche products. Likewise, as globalization continues to drive the demand for education, the need for educational products and services will increase.

CONCLUSION

The last half of the 20th century saw the development of "globalism," a world in which free trade made possible by technological and political changes created a competitive world marketplace of goods and services. Although the human construct of countries and regions as seen on a map demarcates economic, governmental, and (sometimes) cultural boundaries at a point in time, the face of the global market is constantly changing. Eventually the shifts in population affect change within and across borders, sometimes changing the borders themselves. In today's rapidly changing and ever consumer-driven world, following the dynamic flow of people is arguably more important than examining countries individually. The convergence of demographic trends, from wealthy aging populations and poor youthful populations to urbanization, to access to education and women's economic participation, will all shape the faces, locations, and lifestyles of future generations. Successful marketers will understand the interrelationship of dynamic global trends and their unique context in a given market to identify current opportunities and long-term trends.

NOTES

1. U.S. Census Bureau, International Database, http://www.census.gov/ipc/www/idb/worldpopgraph.php: 1.

2. GeoHive: Global Statistics, http://www.geohive.com/default1.aspx.

3. "2009 World Population Data Sheet," Population Reference Bureau, http://www.prb.org/pdf09/09wpds_eng.pdf: 2.

4. U.S. Census Bureau, International Database, http://www.census.gov/ipc/www/idb/country.php: 1.

5. "2009 World Population Data Sheet," Population Reference Bureau, http://www.prb.org/pdf09/09wpds_eng.pdf.

6. U.S. Census Bureau, International Database, http://www.census.gov/ipc/www/idb/worldgrgraph.php: 1.

7. Ageing in Asia—The Japan Experience: 9–11. Jacques J. Siegers, "An Economic Analysis of Fertility," *De Economist*, 1987: 135, NR. 1.

8. Jenny Wiggins, "World's Next Top Brands Set to Rise in the East," *Financial Times*, July 20, 2009, 19.

9. Geohive: The Demographic Status of the World's Population. http://www.geohive.com/earth/pop_growth.aspx.

10. CIA World Factbook, https://www.cia.gov/library/publications/the-world-factbook/geos/xx.html.

11. Geohive: The Demographic Status of the World's Population. http://www.geohive.com/earth/pop_growth.aspx.

12. National Intelligence Council, "Global Trends 2025: A Transformed World," November 2008, 21.

13. Cris Prystay and Sarah Ellison, "Time for Marketers to Grow Up?," *Wall Street Journal*, February 27, 2003, B1.

14. Census 2001, Office for National Statistics, General Register Office for Scotland, Northern Ireland Statistics & Research Agency.

15. Population Reference Bureau, "Population Age 65+ (%)" http://www.prb.org/Datafinder/Topic/Bar.aspx?sort=v&order=d&variable=119.

16. Norifumi Tsuno and Akira Homma, "Ageing in Asia—The Japan Experience," *Ageing International*, May 13, 2009, Springer International: 2.

17. "Global Trends 2025: A Transformed World."

18. Ageing in Asia—The Japan Experience: 9.

19. Franco Modigliani, "The Life Cycle Hypothesis of Saving and Intercountry Differences in the Savings Ratio," in *Induction, Trade and Growth: Essays in Honour of Sir Roy Harrod*, ed. W. Eltis et al. (Oxford: Oxford University Press, 1970).

20. Elizabeth Leahy, Robert Engleman, Carolyn Gibb Vogel, Sarah Haddock, and Todd Preston, "The Shape of Things to Come: Why Age Structure Matters to a Safer, More Equitable World," *Population Action International* (2007): 10.

21. Tsuno and Homma, "Ageing in Asia—The Japan Experience," 10–12.

22. Ibid.

23. Sheung-Tak Cheng and Kenneth Heller, "Global Aging: Challenges for Community Psychology," *American Journal of Community Psychology* 44, no. 1/2: 163–65.

24. Monika E. Von Bonsdorff, "The Choice between Retirement and Bridge Employment: A Continuity Theory and Life Course Perspective," *International Journal of Aging and Human Development* 69, no. 2: 79–100.

25. John Knodel and Napaporn Chayovan, "Intergenerational Relationships and Family Care and Support for Thai Elderly," *Ageing*, March 4, 2009, 16–17.

26. Cris Prystay and Sarah Ellison, "Time for Marketers to Grow Up?," *Wall Street Journal*, February 27, 2003, B1.

27. Ibid.

28. Prystay and Ellison, "Time for Marketers to Grow Up?," B1.

29. Carolyn Yoon, Catherine A. Cole, and Michelle P. Lee, "Consumer Decision Making and Aging: Current Knowledge and Future Directions," *Journal of Consumer Psychology* 19 (2009): 2–16.

30. Prystay and Ellison, "Time for Marketers to Grow Up?," B1.

31. "Global Trends 2025: A Transformed World," The National Intelligence Council, November 2008, http://www.acus.org/files/publication_pdfs/3/Global-Trends-2025.pdf: 21.

32. Navtej Dhillon, "The Role of the U.S. in the Middle East" (congressional briefing), May 2008.

33. Leahy, Engleman, Vogel, Haddock, and Preston. "The Shape of Things to Come: Why Age Structure Matters to a Safer, More Equitable World," *Population Action International* (2007): 15.

34. "Mapping the Global Future: Report of the National Intelligence Council's 2020 Project," December 2004.

35. Leahy, Engleman, Vogel, Haddock, and Preston. "The Shape of Things to Come: Why Age Structure Matters to a Safer, More Equitable World," 34.

36. Rubeiz Ghassan, "Why Is Development Evading the Arabs?," *The Arab American News* 25, no. 1228 (August 22–28, 2009): 10.

37. Fareed Zakaria, "The Politics of Rage: Why Do They Hate Us?," *Newsweek*, October 15, 2001, 24.

38. D. Bloom, D. Canning, and J. Sevilla, "The Demographic Dividend: A New Perspective on the Economic Consequences of Population Change," RAND (2003): 30–42.

39. Prystay and Ellison, "Time for Marketers to Grow Up?," B1.

40. Ibid.

41. Media: Asia's Media & Marketing Newspaper, "Tapping into the Media Trends of Asia's Youth," August 13, 2009, 20–21.

42. Ibid.

43. Brian Goesling, "Changing Income Inequalities within and between Nations: New Evidence," *American Sociological Review* 66 (October 2001): 745.

44. Kenneth W. Clements and Ye Qiang, "The Economics of Global Consumption Patterns," *Journal of Agricultural and Applied Economics* 35 (2003): 34–35.

45. Nancy Birdsall, "Income Distribution: Effects on Growth and Development" (working paper, no. 118, April 2007, Center for Global Development).

46. Clements and Qiang, "The Economics of Global Consumption Patterns," 34–35.

47. Distribution of Family Income—Gini Index, The CIA World Factbook, https://www.cia.gov/library/publications/the-world-factbook/fields/2172.html.

48. Joachim Von Braun, "The 2009 Global Hunger Index: More Attention to Women's Rold Needed," 89 (December 2009): 5.

49. Joseph Schmidhuber, "The Outlook for Long-Term Changes in Food Consumption Patterns: Concerns and Policy Options" (FAO Scientific Workshop on Globalization of the Food System: Impacts on Food Security and Nutrition, FAO, Rome, October 8–10, 2003), 2.

50. Marleke Mooj and Geert Hofstede, "Convergence and Divergence in Consumer Behavior: Implications for International Retailing," *Journal of Retailing*, 78, no. 1 (Spring 2002): 61–69.

51. "Global Economic Prospects: Managing the New Wave of Globalization," World Bank, (2007), xvi, http://siteresources.worldbank.org/INTGEP2007/Resources/GEP_07_Overview.pdf.

52. Ibid., xiii.

53. "Global Trends 2025: A Transformed World."

54. Yuval Atsmon and Vinay Dixit, "Understanding China's Wealthy," *McKinsey Quarterly*, July 2009.

55. Eric D. Beinhocker, Diana Farrell, and Adil S. Zainulbha, "Tracking the Growth of India's Middle Class," *McKinsey Quarterly* no. 3 (2007): 50–61.

56. Ibid.

57. "Global Trends 2025: A Transformed World," http://www.acus.org/files/publication_pdfs/3/Global-Trends-2025.pdf: 51.

58. Atsmon and Dixit, "Understanding China's Wealthy."

59. Beinhocker, Farrell, and Zainulbha, "Tracking the Growth of India's Middle Class," 50–61.

60. "Global Trends 2025: A Transformed World," http://www.acus.org/files/publication_pdfs/3/Global-Trends-2025.pdf: 23.

61. http://www.geohive.com/earth/pop_urban.aspx.

62. "Global Trends 2025: A Transformed World," http://www.acus.org/files/publication_pdfs/3/Global-Trends-2025.pdf: 23.

63. Population Reference Bureau, "Average Annual Rate of Change of Urban Population, 2005–2010 (%)."

64. Ben Sutherland, "Slum Dwellers 'to Top 2 Billion,'" BBC News, June 20, 2006, http://news.bbc.co.uk/2/hi/in_depth/5099038.stm.

65. Population Reference Bureau, "Urban Population Living in Slums: 2005," http://prb.org/Datafinder/Topic/Bar.aspx?sort=v&order=d&variable=135

66. Atsmon and Dixit, "Understanding China's Wealthy."

67. Hengun Ma, Jikun Huang, Frank Fuller, and Scott Rozelle, "Getting Rich and Eating Out: Consumption of Food Away from Home in Urban China," *Canadian Journal of Agricultural Economics* 54, no. 1 (2006): 101–19.

68. Ibid.

69. Dilip Ratha and W. Shaw, "South-South Migration and Remittances" (World Bank working paper, January 19, 2007), http://siteresources.worldbank.org/INTPROSPECTS/Resources/South-SouthmigrationJan192006.pdf.

70. Census 2001, Office for National Statistics, General Register Office for Scotland, Northern Ireland Statistics & Research Agency.

71. "Global Trends 2025: A Transformed World," http://www.acus.org/files/publication_pdfs/3/Global-Trends-2025.pdf: 23.

72. Ibid., 21.

73. Eurobarometer, Report Number 53, http://ec.europa.eu/public_opinion/archives/eb/eb53/eb53_en.pdf: 88–89.

74. "First French Racism Poll Released," BBC, January 31, 2007, http://news.bbc.co.uk/2/hi/europe/6317799.stm.

75. Andrea Lauser, "Philippine Women on the Move: Marriage across Borders," *International Migration* 46, no. 4 (2008): 86.

76. Hein De Haas, "International Migration and Regional Development in Morocco: A Review," *Journal of Ethnic and Migration Studies* 35 (2009), no. 10: 1571–76.

77. Ibid.

78. Emily Bazar, "World's Talent Opts to Leave USA," *USA Today,* September 21, 2009, News section: 1A.

79. "Largest Global Survey of Women Finds That No Matter Where They Live, Women Are Over-worked, Over-extended, Over-stressed, and Under-served by Businesses," The Boston Consulting Group, http://www.womenwantmorethebook.com/press/august3.aspx.

80. "Global Employment Trends for Women," March 2009, International Labour Office, Geneva: ILO, 2009, http://www.ilo.org/wcmsp5/groups/public/—-dgreports/—-dcomm/documents/publication/wcms_103456.pdf.

81. "Progress for Children: A Report Card on Gender Parity and Primary Education," UNICEF, April 2005, 4.

82. "Growing Unequal? Income Distribution and Poverty in OECD Countries," OECD, October 2008.

83. "Largest Global Survey of Women Finds That No Matter Where They Live, Women Are Over-worked, Over-extended, Over-stressed, and Under-served by Businesses," The Boston Consulting Group.

84. "Global Employment Trends for Women," http://www.ilo.org/wcmsp5/groups/public/—-dgreports/—-dcomm/documents/publication/wcms_103456.pdf: 10.

85. Ageing in Asia—The Japan Experience: 10.

86. "Global Employment Trends for Women," http://www.ilo.org/wcmsp5/groups/public/—-dgreports/—-dcomm/documents/publication/wcms_103456.pdf: 17.

87. "Progress for Children: A Report Card on Gender Parity and Primary Education," 2.

88. Joachim Von Braun, "The 2009 Global Hunger Index: More Attention to Women's Role Needed," 89 (December 2009): 6.

89. Ghassan, "Why Is Development Evading the Arabs?," 10.

90. "Global Trends 2025: A Transformed World, the National Intelligence Council."

91. Ibid.

92. Sophia Pandya, "Religious Change among Yemeni Women: The New Popularity of 'Amr Khaled," *Journal of Middle East Women's Studies* (2009): 276.

93. "Progress for Children: A Report Card on Gender Parity and Primary Education," 9.

94. Ibid., 276.

95. Ibid.

96. Jennifer Van Hook, "Immigration and Living Arrangements: Moving beyond Economic Need Versus Acculturation," *Demography* 44, 2 (May 2007): 225.

97. United Nations, Divorces and crude divorce rates by urban/rural residence: 2003–2007. Table 23.

98. K. Kiernan, "Redrawing the Boundaries of Marriage," *Journal of Marriage and Family* 66 (2004): 980–87.

99. Oystein Kradval, "Child Mortality in India: The Community-level Effect of Education," *Population Studies* 58, no. 2 (2004): 179–90.

100. "Progress for Children: A Report Card on Gender Parity and Primary Education," 7.

101. Kradval, "Child Mortality in India: The Community-level Effect of Education," 179.

102. Central Bureau of Statistics, State of Israel, http://www.cbs.gov.il/reader/cw_usr_view_Folder?ID=141.

103. Bloom, Canning, and Sevilla, "The Demographic Dividend: A New Perspective on the Economic Consequences of Population Change," 30–42.

104. Katarina R. I. Keller, "How Can Education Policy Improve Income Distribution? An Empirical Analysis of Education Stages and Measures on Income Inequality," *Journal of Developing Areas* 43, no. 2 (Spring 2010).

105. Ibid.

106. UNESCO. EFA Global Monitoring Report 2009: 274.

107. Guillermo Sunkel, Las tecnologías de la información y la comunicación (TIC) en la educación en América Latina. Una exploración de indicadore2, United Nations (December 2006): 15.

Chapter 13

The Logistics Challenge in International E-Commerce

Kefeng Xu, Timothy J. Wilkinson, and Lance Eliot Brouthers

THE DARK SIDE OF INTERNATIONAL E-COMMERCE: LOGISTICS

At the height of post–World War II American economic prosperity, Peter Drucker described distribution/logistics as the U.S. economy's "dark continent."[1] He meant that it was one of the most neglected, least understood, yet potentially most promising areas of American business. Drucker encouraged American managers to raise the effectiveness/ efficiency of the U.S. distributive system as a means to combat foreign competition and improve profitability.

Internet usage and e-commerce have become ubiquitous in developed countries and continues to grow in emerging markets.[2] International e-commerce is touted as something which will revolutionize international business. By using internal and external networks to create market efficiencies, large and small firms will become lean organization's able to leverage their dynamic capabilities in order to positively influence performance.[3] Many Internet start-up companies believe that e-commerce will eliminate the middleman (wholesalers, retailers, etc.), allowing e-businesses to effortlessly sell their goods in many national markets simultaneously. People from anywhere in the world will be able to buy a company's product by logging in, pointing, and clicking.

Retailers are responding by forming partnerships with e-commerce businesses like Google, Yahoo!, and AOL. Most business schools offer a number of courses in e-commerce even as academics are scrambling to keep up with new developments in social networking. In short, e-commerce is seen as something that has already altered the manner in which business is conducted in the 21st century.

Although e-commerce has proven to have staying power, particularly in the domestic context, it has turned out to present a series of challenges for international companies. International business is quite different from domestic commerce and these differences constitute major obstacles to the click and point philosophy of international trade.

E-business as a research domain for academics is relatively new. A great deal of work, both theoretical and empirical, needs to be undertaken so that the commercial possibilities afforded by the Internet can be fully exploited by the business sector. Certainly much of the work that is being done in this area has implications for international firms. However, there exists an acute need for research specifically focused on questions relevant to international e-business firms. It has been suggested that the lack of such research challenges the accuracy of our very understanding of international business.[4] With the globalization of the economy, and with the contribution that the Web has already made to the internationalization of many firms, such research is past due. As a result, multinational corporations are not receiving the benefits of the kind of theoretically verifiable and systematized analysis that should be available.

In this paper we partially address the problem described previously by discussing logistical barriers which impede the successful development of global e-business and thus, represent the dark side of international e-commerce. We begin by describing how international e-commerce differs from domestic e-business and traditional international business. The major challenges of international logistics are then discussed. Finally, several major problems faced by international e-commerce firms are described and solutions to those problems are offered.

E-Business, International Business and International E-Business

Many issues important to international e-business firms are also relevant to traditional companies working overseas as well as traditional

Table 13.1
Differences between Domestic and International E-Commerce

Areas	Domestic E-Commerce	Traditional international business	International E-Commerce
Complexity of calculating cross-border taxes, quotas, and tariffs	N.A.	Low	High
Quality of infrastructure	High	Adequate	Low
Availability of appropriate warehousing	High	Adequate	Low
Adequacy of information technology	High	Adequate	Low
Cost uncertainty	Low	High	High
Customer expectations	High	Low	High
Timely delivery	High	Adequate	Low
Complexity of reverse logistics	Low	Low	High
Fraud	Medium	Low	High

businesses operating in domestic markets. At the same time, the problems and opportunities faced by an international e-business may be quite different from those faced by traditional firms. Table 13.1 delineates the differences between these three possibilities.

Domestic E-Business vs. International E-Business

The primary difference between domestic e-business and international e-commerce is one of complexity. Compared to domestic e-business, international e-business operates in an intricate and often confusing, environment.

Indicative of this complexity is the comparative ease in which domestic e-firms calculate shipping costs. Domestic e-businesses typically tack an average shipping-handling fee along with a tax surcharge onto sales. National or state sales taxes are generally waived for physical goods in major developed countries. Because shipments take place within national borders, tariffs, quotas, and customs clearance are non-issues. In addition, transport and insurance costs are often low.

For international e-businesses, transport and insurance costs are high. Country and regulation differences mean that international e-commerce firms face extreme difficulties in calculating shipping costs before the actual time of order execution. It is often hard to determine national and subnational sales taxes, let alone taxes on cross-border payments and value-added taxes.

Operating an e-business globally also adds complexity in terms of packaging, documentation, and labeling requirements. These requirements exist because of a tragic accident that took place over a century ago. An unmarked crate of nitroglycerin was shipped from Scandinavia to the United States in 1872. A deadly explosion resulted when the crate was opened with hammers and crowbars.[5] Therefore, documentation, packaging, and labeling requirements are taken seriously in international commerce. However, what is relatively simple for an e-business to do domestically is fraught with potential error in the international environment. Noncompliance with often-detailed requirements may result in delays or even legal culpability.

Finally, in contrast to the domestic sphere, there is not an agreed upon set of laws to regulate international e-commerce. Markets operate successfully only within the context of corresponding rules. The lack of international e-commerce regulation constitutes a substantial barrier to the successful implementation of international e-business strategies.

If e-businesses can solve these problems, the potential rewards are great. As of 2010 more than 85 percent of Web users reside outside the United States.

International Business vs. International E-Business

For both international firms and global e-businesses, logistical operations present numerous challenges not commonly fund in domestic settings. The level of uncertainty, the number of activities, and the complexity of operational constraints, often reduce the e-commerce firm's international operating efficiency. For example, freight is damaged or lost more often. Packaging, documentation, and labeling are more complex. Cycle times get longer, and international transportation and insurance are more expensive. Companies doing business overseas face language, cultural, and time barriers as well as distinct sets of foreign rules for packaging and transporting products.

Forrester Research interviewed 40 vice presidents of operations from retail, Internet, and manufacturing companies with an online presence.[6] They found that 85 percent cannot fill international orders because of complexities in shipping across borders. Barriers include local taxes, different currencies, language barriers, and customs procedures. Although these problems are common to international business they have often been ignored in discussions about international e-commerce firms.

Another complication for an international e-business is the quick transition it must make from a domestic firm to an international firm. Several studies indicate that firms progress through a number of stages before they become internationalized. The early stages are: (1) passive exporting, (2) export management, (3) export department, and (4) sales abroad.[7] By going through these stages a traditional firm has time to grow into a multinational corporation. In contrast, an e-business goes global as soon as it puts up its web site. This means that the challenges of e-commerce descend upon the newly minted international firm the moment it goes online. However, it is unrealistic for the managers of non-exporting firms to believe that they can become successful exporters by simply producing and maintaining a web site. Until a fairly developed and costly export specific infrastructure is developed within the firm, an Internet presence can be more trouble than it is worth.[8]

Finally, many Internet executives ignore the role of logistics in international e-business because of their professional backgrounds. These individuals were previously technical wizards who believe fancy web site designs are the key to their business successes, or marketers who think that attracting customers to the web site or being the first to the market is paramount, or financiers who focus much more on getting the first several rounds of venture capital or going public. They may have only learned the real pain of logistics execution after serious business losses. The challenges that these executive face, which are the same those faced by traditional firms operating internationally, are described next.

Challenges of International Logistics

Logistics is that part of the supply chain process that plans, implements, and controls the efficient, effective flow and storage of goods, services, and related information from the point of origin to the point of consumption in order to meet customers' requirements.[9] Logistics are relatively simple when inputs are close to production facilities and markets. Complexity occurs when natural factors, such as long distances, or manmade factors, such as laws and regulations, separate supplies, and markets from production.[10] The international dimension adds a series of impediments which can be overcome only through managerial expertise or through the actions of governments. These impediments are described next.

Trade Barriers and Exchange Rates

Tariff and non-tariff trade barriers constitute significant logistical obstacles in international business. In addition to explicit governmental trade barriers (tariffs, quotas, local content laws, value added taxes, embargoes, etc.), implicit barriers exist. Obstacles, such as inspection laws, can be manipulated to prevent or delay products' entry to the market. Distribution channels may be owned by the maker of a competing product or service.[11] Such an environment increases the opportunities for business abuses, disputes, and even crimes.

When exchange rates are volatile (the value of money made today may be different from money made tomorrow) and there is economic instability, international firms are exposed to high inventory costs, component obsolescence, and non-fixed-asset sheet costs.[12]

Infrastructure

To most shippers distributing products (or sourcing raw materials or components from less developed countries), the most obvious obstacle to successful international logistical operations is inadequate or stretched transport infrastructures in almost all modes of transportation. Brisk economic growth in most of Asia is pushing port, road, and rail infrastructure across the region to the limit.[13] Few highways, railroads, or road/rail links are appropriate for international trade flows. Road conditions are often intolerably poor, which inhibits traveling speed and tends to damage transported goods. These barriers make it difficult to use coordination-based logistics strategies such as just-in-time (JIT).

The United States has an international logistics infrastructure problem of a different kind. Almost all U.S. imports and exports pass through a computer system built 15 years ago, known as the Automated Commercial System (ACS). But today, ACS simply cannot keep up with the growth in international trade. What's more, ACS cannot support modern business inter-connectivity or provide real-time, online information. It does not support the Internet or many other innovations. The ACS is not merely old; it is decrepit—so much so that it could fail at any moment. If it does fail, nothing will be able to move in or out of U.S. ports. Although ACS is currently experiencing slowdowns and brownouts, the U.S. government has yet to take any major action to correct this problem.[14]

Warehousing

In a majority of Asia and Latin American countries, there is little availability of warehousing which meets North American standards. Those few local companies which operate well-furnished and spacious facilities often lack necessary information systems.[15] Warehouses are rarely automated and even less frequently computerized.[16]

Outdated Information Technology

In international e-business logistics process, the information flow is often as important as the flow of physical goods involved. Thus, the rise of the global supply chain has created tremendous pressure on the freight-forwarding business and on information technology. Currently, information about shipments in the international supply chain is inadequate or sluggish. Often the culprit is an outdated and incomplete international information technology system. Ideally, a parts or product database has unique item identifiers. These include parts numbers, product descriptions which aid in tariff classification, an accurate value for customs purposes, and correct country of origin information. Unfortunately such databases are typically nonexistent. On the hardware side, although the use of advanced communication tools such as electronic data interchange (EDI), satellite transmission, and the Internet are becoming more and more common in North American carriers, they are still relatively scarce in emerging markets, including most of Asia.

Many logistics service firms involved in global commerce (on which many e-businesses rely) exaggerate the level of service they can actually provide. Third party logistics (3PL) providers, hungry for business in a competitive market, have been known to promise more than they can deliver. This type of behavior can result in glitches in complex software and communications packages, can destroy an outsourcing partnership in its early stages, and is a major reason why many logistics contracts are prematurely canceled.[17]

Cost Uncertainty

One of the biggest barriers to retailing in international markets is cost uncertainty. This makes it difficult to accurately price goods.[18] A $15 order can balloon to $50 once duties, taxes, and other landed costs are added. Valuation and classification are tough enough in the United States, but to keep current, foreign government publications that list tax and tariff classification data must be monitored daily. Binding rulings, such as those made by the U.S. Customs Service with regard to classification of goods, must also be checked regularly.

Overcoming International Logistics Barriers

Many of the challenges of international logistics will be overcome in the next several years. Emerging markets such as China and Brazil have invested heavily in infrastructure improvements and have started transportation sector deregulation or privatization. Expected continuation of these activities should provide more efficient logistical operations to, from, and within those countries. In the near future, many key transportation corridors in Asia and Latin American will receive upgrades to standards similar to those found in the United States or Europe, easing some immediate pressure of trade traffic. These and other positive trends are outlined next.

Privatization

One method for achieving improved infrastructure is privatization. For instance, in a few years it is expected that almost every major port in Mexico, Central America, and South America will be privately operated. Mexico, Guatemala, Brazil, Peru, Bolivia, Paraguay, and Argentina have already awarded franchises to private companies.[19] Privatization will bring more efficient operations, faster turnaround times, improved labor relations, and updated infrastructures.

In emerging markets with generally overloaded transportation infrastructure, unique niche strategies may work. For instance, although China has many airports, most of these are under-utilized. The Chinese government is spending $17.4 billion to build 42 new airports and to expand 73 to improve cargo-handling capabilities and increase runway capacity.[20] An e-business could pursue an effective niche logistical strategy by utilizing these new transport capabilities to reach the Chinese markets.

VMI Arrangements

To ward off the effects of economic instability and volatile currencies, traditional firms and e-businesses may wish to consider using vendor-managed inventory (VMI) arrangements and the use of a vendor hub. VMI shifts the responsibility for inventory management back to the supplier. Suppliers continue to supply their e-business clients based on their client's demand forecast; however, change of ownership is recognized only at the point where the goods are ordered by the e-business. The vendors share and pay for space use at a hub, typically owned by a 3PL firms such as Circle International. A vendor hub helps to bring greater efficiency to the whole system.

Similar arrangements can be observed in the partnership between Amazon.com and Toys 'R' Us. Amazon helps sell may product lines of Toys 'R' Us online, but in its distribution centers these toys are owned and replenished by Toys 'R' Us until the products are sold. Amazon believes that this relationship is mutually beneficial because it allows both firms to concentrate their efforts most appropriately.

Evolution of Intermediaries

To tackle the requirements of effectively managing a global supply chain, freight forwarders need to expand their own coverage of services and territories, either through internal growth, acquisition, or merger. The decline in trade barriers and improvements in information technology have led shippers to actively expand their international operations, altering dramatically their expectations of freight forwarders. Large international shippers with complex supply chains still insist on low rates and on-time service but now they also expect forwarders to provide customs brokerage and multi-modal, one-stop shopping for logistics services. In addition to increased client expectations, competition across modes such as integrators (e.g., FedEx and UPS) and ocean shipping lines (e.g., APL, Maersk, NYK, SeaLand) have fostered rapid consolidation within the freight forwarding industry. These all point to the eventual disappearance of industry barriers between forwarders, international carriers, and logistics providers. Thus, the evolution of intermediaries into broad-based contract logistics providers will increase overall competition.

Clearly, progress is being made by governments and business working in the complex area of international logistics. Next we examine how this complicated environment is altered for international firms operating as e-businesses.

Challenges and Solutions in International E-Business

If the Web makes any company instantly global, then why don't more e-businesses ship overseas? Why don't more companies make their Internet-powered supply chains globally accessible? The complexity of international logistics increases exponentially for e-business firms. The overarching problem is that companies cannot manage the complex logistics and financial and regulatory requirements of global trade.

Our general recommendation is that international firms adopt a best practices approach to e-commerce. Almost all best practices (i.e., adapt to customer needs, personalize site, build trust) for domestic e-business are applicable in the area of international e-commerce. However, several practices have particular potency in the global arena. The best web sites are simple, and are easy to navigate. Simplicity is even more important in the international environment because of the inherent complexities of cross cultural communications. The use of focus groups consisting of people of from different countries, e-mail surveys, and the statistical analysis of usage patterns should be conducted throughout the lifetime of a web site.[21] In the following section specific problems and potential solutions are discussed.

Cost Uncertainty

Problem

As mentioned earlier, many American e-retailers cannot fill international orders because of barriers faced in cross-border commerce. These include local taxes, different currencies, language barriers, and customs procedures.[22] One of the biggest barriers to e-tailing in international markets is cost uncertainty. Continually changing duties, taxes, and other landed costs make international pricing quite difficult.

Pricing in multiple currencies in international e-commerce is particularly challenging. Most online businesses don't want to assume the risk of currency fluctuations between the time the customer's bank authorizes a credit-card transaction and when the sale's proceeds are deposited into the merchant's account. Therefore, extremely accurate and updated exchange rates must be continually fed into web sites. To make matters worse, online businesses cannot quote only the approximate customer charges because most countries prohibit this type of "ballpark" pricing. This issue is related to the landed cost calculation discussed below where logistics costs could be a big part of uncertainty in the whole formula.

The data infrastructure required to provide real-time, online shipping cost calculations for international e-commerce is very complicated. Input requirements include information about ever-changing regulations, taxes like the value-added tax (VAT), various duties, and many other components of the landed cost. These data requirements are much less of an issue in traditional international trade due to the long time frame and the amount of interactions allowed among the parties involved.

Solution

Shipping Solutions, Inc., offers e-tailers a potential solution to cost uncertainty. It has created an online tool that allows users to calculate tariffs, duties, and other landed costs in real time, over the Internet, on a transaction-by-transaction basis.[23]

Shipping Solutions, Inc., helps to solve the cost uncertainty problem. People buy imported goods for reasons such as brand, increased functionality or features, better performance, or simply lower total cost of ownership (even though the shipping cost is higher). For products of similar brands, features, and performance, customers are mostly concerned with the total cost of ownership (i.e., after receiving and being able to fully use the product or service). That is exactly why the LCE is so important in international e-business—product price is no longer the major part of the total cost of ownership.

An even more comprehensive solution for online businesses is looming on the horizon. CommerceZone plans to establish local portals in overseas markets that will lead international customers to the websites of U.S. retailers. In a third-party capacity CommerceZone will handle payment and reconciliation of customs duties, tariffs, and value-added taxes, providing customers a guaranteed total-landed-costs calculation in their local currencies.

Warehousing

Problem

Although some believe that international e-business logistics are not different from international mail-order logistics, Todd Carter, vice president of customer solutions for GATX Logistics Inc., suggests this really isn't so. He contends that e-commerce is very different from both traditional retail and mail-order businesses. To manage faster throughput, entirely different warehousing layouts are necessary because customized, smaller, and more frequent batch sizes are required. Carter asserts that what is needed does not even resemble the old model of warehousing.

Manufacturers and wholesalers want consignments delivered fast to schedules that should normally, but not always, be predictable. Warehouses dealing with Internet orders need to handle small volumes of dissimilar items efficiently and accurately using streamlined picking and dispatch processes.[24] Fortunately, many B2B firms have gained such experience through previous use of the electronic data interchange (EDI) systems that were devised for just-in-time (JIT) deliveries.

For international e-tailing to succeed, logistics support has to be tailored to the "bulk in, singles out" need. International e-tailors can also solve warehousing problems by using local or regional fulfillment centers. For instance, UPS offers numerous services that help companies streamline supply chain operations, including warehousing, back-office operations, return processing, and even account receivables. They literally help companies redesign their international operations in order to achieve the greatest efficiencies possible. Another example is Amazon.com, which serves the UK and German markets from its UK- and German-based subsidiaries, which consist of distribution centers and customer service centers. For smaller firms that cannot afford to set up a distribution/fulfillment center in every country they do business in, 3PL service firms can provide a way to handle the warehousing component international logistics.

Timely Delivery

Problem

Speed, fulfillment, and cost of delivery appear to rule in the new e-business-to-consumer market.[25] Customers in the e-commerce world have higher service expectations compared to customers of traditional retailing. Compared with the U.S. domestic market, international fulfillment appears to be a black hole. Most "global" e-businesses ship to just a few countries in Europe and Asia. Of the globally incapacitated, 75 percent cite their systems' inability to register international addresses accurately or price total delivery cost. For instance, users checking into a web site to purchase products expect full product availability, timely delivery, quality packaging, complete order accuracy, and ease of returning the products. E-commerce customers are addicted to real-time information and continuing visibility about their orders. Thus, providing order tractability is a necessity rather than a luxury in e-commerce. This, unfortunately, requires all parties (suppliers, carriers, 3PLs, etc.) involved in a supply chain to be fully integrated with the Internet capabilities needed to provide this information.

In addition, in international business where freight is damaged or lost more often, cycle times get longer, and other operating errors occur with greater frequency, carrier or logistics companies need to understand which logistics service attributes are more important to e-business clients and plan their operational focus accordingly. In general, previous research clearly shows that the reliability of delivery is more critical than the speed of delivery. The reason for this is that time-definite transportation makes it possible to plan just-in-time material flow.[26]

Solution

To deal with the issue of customer responsiveness and shipment tracking in international e-commerce, several basic steps are required.[27] First, it is vital to communicate to customers the importance of planning early so that on-time delivery can be assured. This means that customers must be educated about complexities of timely delivery in the international context. Second, make system integration an absolute priority. The dependence of logistics operations on accurate and timely operational data suggests that everything from the software packages to the database systems that an e-business uses must be fully integrated within the firm and across its supply chain partners. Third, build the best, most compatible databases possible.

Databases are the essential ingredients of e-logistics operations. Not only must they be fully integrated into whatever systems a firm is running, they must also be scalable, so that they can expand to meet a growing business' needs. For instance, Dell Computer sold direct mainly to business end users from its manufacturing base in Limerick before the facilities were relocated to Poland (and eventually sold in 2009). Sales were downloaded from the Internet three times a day and, from there, the computers were scheduled, built, and dispatched. Because the factory had no storage areas, finished goods were sent straight onto the lorries. Through sharing information with trusted suppliers online, the manufacturing department was able to carry just six days' worth of raw materials and components inventory.

By combining speed and reliability, supply chain managers can devise inventory strategies that counter the uncertainty of demand with the certainty of supply. For logistics companies servicing international e-businesses, proper inventory management and timely delivery are basic requirements in order to maintain customer loyalty and control costs.

Reverse Logistics

Problem

Reverse logistics (customers returning the products) are also a nightmare for an e-commerce firm. Companies typically do not have the efficient means and locations to handle returns, unlike a brick-and-mortar firm. Between 20 and 40 percent of all Internet-ordered items are returned because they are faulty, damaged in transit, or simply inappropriate. It has been estimated that return rates on international shipments are as high as 30 to 50 percent.[28] For example, online sellers of apparel experience return rates of up to 45 percent of their orders.

Solution

Two notable international logistics trends should help to alleviate the reverse logistics challenge. First, there is an increase in one-stop shopping for third-party logistics services such as 3PL providers (e.g., Ryder Logistics) and freight-forwarders.[29] Global trade is a fertile breeding ground for 3PL providers. Nowhere is the trend toward outsourcing logistics stronger or more logical than in global commerce. Experienced 3PL providers can give smaller firms (shippers) a more level playing field, by offering similar international capabilities that large multinationals have.

Second, there is a rapid increase in integrated express air cargo companies. The top six global carriers—UPS, FedEx, Emery Worldwide, Burlington Air Express, Airborne Express, and DHL—grew rapidly during the last decade of the 20th century. These firms are integrated in the sense that they provide shippers with full logistics services. These include: transportation, warehousing, customs clearance, freight tracking and tracing, the ability to provide and control information, order purchasing, inventory control, and even assembling merchandise.[30]

Fraud

Problem

Fraud represents another major challenge for international e-businesses. In most developed countries the use of credit cards has minimized the risk to businesses of customer fraud. However, customer fraud is high for international e-commerce transactions with online merchants. This is because customer addresses are impossible to verify and the responsibility of fraudulent charges on credit cards often resides with online merchants. Concerns about Web security have grown in tandem with increasing numbers of Internet shoppers. During the past decade Web security has become a worldwide concern. Although avenues of redress are available to victims of Internet fraud, awareness of such avenues is low. People are not informed about the governmental and non-governmental organizations that can help them deal with unethical or fraudulent e-retailers.

Solution

Best practices concerning Web security are essential for international e-business firms. An important source of information on Web security is *E-Commerce Security-Enterprise Best Practices*, published by Deloitte & Touche. These best practices, which are entirely applicable to international e-commerce, can be summarized as follows:

Establish a process whereby participants in an e-commerce transaction can be identified uniquely and positively. Put procedures in place to control changes to an e-commerce presence. Maintain logs of e-commerce use, and have responsible personnel monitor them. Put features in your e-commerce applications to reconstruct the activity performed by the application in case information is lost. Make sure you have a way to ensure confidentiality of the data communicated between customers and vendors. Put features into your system architecture to prevent components from failing and to repair themselves in they should fail.[31]

American Express has successfully addressed the problem of customer fraud by conducting original research in an effort to identify best practices for secure e-business transactions. It has formed the E-Commerce Fraud Prevention Network through which it provides e-commerce firms with the tools needed to blunt customer fraud. Tools include the creation of secure web sites and the validation of customer shipping addresses.[32]

CONCLUSION

The logistical barriers which may impede the successful development of global e-business represent the dark side of international e-commerce. Many firms attempt to focus on their core business and outsource their international logistics functions. Unfortunately, given the current state of international logistics, it may be somewhat premature to believe that international e-business can currently turn over the international logistics/distribution aspects of their business to others. What is needed is an awareness of global logistic trends and practices in order that an effective and efficient international e-business logistics strategy can be formed, implemented, and monitored.

E-commerce can give companies in industry sectors or countries the opportunity to provide superior customer service (a major component of a firm's logistics arm), but it can also serve as a cost cutting strategy.[33] E-commerce has radically changed the way in which companies reach and engage their customers. In the case of international e-commerce with the language capability of the customers (e.g., if the web site is multilingual and is supported by multilingual customer service staff), customer service would be better than that in traditional international trade environment, because e-commerce can provide timely, contents-rich information to customers. For instance, companies can reduce costs by launching an online catalog, which eliminates two major expenses, printing and distribution, and people to capture orders. Customer service is also less expensive on the Internet, because customers can look up their own orders and find order tracking information even outside of business hours. This easily translates into fewer calls into call centers and fewer overtime hours and customer service representatives.

In addition, although language and cultural differences are major obstacles confronting multinational firms, such differences are less important in cyberspace. This is because the primary language of the Web is English. In order to be competitive, firms must have English-language web sites. The availability of translation software has made it easy to fulfill this requirement. Moreover, communicating with global customers over the Web is easier, not more difficult, than is cross-cultural communication in traditional venues. Once again, translation software used in conjunction with e-mail has simplified the communication challenge.

As pointed out earlier, the absence of well-accepted regulation on international e-commerce presents both opportunities and challenges. Within this kind of context and environment, a multi-domestic logistical strategy seems to have higher chance of success than a uniform international logistical strategy. Examples of multi-domestic logistical strategy abound, including those of Amazon.com, Dell, and DHL.

Because of the lack of enforcement authority by supranational organizations it is unlikely that this situation will change.

E-businesses wishing to operate in the emerging global environment need to be able to react quickly, both (1) to take advantage of new opportunities for sourcing or sales and (2) to deal with the sudden emergence of new or unexpected problems. This suggests that supply chain/logistics management is a major component of building customers; efficient logistics strategies may prove to be more important than brand names in finding and keeping Internet consumers.[34]

The implication for global logistics companies is equally compelling. In order to better serve their e-business clients, broad-based contract logistics providers need to offer value-added services like Web-trackable, time-definite delivery, and customized logistics solutions. For an e-business to succeed globally, it needs a logistics network that can provide exact inventory (no matter where the customer is located) and instantaneous information. Internet e-business promises much; effectively, efficiently, and strategically managing the logistics function is what will allow e-commerce to "deliver."

In summary, we suggest that successful international e-businesses pursue multiple logistics strategies. This means staying sensitive, innovative, and flexible in designing, implementing, and monitoring global logistical strategies. Although the logistical problems faced by managers of international e-commerce firms may seem daunting, cutting-edge solutions to these problems are being generated by people working in the logistics field.

NOTES

This chapter is adapted from "The Dark Side of International E-Commerce: Logistics," published in the *Marketing Management Journal*, 12(2), 2002, 123–134.

1. P. F. Drucker, "The Economy's Dark Continent," *Fortune*, April 1962, 265–70.

2. Syed Akhter and Pervaiz Alam, "Information Acquisition and Investment Decisions on the Internet: An Empirical Investigation," *Marketing Management Journal* 11, no. 1 (Spring 2001). Also see http://www.internetworldstats.com/stats.htm and http://www.witiger.com/ecommerce/ecommercestatistics.htm.

3. S. Nitish and S. Kundu, "Explaining the Growth of E-Commerce Corporations (ECCS): An Extension and Application of the Eclectic Paradigm," *Journal of International Business Studies* 33, no. 4 (2002): 679–97.

4. J. Hamill, "The Internet and International Marketing," *International Marketing Review* 14, no. 5 (1997): 300–23.

5. David M. Neipert, *A Tour of International Trade* (Upper Saddle River, NJ: Prentice Hall, 2000).

6. Forrester Research, http://www.forrester.com.

7. J. B. Cullen, *Multinational Management: A Strategic Approach* (Cincinnati, OH: South-Western College Publishing, 1999).

8. S. Samiee, "Exporting and the Internet: A Conceptual Perspective," *International Marketing Review* 15, no. 5 (1998): 413–26.

9. Council of Supply Chain Management Professionals, http://www.clm 1.org.

10. M. Mendenhall, B. J. Punnett, and D. Ricks, *Global Management* (Oxford: Blackwell Publishers, 1995).

11. Anonymous, "Creating the Right E-Business Model," *Chief Executive*, February 2000, 30–31.

12. Ann Saccomano, "So You've Got a Web Page. Now What Do You Do?," *Traffic World* 259, no. 4 (July 26, 1999): 28–30.

13. John Parker, "In the Global Zone," *Traffic World*, March 13, 2000, 20–21.

14. David Biederman, "The LCE Has Arrived," *Traffic World*, January 10, 2000, 18.

15. John R. Johnson, "Surviving the E-Commerce Transition," *Warehousing Management* 7, no. 11 (2000): WM3–WM6.

16. Anonymous, "Creating the Right E-Business Model."

17. Geoff Tyler, "Get up to Speed," *Supply Management* 5, no. 6 (March 23, 2000): 41–43.

18. Annie Gregory, "E-fulfillment Is Delivering . . . Oh No It Isn't!," *Works Management* 54, no. 3 (2001): 20–24.

19. Johnson, "Surviving the E-Commerce Transition."

20. Anonymous, "China in a Flurry of Airport Construction," *USA Today*, October 2, 2006, http://www.usatoday.com/travel/flights/2006-10-02-china -airports-usat_x.htm.

21. Anonymous, "Creating the Right E-Business Model."

22. Parker, "In the Global Zone."

23. http://www.exportcompliance.com/landed_cost_calculator.asp.

24. Tyler, "Get up to Speed."

25. Marcia Jedd, "Reverse Logistics Online: Returns Happen," *Inbound Logistics* 20, no. 2 (February 2000): 22–30.

26. Anonymous, "Creating the Right E-Business Model"; Saccomano, "So You've Got a Web Page."

27. Tony Seideman, "Weapons for a New World," *Logistics Management and Distribution Report*, April 2000, E33–E36.

28. Parker, "In the Global Zone"; Ong, Cin Eang, and Singh Mohini, "The Role of Redress in B2C E-Business" (22nd Bled eConference eEnablement: Facilitating an Open, Effective and Representative eSociety, June 14–17, 2009), http://www.bledconference.org/proceedings.nsf/Proceedings/ 18F571429D2455D5C125760000410AEE/$File/37_Ong.pdf.

29. Seideman, "Weapons for a New World."

30. Anonymous/Caldwell, "Transportation Policy is Key to Global Trade," *Transportation and Distribution*, June 1997, 84–90.

31. Kathy Williams, "Preparing Your Business for Secure E-Commerce," *Strategic Finance*, 2000, 21–23.

32. M. Hartnett, "New Anti-Fraud Initiative Focuses on E-Commerce Transaction Security," *Stores* 82, no. 12 (December 2000): 64–66.

33. S. DeCovny, "The Electronic Commerce Comes of Age," *The Journal of Business Strategy* 19, no. 6 (November/December 1998): 38–44; Paula Saunders, Herbert Brown, Roger Brucker, and Richard Bloomingdate, "Disintermediation and the Changing Distribution Landscape," *Marketing Management Journal* 11, no. 2 (2001).

34. Parker, "In the Global Zone."

Chapter 14

The Development and Future Potential of the Maquiladoras

John P. McCray, Lance Eliot Brouthers and Timothy J. Wilkinson

Maquiladora factories in Mexico have experienced phenomenal growth during the past four decades. Initially employing about 3,000 workers in 1965, their total workers today number more than one million. Their establishment and subsequent growth represent a major change in Mexico's import substitution and foreign investment policies.

Before maquiladoras, direct investment in Mexico required complex governmental approval, 51 percent Mexican ownership, and often a percentage of local content. Exporting to Mexico was made difficult by the country's import permits (which were expensive and required long periods of time and appropriate governmental connections to obtain) and high tariffs, often exceeding 20 percent of product value.

Maquiladora manufacturing has expanded in six distinct stages, each characterized by increasing competitiveness. In stage I, entrepreneurial expansion, Mexican entrepreneurs experimented with the creation of industrial parks, U.S. entrepreneurs experimented with manufacturing in Mexico, and Mexican officials experimented with the creation of maquiladora rules and laws establishing duty-free processing zones in the country. Stage II, regional expansion, was characterized by more favorable Mexican laws, while Stage III, multinational expansion, saw significant devaluations of the peso which lowered maquiladora wage rates. In Stage IV, NAFTA maquiladora manufacturing increased dramatically as Mexican wages continued to fall. This continued in Stage V, wherein maquiladora employment reached its peak. Finally, in Stage VI, low-wage competition from China put a dent in what had seemed to be an inexorable expansion of the maquiladoras.

How have such dramatic changes occurred? What will maquiladoras look like by the middle of the century? Which industries will likely benefit from the maquiladoras of the future? We address these questions by first examining the historical development of manufacturing along the northern border of Mexico, discussing the major ethical and social issues confronting the factories, and examine job and plant displacement.

ORIGINS OF THE MAQUILADORA

Far from the populated center of Mexico lay the northwestern frontier known as the "Zona Libre," or free zone. It consisted of the state of Baja California and certain cities in Sonora that functioned as free ports. Official Mexican import substitution policies (high tariffs, import permits, and restrictions on foreign investment) were not followed in the Zona Libre because the government found it too difficult to enforce them in the regions along the westernmost U.S./Mexico border. For that reason, U.S. trade and investment in the free zone was, for the most part, unrestricted.

Zonas Libres

The concept of the Zona Libre allowed U.S. and Mexican entrepreneurs to develop their businesses with little regard for the border between the two countries. These infant businesses in the Zona Libre, which manufactured in Mexico using inputs from the United States (with no formal recognition from either the U.S. or Mexican governments), set the stage for the more formalized maquiladora factories that followed. The name "maquiladora" came from the Spanish term *maquila*—the payment in corn that a miller keeps for milling. Often the term is shortened to just "maquila."

In addition to the favorable conditions created by the concept of the Zona Libre, unemployment in Mexico along its border with the

United States became a concern for the Mexican government when the United States ended the Bracero program in 1964.[1] The Bracero program had allowed Mexican workers to enter the United States temporarily, work on U.S. farms, and return to Mexico at the end of the season. Without this program to provide jobs, and with little industrial development in Mexico along the border, Mexican officials were concerned that high unemployment would plague the border cities. So the government commissioned a series of studies to determine how to increase industrialization and employment along the border. One such study, completed by Arthur Little de Mexico in 1964, recommended the establishment of manufacturing within "free zones" in the northern border cities.[2]

U.S. Policy

The United States has never passed any specific law to promote maquiladoras in Mexico. However, two provisions of U.S. Customs laws and domestic transportation policy contribute to the development of maquila manufacturing. Items 806.30 and 807.00 of the 1963 Tariff Schedules allow reimportation into the United States of products assembled abroad with American components, charging a duty only on the value added by foreign assembly. These laws apply to all non-U.S. countries and were enacted before any formally recognized maquiladora plants existed in Mexico.[3]

Second, the completion of the U.S. interstate highway system in the late 1960s and early 1970s reduced the cost of transportation in the United States. This made maquila manufacturing attractive by reducing the cost and time associated with moving (1) inputs from factories in the United States to the maquiladoras and (2) finished products to where they were needed in the United States.

MAQUILADORA DEVELOPMENT

As mentioned before, the development of maquiladoras occurred in four distinct and recognizable stages of expansion: (1) entrepreneurial, (2) regional, (3) multinational, and (4) NAFTA. In the following discussion, we point to three primary drivers of maquila expansion: Mexican economic policy, currency devaluations, and relative wages. The influence of these factors on each stage of development is summarized in Table 14.1.

Table 14.1
Development of the Maquiladoras

	Mexican Maquiladora and trade policy	Total Peso devaluation	End-of-stage comparative wages	Growth in number of workers	
				Average annual growth	End-of-stage employment
Stage I 1965–1971 Entrepreneurial Expansion	Experimenting with maquiladora rules and regulations; imports to non-maquiladora factories require import permits, very high tariffs, and significant Mexican content	None	Mexico $ .57 Hong Kong .36 Singapore .30 Korea .26 Japan 1.34 United States 3.56	4,369	29,214
Stage II 1972–1981 Regional Expansion	Law establishing tariff-free imports for maquiladoras; imports to non-maquiladora factories require import permits, very high tariffs, and significant Mexican content	49%	Mexico $ 2.82 Hong Kong 1.55 Singapore 1.80 Korea 1.02 Japan 6.08 United States 10.87	9,213	130,973
Stage III 1982–1988 Multinational Expansion	More favorable maquiladora laws; Mexico joins GATT; tariffs lowered for non-maquiladora factories;	98%	Mexico $ 1.25 Hong Kong 2.40 Singapore 2.67 Korea	40,407	369,489

Stage	Description	%	Country	Hourly compensation		
	most import permits removed		Japan	2.20		
			United States	12.63		
				13.91		754,858
Stage IV 1989–1996 NAFTA Expansion	Maintenance of favorable maquiladora laws; Mexico initiates and negotiates NAFTA; maquiladoras have clear regulations and the most favorable tariffs	68%	Mexico	$1.50	46,448	754,858
			Hong Kong	5.14		
			Singapore	8.32		
			Korea	8.23		
			Japan	8.23		
			United States	21.04		
				17.74		
Stage V 1997–2000 Extension of NAFTA Expansion	Maintenance of favorable maquiladora laws	4.6%	Mexico	$2.89	144,091	1,331,224
			Hong Kong	—		
			Singapore	11.65		
			Korea	9.26		
			Japan	25.34		
			United States	24.63		
Stage VI 2001–2006 Competition with China	China is a member of WTO which increases U.S.-China trade; U.S. in recession	37%	Mexico	$3.72	(22,843)	1,194,167
			China	0.81		
			Singapore	13.77		
			Korea	16.59		
			Japan	24.32		
			United States	29.98		

Source: International Comparisons of Hourly Compensation Costs in Manufacturing, Bureau of Labor Statistics, U.S. Department of Labor, March 26, 2009.

Stage I, 1965–1971: Entrepreneurial Expansion

The initial push that set maquiladora manufacturing in motion came from Mexican and U.S. entrepreneurs who possessed the capability to build, finance, and run industrial parks and factories in Mexico. Beginning with 3,000 workers in 1965, the entrepreneurs established factories in Mexico along its northern border. With loose, informal arrangements there, Mexico required few if any tariffs as the component parts used by the maquiladoras entered Mexico. When the products made in the factories entered the United States, tariffs were generally due only on the value added to the U.S. components. During this stage, Mexican officials began to experiment with regulations to establish legal duty-free manufacturing processing zones. But with no devaluations and Mexican wages above those in Asian countries, maquila employment grew only slightly.

The early entrepreneurs represented both small and large businesses. The initial small maquiladoras were concentrated in sewing and furniture making, whereas larger firms such as Raytheon developed electrical and electronic manufacturing.

Mexican Policy in Stage I

Mexico's experimentation with border manufacturing regulations began with an announcement in May 1965 of a Border Industrialization Program.[4] Over the next few years, entrepreneurs established maquiladora factories by working out investment and customs procedures in Mexico in conjunction with local officials at the border. The first maquiladora law was passed in 1971, permitting the plants in border cities and along the coast, 100 percent foreign ownership; foreign technicians; and duty-free importation of raw materials, supplies, and machinery.[5] As a consequence, Mexican entrepreneurs began to build larger and more competitive industrial parks, stimulating the growth of maquiladora factories and employment.[6]

Comparative Wages and Employment in Stage

During the entrepreneurial stage, Mexican manufacturing wages were about 25 percent of U.S. wages, but higher than those in many Asian countries, such as Singapore and Korea. Although advocates of the Border Industrialization Program in the United States and Mexico stressed the comparative savings of maquiladora wages over United States wages with some success, Mexican labor continued to lose out to its Asian competition.

Also during this stage, maquila employment grew from 3,000 to 29,214 people, with an average annual increase of 4,369 workers. Thus, by the end of stage I, maquiladoras still played a minor role in the Mexican economy.

Stage II, 1972–1981: Regional Expansion

The passage of the 1972 maquiladora law in Mexico marked the beginning of regional expansion for the maquilas. American firms began to move labor-intensive aspects of their manufacturing operations to Mexico to improve their competitiveness in the United States. The comprehensive new law allowed maquilas throughout Mexico, except in densely populated cities like Mexico City and Monterrey. U.S. companies, however, continued to flock to the border, especially those in labor-intensive industries seeking cheap, non-unionized workers. The dominant businesses were electrical assembly and apparel plants, which by 1979 comprised 71 percent of total maquila employment.[7]

Mexican Policy

In 1972, as the maquila program began to generate much-needed foreign exchange, Mexico passed the comprehensive law setting in place the fundamentals of maquiladora manufacturing. The law not only allowed maquilas anywhere in Mexico, it also permitted 100 percent foreign ownership; practical ownership (foreign firms could hold land in trust within the border region); and importation of tariff-free raw materials, components, and machinery. In response, larger firms began to replace smaller firms as the dominant maquiladora manufacturers, and about 30 percent of the maquilas became non-American owned.[8]

Devaluations, Comparative Wages, and Employment

From 1972 through 1975, no Mexican currency devaluations occurred. But in 1976, the peso fell 19 percent, and 1977 saw a drop of 32 percent. Despite these two devaluations, Mexican hourly wages remained higher than those of Hong Kong, Korea, and Singapore. But they were still low compared to U.S. wages, which averaged over $10.00 an hour at that time.

During this regional expansion stage, maquila employment grew from 48,060 to 130,973 workers, with an average annual increase of

9,213 workers—about twice that of the preceding stage. Although still a small percentage of the overall Mexican workforce, maquilas were beginning to grow in importance, especially for companies interested in lowering their labor costs for goods bound for U.S. markets.

Stage III, 1982–1988: Multinational Expansion

The third stage of maquila development, which came about in part because of the world oil crisis, was noteworthy because of two situations: (1) new Mexican policies favoring maquiladora owners, and (2) significant devaluations of the peso, which created more favorable relative wage rates for maquilas. For the first time, Mexican wages fell below those in Asia. As a result, average annual job growth increased dramatically. Lower relative Mexican wages plus easy access to the U.S. market allowed the maquilas to become one of the world's most desirable manufacturing arenas.

Maquiladora manufacturing saw a dramatic increase in the number of larger, non-U.S. global corporations, such as Sony, Matsushita, and Samsung.[9] It was not unusual for a single new factory to employ 3,000 or more workers.

Mexican Policy

During this stage, declining international oil prices (and the resulting domestic financial crisis), coupled with a maquiladora program that offered successful alternatives to traditional import substitution, inspired Mexico to change its historic trade policies. Unilaterally, the country scrapped fundamental policies of import substitution and joined the General Agreement on Tariffs and Trade (GATT)—now known as the World Trade Organization (WTO)—in August 1986.[10] With this move, a comprehensive trade treaty existed between the United States and Mexico for the first time. This set the stage for considering and negotiating the North American Free Trade Agreement (NAFTA).

Devaluation, Comparative Wages, and Employment

Currency devaluations occurred in every year of Stage III, driving Mexican hourly wages well below those of Hong Kong, Korea, Singapore, and other low-wage competitor nations. Mexican wages, which had been about 15 percent of U.S. wages, dropped to 10 percent. Combined with access to the U.S. market, these new wage rates established maquiladora manufacturing as one of the more competitive manufacturing platforms in the world. The average annual increase in maquila employment was 40,407 workers per year—nearly four times the annual growth in the preceding stage.

Stage IV, 1988–1996: NAFTA Expansion

A continued reduction in labor costs resulting from additional peso devaluations characterized the fourth expansion stage. NAFTA provisions also benefitted maquila manufacturing, creating additional demand for maquila plants from firms committed to the North American marketplace.

The NAFTA contained three provisions that were critical for maquiladoras. First, in order to receive preferential NAFTA tariffs, a minimum of 50 percent of most products' content had to come from Mexico, Canada, or the United States for most products. For autos and light trucks, the figure was a whopping 62 percent. Second, NAFTA provided for the eventual reduction of tariffs to zero for products containing sufficient North American content. Third, special import and tariff provisions, such as those enjoyed by the maquiladoras, were required to be phased out by 2001. No doubt, it is because of this provision that many thought NAFTA would doom the maquilas.

The irony was that content requirements and tariff reductions, coupled with the already existing maquiladora laws in Mexico, made maquila manufacturing even more competitive under NAFTA. Content requirements favored North American manufacturers, and Mexico was the most cost-effective place in North America to locate new manufacturing.

Both U.S. and Mexican tariffs were being phased out over a period of time under NAFTA, but Mexican tariffs started from a higher base percentage. Although Mexico would eventually remove its tariffs, many were still significant as NAFTA was implemented. Thus, maquilas could still benefit from duty-free imports into the country as provided by maquiladora laws.

Finally, maquilas were in a very competitive position because the laws governing them were well-established and working smoothly by the time NAFTA went into effect in January 1994. In contrast, NAFTA rules and tariffs were new, and some provisions, such as the transportation provisions to open the border to trucking on December 17, 1995, were delayed. So the maquiladora was still the "smart bet" for new investors in Mexico; the rules of the game were in place and the plants still received preferential tax treatment.

Devaluation, Wages, and Employment

Devaluations occurred every year in this stage, with the net effect of making Mexican wages among the lowest in the world and maquiladoras among the most cost-competitive manufacturers. With wages more favorable than most Asian competitors and NAFTA giving tariff preferences to all products manufactured in North America, maquiladoras became firmly established as an essential part of the North American global manufacturing mix.

During this expansion stage, large, efficient maquila factories owned by large U.S. and Japanese firms dominated. Maquila employment grew from 429,725 workers in 1989 to 754,858 workers in 1996. The average annual increase in the number of workers was 46,448, the highest of all four states.

Stage V, 1997–2000: Extension of NAFTA Expansion

This stage can be characterized as a simple extension of the expansion that took place in the 1990s. During this time maquila employment and overall maquila operations continued to expand, reaching an all time high of 1,331,224 by the year 2000. It is interesting to note that little attention was being paid to new developments taking place in China, which would soon place the maquilas at a competitive disadvantage vis-à-vie their Chinese counterparts. Essentially the Middle Kingdom was taking a page out of the Mexican playbook by creating economic zones that were organized and function very similarly to the Maquiladoras. The largest of these was developed in Shenzen, adjacent to Hong Kong. During this period trade between the United States and Mexico continued to grow, but U.S. and China trade grew even more rapidly.

Devaluation, Comparative Wages, and Employment

During this stage the peso was devalued by only 4.6%. However, Mexican wages, at $2.89 an hour, remained well below those of Korea, its closest competitor. This period also exhibits the largest average annual growth in the number of Maquila workers. Each year 144,091 new employees were added, almost three times the average of the previous stage.

Stage VI, 2001–2006: Competition with China

In 2000 China became a member of the World Trade Organization (WTO). This resulted in dramatic changes for the maquiladoras. Just as the NAFTA caused an increase in U.S. Mexican trade—including maquila trade—the admission of China into the WTO resulted in a substantial increase in trade between the United States and China.

Devaluation, Comparative Wages, and Employment

U.S. companies were not slow to embrace the low-wage option of Chinese contract manufacturing. Average end-of-stage wage rates in China were a mere $0.81 per hour. Mexico, with an hourly rate of $3.72, was no longer the low price leader, even after a 37% currency devaluation during stage VI.

The results are not surprising. During this stage a significant decrease in maquiladora employment took place: from 1,331,224 in 2000 to 1,087,664 in 2001. To make matters worse for Mexico, the United States was also in a recession in 2001. The combination of increasing U.S. trade with China as a result of China joining the WTO and the U.S. recession resulted in maquila employment falling to 1,084,230 in 2002, 1,067,160 in 2003, and a low of 1,151,610 in 2004. After 2004, employment began to recover. In 2006, the last year for which reliable statistics are available, maquila employment stood at 1,194,167. Not surprisingly, 18% of maquila factories shut down between mid-2000 and August of 2003.[11] It is safe to assume that employment dropped further after the worldwide financial implosion that began in 2008.

The Once and Future Maquiladoras

Mexico Peso devaluations have continued almost every year, as shown in Table 14.2. In 1996, 7.60 pesos could purchase one dollar. Between 1996 and 2006 the Mexican peso had devaluated and it took 13.50 pesos to purchase one U.S. dollar. The effect of this devaluation was to make Maquiladora wages less and less relative to U.S. wages.

Although China has clearly put a dent in the maquilas, the maquiladoras do have strategic advantages such as the close proximity of these factories to the United States and a greater ability to control intellectual property. The maquilas have also been drawn into the U.S.-China trade relationship. There was a significant shift in maquiladora inputs from the United States to Asia after China was admitted to the WTO, when Chinese imports to the United States were growing dramatically. Maquiladoras use numerous components that are cheap in Asia. About one-half of the U.S. trade that is southbound (U.S. exports) at El Paso are re-exports. This means that they were imported into the United States and then

Table 14.2
Pesos per U.S. Dollar

Year	Average annual Mexican Pesos per U.S. dollar
1996	7.60
1997	7.92
1998	9.15
1999	9.55
2000	7.95
2001	9.34
2002	9.67
2003	10.79
2004	11.29
2005	10.89
2006	10.90
2007	10.93
2008	11.15
2009	13.50

without being altered or changed in any way. Although re-export data is identified in trade data, country of origin is not specified. However, that a large portion of re-exports headed to Mexico are Chinese in origin is no secret among U.S. Customs officials as well as others familiar with cross-border trade with Mexico.

What changes can international managers expect to take place in maquiladoras during the 21st century? Companies and governments alike will have to grapple with four major issues in the next few decades. First, how will business and political leaders address the ethical and social issues that arise from further concentration of industry along the northern border of Mexico? Second, how will NAFTA affect the maquilas? Third, which areas of the world will lose jobs to the maquilas? And fourth, what industries will be drawn to them in the future?

Ethical and Social Issues

Despite the benefits enjoyed by government and industry, the situation has not always been bright for the low-wage maquila workers. Disturbing reports of human rights abuses raise the question of how managers and government officials should address the ethical issue of labor exploitation and the social issues surrounding living conditions along the northern border. Labor groups protest the low wages, unsafe working conditions, and sexual and other forms of harassment that take place.[12] Martha Ojeda, an organizer for the Coalition for Justice in the maquiladoras, complains, "There are many companies along the border which treat their employees like trash."[13]

Economist Stephen Golub illustrates the complexity of the human rights issue by pointing out that "developing countries have expressed concern that the industrial countries' new emphasis on labor standards is just protectionism in disguise."[14] He argues that mandating labor conditions on a par with those of the developed world only makes things worse by forcing people to live in even shabbier conditions. For example, while child labor is an appalling practice, says Golub, "the earnings of these children may be important to their families' and their own survival."[15] By proscribing work in the formal sector, children may end up engaging in illegal activities that are even more degrading. Moreover, regulating labor conditions can have unintended, negative consequences. For example, minimum wages comparable to those of developed countries can result in high unemployment, with too few people being paid excessively high wages.

Golub suggests that labor and trade policies encouraging high growth, as well as government funds targeted for education and training, should be pursued as an alternative to counterproductive legislation.[16] And if such actions do not improve living and working conditions among the maquilas, the U.S. government has the option of passing laws specifically designed for American firms on the Mexican border. Such extraterritoriality has proven to be popular in the U.S. Congress in recent years, from the prohibition of foreign firms dealing with Cuba to attempts to enforce antitrust laws outside its borders. Selective application of American standards for companies operating so close to the United States might be a direct way of addressing some of the human rights issues facing the maquilas.

NAFTA and the Maquiladoras

Mexican and U.S. firms are likely to dominate the maquiladora scene in the foreseeable future. Local content requirements coupled with tariff reductions and the close proximity of company headquarters favor North American manufacturers. In addition, there will likely be dramatic increases in the number of small to medium-sized firms in the program. This is because maquilas serve as low-cost export platforms that help companies gain valuable international experience.

Maquiladoras can and do produce NAFTA products. A significant change took place in the years since NAFTA came into effect in January 1994 and the first increment of tariffs was removed. NAFTA contained two principal provisions related to products that could be traded. The first was the tariff—what would be the tariff rate on day one of the NAFTA (actually there technically was no day one since the treaty was late being signed) and what would be the phase out period before the tariff became zero. The other provision was content—how much of the value of the product must originate in any combination of the three North American countries. Even a tariff of 20%, which was very high, stood at only about 3% by 2010. If a firm wants to have the North American market available at essentially zero tariffs, it must insure that it has the appropriate North American content—50% for most products, 62.5% for autos and light trucks. Since many Asian components are cheap, a combination of Asian components, maquiladora assembly and final manufacturing in the United States often make a competitive combination.

Job and Plant Displacement

In terms of employment displacement, facts are not easy to ascertain. Estimates of U.S. job losses as a result of maquila production depend on the type of estimation method used.[17] The Clinton administration claimed that of the 2.3 million jobs supported by exports of U.S. goods to Mexico, 322,000 could be attributed to increased trade under NAFTA.[18] Estimates of the number of American jobs displaced by the agreement were not included in the report. However, during the same time period, the Economic Policy Institute, a critic of NAFTA, placed job losses at 250,000, whereas the International President of the United Steelworkers of America estimated the number at approximately 2 million.[19] The debate has continued up to the present day. After Barak Obama claimed that millions of manufacturing jobs had been lost due to NAFTA, John Engler, of the *Wall Street Journal* wrote an op-ed piece which states, "What the anti-trade advocates have been hiding from the candidates (or maybe don't know themselves) is that almost all of the increase in our NAFTA deficit since 2000 has been in increased U.S. imports of energy from Canada and Mexico. In fact, $58 billion of the $62 billion increase in our NAFTA deficit has been in energy imports. That's 95% of the total increase."[20]

Clearly, the number and location of job displacements in North America is a matter of considerable dispute.

Maquilas of the Future

When we first wrote about the maquiladoras in 1999, we stated the following:

The future of maquiladora manufacturing appears to be rosy. Maquilas operate as free trade zones within Mexico, permitting the exporting of assembled products to the U.S. and Canada under the favorable conditions of NAFTA, and exporting to non-NAFTA countries with no more restrictions than other exports. Regardless of potentially strengthened local content or value-added content stipulations, many foreign firms are likely to continue investing in maquilas for three reasons: a plentiful labor supply, low labor costs, and easy access to U.S. markets.

Although it is not possible to predict exactly which industries will be drawn to the maquilas, one of two scenarios is likely to be played out. First, Mexico's corporatist political system may decide to pursue export-led growth that depends on something besides cheap labor. Currently, in terms of the sheer number of plants, textiles, clothing, and electronics make up almost half of the total. By directing foreign investment to more desirable industrial sectors, upgrading technology, and eventually engaging in local R&D, Mexico's maquilas could be transformed into leading-edge producers of high-tech products. Computerization, microelectronic technology, and flexible manufacturing systems have been incorporated in some electronic and automotive plants.[21] Under this scenario, the government will implement policies which move the maquilas beyond assembling components to a point at which national inputs are a substantial part of the production process. Through such "backward linkages," says Wilson, the maquilas would cease to exist as the world's low-wage leaders, instead pursuing a development path similar to that of the Asian tigers.[22]

The second, more likely scenario, is that the maquilas remain merely "enclaves" in which components are assembled using low-wage laborers and then exported. Arguments suggesting these factories are in the process of modernizing have been rigorously disputed. Automation and skill development for workers are key elements in the development of the previously mentioned backward linkages; yet in newer maquila operations, 80 percent of the workers are classified as being low-skilled. Management has shown little interest in activities that would upgrade the labor force because cheap labor is, after all, the most attractive aspect of the maquiladora. Introducing the most efficient technologies, says Kopinak, would not be cost effective.[23] Therefore, unless Mexico's political forces change the rules of the game, a comparatively inexpensive labor pool will continue to draw those industries that are not dependent on a highly skilled work force. Barring a move up in the "food chain" of international production, the industries that are attracted to the maquilas should remain the same.

As it turned out, because of China, the future did not turn out to be all rosy for the maquiladoras. A great deal of manufacturing, and the accompanying employment, went overseas. The maquilas did not end-up being the low-wage champions of the world, and neither did Mexico successfully use the maquilas to improve their labor force or help their companies to rapidly move up the value chain in terms of innovation and manufacturing. At the same time, an important trend can be seen in terms of the aggressiveness that some developers have undertaken to maintain and expand maquila manufacturing. The result of this is that some maquila developers, especially in the city of Mexicali, have moved up scale from SONY TV production to jet engine blade manufacturing. Again if a firm is concerned about their intellectual property in China, the maquila is a good bet.

Competition from the Chinese has belatedly led to a shift away from low value-added products to a product mix that emphasized just-in-time products, products with short cycle requirements and heavy goods that are too expensive to source from across the ocean. Over time the goal is to leverage Mexico's large number of university-trained engineers and its strong affirmation of intellectual property rights in order to produce higher value added products.[24]

CONCLUSION

Through their various stages of development and expansion, maquiladoras appear to have benefitted from a wide variety of economic policies and fluctuations. Historically, what has been good for

Mexico has been good for the maquilas, and what has been bad for Mexico has *also* been good for the maquilas.

Which scenario will fit the performance of the maquilas of the next century? Will they pursue a developmental strategy similar to that taken by Asia's Four Tigers—technological development, improvements in human capital, backward linkages, involvement in R&D, and the eventual development and export of high-tech products? Or will they remain much as they are, assembly points for mainly foreign manufacturers? The circumstances that have allowed them to become the world leader in low labor costs would appear to favor the second scenario. As a result, maquiladoras could be a place of opportunity for foreign firms—and sometimes deplorable working conditions—well into the twenty-first century.

NOTES

This chapter is adapted from the article, "Maquiladoras: Entrepreneurial Experimentation to Global Competitiveness," published by Business Horizons, pages 37–44. March–April 1999. Copyright © 1999 Kelly School of Business, Indiana University. All rights reserved. Reprinted with permission from Elsevier.

1. Leslie Sklair, *Assembling for Development* (San Diego: Centèr for U.S. Mexican Studies, University of California, 1993).

2. Joseph Grunwald, "The Assembly Industry in Mexico," in *The Global Factory: Foreign Assembly in International Trade*, ed. Joseph Grunwald and Kenneth Flamm (Washington, DC: Brookings Institute, 1985), 137–79.

3. U.S. Tariff Commission, *Economic Factors Affecting the Use of Items 807.00 and 806.30 of the Tariff Schedules of the United States* (Washington, DC: U.S. Tariff Commission, 1970).

4. Sklair, *Assembling for Development*.

5. Secretaria de Industria y Comercio, *Mexican Border Industrialization Program* (Mexico, D.F.: Secretaria de Industria y Comercio, 1971), 82.

6. Richard L. Bolin, "The Mexican Example Can be Applied Elsewhere," *Caribbean Business*, February 29, 1984.

7. INEGI, *Estadistica de la Industria Maquiladora de Exportacion 1975–1985* (Mexico, D.F.: Instituto Nacional de Estadistica Geografia e Informatica, INEGI, 1986).

8. "Mexico: Surge in Foreign Investment," *Institutional Investor*, July 10, 1991.

9. Larry Waller, "Japanese Manufacturers Flock to Mexico," *Electronics*, March 31, 1988, 46–47.

10. USITC, *The Impact of Increased United States—Mexico Trade on Southwest Border Development* (Washington, DC: United States International Trade Commission (USITC) Publication 1915, November 1986), 47–48.

11. Ernesto Acevedo, "Causes of Recession in Maquiladora Industry" (presentation at El Paso for the Federal Reserve Bank of Dallas, November 2003).

12. David Bacon, "Workers in Maquiladoras from Tijuana to Juarez Are Fighting Back against NAFTA-Driven Exploitation," *SF Bay Guardian*, March 5, 1997.

13. S. L. Smith, "Alcoa Scruitinizes Maquiladoras," *Occupational Hazards*, March 1997, 20.

14. Stephen Golub, "Are International Labor Standards Needed to Prevent Dumping?," *Finance & Development*, December 1997, 20.

15. Ibid., 22.

16. Ibid.

17. Gregory K. Schoepfle and Jorge F. Perez-Lopez, "The Impact of Macquiladoras on U.S. National Employment and Employment in Selected Industrial Sectors," in *The Maquiladora Industry: Economic Solution or Problem?*, ed. Khosrow Fatemi (New York: Praeger, 1990).

18. Executive Office of the President (EOP), *Study on the Operation and Effects of the North American Free Trade Agreement* (report to Congress, 1997).

19. David Adams, "Workers Lose in Race for Profit, Leader Says," *Akron Beacon Journal*, September 18, 1998.

20. John Engler, *Wall Street Journal* (Eastern edition), April 21, 2008, A.15

21. J. C. Ramírez and N. Fuentes Flores, "La Nueva industria sonorense: El Caso de las Maquilas de Exportaciòn," in *Industrializaciòn en Sonora: El Caso de los Sectores de Alta Tecnologìa*, coordinator J. Ramírez, *La Nueva* 170132 (Hermosillo: El Colegio de Sonora, 1989); Harvey C. Bunke, "In Search of Gold and Sanctuary in Tijuana," *Business Horizons*, January–February 1992.

22. Patricia A. Wilson, *Exports and Local Development: Mexico's New Maquiladoras* (Austin: University of Texas Press, 1992), 23, 33–35.

23. Kathryn Kopinak, *Desert Capitalism* (Tucson: The University of Arizona Press, 1996), 145.

24. ProLogis Research Bulletin, "Mexico's Maquiladoras—Climbing the Ladder of Success," Spring 2008.

Chapter 15

Using Social Media to Promote Global Organizations

Kristi Drake and Sarah N. Keller

INTRODUCTION

Facebook, Twitter, and YouTube among others, provide entertainment and connectivity around the globe. Their popularity in this global society, where face-to-face social interaction narrows to work and family, is no surprise. Now cable shows, news, amusing videos, and novel productions are free to nearly anyone with an Internet connection. Old friends find each other and incumbents update one another on their latest whereabouts, through social media. Through this vast network of high-volume, fast-paced messaging, communities are built and relationships are strengthened.

Domestic and multinational organizations have found that the online community often welcomes their presence, and is invited to join the dialogue to promote or address issues. Individuals have long traded information about organizations, products, and causes that catch their attention through social media connections. Businesses and nonprofits are now learning to talk *with* viewers, instead of simply being talked *about*.

The Internet and social media have brought on new opportunities for organizational promotion to global audiences. These media are not only accessible for users and organizations, their use is expanding among many demographic audiences, and can be a preferred source of information to enhance traditional media.

Social media include mobile phone text messaging, social networking sites, blogs, message boards, etc. More than 600 million users existed on the social networking web sites (Facebook, MySpace, LinkedIn, etc.) in late 2009, a number that grows 6 percent monthly.[1] Although the major segment of users is under 25, users can vary in age from preteens to the elderly, and live in areas as remote as Nepal or Bhutan. Users of social networking sites are divided along age and class lines. More than 25 percent of all Americans visit MySpace monthly. Of these, 63 percent are female; 14 percent are 17 and under. Facebook tends to appeal to an older, more gender-balanced audience.[2]

The term *social media* refers to the connectivity and interaction with others these sites offer to users. On a given day, a Twitter user will have updated his or her personal profile several times, with information about where (s)he is going, what (s)he has done, or his or her observations about the day. Perhaps (s)he will come across an entertaining story on the Internet and will pass it on to friends via a Twitter update. Articles and videos can originate from news feeds, YouTube videos, and podcasts, and are passed from peer to peer, and across media platforms. Of course, these messages know no boundaries in the digital world, so localized information can travel across the globe and reach multitudes of cultures in seconds.

The style of communication among audiences and platforms is quite varied. For example, there are five ways to communicate on Facebook: status updates, bulletins, blogs, comments, and one-on-one messaging. Many messages have to do with social responsibility, personal life, fan clubs, jokes, and news.

Research shows that most people connecting to these sites are from the socially conscious millennial generation.[3] Their propensity for constant social connections makes them a good market for social causes and cause marketing.

Boyd[4] found that U.S. youth use a variety of social media to develop and maintain broader communities of peers. Teen practices when using social media mirror those of other places where teens gather with peers; in parking lots and shopping malls, teens gather in public spaces to negotiate identity, gossip, support one another, jockey for status, collaborate, share information, flirt, joke, or just "hang out." By providing tools for mediated interactions, social media allow teens to extend their interactions beyond physical boundaries. Conversations and interactions that begin in person do not end when friends are separated.

People accessing Facebook, Twitter, and other sites belong to a vast population of global consumers. A U.S. cluster analysis of the National Consumer Study by Simmons Research, an Experian company, reveals nine distinct types of social media consumers: (1) socially isolated users; (2) approval seekers (who buy what others are buying and like to follow styles and trends); (3) health and image leaders (who are eager to try health and wellness products, experiment with diets, and spend to look younger); (4) smart green users (prefer to buy products in recycled packages and eschew products that pollute); (5) brand-loyal users; (6) stay-at-home moms (who use social media for a variety of reasons, including staying in touch and parental guidance); (7) upscale grays (50-plus consumers with college degrees and household incomes of more than $100,000 are low-level social-media users); (8) first-time home-buyers; and 9) divorcees.[5]

Social Media Is Transforming Marketing and Public Relations

Public dialogue about products, experiences and social causes is impetus for organizations to join the discussion and build relationships. Those who do not engage in popular public commentary can be overlooked, forgotten, or worse, targeted by users or competitors without much opportunity for appeal.[6]

Social media can be an effective way to market an organization on an international scale. Companies and nonprofits are harnessing the power of this vastly accessed medium to introduce their concepts into the global marketplace of ideas. Furthermore, the interpersonal feature of social media allows companies to not only speak directly to audiences, but also to gather useful information from them to further develop their appeal.

Skype, the worldwide Internet phone company based in Luxembourg, marketed its wares to an international audience in 2008, using various social media sites to demonstrate its capability for easy connection around the world. The "Skype Nomad," a 26-year-old Australian woman, traveled the world in 33 days and updated readers simultaneously on a blog, Facebook, YouTube, Flickr, Twitter, MySpace, and Dopplr. This resulted in "800,000 unique visitors to the Skype Nomad blog; 140,000 page views on Flickr; 300,000 YouTube video views; global coverage on blogs, in the press and on TV—more than 175 stories; and a significant increase in awareness of Skype's mobile capabilities, including a 9 percent increase in the U.K. and an 18 percent increase in the U.S."[7]

Corometrics' "Face of the New Marketer" study found that 78 percent of marketers see social media as a way to gain a competitive edge, but fewer than 8 percent have budgets devoted to it.[8] Currently, this picture is changing; some 88 percent of marketers who use social media plan to spend more on it this year.[9]

Thus, in this digital age, it is imperative that organizations strongly consider incorporating digital relationship-building into their overall promotional strategy. According to Tsai, using social media for marketing is a valuable and increasingly crucial tool in promoting a business. Capitalizing on this enterprise gives organizations a chance to increase awareness about their brand and deepen loyalties with consumers.

Key Strategies Using New Media for Promotion of For-Profit and Non-profit Organizations

Personal Appeal

Along with the personal benefits that users derive from connecting on a personal level, social media sites have created opportunities for organizations to connect and promote themselves on a personal-yet-global level.

Viral Marketing

The social media dimension of promotional messaging not only offers companies the chance to make direct appeals to audiences, it enhances the word-of-mouth factor that gives an organization added credibility as individuals receive endorsements through their mobile devices from peers. Organizations can use social networking sites to reach a new audience that is global in scope, to drive traffic to their website, to build their e-newsletter lists, to fundraise, to drive "friends" to other social networking communities, to gather consumer data, to promote e-advocacy campaigns, and to allow supporters to interact with an organization and promote its Facebook or MySpace site.

Organizations that catch online reader attention can become the subject of discussion through networking. When a message has a certain appeal, it serves as a type of "social currency" that audience members collectively enjoy, point out, or sometimes, demonize.[10] When it attracts enough interest among online community members, organizational messages forwarded to others can go "viral." This word-of-mouth promotion via individual mobile devices has been termed *brand in the hand* marketing.[11] Having a marketing message pass from peer to peer is an ideal situation because individuals are more likely to read a message from an acquaintance than an ad sent by a marketer;[12] however, as control over the message is in the hands of the audience, it can sometimes work to an organization's disadvantage.

Public Relations

Social media is a unique blend of public relations and marketing. Here, the top-down advertising approach is less effective because social media users are engaged for the purpose of connecting on a social level.[13] For this reason, organizations should create a social media marketing strategy with a major focus on public relations, which incorporates lessons learned about both social media usage and cross-cultural communication practices.

Public relations scholars concur that the key strategy in promoting an organization is building relationships with stakeholders.[14-16] Many relationships are cultivated through two-way symmetrical communication, where organizations can listen and respond to audience concerns, with a goal of creating an acceptable solution for both themselves and their stakeholders. Grunig suggested that symmetrical communication requires individuals, organizations, and publics "to adjust their ideas and behavior to those of others rather than to try to control how others think and behave."[17]

Social media provide an ideal platform for attaining such a level of concurrence, as they enable "two-way" contact with stakeholders. As organizations connect with their audiences on a more personal level, they can learn qualitative information that can help them adjust their strategies to create solutions and reconcile differences.

Hyundai exemplified this strategy when it launched its "Think Tank" in 2008. This social media campaign gave the community a chance to communicate directly with top management and even the company's president for an hour to discuss their ideas and opinions about their products and services. When the automaker invited its customers to share thoughts about marketing solutions and product names, "everyone liked having access to the highest person in the company," according to Eileen Mahdi, manager of consumer insights for the company.[18]

Dell computers, albeit a bit late for the trouble it endured, learned the lesson of engaging its public back in 2006. Customer service trouble drove blogger Jeff Jarvis to go to war with Dell on the Internet. Many concurred with the "Dell Hell" blog, and according to Feng and Li, this "effectively brought the power of blogs to international attention for almost the first time."[19] Dell responded with a blog of its own called Direct2Dell, which addressed the customer service problem and was available in a multitude of languages. Dell went further and launched IdeaStorm in 2007, which invited users to tell the company where they needed to improve. Jarvis condoned this move in his 2007 *Business Week* article, and commented on Michael Dell's willingness to admit problems, ask consumers for advice, and be responsive to suggestions. In fact, he described the improvements at Dell: "The crucial word you hear at Dell is 'relationship.' Dell blogger Menchaca has led the charge in convincing bloggers that 'real people are here to listen,' and so he diligently responds and links to critics, and holds up his end of the conversation. 'You can't fake it,' he says. Dell's team is stanching the flow of bad buzz. By Dell's measure, negative blog posts about it have dropped from 49% to 22%."[20]

Certainly, communicators who are engaged with the community via social media will be more adept at noticing, negotiating, and moderating adversity. Communities form both on- and offline when individuals find they share interests or problems. According to public relations theory, stakeholders manifest into a defined group when a few people perceive that an organization has an impact on an issue that concerns them. Online, their voices can attract attention and supporters to the cause. "Aware" publics recognize problems and evolve into "active" publics when they attempt to resolve problems.[21] Grunig[22] found that environmental scanning and segmenting publics by behavior, not demographics, are two components of excellent, effective public relations practices. This will be facilitated through dialogue with online community members, and other voices that may turn up in that medium. The "value of hearing external voices in the strategic management process—voices amplified by public relations professionals who scan the publics in the organization's environment," is a valuable tool in learning how to make sound decisions.[23] Thus, a professional communicator is in a better position to demonstrate the organization's transparency and willingness to listen.

Pitfalls and Considerations of Social Media Promotions

Although evidence seems to clearly illustrate a strong argument for entering the social media arena, a sure-fire formula is yet undeveloped. In addition to the lack of roadmap, global usage of social media exposes companies to heightened consumer expectations, increases pressure for cause marketing, and introduces more risk of cross-cultural miscommunication due to the interactive nature of the medium. In addition, social media management is time-consuming, requiring organizations to commit extra staff to maintaining sites or trusting a company outside of the organization to manage and represent it online.

Lack of a Roadmap

Management Issues.   Different models exist for social media management. Content can be maintained by various levels of individuals within the organization, or can be outsourced by a professional manager, such as a public relations firm. Grunig[24] suggests that public relations matters should be handled by in-house public relations people who have the autonomy to make strategic organizational decisions; Tsai[25] notes that many companies often give the social media management role to junior-level employees who have little decision-making power; however some CEOs recognize the importance that social media plays in promoting their organization and act in a kind of partnership with social media-savvy employees, suggesting a team approach. Each model has benefits and drawbacks.

A review of corporate marketing through social media revealed an analysis of three prominent models, used by Kodak, Ford, and Best Buy: (1) centralized social media departments; (2) distributed social media functions; and (3) combined social media approaches.[26] In the centralized model, the social-media department functions at a senior level, reporting to the CMO or CEO, and is responsible for all social-media activation for the brand. This approach is used by Ford. One disadvantage of this approach is that the social-media director might not pay adequate attention to departments outside their scope, such as customer service. In the distributed model, used by Best Buy, no one person technically owns social media. Instead, all employees from customer care, marketing, media, and beyond represent the brand and work social media into their roles. This model risks veering a brand off message. The combined approach, used by Kodak, involves centralized best practices and decentralized execution, in which planning for social media might take place in one department and execution in another. This approach lacks accountability.[27]

A non-profit social network survey conducted in 2010 reported that organizations whom dedicated two or more staff to managing online social network communities experienced the highest level of satisfaction with their efforts, and associated value in successful campaigning with committing heavily to social media networking.[28]

Social Media Site Preference Is Dynamic.   The popularity of social media sites is capricious. The nature of this medium involves following what everyone else is doing: running along with the pack. Knowing which sites are preferred at a given time requires constant vigilance about trends.

A recent informal poll at a non-profit managers symposium indicated that the most used social media sites by non-profit managers were personal Twitter accounts along with group Twitter accounts tied to their organization. Only 70 to 75 percent of the managers used Facebook for their organization, and even fewer blogged.[29] In fact, a formal survey of 1,173 nonprofit communicators showed that Twitter usage grew 38 percent from 2009 to 2010. It confirmed the informal poll in finding that the rise in new Facebook accounts grew at a smaller percentage (only 16 percent over the prior year) than did new Twitter accounts. Yet that same survey indicated significant use of Facebook, reporting that it was the most popular site used by non-profits and international nonprofits, 97 percent of whom used Facebook. It seems that these nonprofits cover many bases—as the data showed most organizations as using a mix of different sites: although the majority of the international respondents used Facebook, 83.3 percent used Twitter and 69.4 percent used YouTube. LinkedIn trailed at approximately 39 percent usage, followed by Flickr and MySpace respectively.[30]

Consumer Expectations

Another concern is the presence of heightened consumer expectations. As organizations enter this social environment, consumers expect more from a company, including transparency, social responsibility, and two-way communication on a more interpersonal level.[31]

Users of social media reject traditional top-down marketing strategies. Businesses should recognize that for many consumers, the top-down approach is no longer sufficient in product promotion. Blogs are a constantly changing, interdependent medium. If the moderator does not update often with interesting or relevant information, the blog will get stale. The fluidity of information exchange makes them a co-dependent relationship between blogger and follower. "The brisker the pace, the more engaged the readership becomes . . . it's an obsessive compulsive codependent relationship."[32]

Cause Marketing and Corporate Social Responsibility

Tsai noted that the millennial generation, which is now driving the consumer market, expects a more personal relationship from companies, and demands more corporate social responsibility (CSR). CSR can include a company's efforts to give back to society, where social causes become a whole campaign in themselves. With this new way of doing business comes the expense to the organization of committing more resources to funding charitable donations, and staff to managing the campaign—however, the civic and financial rewards may be worth the effort.

The Pepsi Corporation recently forged the way in joining social media with cause-marketing to appeal to this audience. In January 2010 Pepsi launched its "Pepsi Refresh Project," a social media campaign which will include cause-related grants to charitable organizations. In this age of CSR awareness, Pepsi hopes to promote an interpersonal, socially responsible image to its audience. This innovative campaign is likely to deepen Pepsi's relationship with its audience, who had previously been accustomed to simply being entertained by advertisements in more traditional media. As they daringly abandon more expensive media with this latest effort, Pepsi is creating an "opportunity to build ongoing connections with consumers who begin to see Pepsi as a brand that supports them rather than just another marketer blanketing the airwaves and Internet with impressions."[33]

Global Social Media and Cross-Cultural Issues

As a social media campaign reaches across national and cultural borders, whether or not a company intends it, message content should be effective and ethical. Given the interactive nature of social media, complex issues in cross-cultural communication are likely to arise. Cultural contexts, values, and local participation are elements of communication an organization should consider when they are promoting across borders.

Cultural values and folk stories play an important role in forming perceptions. The motives that drive behavior, and the use of symbols and metaphors will undoubtedly differ from culture to culture. When communicating with foreigners, an important component of a well-designed international campaign includes a comprehensive cultural adaptation to messages, which may be more accurately accomplished by someone who is native to the target culture.[34]

In promoting an organization effectively, information must not only be translated, it should be *localized*.[35] In fact, *radical localization*, which "incorporates cultural differences that affect the way users think, feel, and act, above and beyond the superficial differences," will make it more likely that a message will be properly assimilated.[36] For instance, it was reported that in training sessions with foreign salespeople, the American message about monthly sales efforts paying off was shifted to properly fit the cultural value in the foreign market. The American motive for selling, which was to make a profit, was *radically localized* for harmony-conscious, process-oriented Japanese salespeople to communicate a different incentive focused on a monthly effort which became their strength." This supported their values of self-discipline and self-mastery which, when compared to the American's, did not sound so "greedy or selfish."[37]

Digital media can be used effectively to create viral campaigns that appeal to certain age groups. However, their appeal among members of one demographic audience can be offensive to others. Using social media to reach a specific demographic audience on an international scope cannot be contained to a target audience. Messages will undoubtedly find their way into the consciousness of different age groups and cultures when a company markets itself internationally. Despite a campaign's success with a certain group, it can set off a backlash from other stakeholders and its racy appeal may even have a short shelf-life with the target audience.

Rahoi-Gilchrest described how one multinational company used social media to deliver "irreverent messages" to people under 30, around the globe. According to Rahoi-Gilchrest, 42 Below vodka "employed viral public relations to simultaneously build and break relationships in what would seem a socially irresponsible corporate fashion."[38]

The New Zealand distillery generated their campaign through young, " 'hip' staff members" who publicized the brand and collected cell phone numbers at promotional events. Irreverent, sarcastic ads that appealed to this younger audience, exemplified the company's "staunch Kiwiness" and "corporate attitude," and were quickly circulated via personal mobile devices. Although the campaign was successful in many young markets around the globe, it tipped off a backlash from the gay community, as well as others who were the subjects of satire in the ads.

A different story from New Zealand exemplifies the success a nonprofit organization enjoyed when it incorporated social media into its campaign to end child poverty in that country by the year 2020. Ideas Shop of Wellington, New Zealand, reported that by using a Facebook "cause," they found a cost-effective way to "influence government policy and position Child Poverty Action Group as expert media spokespeople." They offered viewers an easy way to donate, provided links to relevant media stories, and updated the site often.[39] By giving the issue an online presence, offering "the latest media coverage and communicating on a direct, personal level," Ideas Shop instigated online dialogue about child poverty and attracted a wider audience.[40]

Last, cultural dimensions play a large role in how different cultures perceive messages and communicate with others. To explain variability in cultural paradigms that affect motives and behavior, cross-cultural communication scholars have identified five main points of dimensionality across cultures, each of which exists along a continuum. They described cultures as predominantly *individualistic* or *collectivistic; masculine* or *feminine; horizontal* and *vertical; low-* vs. *high-context; power distance;* and *individual values* and *self-construals*, as necessary considerations in predicting cultural tendencies.[41, 42] Cultures with a highly *collectivist* orientation are group-oriented; whereas those from *individualistic* cultures perceive themselves as separate from others and responsible for their own decisions; *masculinity* (accomplishing, doing) vs. *femininity* (nurturing, being) indicates whether a culture focuses on aggression and materialism vs. compliance and cooperation. In *high-context* cultures like the Middle East, much communication is implied and non-verbal: from subtle gestures, to family or social status, to adornment and other environmental queues.[43, 44] In *low-context* cultures like the United States, individuals rely on concise explanations for meaning.

Societies that have been identified as leaning toward collectivism include many African, Arab, Asian, Latin, and southern European cultures. Cultures that tend toward individualism include the United States, Canada, Australia, New Zealand, and northern Europe.[45]

Smiramesh and Vercic described two other important cultural variables which will have an impact on how public relations is best practiced in specific cultures: infrastructure and media environment. Infrastructure encompasses a nation's politics, economics, and activism.

These variables will determine how private enterprise is conducted in a society and how free individuals are to communicate ideas. The media environment will affect the channels for message dissemination, the types of messages allowed, and how the media interact with promotional communicators.[46]

When communicating across cultures, especially on an interpersonal level within social media, it is important to take cultural dimensions into consideration to ensure that messages are understood clearly and to avoid conflicts. See Table 15.1 for a brief summary of cultural dimensions and some issues to consider for communicating cross-culturally.

Table 15.1
Adapted from Hofstede's Cultural Dimensions[47]

Cultural dimensions	Cultural models	National tendency ranked in order along continuum	
Power distance	How much individuals accept hierarchical/ unequal distribution of power	*Lowest acceptance* 1. New Zealand 2. England 3. Germany 4. Australia 5. Canada 6. United States	*Highest acceptance* 1. Mexico 2. Arab world 3. China 4. France 5. India 6. Japan
Individualism/ collectivism	Individuals identify themselves as separate from others or as part of a group	*Individualism* 1. United States 2. Australia 3. England 4. Canada 5. New Zealand 6. France	*Collectivism* 1. China 2. Mexico 3. Arab world 4. Japan 5. India 6. Germany
Masculine/ feminine	Aggressive, materialistic behavior vs. solidarity, emotional displays, relationships & compromise	*Masculinity* 1. Japan 2. Mexico 3. China 4. England 5. Germany 6. United States	*Femininity* 1. France 2. Arab world 3. Canada 4. India 5. New Zealand 6. Australia

Table 15.1 (Continued)

Uncertainty avoidance	Prefer the known over the unknown, work with people they are familiar with, rather than strangers	*Accept Unknown* 1. China 2. England 3. India 4. New Zealand 5. United States 6. Canada	*Prefer Known* 1. Japan 2. France 3. Mexico 4. Arab world 5. Germany 6. Australia
Long-term v. short-term orientation	Defer gratification to achieve long-term success	*Long-term (defer gratification)* 1. China 2. Japan 3. India	*Short-term (live for now)* 1. Canada 2. England 3. United States 4. New Zealand 5. Australia 6. Germany

Recommendations for Global Social Media Promotion

Ethical models of international public relations have been the focus of international communication scholars for the past few decades. As communication technology brings cultures closer together, ethical theory has evolved. Little yet is known about the effects of cultural dimensions, such as high-context vs. low-context orientations, on social media usage, and how organizations can most effectively use this new medium to their benefit—both in the non-profit and for-profit sectors. A few lessons learned are summarized below.

Cultivating positive relationships with publics is a key strategy in ensuring the longevity of an organization. Using social media can be a crucial tool in this venture, if done properly. In fact, having a strong positive relationship can be counted as one of a company's intangible assets, according to Grunig.[48]

As organizations consider implementing social media campaigns into their promotional master plan, we suggest these steps, adapted from a guide for mobile phone electoral campaign promoters:[49] (1) Analyze benefits and determine objectives (i.e., analyze the uses and benefits of social media for your organization). (2) Understand the target audience and potential publics. What media sites do they use? How do they access them? What language do they speak? What are their cultural values? A qualitative survey of a sample audience may provide important information for content, usage, interests, and demographics. (3) Create a clear plan for how it will be used, who will manage it, and objectives to be attained through its use. (4) Determine costs of technology, staffing, and other elements to create a campaign budget. (5) Create a communication plan that includes: how to respond to suggestions; who will make decisions about making changes; how to respond to negativity or other crises; how often to update and what type of information is worth audience attention; what type of context, language, or regional/demographic colloquialisms are used. (6) Clearly state the message or purpose in the communication. Have someone on staff to monitor the community—to scan for emerging audiences, respond to negative messages immediately and appropriately. Depending on the organization and its public, consider giving the audience access to the top executive every so often. Expand the message by asking community members to "tell a friend." (7) Be considerate of the audience (i.e., be prepared to be flexible and transparent to the public); respect the opt-in and opt-out policies of media providers, and give the audience an easy way to stop receiving e-mail or text messages. (8) Don't be afraid to jump in, otherwise, the organization may be ignored. If a reader catches a mistake, most often they will correct it without a lot of fuss. By the same token, don't fake it: flashy technology should be used well. The audience may have little patience for poor production quality.

Finally, communicators are advised to be culturally sensitive when practicing internationally. Multinational organizations can be viewed by foreign locals as the "others," who take assets from the local environment without reciprocating any perceived value.[50] Multinationals might find that if done with diplomacy, social media can enhance an organization's appearance as a local presence, as friendly local stakeholders promote it to their peers; or they may appeal directly to locals as a "good guy," who gives back to a community that supports them. Success at this delicate situation will most likely involve two-way, symmetrical communication and quick responsiveness.

In other cases, companies can use their cultural identity as a "personality attribute" to market to other cultures.[51] Sarcasm, political incorrectness or quirky humor can be the magic ingredient that makes a message "go viral" among some audiences, as was the case in the 42 Below campaign. Companies that think they might have global impact through social marketing must continually scan for potential stakeholders, and try to predict any long-term effects their corporate decisions may have on those publics.[52,53] During their environmental scanning, public relations practitioners should be aware of which cultures are discussing or adopting their messages, and might work with someone from that culture to make sure they don't affect them adversely. However, with so many publics being exposed to messages through the digital communication world, pleasing all will be nearly impossible.[54] Professional communicators should be adequately trained to build multicultural relationships and respond to activist publics.

Public relations and marketing practitioners should have the authority to make management decisions in guiding the cultivation of positive relationships.[55] These professionals must have the autonomy to freely build relationships both within the company and with external publics, and they should have some experience with social media for this purpose.[56]

Further Research

Clearly, more needs to be learned about how organizations can use social media effectively for various promotional purposes. More research is needed to look into how cultural dimensions play into message dissemination to peers, what audiences are most likely to use social media, and which demographics are likely to pass on which kinds of messages to their peers.

Research examining how people from different cultures interact with and respond to socially mediated messages will be essential for evolving global marketing to efficient social media practice. For example, researchers studying how collectivism affects individual learning found that people from collectivist cultures accept new behaviors when they are adopted by their group, where those from individualist cultures tend to accept new behaviors when they believe it will enhance their personal life.[57] This finding may or may not have significance in how cultural dimensions influence new behavior adoption when it is promoted through social media.

CONCLUSION

As social media come to dominate consumer and public discussions, marketing experts will be obliged to meet them halfway. Already, global conversations are taking place on social networking sites, cell phones, and other social media. If organizations remain absent or minor in these discussions, they will lose out to competitors who are craftily and boldly embracing this new wave of technology.

Marketing global organizations in the social media arena will require a new style of messaging; one that builds community from the bottom up rather than the top down. To do this well, organizations may be forced to spend precious resources learning how to walk the social media "walk" and talk the social media "talk."

NOTES

1. DIOSA Communications. "MySpace Usage Rates," www.diosacommu nications.com, (accessed April 7, 2010).

2. DIOSA, "MySpace Usage Rates."

3. Jessica Tsai, "Marketing and Social Media: Everyone's Social (Already)," *Customer Relationship Management* (2009): 34–38.

4. Danah Boyd, "White Flight in Networked Publics? How Race and Class Shaped American Teen Engagement with MySpace and Facebook," in *Digital Race Anthology,* ed. Lisa Nakamura and Peter Chow-White (Routledge, In Press).

5. B. Bulik, "Is Your Consumer Using Social Media?," *Advertising Age* 79 (2008): 12–13.

6. Tsai, "Marketing and Social Media: Everyone's Social (Already)," 34–38.

7. Christopher Carfi, "Collective Consciousness," *Communication World* 26 (2009): 16–20, p. 18.

8. Corometrics. "Survey Reveals Disconnect in Social Media Marketing Programs," www.corometrics.com (accessed April 8, 2010).

9. Bulik, "Is Your Consumer Using Social Media?," 12–13.

10. Carfi, "Collective Consciousness," 18.

11. Rita L. Rahoi-Gilchrest, "The 42 Below Story (A Company That Breaks the Rules of Corporate Social Responsibility—and Just Doesn't Care)," *International Journal of Communication* 17 (2007): 79–93.

12. Joseph E. Phelps, Regina Lewis, Lynne Mobilio, David Perry, and Niranjan Raman, "Viral Marketing or Electronic Word-of-Mouth Advertising: Examining Consumer Reponses and Motivations to Pass along Email," *Journal of Advertising Research* 44 (2004): 333–48.

13. DIOSA, "MySpace Usage Rates."

14. James E. Grunig, "Furnishing the Edifice: Ongoing Research on Public Relations as a Strategic Management Function," *Journal of Public Relations Research* 18 (2006): 151–76.

15. Lan Ni, "Strategic Role of Relationship Building: Perceived Links between Employee–Organization Relationships and Globalization Strategies," *Journal of Public Relations Research* 21 (2009): 100–120.

16. Robert I. Wakefield, "Theory of International Public Relations, the Internet, and Activism: A Personal Reflection," *Journal of Public Relations Research* 20 (2008): 138–57.

17. Grunig, "Furnishing the Edifice: Ongoing Research on Public Relations as a Strategic Management Function," 156.

18. Tsai, "Marketing and Social Media: Everyone's Social (Already)," 37.

19. Bingqi Feng and Han Li, "An Analysis of Consumer Generated Media's Application in Multicultural Public Relations Practice," *China Media Research* 5 (2009): 20–30, p. 26.

20. Jeff Jarvis, "Dell Learns to Listen," *Business Week*, October 17, 2007, http://www.businessweek.com/bwdaily/dnflash/content/oct2007/db20071017_277576.htm?chan=top+news_top+news+index_top+story, p. 2.

21. Feng and Li, "An Analysis of Consumer Generated Media's Application in Multicultural Public Relations Practice," 26.

22. Grunig, "Furnishing the Edifice: Ongoing Research on Public Relations as a Strategic Management Function," 156.

23. Ibid., 162.

24. Ibid., 156.

25. Tsai, "Marketing and Social Media: Everyone's Social (Already)," 37.

26. Advertising Age, "Three Marketing Models for Social Media," *Advertising Age* 81 (2010): 8.

27. Advertising Age, 2010.

28. Nonprofit Technology Network. Nonprofit Social Network Benchmark Report 2010, http://www.nonprofitsocialnetworksurvey.com/download.php (accessed April 9, 2010).

29. Carlos Bergfeld, "Social Media Veterans Tell What Works, What Doesn't" (report from the 2010 Nonprofit Technology Conference blog), http://blog.techsoup.org/node/1237 (accessed April 9, 2010).

30. Nonprofit Technology Network. Nonprofit Social Network Benchmark Report 2010.

31. Tsai, "Marketing and Social Media: Everyone's Social (Already)," 37.

32. X Andrew (2010). "Live Notes from Journalist Andrew Sullivan's Opening Plenary," http://blog.techsoup.org/node/1242 (accessed April 9, 2010).

33. N. Zmuda and K. Patel, "Pass or Fail, Pepsi's Refresh Will be Case for Marketing Textbooks," *Advertising Age* 81 (2010): 1–18.

34. James E. Grunig, Larissa A. Grunig, K. Sriramesh, Yi-Hui Huang, and Anastasia Lyra, "Models of Public Relations in an International Setting," *Journal of Public Relations Research* 7 (1995): 163–86.

35. N. Hoft, *International Technical Communication: How to Export Information About High Technology* (New York: Wiley, 1995).

36. Hoft, *International Technical Communication: How to Export Information about High Technology,* 12.

37. Ibid.

38. Rahoi-Gilchrest, "The 42 Below Story (A Company That Breaks the Rules of Corporate Social Responsibility—and Just Doesn't Care)," 90.

39. www.ideashops.co.nz.

40. Ibid.

41. Geert Hofstede, *Culture's Consequences: International Differences in Work-Related Values* (Beverly Hills: Sage, 1980).

42. F. Kluckholn and F. Strodtbeck, *Variations in Value Orientations* (Chicago: Peterson & Co, 1961).

43. Martin J. Gannon, *Understanding Global Cultures: Metaphorical Journeys Through 23 Nations*, 2nd ed. (Thousand Oaks: Sage Publications, 2001).

44. Judith N. Martin and Thomas K. Nakayama, *Intercultural Communication in Contexts* (Mountian View: Mayfield Publishing Company, 2000).

45. Sudith Martin and Thomas Nakayama, *Intercultural Communications in Context* (Mountain View, CA: Mayfield Publishing Co., 2000).

46. Krishnamurthy Sriramesh and Dejan Vercic, *The Global Public Relations Handbook: Theory, Research and Practice* (Mahwah: Lawrence Erlbaum Associates, Inc., 2003).

47. Geert Hofstede, "Geert Hofstede™ Cultural Dimensions," http://www.geert-hofstede.com/hofstede_dimensions.php (accessed April 13, 2010).

48. Grunig, "Furnishing the Edifice: Ongoing Research on Public Relations as a Strategic Management Function," 151–76.

49. MobileActive.org Strategy Guide #1: Using Mobile Phones in Electoral and Voter Registration Campaigns (English, French, Arabic) 2007, http://www.mobileactive.org/strategy-guide-1-using-mobile-phones-electoral-and-voter-registration-campaigns-0 (accessed April 9, 2010).

50. Yoonhyeung Choi and Glen T. Cameron, "Overcoming Ethnocentrism: The Role of Identity in Contingent Practice of International Public Relations," *Journal of Public Relations Research* 12 (2005): 171–89.

51. Rahoi-Gilchrest, "The 42 Below Story (A Company That Breaks the Rules of Corporate Social Responsibility—and Just Doesn't Care)," 90.

52. James E. Grunig and Larissa A. Grunig, "Implications of Symmetry for a Theory of Ethics and Social Responsibility in Public Relations" (paper presented at the meeting of the International Communication Association, Chicago, 1996).

53. Seong-Hun Yun, "Toward Public Relations Theory-Based Study of Public Diplomacy: Testing the Applicability of the Excellence Study," *Journal of Public Relations Research* 18 (2006): 287–312.

54. Wakefield, "Theory of International Public Relations, the Internet, and Activism: A Personal Reflection," 138–57.

55. Grunig, "Furnishing the Edifice: Ongoing Research on Public Relations as a Strategic Management Function," 151–76.

56. Tsai, "Marketing and Social Media: Everyone's Social (Already)," 37.

57. B. Yang, Y. Wang, and A. W. Drewry, "Does It Matter Where to Conduct Training? Accounting for Cultural Factors," *Human Resource Management Review* 19 (2009): 324–33.

Index

About the Editors and Contributors

EDITORS

BRUCE D. KEILLOR is Associate Professor of Marketing at Youngstown State University. Dr. Keillor received his bachelor of arts (economics/Japanese studies) from the University of Minnesota in 1987, his MBA (marketing concentration) from Minnesota State University in 1989, and his PhD (Marketing) from the University of Memphis in 1994. Prior to joining the Marketing Department at YSU he was, for the past 9 years, professor of marketing and international business, and both associate director and director of the Institute for Global Business, at the University of Akron. Dr. Keillor has published over 100 referred journal articles, conference papers, books, and book chapters over the last 15 years. His primary area of research is international marketing strategy, cross-cultural research methodology, and global consumer behavior. In addition he has served, or is currently serving, on a number of review boards including *Journal of International Business Studies*. Dr. Keillor is also the founding editor of *Direct Marketing: An International Journal* published by Emerald Publications and a research fellow in the Center for International Business at Michigan State University. Outside of his academic activities, Dr. Keillor is an active consultant, with clients that include *Fortune 500* firms, and a successful software entrepreneur.

TIMOTHY J. WILKINSON is professor of marketing and interim dean at Montana State University—Billings. He earned a PhD from the University of Utah, with a doctoral dissertation that examined subnational export promotion policy. Before returning to the Rocky Mountain region, Professor Wilkinson taught for eight years at The University of Akron, where he served as the associate director of the Institute for Global Business. In addition, he has lectured in the doctoral programs at the University of Texas at El Paso and Kennesaw State University. Wilkinson is the co-author of the AMA-Berry Award winning book, *The Distribution Trap*, and the editor of *New World Marketing*, the first volume of the series, *Marketing in the 21st Century*. His academic papers include publications in *Long Range Planning, Journal of Business Research, Journal of International Business Studies, International Business Review*, and the *Journal of Small Business Research*. Other articles have been published in *Business Horizons*, *MIT Sloan Management Review*, and the *Wall Street Journal*.

CONTRIBUTORS

LANCE ELIOT BROUTHERS is professor of management and research coordinator for the DBA program in the Coles College of Business at Kennesaw State University. He has consistently been ranked among the top international business scholars in the world and has appeared in print over 90 times. His research examines international strategy issues, particularly the impact of the international business environment, mode choice, exporting, and product strategy and has appeared in leading journals including: *Strategic Management Journal, Journal of International Business Studies, Journal of Management, Journal of Management Studies, Entrepreneurship: Theory and Practice, Journal of Business Ethics, Management International Review, Journal of International Marketing, Industrial Marketing Management, Long Range Planning*, and the *Journal of World Business*. He currently serves on six editorial review boards: *Journal of International Business Studies, Journal of Management, Journal of Management Studies, Management International Review, Management and Organization Review*, and *Journal of International Management*.

MICHAEL R. CZINKOTA teaches international business and marketing at Georgetown University in Washington, DC, and holds the chair in international marketing at the University of Birmingham in the United Kingdom. He served in the U.S. government as deputy assistant secretary of commerce and was a partner in a trading firm. Aside from more than 100 articles on export management and trade policy, his key books are *International Marketing* (9th edition) and *International Business* (8th edition), and *Emerging Trends, Threats, and Opportunities in International Marketing*. He has served the Academy of Marketing Science for 22 years as a member of the Board of Governors. He is a graduate of the University of Nürnberg (Germany) and The Ohio State University.

KRISTI DRAKE is a graduate student of public relations at Montana State University—Billings. Her focus in communication studies has leaned toward issues related to cross-cultural understanding, ethical nonprofit advocacy, and relationship-building. Before attending Montana State University—Billings, she worked in advertising, public relations, event planning, and fundraising. Drake has experienced many cultures firsthand and speaks several languages.

GARY GARRISON is an assistant professor of information systems management at Belmont University. His research is focused on virtual team collaboration and organizational identification and adoption of disruptive technology. Dr. Garrison's publications can be found in *Information Systems Research, The DATA BASE for Advances in Information Systems, Information Systems Frontiers*, and *Computers in Human Behavior*, among others.

TRACY L. GONZALEZ-PADRON is the director of the College of Business Ethics Initiative and an assistant professor of marketing at the University of Colorado at Colorado Springs. She received her PhD in marketing and international business from Michigan State University. Her research interests include marketing strategy, global marketing, and corporate social responsibility. She has published research in *Industrial Marketing Management, Journal of International Business Studies, Journal of Macromarketing, Journal of Public Policy & Marketing*, and *British Journal of Management*, and presented at international conferences. She has considerable managerial business experience relating to new business development in North America, Europe, Latin America, India, and China.

MICHAEL HARVEY received his PhD at the University of Arizona. Currently he is distinguished chair of global business at the University of Mississippi and professor of global management at Bond University,

Queensland, Australia. Professor Harvey's (PhD University of Arizona) teaching interests are in global business policy and international human resource management. He has published over 300 articles in such academic journals as: *Sloan Management Review, Journal of International Business Studies, Journal of World Business, International Journal of Human Resource Management*, and *Human Resource Management*, among others. Mike also serves on eight editorial review boards. Mike was a faculty member at Southern Methodist University for 17 years and more recently held the Puterbaugh Chair of American Free Enterprise at the Michael F. Price College of Business at the University of Oklahoma for 9 years.

LLEWELLYN D. HOWELL is Emeritus Professor of International Management at Thunderbird School of Global Management in Glendale, Arizona, Senior Advisor for the PRS Group in Syracuse BY, and President and CEO of Howell International Inc., a political risk consulting firm in Glendale, Arizona. Since 1991 he has been the International Affairs Editor of *USA Today Magazine,* published by the Society for the Advancement of Education.

SARAH N. KELLER has developed a service learning curriculum that has been well attended by students and enthusiastically received by the community at Montana State University—Billings. Dr. Keller began this process at Emerson College, where she taught in a master's program in health communication. The curriculum allows her to apply professional experiences from overseas entertainment educa- tion and health communication campaigns with Population Commu- nication International, USAID, and Family Health International. Her students have collectively produced three social marketing cam- paigns over the past three years: 1) "Get Tested!" to promote HIV testing; 2) "Open Your Eyes" to prevent domestic violence; and 3) "Go Play!" to promote physical activity and nutrition. Each campaign has been supported by external grants and in-kind services from area broadcast and media professionals, solicited by the professor. Her media work is informed by her background as a professional news- paper reporter for several small and midsized daily newspapers around the country, and as a freelance reporter internationally for McGraw-Hill, the *Washington Post*, and *United Press International*. Research on her campaigns has resulted in papers appearing in the *Journal of Marketing Education, Nursing & Health Sciences, Journal of Advertising*, and *Health Knowledge, Attitudes and Practices* by Nova Press.

Her ongoing research agenda centers on examining the use of mass media to promote health behavior and attitude change on a variety of public health topics.

MASAAKI KOTABE holds the Washburn Chair Professorship in international business and marketing, and is director of research at the Institute of Global Management Studies at the Fox School of Business and Management at Temple University. Prior to joining Temple University in 1998, he was Ambassador Edward Clark Centennial Endowed Fellow and professor of marketing and international business at the University of Texas at Austin. Dr. Kotabe served as the vice president of the Academy of International Business in 1997–98. In 1998, he was elected a fellow of the Academy of International Business for his significant contribution to international business research and education. Dr. Kotabe has written more than 100 scholarly publications, including the following books: *Global Sourcing Strategy: R&D, Manufacturing, Marketing Interfaces* (1992), *Anticompetitive Practices in Japan* (1996), *Global Supply Chain Management* (2006), and *Global Marketing Management*, 5th ed. (2010).

DANA-NICOLETA LASCU is professor of marketing and chair of the Marketing Department at the Robins School of Business, University of Richmond. Her doctorate is from the University of South Carolina and her master's of international management is from the Thunderbird Graduate School of International Management. She has published articles in journals such as *International Business Review, Journal of Business Ethics, International Marketing Review, European Journal of Marketing*, and has consulted for Yellow Book North America and Ford Motor Company, among others.

ANNA McALISTER (PhD, University of Queensland, Australia) is a lecturer at the University of Wisconsin–Madison. Prior to joining the Department of Consumer Science at UW, she was postdoctoral research fellow and lecturer in marketing at the University of Queensland, Australia. Her research focuses on consumer behavior. Having earned a PhD in developmental psychology, Anna's special interest is the application of theories of developmental psychology to the study of children's consumer socialization. Recent papers are published in *Journal of Public Policy & Marketing, Psychology & Marketing, Cognitive Development*, and *British Journal of Developmental Psychology.*

JOHN P. McCRAY is an associate professor of management at the University of Texas at San Antonio. He received a PhD from Texas A&M University (1985) in strategic management. He also holds an MBA. from Northwestern Louisiana State University; a B.A. (Cum Laude) from Chapman College, Orange, California; and is a professional engineer, California License 18510. Dr. McCray served as an infantry, civil affairs, and logistics officer in Vietnam and worked as a professional civil engineer in California designing and building roads, bridges, and other projects. His research interests include the Maquiladora factories in Mexico; the United States–China and United States–Mexico trade and transportation; developing inland ports in the United States, Mexico, and China; and strategic market opportunities created by the growing trade between the United States, Mexico, and China.

MARY McNALLY is a Professor of Management in the College of Business at Montana State University—Billings. She has been on the faculty for 23 years, teaching management, business and the environment, and international business. Dr. McNally has also served as Interim Dean of the College of Business at MSU—Billings.

NANCY NAPIER is professor of international business and executive director of the Centre for Creativity and Innovation at Boise State University, USA. She managed Boise State's nine-year involvement in an $8.5 million capacity building project at the National Economics University in Hanoi, Vietnam, funded by the Swedish International Cooperation Development Agency (SIDA) and the United States Agency for International Development (USAID). Her most recent books are *Insight: Encouraging Aha! Moments for Organizational Success*, and *The Creative Discipline: Mastering the Art and Science of Innovation*. Her articles appear in such journals as *Creativity and Innovation Management, Journal of Management Psychology, International Journal of Cross-Cultural Management, Academy of Management Review*, and *Journal of International Business Studies*.

TED BARBER RANDALL is co-founder and president of NuVision Pharmaceuticals, LLC, and marketing manager for Saudi Aramco. He has 19-plus years experience in the petrochemicals and polymers industry, the last several years spent developing new business. Mr. Randall graduated with a B.S. in design engineering from Brigham Young University, earned his MBA from Kennesaw State University, and is currently working on a DBA with a focus on international business, strategy, and entrepreneurship. In 2008 Mr. Randall and colleagues launched NuVision Pharmaceuticals, LLC, bringing a revolutionary new product to the diabetic and assisted living segments of healthcare. Mr. Randall and his family reside in Saudi Arabia where he is assisting in the launch of Saudi Aramco's new chemicals business.

TERRI L. RITTENBURG is associate professor of marketing and adjunct associate professor of international studies at the University of Wyoming in Laramie, Wyoming. Prior to joining the University of Wyoming faculty in 1989, she was a faculty member at Iowa State University. She has been an active contributor to literature in the areas of business ethics and macromarketing throughout her career. Her work appears in a number of academic journals, including the *Journal of Business Ethics, Journal of Macromarketing, Journal of Public Policy & Marketing*, and *Psychology & Marketing*. She serves on the editorial policy board for the *Journal of Macromarketing*.

ILKKA A. RONKAINEN serves on the faculty of marketing and international business at Georgetown University's McDonough School of Business as well as docent of international marketing at the Helsinki School of Economics. He received his PhD from the University of South Carolina. He is co-author of multiple texts, two of which, *International Business* and *International Marketing*, are among the leading ones used in schools in the Americas, Asia, and Europe. In 1995, his co-authored text, *The Global Marketing Imperative*, was a winner of the Choice award given to the best research books of the year. His international marketing work has been published in *the Journal of International Business Studies, Journal of International Marketing*, and the *International Marketing Review*.

TRACY SCOTT has 10 years of strategic marketing and consulting experience with *Fortune 500* brands. Tracy is currently completing her master's degree with the Robins School of Business at the University of Richmond through the International MBA program at Tsinghua University in Beijing. She holds undergraduate degrees in international studies and business administration from Trinity University. Most recently, she served as the director of Marketing and New Business for McClain Finlon, a large private ad agency headquartered in Denver, Colorado. Prior to McClain Finlon, Tracy was an account strategist at Ogilvy. Her clients included Motorola, Otis Elevator Company, Dell Inc, Qwest Communications International, Best Buy, Suncor, and Salomon.

NITISH SINGH (PhD, Saint Louis University) is an assistant professor of international business at the Boeing Institute of International Business, St. Louis University. His research emphasis is in the area of international e-business, cross-cultural research, and emerging markets. He has publishing activity in a variety of journals including the *Journal of International Business Studies, Journal of Business Research, Psychology & Marketing, International Marketing Review, European Journal of Marketing, Journal of Advertising Research, Journal of Electronic Commerce Research, Journal of Global Information Management, Journal of Computer Mediated Communication, Multinational Business Review, Thunderbird International Business Review*, and others. He is also a co-author of the book *The Culturally Customized Website* and the book, *Proliferation of Internet Economy*.

ANDREW R. THOMAS is assistant professor of international business at the University of Akron. A bestselling business writer, he is author, co-author, or editor of more than 15 books, including *The Handbook of Supply Chain Security, Aviation Security Management: 3 Volumes*, and *Supply Chain Security: International Practices and Innovations for Moving Goods Safely and Efficiently*. Professor Thomas writes, consults, and speaks extensively on building the sustainable global enterprise, from supply chain security, production and operations to marketing, sales, and distribution. His research has appeared in the *Wall Street Journal, MIT Sloan Management Review*, and *Business Horizons*. Andrew is founding-editor-in-chief of *Journal of Transportation Security* and a regularly featured media analyst for MSNBC, CNN, BBC, and FOX NEWS.

SCOTT WIDMIER, PhD, researches and teaches in the area of selling, sales management, business negotiations, and international sales strategy. He has over 20 research publications in top academic and practitioner journals. He has spent over 15 years teaching undergraduates, graduates, and executives including custom training courses for *Fortune 500* companies. In total, he has taught over 3,000 people the art of sales, sales management, and business negotiations. Dr. Widmier gained sales experience in the financial industry earning his series 7 and series 63 licenses before returning to the university in order to learn and improve the sales profession. After earning his doctorate in business at Arizona State University, he accepted a position at the University of Akron where he became associate director for the Fisher Institute for Professional Selling. He then moved to Kennesaw State University where he was the associate director for the center for professional selling in charge of consulting services, technology, facilities expansion, and directs the Center's efforts in international studies abroad. He now applies his administrative and research expertise as director of the Coles College of Business DBA program.

KEFENG XU is an associate professor of operations and logistics management at the University of Texas at San Antonio (UTSA). He received his PhD with double majors in operations management and logistics/transportation from the University of Maryland. His publications have appeared in refereed academic journals such as *Journal of International Business Studies, Journal of Business Logistics, Transportation Research, Journal of Transportation Economics & Policy, International Journal of Physical Distribution & Logistics Management, European Journal of Operational Research, International Journal of Production Economics, International Journal of Production Research,* and *Computers & Operations Research, etc.* His research interests include international logistics, service and manufacturing strategy; supply chain modeling; transportation policy, service, cost and demand studies. He has won many research and teaching awards, including the Plowman Award (Best Paper Award) in Council of Logistics Management Educators Conference, and Col. Jean Migliorino and Lt. Col. Philip Piccione Endowed Research Award at UTSA.

HONGXIN ZHAO (PhD, George Washington University) is the David Orthwein Professor of International Business, Boeing Institute of International Business at the John Cook School of Business, Saint Louis University. His research focus is in FDI and international business strategy. His publications appear in *Journal of International Business Studies, Journal of International Marketing, Management International Review,* and *International Business Review,* among others. Dr. Zhao taught previously at National University of Singapore and was the international program coordinator at the Chinese Ministry of Foreign Trade (now Ministry of Commerce) and the Chinese Ministry of Science and Technology, respectively.